The first page of 'Pa gur yw y porthaur' from Peniarth MS 1, f 47b
(The Black Book of Carmarthen)
(By permission of the National Library of Wales)

THE ARTHUR

OF THE WELSH

THE ARTHUR
OF THE WELSH

THE ARTHURIAN LEGEND IN MEDIEVAL WELSH LITERATURE

edited by

Rachel Bromwich, A.O.H. Jarman, Brynley F. Roberts

CARDIFF
UNIVERSITY OF WALES PRESS
1991

British Library Cataloguing in Publication Data
The Arthur of the Welsh : the Arthurian legend in medieval
  Welsh literature.
  1. Wales. Tales
  I. Roberts, Brynley F. (Brynley Francis) 1931 – II.
  Jarman, A.O.H. (Alfred Owen Hughes) 1911 – III.
  Bromwich, Rachel 1915 –
  398.22

ISBN 0-7083-1107-5

Typeset by the Vinaver Trust, and Afal, Cardiff.
Printed in Great Britain by Antony Rowe Ltd, Chippenham, Wiltshire

Cyflwynir y gyfrol hon

i goffadwriaeth annwyl

yr Athro Thomas Jones

CONTENTS

THE CONTRIBUTORS

RACHEL BROMWICH, Emeritus Reader in Celtic Languages and Literature, University of Cambridge.

THOMAS CHARLES-EDWARDS, Fellow and Tutor in History, Corpus Christi College, University of Oxford.

DANIEL HUWS, Keeper of Manuscripts and Records, National Library of Wales.

A.O.H. JARMAN, Emeritus Professor of Welsh, University College, Cardiff.

CERIDWEN LLOYD-MORGAN, Assistant Archivist, Department of Manuscripts and Records, National Library of Wales.

IAN C. LOVECY, Librarian, University College of North Wales, Bangor.

ROGER MIDDLETON, Lecturer in French, University of Nottingham.

O.J. PADEL, Research Assistant, Department of Welsh History, University College of Wales, Aberystwyth.

BRYNLEY F. ROBERTS, Librarian, National Library of Wales.

PATRICK SIMS-WILLIAMS, Fellow of St John's College, Cambridge.

ROBERT L. THOMSON, formerly Reader in Celtic, University of Leeds.

J.E. CAERWYN WILLIAMS, Emeritus Director, University of Wales Centre for Advanced Welsh and Celtic Studies, Aberystwth.

ABBREVIATIONS

AB   *Annales de Bretagne.*

AC   *Annales Cambriae; Cy.,* 9 (1888), 141ff.; ed. and trans. J. Morris, *Nennius's British History and the Welsh Annals* (London and Chichester, 1980).

ALMA   *Arthurian Literature in the Middle Ages,* ed. R.S. Loomis (Oxford, 1959).

AP   *Armes Prydein: 'The Prophecy of Britain',* ed. Ifor Williams. English edition translated by Rachel Bromwich, DIAS Medieval and Modern Welsh Series VI (Dublin, 1972, 1982).

Ast.H   *Astudiaethau ar yr Hengerdd,* ed. Rachel Bromwich and R. Brinley Jones (Cardiff, 1978).

ATC   R.S. Loomis, *Arthurian Tradition and Chrétien de Troyes* (New York, 1949).

B   *Bulletin of the Board of Celtic Studies.*

BB   *Brut y Brenhinedd* (Llanstephan I Version), ed. B.F. Roberts (DIAS 1971).

BBC   *The Black Book of Carmarthen,* ed. J. Gwenogvryn Evans (Pwllheli, 1907).

BBIAS   *Bibliographical Bulletin of the International Arthurian Society.*

BD   *Brut Dingestow,* ed. Henry Lewis (Cardiff, 1942).

BR   *Breudwyt Ronabwy,* ed. Melville Richards (Cardiff, 1948).

BT   *The Book of Taliesin: Facsimile and Text,* ed. J.G. Evans (Llanbedrog, 1910).

BWP   *The Beginnings of Welsh Poetry: Studies by Sir Ifor Williams,* ed. Rachel Bromwich (Cardiff, 1972, 1980, repr. 1990).

CA   *Canu Aneirin,* ed. Ifor Williams (Cardiff, 1937, 1961, repr. 1989).

CBB   John Jay Parry, *Brut y Brenhinedd: Cotton Cleopatra Version* (Cambridge, Mass., 1937).

CF   John Rhŷs, *Celtic Folklore: Welsh and Manx* (Oxford, 1891).

Ch.Br.   Joseph Loth, *Chrestomathie Bretonne* (Paris, 1890).

CLlLl   *Cyfranc Lludd a Llefelys,* ed. B.F. Roberts, DIAS Medieval and Modern Welsh Series VII (Dublin, 1975).

CLlH   *Canu Llywarch Hen,* ed. Ifor Williams (Cardiff, 1935, 1953, repr. 1990).

CMCS   *Cambridge Medieval Celtic Studies.*

CO/CO(1)*Culhwch ac Olwen: Testun Syr Idris Foster*, ed. and completed by Rachel Bromwich and D. Simon Evans (Cardiff, 1988) (*CO*(1)). An enlarged English edition with new introduction and notes is in the Press: references to line numbers in the text of the tale will correspond in the two editions.

CS   *Celt and Saxon*, ed. N.K. Chadwick (Cambridge, 1963).

Cy.   *Y Cymmrodor.*

DIAS   Dublin Institute for Advanced Studies.

EAR   J.D. Bruce, *The Evolution of Arthurian Romance* (Göttingen, 1927).

ÉC   *Études Celtiques.*

EHR   *English Historical Review.*

EWGT   *Early Welsh Genealogical Tracts*, ed. P.C. Bartrum (Cardiff, 1966).

G   *Geirfa Barddoniaeth Gynnar Gymraeg*, ed. J. Lloyd-Jones (Cardiff, 1931-1963).

GMW   D.Simon Evans, *A Grammar of Middle Welsh*, DIAS, (Dublin, 1964).

GPC   *Geiriadur Prifysgol Cymru: A Dictionary of the Welsh Language* (Cardiff, 1950-).

Guide   A.O.H. Jarman and G.R. Hughes, *A Guide to Welsh Literature* (Swansea, 1976).

HB   *The Historia Brittonum*, (i) ed. Mommsen, *Chronica Minora Saec*, IV-VII (MGH AA xiii); (ii) ed. F. Lot, *Nennius et L'Historia Brittonum* (Paris, 1934); (iii) ed. D.N. Dumville, *The Historia Brittonum: The Vatican Recension* (Woodbridge, 1985); (iv) ed. and trans. J. Morris, *Nennius's British History and the Welsh Annals* (see above under *AC*).

Hend.   *Llawysgrif Hendregadredd*, ed. J. Morris-Jones and T.H. Parry-Williams (Cardiff, 1933, repr. 1978).

HLCB   *Histoire littéraire et culturelle de la Bretagne*, ed. Jean Balcou et Yves le Gallo (Paris-Geneva, 1987).

HRB   *Historia Regum Britanniae*, I: Bern Burgerbibliothek MS 568, ed. Neil Wright (Cambridge, 1984).

HRB(T)   *Historia Regum Britanniae*, trans. Lewis Thorpe, *The History of the Kings of Britain* (Harmondsworth, 1966).

HRB(V)   *Historia Regum Britanniae*, II: The First Variant Version, ed. Neil Wright, (Cambridge, 1988).

HW   J.E. Lloyd, *A History of Wales* (Oxford, 1911).

IPT   Kenneth Jackson, *The International Popular Tale and Early Welsh Tradition* (Cardiff, 1961).

LA   E. Faral, *La Légende arthurienne*, 3 vols. (Paris, 1929).

LAMA   *The Legend of Arthur in the Middle Ages*, ed. P.B. Grout *et al.* (Cambridge, 1983).

LBS   S. Baring-Gould and J. Fisher, *Lives of the British Saints*, 4 vols. (London, 1907-13).

Leg. Hist. J.S.P. Tatlock, *The Legendary History of Britain* (California, 1950).

LHEB   Kenneth Jackson, *Language and History in Early Britain* (Edinburgh, 1953).

LL   *Liber Landavensis: The Book of Llandaf*, ed. J. Rhŷs and J.G. Evans (Oxford, 1883).

LlC   *Llên Cymru.*

LlDC   *Llyfr Du Caerfyrddin*, ed. A.O.H. Jarman (Cardiff, 1982).

MA(2)   *The Myvyrian Archaiology of Wales*, 2nd edn. (Denbigh, 1870).

Mab.   *The Mabinogion*, trans. Gwyn Jones and Thomas Jones (Everyman: London, 1949).

MLN   *Modern Language Notes.*

MLR   *Modern Language Review.*

MP   *Modern Philology.*

NLW   National Library of Wales.

NMS   *Nottingham Medieval Studies.*

Owein   *Owein* or *Chwedyl Iarlles y Ffynnawn*, ed. R.L. Thomson, DIAS Medieval and Modern Welsh Series IV (Dublin, 1968).

PBA   *Proceedings of the British Academy.*

PKM   *Pedeir Keinc y Mabinogi*, ed. Ifor Williams (Cardiff, 1930, 1964, repr. 1989).

PT   *The Poems of Taliesin*, ed. Ifor Williams. English edition trans. J.E. Caerwyn Williams, DIAS Medieval and Modern Welsh Series III (Dublin, 1968).

RBB   *The Text of the Bruts from the Red Book of Hergest*, ed. J. Rhŷs and J.G. Evans (Oxford, 1890).

RBP   *The Poetry from the Red Book of Hergest*, ed. J.G. Evans (Llanbedrog, 1911).

RC   *Revue Celtique.*

RM   *The Text of the Mabinogion from the Red Book of Hergest*, ed. J. Rhŷs and J.G. Evans (Oxford, 1887).

RWM   *Report on Manuscripts in the Welsh Language*, ed. J.G. Evans (London, 1898-1910).

SC   *Studia Celtica.*

SEBC   *Studies in the Early British Church*, ed. N.K. Chadwick (Cambridge, 1958).

SEBH   *Studies in Early British History*, ed. N.K. Chadwick (Cambridge, 1954).

THSC   *Transactions of the Honourable Society of Cymmrodorion.*

TRh   *Y Traddodiad Rhyddiaith yn yr Oesau Canol*, ed. Geraint Bowen (Llandysul, 1974).

TYP   *Trioedd Ynys Prydein*, ed. and trans. Rachel Bromwich (Cardiff, 1961, 1978, 1991).

VM   *The Life of Merlin* (Geoffrey of Monmouth's *Vita Merlini*), ed. and trans. Basil Clarke (Cardiff, 1971).

VSB   *Vitae Sanctorum Britanniae et Genealogiae*, ed. and trans. A.W. Wade-Evans (Cardiff, 1944).

WAL   R.S. Loomis, *Wales and the Arthurian Legend* (Cardiff, 1956).

WHR   Welsh History Review.

WM   *The White Book Mabinogion*, ed. J.G. Evans (Pwllheli, 1907). Second edition with introduction by R.M. Jones (Cardiff, 1973, repr. 1977).

YB   *Ysgrifau Beirniadol*, ed. J.E. Caerwyn Williams (Denbigh, 1965-).

YMTh   *Ymddiddan Myrddin a Thaliesin*, ed. A.O.H. Jarman (Cardiff, 1967).

ZCP   *Zeitschrift für Celtische Philologie.*

LAMA *The Legend of Arthur in the Middle Ages*, ed. P.B. Grout *et al.* (Cambridge, 1983).

LBS S. Baring-Gould and J. Fisher, *Lives of the British Saints*, 4 vols. (London, 1907-13).

Leg. Hist. J.S.P. Tatlock, *The Legendary History of Britain* (California, 1950).

LHEB Kenneth Jackson, *Language and History in Early Britain* (Edinburgh, 1953).

LL *Liber Landavensis: The Book of Llandaf*, ed. J. Rhŷs and J.G. Evans (Oxford, 1883).

LlC *Llên Cymru.*

LlDC *Llyfr Du Caerfyrddin*, ed. A.O.H. Jarman (Cardiff, 1982).

MA(2) *The Myvyrian Archaiology of Wales*, 2nd edn. (Denbigh, 1870).

Mab. *The Mabinogion*, trans. Gwyn Jones and Thomas Jones (Everyman: London, 1949).

MLN *Modern Language Notes.*

MLR *Modern Language Review.*

MP *Modern Philology.*

NLW National Library of Wales.

NMS *Nottingham Medieval Studies.*

Owein *Owein* or *Chwedyl Iarlles y Ffynnawn*, ed. R.L. Thomson, DIAS Medieval and Modern Welsh Series IV (Dublin, 1968).

PBA *Proceedings of the British Academy.*

PKM *Pedeir Keinc y Mabinogi*, ed. Ifor Williams (Cardiff, 1930, 1964, repr. 1989).

PT *The Poems of Taliesin*, ed. Ifor Williams. English edition trans. J.E. Caerwyn Williams, DIAS Medieval and Modern Welsh Series III (Dublin, 1968).

RBB *The Text of the Bruts from the Red Book of Hergest*, ed. J. Rhŷs and J.G. Evans (Oxford, 1890).

RBP *The Poetry from the Red Book of Hergest*, ed. J.G. Evans (Llanbedrog, 1911).

RC *Revue Celtique.*

RM *The Text of the Mabinogion from the Red Book of Hergest*, ed. J. Rhŷs and J.G. Evans (Oxford, 1887).

RWM *Report on Manuscripts in the Welsh Language*, ed. J.G. Evans (London, 1898-1910).

SC *Studia Celtica.*

SEBC *Studies in the Early British Church*, ed. N.K. Chadwick (Cambridge, 1958).

SEBH   *Studies in Early British History*, ed. N.K. Chadwick (Cambridge, 1954).

THSC   *Transactions of the Honourable Society of Cymmrodorion.*

TRh   *Y Traddodiad Rhyddiaith yn yr Oesau Canol*, ed. Geraint Bowen (Llandysul, 1974).

TYP   *Trioedd Ynys Prydein*, ed. and trans. Rachel Bromwich (Cardiff, 1961, 1978, 1991).

VM   *The Life of Merlin* (Geoffrey of Monmouth's *Vita Merlini*), ed. and trans. Basil Clarke (Cardiff, 1971).

VSB   *Vitae Sanctorum Britanniae et Genealogiae*, ed. and trans. A.W. Wade-Evans (Cardiff, 1944).

WAL   R.S. Loomis, *Wales and the Arthurian Legend* (Cardiff, 1956).

WHR   Welsh History Review.

WM   *The White Book Mabinogion*, ed. J.G. Evans (Pwllheli, 1907). Second edition with introduction by R.M. Jones (Cardiff, 1973, repr. 1977).

YB   *Ysgrifau Beirniadol*, ed. J.E. Caerwyn Williams (Denbigh, 1965-).

YMTh   *Ymddiddan Myrddin a Thaliesin*, ed. A.O.H. Jarman (Cardiff, 1967).

ZCP   *Zeitschrift für Celtische Philologie.*

INTRODUCTION

The Editors

with a contribution by Daniel Huws

AT a meeting of the British Branch of the International Arthurian Society held in Manchester in 1985, the trustees of the Eugène Vinaver Memorial Trust announced the Trust's intention to commission a series of volumes to supplement and revise *Arthurian Literature in the Middle Ages*, edited by the late R.S. Loomis (Oxford, 1959), a work to which a number of writers contributed. During the years which have intervened since that book appeared the results have been made available of major advances in research in many of the relevant fields of study, and this has necessitated an up-date of much of the material assembled in ALMA. It was decided that the first of the projected volumes to be undertaken should offer a revision of the earlier chapters in ALMA, which are concerned with various aspects of the Celtic sources and affinities of the Arthurian Legend. The three editors of the present volume were appointed by the trustees, and together agreed to organize the revision of these chapters by an appropriate panel of specialists. By the decision of the editors this first volume has been entitled *The Arthur of the Welsh*. The editors wish to thank Dr W.R.J. Barron for his initiative in organizing the project, and for setting the text and producing the camera-ready copy. Our thanks also go to the Manchester University Research Support Fund for financing the production of the text. The editors are grateful to the University of Wales Press, and especially to Ceinwen Jones, for their invaluable assistance.

Our purpose has been to revise and/or to supplement chs.1-8, 12 and 16 of ALMA in the light of more recent work which has been accomplished during the last thirty years. Some of the material in the earlier volume has been differently arranged: certain subjects have been treated more fully and others less fully. The early Welsh poems which make allusion to Arthur have been examined in greater detail, and a complete chapter has been allotted to each of the 'Three Romances' *Geraint*, *Owain*, and *Peredur*. These tales have been primarily considered in their Welsh context, rather than in their relation to the poems of Chrétien de Troyes (the so-called 'Mabinogionfrage' has however received brief mention in the final chapter). Since *Trioedd Ynys Prydein* (1961, revised edn. 1978) appeared after ALMA, it has no longer been considered necessary to devote a separate chapter to the Triads, though these have been cited individually as occasion required, and as a collection they have been briefly noticed in association with *Culhwch ac Olwen*. With *Culhwch* also have been considered the Welsh Saints' Lives and the 'Thirteen Treasures of the Island of Britain', two Arthurian sources which were only incidentally mentioned in ALMA. Geoffrey of Monmouth's *Historia Regum Britanniae* has been discussed in conjunction with its Welsh adaptations in *Brut y Brenhinedd*: these Welsh versions of the *Historia* possess a unique interest, and they received no more than a bare mention in the earlier work. In the later chapters reference is made to such twelfth-century works in Old French as warrant consideration in view of their original context in Brittany, and in some cases (conjecturally) in the Breton language. A full and separate chapter has been allotted to a discussion of the Breton contribution to Arthurian literature. The discussion of *Breuddwyd Rhonabwy* has been combined with that of recent research concerning the later adaptation of French romance material into Welsh: this is another new departure. More recent work on the Myrddin cycle has been cited, as also have some new opinions concerning the genesis of the Tristan legend (including a fresh examination of the relation between the insular sources and the Irish tale of *Diarmaid and Gráinne*). Progress in archaeological research, combined with place-name study has led to a reassessment of the original purpose of the site at Tintagel, and has also demolished misconceptions concerning the other supposedly Arthurian sites at South Cadbury and Castle Dore, while new light has been cast on the possible localization of Celli Wig. Significant parallels from early Irish literature have been frequently cited for purposes of comparison, though a later generation is less ready than were its predecessors to accept as inevitable an Irish origin, in place of a common Celtic inheritance for mythical themes which reappear in the Continental Arthurian romances. In contrast with these many amplifications, we have devoted less attention than did the late R.S. Loomis to the subject of Arthurian cave-legends and other aspects of Arthurian folklore, together with the different manifestations of the messianic hope for Arthur's return. Where variant opinions may have been expressed by the contributors, the editors have made no attempt to impose consistency.

Kenneth Jackson's discussion in the opening chapter of ALMA of the primary sources which relate to Arthur's historicity has been supplemented but in no way replaced by the observations of subsequent writers. Jackson showed that the twelve victories assigned to Arthur in the *Historia Brittonum* can only in a very few instances — *Cat Coit Celidon, Bellum in urbe legionis* — be certainly identifiable with existing place-names in Britain, and that the same may be said, though with less positive assurance, of the *bellum Badonis* (*ann.* 518) and *Gueith Camlann* (*ann.* 539) of the *Annales Cambriae*. Even though these names may all recall once-famous battles, it is not necessary, and it is indeed hardly possible, that they can have all been fought by Arthur.[1]   Jackson endorsed the suggestion originally made by the Chadwicks[2] that their source may well have lain in 'some antiquarian poem on the long-dead hero'.   He described the famous allusion to Arthur in the *Gododdin* poem as 'what may well be one of the most convincing pieces of evidence for a historical Arthur'.   He stressed also the potential significance of the occurrence of four (possibly five) historical figures whose names appear to commemorate the otherwise rare name of Arthur, and who are recorded as having lived in the late sixth and early seventh centuries.   This point had also been made earlier by the Chadwicks and others.[3] Jackson concluded: 'He (Nennius) could hardly have invented Arthur himself, for Nennius was no Geoffrey: he was not capable of creating a character out of nothing at all.'

Each of these three testimonies in the 'case for the defence' for Arthur's historicity has in the mean time been pursued further by subsequent writers.   Indeed one of the most important surveys of the subject appeared almost concurrently with the publication of ALMA, though it was not seen by Jackson.   This was Thomas Jones's 'Datblygiadau Cynnar Chwedl Arthur', first published in the *Bulletin of the Board of Celtic Studies*, 17 (1958), and later translated by Gerald Morgan, to appear in 1964 as 'The Early Evolution of the Legend of Arthur' in *Nottingham Medieval Studies*, 8.   Like Jackson, Thomas Jones supported the suggestion first made by the Chadwicks that an early Welsh poem in retrospective praise of Arthur would be a likely source for the list of Arthur's battles in the *Historia Brittonum*.   This is a type of poem for which there are significant analogies in praise-poems addressed to other early Welsh heroes, but even when such poems preserve the names of authentic battles, these battles need not always have been correctly appropriated to the hero in question, nor need they always have been fought against the Angles or Saxons.   Jones cast doubt on the ascription to Arthur of the victory of *bellum Badonis* in the *Annales Cambriae* (*in monte badonis* in the *Historia Brittonum*), observing that the allusion to Arthur's carrying the Cross on his shoulders (more probably on his shield) 'savours of a religious legend'.   For Jones the allusion in the *Annales* to *Gueith Camlann* was 'perhaps the most authentic historical reference to Arthur'.   It is indeed noticeable that the sparse allusions made by the Welsh court-poets of the twelfth to the fourteenth centuries to the Battle of Badon do not associate it with Arthur,[4] nor is any mention of the battle made in the Triads — whereas Welsh poets frequently revert to the memory of Camlan as a cataclysmic disaster for the Britons.   It has subsequently been shown that these early entries in the *Annales* cannot be drawn from a contemporary, or even from a nearly contemporary, source for the period.[5] There is no reason to doubt the identity of *Bellum Badonis* with the *obsessio*

Badonici montis of Gildas, but the latter's silence as to Arthur's presence at this battle (or indeed to Arthur's very existence) lends some support to Thomas Jones's suggestion that Badon was not in fact fought by Arthur.

Recent studies have envisaged the earliest sources for Welsh history 'subjectively' as expressive of their authors' intentions and circumstances, rather than 'objectively' as prime sources of reliable information for events which occurred many years before the time when they were written. Dr D.N. Dumville has published an important sequence of articles from this viewpoint as preliminary studies to his series of editions (now in progress) of the different versions of the *Historia Brittonum*.[6] The results of this innovatory research are naturally of crucial importance for a correct interpretation of the significance of the passage in the *Historia Brittonum* on Arthur's battles. It is in relation to Dr Dumville's work that this subject is re-assessed in our first chapter by Dr Charles-Edwards. He concludes, however, on a note of qualified optimism by raising the query as to whether the *Historia Brittonum* can be *entirely* dismissed as consisting of no more than 'synthetic history'. Where the underlying sources are completely unknown, there must always remain an element of doubt as to their provenance.

The second item of evidence which has been frequently advanced in support of the case for Arthur's historicity is the allusion to Arthur in the *Gododdin* (*Canu Aneirin*, line 1241), where the warrior Gwawrddur is commemorated for his great deeds 'though he was no Arthur'. Most previous writers, including Jackson and Dumville,[7] have laid considerable stress on the potential importance of this allusion. Whatever may be the date at which the line first became incorporated into the poem, its reference to Arthur plainly emanates from a tradition which is independent of the account of Arthur's activities in the *Historia Brittonum* or that in the *Annales*: it could quite probably be as old as the ninth-century redaction of the *Historia Brittonum*, even if it formed no part of the original *Gododdin* poem. Whether the reference is to a contemporary or to an earlier figure, it constitutes proof for the existence of a man named Arthur, since as Thomas Jones pointed out, early Welsh praise-poetry makes no allusion to characters not regarded as historical for purposes of eulogistic comparison.

The *Gododdin* emanated from one of the British kingdoms in the 'Old North'. Can this mean that the original field of Arthur's activities lay also in north Britain (that is in Cumbria and southern Scotland)? In his study of the *Gododdin* Jackson categorically rejected this view, for he regarded Arthur as 'the great national hero of the entire British people'.[8] But the probability of an ambience in the 'Old North' for the genesis of the earliest traditions concerning Arthur's activities is consistent with the transference to Wales and fresh localization there of the traditions of a number of other northern heroes, and it has received tentative support from Thomas Jones and others.[9] The full implications of the *Gododdin* allusion have been most recently and comprehensively discussed by A.O.H. Jarman in 'The Arthurian Allusions in the Book of Aneirin', *SC*, 24/5 (1989-90), 15-25.

It is also relevant to mention here a further allusion to Arthur in an early poem which would be almost as significant as that in the *Gododdin* if only its textual authority were more securely established. An elegy for Cynddylan, a seventh-century prince of Powys, has survived only in copies from the seventeenth century and later, but it is composed in a language, idiom and metre closely resembling that of the *Gododdin*, while its text has orthographical features which suggest it was copied from a manuscript as old as the thirteenth-century Book of Aneirin. One of its lines describes Cynddylan and his brothers as *canawon Artur Fras, dinas dengyn*, 'whelps of stout Arthur, a strong fortress'.[10]

The final item in the 'case for the defence' of Arthur's historicity consists in the record in Gaelic sources of four (or five) historical figures named Arthur who are said to have been born in the late sixth or early seventh centuries — though this name is of extremely rare occurrence either before or after that date. Two of these men are conjectured to have been born *c. 570*: *Arturius* son of *Aedán mac Gabráin* of Dál Riada in Scotland enters into Adomnan's *Life of Columba*[11] — a seventh-century and therefore a near-contemporary source — and *Artúr mac Petuir* (*var. Retheoir*) is named in the eighth-century Irish genealogy of the immigrant tribe of the Deisi,[12] and appears also as *Arthur map Petr* in the Harleian genealogy of Dyfed. The Irish descent of this line of the early rulers of Dyfed is a well-established and recognized fact,[13] and Arthur map Petr is one of a series of twelve names for which there is close correspondence between the Welsh form of this genealogy and the Irish version. These names have been taken to commemorate the British hero Arthur, the Arthur who is alluded to in the *Historia Brittonum*, the *Annales Cambriae*, and the Welsh poems — though such a commemoration by name of an earlier and unrelated hero would be hard to parallel elsewhere in Celtic sources. Its likelihood must turn on the question whether Arthur was in fact, already by the eighth century, 'the great national hero of the entire British people' (Jackson), or whether he was originally a purely local war-lord whose original sphere of activity lay in the 'Old North'. Some have indeed gone so far as to propose the identification of the Scottish Arthur of Dalriada with the Arthur famous in Brythonic tradition.[14] The difficulty presented by these widespread and relatively early Arthurian 'namesakes' is likely to remain a lasting crux: one possible solution would be to postulate a derivation for the Gaelic names other than the commonly accepted derivation of 'Arthur' from the name of the Roman *gens Artorius*. The Irish word *art* and Welsh *arth*, 'bear', were frequently used figuratively in both languages to denote a warrior, and *Art* actually survived as a personal name in Irish, and as the first element in such early Welsh names as *Arthgen, Arthgal, Arthgloys*.[15] We are reminded also of the ancient Gaulish names *Dea Artio*, 'Bear Goddess', and *Artgenos*, 'Son of a Bear'.[16] And this alternative possibility could also apply to the Arthur of the *Gododdin*. As Jean Markale has pointed out,[17] it is significant that Latin writers always refer to Arthur as *Arturus* or *Arturius*, never as *Artorius*.

Attempts have been made to find a prototype for the Arthur of the Britons by identifying him with historical figures whose names have come down in early and independent records. It is commonly accepted that the most likely derivation of his name is from the Latin *Artorius*, and there is evidence that this name was known in Britain in the second century, for an inscription records that in this century a certain Lucius Artorius Castus, *praefectus castrorum* of the Sixth Legion stationed at York, was sent at the head of two legions to Armorica to suppress a rebellion.[18] It would, however, be merely wishful thinking to identify this officer with the hero of the Britons: his date is much too early. But the existence of the inscription proves that the name *Artorius* was known in this country from an early date: Lucius Artorius could have left descendants or possibly namesakes in Britain.

More recently Geoffrey Ashe has advanced the claims of a different historical prototype for Arthur, and one who approximates more closely to the requirements of the chronology implied by the native records. In the late fifth century a shadowy figure called *Riothamus*, who is said to have been a 'king' of the Britons (that is, he was not *dux bellorum*) is briefly alluded to by the writers Gregory of Tours, Jordanes, and Sidonius Apollinaris, who between them testify that he led an army of sea-borne troops from Britain (less probably, from Brittany) to Gaul[19] in order to oppose the Visigothic king Euric. It appears that Riothamus was betrayed by the Gaulish prefect Arvandus, that he was defeated by Euric near Bourges in 469-70, and that he fled afterwards to Burgundy. Henceforth he disappears from history — though the Burgundian town of Avallon (the Gaulish *Aballone*, the 'place of apples') is proposed as commemorating his demise. It is possible that *Riothamus*, 'supreme king', might be a title, rather than a personal name: hence the proposed conflation with the figure of Arthur.[20]

Such suggestions as these can at best be no more than straws in the wind. Earlier than Geoffrey of Monmouth, Welsh traditions do not attribute any overseas expeditions to Arthur (that is, apart from the dubious testimony of the porter in *Culhwch ac Olwen* — hardly a credible 'historical' witness), but represent him as fully occupied in opposing human and non-human enemies in the Island of Britain. Undoubtedly a composite memory of the foreign expeditions led by Romano-British leaders of long ago must have contributed to Geoffrey of Monmouth's portrayal of the great leader. Among these we should not forget the powerful legend of the Emperor Maximus, the Welsh 'Maxen Wledig', who was believed to have conquered Rome and afterwards to have left his troops as the first colonizers of Brittany.[21]

We may conclude by paraphrasing the words of the late Thomas Jones in his review-article of ALMA in *Llên Cymru*, 5 (1959), 99. He observes that there is an abiding mystery in the survival over so many centuries and in the literatures of so many countries of the memory of a hero about whom we can in reality know next to nothing. Arthur's name has left a deep imprint not only on literature but on the topography and popular traditions of Wales, Cornwall, and England, and in a few instances such localizations have even spread as far as the Continent. Thomas Jones suggested that it was not the raw material of the tales which was the most important element in this miracle, but rather some inexplicable creative impulse on the part of society as a whole, which found its expression through individual authors. But to conclude in this way does no more than raise a host of additional questions.

The texts of the Welsh poems and stories to be discussed are with few exceptions to be found in one or more of five manuscript volumes containing Welsh literary material. These are the Black Book of Carmarthen, the Book of Aneirin, the Book of Taliesin, the White Book of Rhydderch and the Red Book of Hergest. These volumes can at best be only approximately dated, and not one of them is older than the thirteenth century. But most of the contents of all five have been shown on linguistic, orthographical and metrical evidence to be copies of earlier prototypes — in some cases prototypes very much earlier — and frequently these contents have evidently been transmitted through more than one intermediary version. It is the more unfortunate that all of these manuscipts, as they have reached us today, lack a number of quires and separate leaves.

Apart from the unique citation of Arthur's name in the thirteenth-century Book of Aneirin (Cardiff MS 2.81) as a paragon of valour in past times, the earliest source for Welsh Arthurian poems is the Black Book of Carmarthen, *Llyfr Du Caerfyrddin* (NLW Peniarth MS 1). This small parchment volume was compiled over a period of years during the latter half of the thirteenth century, apparently by a single somewhat eccentric scribe, whose handwriting alters considerably as the book progresses. Its contents comprise religious poetry, early praise-poems addressed to patrons, prophetic verse belonging to the cycle of Myrddin, and poems such as 'Pa gur yw y Porthaur' which evidently relate to stories concerning Arthur and other legendary heroes. The Black Book was known by its present title to sixteenth-century scholars, and the first of these, Sir John Prys, records that it came from the Priory of St John the Evangelist at Carmarthen.[22]   A *Facsimile of the Black Book of Carmarthen* was published by J. Gwenogvryn Evans (Oxford, 1888), and subsequently a diplomatic edition was produced by the same editor (Pwllheli, 1907).   More recently the text has been republished by A.O.H. Jarman, *Llyfr Du Caerfyrddin* (Cardiff, 1982).   His introduction provides a guide to the many earlier editions and translations of individual poems. It also includes on pp. xiii-xxiv an authoritative description of the manuscript by the late E.D. Jones. A.O.H. Jarman's Sir John Rhŷs Memorial Lecture, 'Llyfr Du Caerfyrddin: The Black Book of Carmarthen', *PBA*, 71 (1985), 333-56, offers a convenient summary in English of E.D. Jones's views and a general survey of the contents of the Black Book.

The Book of Taliesin (NLW Peniarth MS 2) was written by a single scribe during the first quarter of the fourteenth century.   Its contents are a disparate collection of religious, prophetic, and historical poems purporting to comprise the collected works of the sixth-century poet Taliesin, as these were envisaged in the later Middle Ages.   The title first appears in Edward Lhuyd's *Archaeologia Britannica* (Oxford, 1707).   The case for a genuine early nucleus, which may represent the poet's authentic work, is based on a group of archaic praise-poems addressed to Urien Rheged and other sixth-century rulers in the 'Old North' and in Wales (for these see Ifor Williams, *The Poems of Taliesin* (*PT*) and *The Beginnings of Welsh Poetry* (BWP). Of more certain date is the tenth-century prophetic poem *Armes Prydein* (*AP*) which foretells the victory of the Welsh with their allies over the English.   But the main content of the manuscript consists of a mass of poems of differing dates which are implicitly attributed to the fictional figure of the omniscient Taliesin as he was conceived by later ages. (Only rarely is the attribution to Taliesin explicitly stated.) Such sparse allusions to Arthur as are found in these poems are invariably presented in the context of the 'Taliesin saga' and are usually to be understood as speech-poems declaimed by the legendary poet.   In the Arthurian context the most meaningful is undoubtedly *Preiddeu Annwn*, 'The Spoils of Annw(f)n', which outlines a lost mythical story whose content (as shown in ch.2 below) can be partly elucidated from other sources. A *Facsimile and Text of the Book of Taliesin* was edited by J. Gwenogvryn Evans (Llanbedrog, 1910), and the manuscript is discussed by M. Haycock, '*Llyfr Taliesin*', *NLW Journal*, 25 (1988), 357-86, and by the same author in her unpublished Ph.D. dissertation, 'Llyfr Taliesin: Astudiaethau ar rai Agweddau' (University of Wales, Aberystwyth, 1982).

Certain other manuscripts have been shown to be in the same hand as that of the scribe of the Book of Taliesin, and these can therefore be similarly dated to within this scribe's life-span. Some of these manuscripts are of especial interest for subjects to be discussed in this book. A large portion of *Chwedl Gereint fab Erbin* is contained in the fragmentary manuscript Peniarth 6, part iv *(WM 206-25, 254)*. This is one of two fragments of the tale contained in this manuscript, and both appear to antedate the complete texts which are found in the White Book and the Red Book. Both fragments, together with others from *Branwen* and *Manawydan*, were printed by J. Gwenogvryn Evans in *The White Book Mabinogion (WM)*. NLW MS 3036B (= Mostyn MS 117) which contains a version of *Brut y Brenhinedd* is also in this hand.

The thirteenth-century MS NLW Peniarth 16, part iv, ff.50-4v, contains the earliest extended version of *Trioedd Ynys Prydein* (the 'Early Version' of the Triads) and *Bonedd y Seint*; it originally formed part of NLW MS 5266B, the Dingestow manuscript of *Brut y Brenhinedd (BD)*, and both manuscripts are in the same hand. See Henry Lewis, *Brut Dingestow* (Cardiff, 1942); *TYP* xviii and B.F. Roberts, 'Fersiwn Dingestow o *Brut y Brenhinedd'*, *B*, 27 (1977), 331-61 (332).

The White Book of Rhydderch (NLW Peniarth MSS. 4 and 5) and the Red Book of Hergest (Oxford, Jesus Coll. MS 111) are two remarkable compendia of medieval Welsh prose and verse which were inscribed during the fourteenth century, the first about the middle of the century and the second towards its close. A substantial part of the content of these two manuscripts corresponds: in particular, they have closely similar versions of the ten 'Mabinogion' tales (to which the Red Book adds one additional tale, *Breuddwyd Rhonabwy*, see below) as well as of the Triads (see *TYP* xxiii-xxviii) and other material. We are indebted to Daniel Huws for the essentials of the following account of these two manuscripts.

The White Book of Rhydderch, *Llyfr Gwyn Rhydderch*, is now bound in two volumes preserved in the National Library of Wales. The medieval foliation shows that originally Peniarth 5 preceded Peniarth 4. Whole quires and a few single leaves are now missing at several points in both volumes. When complete, Peniarth 5 contained religious texts, the Welsh Charlemagne cycle, the Welsh version of 'Bevis of Hampton' *(Bown de Hamtwn)* and other matter. Peniarth 4 contained the earliest complete text of the 'Mabinogion' tales. These are found in the following order: the Four Branches of the *Mabinogi*, *Historia Peredur fab Efrawc*, the *Dream of Macsen Wledic*, *Lludd and Llefelys*, *Owein* or *Chwedl Iarlles y Ffynnawn*, followed by *Trioedd Ynys Prydein*, *Bonedd y Saint*, Proverbs, early poetry or Hengerdd, and finally by *Chwedl Gereint fab Erbin* and *Mal y kavas Kulhwch Olwen*. The White Book thus provides the earliest texts of much of the best of Welsh medieval secular prose (the religious texts for the most part survive in earlier manuscripts). Unfortunately much of the early poetry once contained in this manuscript has come down only in later copies.[23] The 'Mabinogion' tales are inscribed in two contemporary hands which are closely similar: one of these wrote the main collection of tales, and the other scribe followed with the two tales *Gereint fab Erbin* and *Culhwch ac Olwen*. As a whole the White Book is a remarkable and unprecedented gathering together of a wide range of medieval Welsh literature, and its creation was an achievement unsurpassed until the Red Book of Hergest came to be produced. It probably derives its name from Rhydderch ab Ieuan Llwyd (*c.* 1324–*c.* 1398) who appears to have been its original owner and may in fact have commissioned it. His home was at Parcrhydderch, Llangeitho, Ceredigion, and he was heir to a notable family tradition of literary patronage, besides being himself one of the most celebrated patrons of the Welsh poets of his day, the friend and patron of Dafydd ap Gwilym. The White Book was in the hands of his descendants until towards the end of the sixteenth century, about which time the title *Llyfr Gwyn i Rydderch* is first recorded. This seems to be good evidence for the White Book's original ownership. In mid-fourteenth-century Ceredigion the first place to have looked for a well-schooled body of scribes would have been Strata Florida Abbey, ten miles from Parcrhydderch, and Ieuan Llwyd's family had associations with the abbey which go back to its founder.

The fullest description of the White Book until now remains that of J. Gwenogvryn Evans in *Report on Manuscripts in the Welsh Language* (RWM, I, pp. 305-16, and 324-5 (the latter pages describe the detached portion in Peniarth MS 12,24 containing the Triads and other material which is now restored to its correct place in the White Book). The tales from Peniarth 4 were published by J. Gwenogvryn Evans in a diplomatic edition entitled *The White Book Mabinogion* (Pwllheli, 1907). This edition was reprinted with a valuable new introduction by R.M. Jones as *Llyfr Gwyn Rhydderch: Y Chwedlau a'r Rhamantau* (Cardiff, 1973). The manuscript is discussed at length by Morgan Watkin in the introduction to his diplomatic edition of *Ystorya Bown de Hamtwn* (Cardiff, 1958). An account of the White Book of Rhydderch by Daniel Huws will appear in *CMCS*, 21 (1991).

The Red Book of Hergest, *Llyfr Coch Hergest*, now preserved in the Bodleian Library at Oxford (Jesus Coll. MS 111) is the largest of the Welsh medieval vernacular manuscripts. It now comprises 362 leaves (measuring 34 by 21 cms.) — all that survives from perhaps about 400 leaves which the manuscript originally comprised. The Red Book has been described as a one-volume library. It is easiest to describe its contents by saying that it includes almost the whole of Welsh literature known to have been committed to writing before 1400, with the exception of religious and legal texts (no doubt deliberate omissions), and the early poetry found in the Book of Aneirin and the Book of Taliesin (these texts were probably not available to the compilers of the Red Book). Another exception is poetry in the newly developed *cywydd* metre, which was perhaps regarded as too new-fangled to deserve a place in a collection which was essentially representative of classical Welsh literature. Like the White Book, the Red Book was evidently a planned and a bespoken work, and there seems no reason to dissent from the view expressed by the late G.J. Williams that it was made for the well-known *uchelwr* Hopcyn ap Thomas, who was an old man in 1403;[25] among his reasons is the fact that the Red Book contains five *awdlau* addressed to Hopcyn and one to his son.

The Red Book contains one of the two major collections of the poetry of the Princes (that of the *Gogynfeirdd*) together with a large amount of early verse in the *englyn* metre, including gnomic and saga poetry, much of it belonging to the cycles of Llywarch Hen and Heledd: these last poems are known also to have been contained in the lost quires of the White Book (see n.23 above). It included also the texts of two poems relating to the story of Myrddin — the *Cyfoesi Myrddin a Gwenddydd y Chwaer* and *Gwasgargerdd Fyrddin yn y Bedd*. The prose contents include *Brut y Brenhinedd* and *Brut y Tywysogion*, preceded by the Welsh verion of *Dares Phrygius*. The Red Book also has the most extensive copy of *Trioedd Ynys Prydein* and in addition to the ten 'Mabinogion' tales it has *Breuddwyd Rhonabwy* (cols.555-71), a tale which is absent from the collection in the White Book. The ten stories which are common to the two manuscripts fall into three distinct groups, which follow each other consecutively in the Red Book (cols.710-844) and in the following order: (i) *Owein, Peredur, Macsen Wledig, Lludd a Llefelys*, (ii) The Four Branches of the *Mabinogi*, (iii) *Gereint fab Erbin* and *Culhwch ac Olwen*. In the White Book the first two of these groups are found in the opposite order, namely (ii), (i), (iii), and each of the three groups is separated from the others by intervening prose items. It seems clear that these three groups already formed three separate entities in the manuscript(s) from which both the White Book and the Red Book were derived. It is worth noting that in both manuscripts *Gereint* and *Culhwch* formed one of these distinct groups and these two tales share certain special features which distinguish them from the other tales.[26]

The Red Book is the work of three professional scribes working in collaboration sometime between 1382 and *c*. 1410. The chief scribe was a certain Hywel Fychan ap Hywel Goch of Builth, whose hand has been identified in several other manuscripts, including Peniarth 11, the earliest text of *Y Seint Greal*. In one manuscript he names himself as 'Hywel Fychan fab Hywel Goch o Fuellt' and refers to his 'master' as 'Hopcyn ap Thomas ab Einion' of Ynys Dawe.[27] Not only did Hywel Fychan write much of the volume, including the three groups of 'Mabinogion' tales listed above, together with *Breuddwyd Rhonabwy* and *Trioedd Ynys Prydein*, but it is evident that he had access also to the White Book at some stage, for his hand has been clearly identified in a brief passage in the White Book text of *Culhwch ac Olwen* (*CO* lines 324-6 = *WM* cols. 467-8) where the original scribe had left a blank space. At one time it was concluded from this that the Red Book scribes must have copied the texts of all these tales from the White Book, but more recently the consensus of opinion has favoured the belief that the texts common to the White and Red Books derive independently, whether directly or indirectly, from a lost common archetype. This subject has been fully discussed by R.M. Jones in his *Rhagymadrodd* to *Llyfr Gwyn Rhydderch*.

The fullest description of the Red Book of Hergest is that of J. Gwenogvryn Evans in RWM II, 1-29. This should be read alongside G. Charles-Edwards, 'The Scribes of the Red Book of Hergest', *NLW Journal*, 21 (1980), 246-56. The association of the Red Book with Hopcyn ap Thomas is proposed by G.J. Williams, *Traddodiad Llenyddol Morgannwg* (Cardiff, 1948), 11-14, 147-8. The history of the Red Book is treated by Prys Morgan, 'Glamorgan and the Red Book', *Morgannwg*, 22 (1978), 42-60. By the mid-sixteenth century the Red Book had already acquired its name and had become known to some of the leading Welsh scholars of the day. It has been one of the famous Welsh manuscripts ever since, and has been all the more influential for having been easily accessible since 1709 in the Library of Jesus College, Oxford, and in more recent years in the Bodleian Library.

The main texts contained in the Red Book have been published in diplomatic editions: John Rhŷs and J. Gwenogvryn Evans, *The Text of the Mabinogion and Other Welsh Tales from the Red Book of Hergest* (Oxford, 1887) (includes *Trioedd Ynys Prydein*), *The Text of the Bruts from the Red Book of Hergest* (Oxford, 1890); and J. Gwenogvryn Evans, *The Poetry in the Red Book of Hergest* (Llanbedrog, 1911). Most of the other contents of the manuscript have also been edited.

NOTES:

1. For Arthur's battles see *HB* ed. Loth, c. 56; ed. Dumville, c. 27. For the suggested localities of the battles see refs. cited in ch.1, n.24 below.

2. ALMA 7-8; see refs. cited in ch.1, n.46. Similarly P. MacCana, *The Learned Tales of Medieval Ireland* (DIAS, 1980), 29, who adds some Irish analogues.

3. H.M. and N.K. Chadwick, *The Growth of Literature*, i (Cambridge, 1932), 161-2; E.K. Chambers, *Arthur of Britain* (London, 1927, 1964), 169-70; ALMA 3-4.

4. Cf. *TYP* 276. The allusion to Badon in *Breuddwyd Rhonabwy* is certainly based on Geoffrey.

5. On the *Annales Cambriae* see K.H. Hughes, 'The *Annales Cambriae* and Related Texts', *PBA*, 59 (1973), 233-58; reprinted in her *Celtic Britain in the Early Middle Ages* (Woodbridge, 1980), 67-85. The writer agrees, ibid. p. 92, that the expansion of the entry on *bellum badonis* 'reads like a gloss'.

6. D.N. Dumville, 'Nennius and the *Historia Brittonum*', *SC*, 10/11 (1975-6), 78-95; 'Sub-Roman Britain: History and Legend', *History*, 62 (1977), 173-92; 'The Historical Value of the *Historia Brittonum*' in *Arthurian Literature*, 6, ed. Richard Barber (Woodbridge, 1986), 1-29.

7. ALMA 3. Cf. D.N. Dumville, 'Sub-Roman Britain', 187-8, L. Alcock, *Arthur's Britain* (Harmondsworth, 1971), 15, 72.

8. K. Jackson, *The Gododdin: The Oldest Scottish Poem* (Edinburgh, 1969), 112.

9. Thomas Jones, *B*, 17 (1958), 238; idem, 'The Early Evolution of the Legend of Arthur', *NMS*, 8 (1964), 6; R. Bromwich, 'Concepts of Arthur', *SC*, 10/11 (1975-6), 163-81 and *TYP* 275; N.K. Chadwick, *Celtic Britain* (London, 1963), 48. Cf. also Charles Thomas, *Britain and Ireland AD 400-800* (London, 1971), 39-41; idem, *Celtic Britain* (London, 1986), 89, 118; D.P. Kirby, *Archaeologia Cambrensis*, 121 (1972), 122.

10. Ifor Williams (ed.), 'Marwnad Cynddylan', *B*, 6 (1931-3), 134-41; discussion and modern Welsh rendering in R.G. Gruffydd (ed.), *Bardos* (Cardiff, 1982), 10-28. It must be recognized, however, that the reading *Art(h)ur Fras* is contingent on the acceptance of the minor textual emendation of *ar tir* to *Artur*. See also A.O.H. Jarman in *An Arthurian Tapestry*, ed. Kenneth Varty (University of Glasgow for the British Branch of the International Arthurian Society, 1981), 4; idem, 'Y Darlun o Arthur', *LlC*, 15 (1984-6), 3-17 (6), and R. Bromwich, 'Concepts of Arthur', *SC*, 10/11, 177.

11. For *Arturius* son of Aedán see A.O. and M.O. Anderson, *Adomnan's Life of Columba* (London, 1961), 228. According to *Seanchus Fir n-Alpain*, ed. J. Bannerman, *Celtica*, 7 (1967), 160, *Artúr* was a grandson of Aedán; see n. *Celtica*, 8, 95-6. The names of Aedán's son and grandson, both called Arthur, may have been conflated.

12. *EWGT* 4, 124. The two versions of the tract *Tucait Indarba na nDessi* are ed. and trans. by Kuno Meyer and published (from Rawl. B. 502) in *Cy.*, 14 (1901), 104-35, and (from Laud 610) in *Ériu*, 3 (1907), 135-42.

13. See Harleian Gen. no. 2 (*EWGT* 10), and cf. HW 261; Wendy Davies, *Wales in the Early Middle Ages* (Leicester, 1982), 95.

14. N.K. Chadwick, *Scottish Gaelic Studies*, 7 (1953), 115-83; Richard Barber, *The Figure of Arthur* (London, 1972); see review of the latter by B.F. Roberts, *SC*, 8/9 (1973-4), 336-9.

15. For refs. see *Annales Cambriae* ann. 807; Harl. Gens. nos. 5 and 26 (*EWGT* 10, 26). Cf.LHEB 437.

16. Cf. Anne Ross, *Pagan Celtic Britain* (London, 1967), 349. Cf. *TYP* (2nd edn.), 544-5.

17. Jean Marcale, *Le Roi Arthur et la societé celtique* (Paris, 1981). Cf. A.O.H. Jarman, 'Y Darlun o Arthur', *LlC*, 15 (1984-6), 8-9. Cf. p.264 below.

18. For Lucius Artorius Castus see S. Frere, *Britannia* (3rd edn. 1987), 150 and n.40; P. Salway, *Roman Britain* (1984), 213 and n. Cf. Jackson, ALMA 2; Kemp Malone, *MP*, 22 (1925), 367-74, Barber, *Figure of Arthur*, 37-8.

19. Geoffrey Ashe, 'A Certain Very Ancient British Book', *Speculum*, 56 (1981), 301-23, and refs. cited in N.J. Lacy (ed.), *The Arthurian Encyclopedia* (New York and London, 1986), 453-5.

20. On Riothamus see N.K. Chadwick, *Early Brittany* (Cardiff, 1969), 195-7, and Jackson, LHEB 13-14; on the name *Riothamus* < *Rigotamos* see LHEB 457. Léon Fleuriot would identify Riothamus with Ambrosius Aurelianus, *Les Origines de la Bretagne* (Paris, 1980), 170-6. The fact that these Britons are described as *super Ligerim sitos* leaves doubt as to whether they came from Britain and had merely camped temporarily on the Loire, or were early emigrants who came from the Armorican colony.

21. Cf. Dumville, 'Sub-Roman Britain', 181.

22. Carmarthen is generally accepted as the place of provenance of the Black Book, and it has much to recommend it, although it cannot be proven owing to the lack of comparative evidence from other manuscripts known to have come from Carmarthen in the twelfth to fourteenth centuries. In view of the traditonal association of Myrddin, the legendary poet, with Carmarthen (see ch.5 below) it is not easy to disregard the significance of the presence of four of the six surviving poems of the Myrddin cycle in the Black Book, including the poem found on its opening pages. R.G. Gruffydd suggested (*YB*, 4 (1960), 16) that the Black Book was the product of a less Norman and more Welsh-orientated monastic establishment than Carmarthen, such as Whitland, Talley, or Ystrad Fflur. But this is to minimize the manifest interest taken by Norman clerics in Welsh secular material, demonstrated at least from the time of Geoffrey of Monmouth onwards, as also by the evidence for their activity in copying manuscripts. Even if it be no more than suggestive evidence, the association of *Bleddri latimer* with the Priory at Carmarthen deserves to be noted (see ch.13, p.286-7 and n.76).

23. Particularly unfortunate is the loss of the cycles of *englynion* relating to Llywarch Hen, Urien Rheged, and Heledd, preserved only in two seventeenth-century copies which are known to be derived from the White Book. See RWM I, 667; *CLlH* xii-xiii, Jenny Rowland, *Early Welsh Saga Poetry* (Woodbridge, 1990), 395-7.

24. The detached pages of the White Book in Peniarth 12 (now correctly replaced) were edited by Egerton Phillimore, *Cy.*, 7 (1884), 123-54. Cf. *TYP* xxiii-iv. Together with the Triads, *Bonedd y Seint* and other material, these pages include a text of *Gwasgarddgerdd Vyrddin yn y Bedd*.

25. On Hopcyn ap Thomas see G.J. Williams, *Traddodiad Llenyddol Morgannwg* (Cardiff, 1948), 9-14, 147-8, *Y Bywgraffiadur Cymreig*, 343.

26. See B.F. Roberts, 'Dosbarthu Chwedlau Cymraeg Canol' *YB*, 15 (1988), 19-46 (22). Cf. introduction to *CO*(2), and on the archaic orthography of *Chwedl Gereint fab Erbin* see R.L. Thomson, *Owein* (DIAS 1968), xxvi.

27. On Hywel Fychan see B.F. Roberts, 'Un o Lawysgrifau Hopcyn ap Tomas o Ynys Dawy', *B*, 22 (1968), 223-8.

1

THE ARTHUR OF HISTORY

Thomas Charles-Edwards

MORE than one question may be asked by an historian about a person such as Arthur.[1] There is the familiar one, asked perhaps a little anxiously: Was Arthur a real person? With a little more knowledge of the ways in which the minds of historians work, a further question may be put: Is there anything valuable which an historian can say about Arthur himself as opposed to his later manifestations in poetry, story and hagiography? And, finally, with even more awareness of the canons of historical criticism, one may ask a question, not about the real, or supposedly real, Arthur, but about the accounts of him given in such texts as the *Historia Brittonum*: what was a given text's perception of Arthur?

The essential, but difficult, truth to learn is that the first question must be asked last and the last question first. Otherwise there will be no critically sifted evidence on the basis of which either of the other questions can be answered. Anyone is entitled to have his hunch, but before a hunch can attain even the modest dignity of an informed guess it needs to be shaped by an understanding of the evidence. Moreover, that understanding will be marred unless ulterior motives are kept firmly in check: the enquiry must first be into the texts themselves without prejudice to any further edifice of argument which may be built upon their foundations.

We may concentrate on the most important of these texts, the *Historia Brittonum*, though there are independent references to Arthur in what may be historical circumstances in two early Welsh poems. The reference in the *Gododdin* to the heroism of a certain Gwawrddur 'although he was not Arthur' (*ceni bei ef arthur*) is only in the B Version; its antiquity is therefore uncertain, for it is only when a passage occurs in both the A and the B Versions that there can be any confidence that it goes back before the ninth or tenth century.[2] The other poem, *Gereint filius Erbin*, although much relied on by the late John Morris, is likewise no earlier than the *Historia Brittonum* (the earliest recension of which is to be dated 829/830). They attest the development of Arthur's reputation in the centuries after the *Historia Brittonum*, but they do not provide an adequate basis for arguments about the historical Arthur.[3] I shall, therefore, concentrate upon the *Historia*

Brittonum, not because everything it contains is historical, but because it is an attempt to make sense of the past by the means then available. I shall, however, leave to one side the section known as the *mirabilia*, although c. 73 refers to a son of Arthur and also to his hound Cabal (Cafall) and the hunting of Twrch Trwyth. The latter is best treated together with *Culhwch ac Olwen* (see ch.3), while the former seems to be an echo of a story telling how a hero killed his son, such as the Irish *Aided Óenfir Aífe*. My principal target will be c. 56 of the *Historia Brittonum*, containing the well-known list of Arthur's battles; but because that chapter can only be understood in the context of the *Historia* as a whole, I shall begin with a consideration of the structure and character of the work.

Our understanding of this 'History of the Britons', however, is in process of being put on a much surer foundation by the series of critical editions of its successive versions now being published by Dr D.N. Dumville.[4] Fortunately, he has also published a number of preliminary studies, including a vigorously polemical essay on 'The Historical Value of the *Historia Brittonum*'.[5] Nothing written at this stage of his great enterprise can pretend to any permanent value, but at least we can review progress to date.

Dr Dumville's main thesis may be summarized as an attack on the 'Heap' interpretation of the *Historia Brittonum*, an attack which is based upon both textual and historiographical premisses. The source from which the Heap theory has been derived is the 'Nennian Preface' which speaks in the first person: 'I, Nennius, a disciple of the holy Elbodugus have taken the trouble to write down some excerpts which the idleness of the people of Britain had caused to be thrown aside . . . I, however, have made a heap of all that I have found, both of the annals of the Romans and of the chronicles of the holy Fathers, and from the writings of the Irish and of the English and from the information handed down by the old men of our people.'[6] The curious mixture of boast and modesty found in this Nennian Preface has been seized upon, both by those who would portray the writer as an ignorant and incompetent compiler and also by those who see in his words a foreshadowing of modern historical attitudes to evidence.[7] Both these interpretations are based upon sandy foundations, for, as Dr Dumville has argued, the Preface was no part of the original text of 829/30 but was added later in a subsequent recension.[8] It is, therefore, the idea of the authorship of the *Historia Brittonum* and of the nature of its contents put forward by a subsequent editor; and it remains to be demonstrated that this editor was any better informed than are modern scholars on the sources and working methods of the original author of the *Historia Brittonum*. It may be that the Preface has commanded respect because it is plainly correct in supposing that the original author used both Irish and English sources;[9] for example, one of the sources it names, a text entitled *Annales Romanorum*, was available to the compilers of the *Collectio Canonum Hibernensis* (alongside another, possibly related text, the *Annales Hebraeorum*) in the early eighth century.[10] Yet, because the Preface is not evidently incorrect in its account of the sources available to our British historian, it does not follow that it is correct in what it says about the way in which those sources were used. The Preface does not, therefore, show that the *Historia Brittonum* was a mere collection of excerpts, a heap of what the author had found.

The argument against the Heap interpretation is also historiographical. It is claimed that the *Historia Brittonum* falls into a genre of historical writing well exemplified in early medieval Ireland, the synthetic history.[11] This form of historical writing is an expression of a sense of national unity projected back into a legendary past. A clear example is the account of the origins of the Irish presented in chapter 13 of the *Historia Brittonum*.[12] This had probably started as an origin legend of the Féni, one of 'the three free peoples' of Ireland. The Féni were divided between a northern branch (to which the Uí Néill and the Connachta belonged) and a southern branch, the ruling people of Munster. Their sense of unity was expressed genealogically, by making them all descend from a single ancestor, Míl Espáine; their divergence was expressed in the same way, by giving Míl two sons, one for the northern, one for the southern branch. The Féni came, by the early eighth century, to claim the status of pre-eminent ruling people in Ireland; but other Irish peoples were to attach themselves to this dominant stock, and, in order to accommodate their claims, the number of Míl's sons had to be expanded from two to three (as in the *Historia Brittonum*) and later six or even eight.[13] The change from an origin legend of a particular Irish people to a history of the origin of the Irish people as a whole entailed the inclusion of the traditions of several peoples, not only the Féni but also the Ulaid, the Laigin and even the Érainn. Furthermore, a sense of the unity of the Irish people required, as a corollary, a sense of the difference between them and neighbouring peoples, Britons, English and Franks. An historical perception of Irish nationality also necessitated a linking of the Irish past with the better-known past of the Romans and of the Jews; the Irish were to have a place, alongside Franks, Britons and English, in the scheme of Christian history and chronology. The full programme of synthetic history included, therefore, not merely the assimilation of different native traditions, but the application of Christian learning. Only some of the raw material would now be origin legends and genealogies; there would also be learned speculation on the descent of the peoples of Europe from Noah and synchronisms between Irish rulers and those of the Romans and the Jews.

Much of this is true, however, not just of the Irish synthetic historians but of Gregory of Tours, Bede and Paul the Deacon. What defines synthetic history as a genre is that its material lies in the pre-Christian past. In the historical perception of Irish scholars from the seventh century onwards there was a convenient, though sometimes only approximate, synchronism between the founders of the currently powerful dynasties and the conversion of the Irish by Patrick and others.[14] The holy man could thus prophesy, and even determine, the rise and fall of dynasties; consequently hagiography depicted the political map of early Christian Ireland. The pre-Christian past, however, was even more malleable than the history of the fourth and fifth centuries, and the synthetic historians' accounts of that more distant past — beyond Patrick and his relationships with the founders of dynasties — were designed to explain and to justify the most general characteristics of the contemporary Irish polity, such as the relationship between the Leinstermen and the Uí Néill. The ostensible subject-matter of the synthetic historian is thus pre-Christian, although statements about the pre-Christian past were intended to make points about the Christian present. Moreover, some of the same preconceptions and techniques were applied to the early Christian period as well. There was no tidy boundary between the period covered by the synthetic historian and that covered by the post-Patrician annals and hagiography.

There is no doubt that the *Historia Brittonum* contains elements comparable to Irish synthetic history, but whether it is best characterized simply as British synthetic history is another matter. This is no mere matter of definition, for Dr Dumville draws a further consequence from his ascription of the *Historia Brittonum* to the genre: no historian, he says, would now place any trust in the literal truth of the narratives offered by such texts; they are interesting for the mentalities and for the political and other interests of the authors, not for the periods about which they purport to write.[15] The *Historia Brittonum* is thus a source for the first half of the ninth century, not for the fifth and sixth centuries. What should concern the historian is what the author of the *Historia Brittonum* said about Germanus, Gwrtheyrn (Vortigern) and Arthur, and why he said it, not whether his statements about such personages have any value as evidence for their careers.

The positive element in this argument is undoubtedly correct: the *Historia Brittonum* is, first and foremost, evidence for the *Historia Brittonum*, for the ideas, sources, culture and intentions of its author. The negative element, however, is much less certain. There are two positions which may be taken: on the one hand one may argue along the sceptical lines taken by Dr Dumville; on the other, one may take the view that it is impossible to prescribe what conclusions may or may not, in the future, be drawn from the text. In particular, it may reasonably be asked how, until the enquiry into the nature and background of the *Historia Brittonum* itself has been brought to a much more advanced stage, one can have such certainty about the value of its evidence for earlier periods. If the crucial rule of method is accepted — first study your source for itself and only then decide what may be the value of its evidence — neither a sceptical nor a non-sceptical position should be adopted at this stage. What has enabled Dr Dumville to take a sceptical position with such confidence is not any rule of historical method, but the proposition that the *Historia Brittonum* is a work of synthetic history.[16]

His most recent statement of historical method is that one may only accept as evidence testimony that is either contemporary or can be shown to be derived from contemporary sources 'by an identifiable and acceptable line of transmission'.[17] This rule seems to me to be too limited. For example, contemporary evidence, imperfectly intelligible on its own, may be explained by information given in a later text. In such a case, there may be good reason to accept the evidence of the later text, even though we are unable to say how it derived its information from a contemporary source. Similarly, there are classic instances in the Carolingian period illustrating an obvious point: a contemporary source may be so constrained by political or other pressures that it cannot tell the truth, whereas a later text, being under less pressure, may be a more reliable source, even though we have no precise idea of the source from which it derived its information.[18]

I have already admitted that the *Historia Brittonum* contains synthetic history, for it is the first text to contain an account of the origins of the Irish, an account later to be worked up into the classical example of synthetic history, the *Lebor Gabála Érenn*, 'The Book of the Conquest of Ireland'.[19] Similarly, the origin of the British people is the first great theme of the *Historia Brittonum* after the opening chronological section on the Six Ages of the World. But if an interest in legends about the origins of peoples is to be enough to brand an entire text as synthetic history and thus as worthless evidence for the period of which it treats, Paul the Deacon and Bede will stand in the dock along with the author of the *Historia Brittonum*. No one will wish to treat Paul the Deacon's account of the dealings of the Lombards with Woden and Frea as sober truth, but the presence of such material in the *Historia Langobardorum* does not make the totality into synthetic history.[20] In any case, the central theme of the *Historia Brittonum* is the relationship between the Gallo-Roman saint Germanus, the British king Gwrtheyrn and the English *dux* Hengest. The Germanus of the *Historia Brittonum* is the pivot between a Roman and a British past, betrayed by a pair of rulers, Maximianus (Maximus) and Gwrtheyrn, and two futures, one Christian and British, the other English, initially pagan but ultimately also Christian. Even though the *Historia Brittonum* declares (c. 22) that the Britons had earlier been converted by a mission sent both by emperors and by the Pope, Gwrtheyrn himself is presented as if he were a pagan:

Germanus fails to convert him to 'his [i.e. Germanus's] Lord' and his guidance comes from the *magus*, the druid, not from the Christian bishop.[21]   The conflict between holy man and pagan king is interwoven with the story of the settlement of the English, led by Hengest, a settlement which took place 'by divine will' (c. 45).   The treatment is reminiscent of the conflict between Patrick and Lóegaire (which, interestingly, the *Historia Brittonum* omits from its account of Patrick in cc. 50-5) and of that between Elijah and Ahab.   Perhaps the main concern of the author of the *Historia Brittonum* is to encourage the Britons to come to terms with defeat and loss of territory.   Not for him the fierce resentment of the tenth-century poem *Armes Prydein* with its hope that the English might yet be driven back into the German Ocean out of which they had come.   He understands such feelings: Gwrthefyr compelled Hengest's men to flee to their boats 'like women' (c. 44).   Yet what concerns him more is the role of the Britons in the providential history not just of their own island but also of Ireland.   A Briton, Patrick, would be sent by the Pope, 'by the advice and persuasion of the holy bishop Germanus' (c. 51) to convert the Irish; a Briton, Rhun ab Urien, would baptize the Northumbrians for forty days (c. 63).   The victories of a Gwrthefyr, or an Arthur, might be glorious, but they had no future; the triumphs of a Patrick and of a Rhun ab Urien would bring whole peoples to salvation.

It may be worth distinguishing two genres of historical writing, both practised by the Irish, sometimes in combination, and both present in the *Historia Brittonum*, synthetic history and synchronistic history.   Synthetic history, as presented in the classic account by MacNeill, has been described already; synchronistic history is concerned to establish a chronological relationship between the histories of different peoples; the model here was Eusebius's Chronicle with its desire to establish the superior antiquity of Judaeo-Christian tradition compared with those of Greece and Rome.   Synthetic history may require synchronisms, but synchronistic history is not necessarily a quasi-historical presentation of a legendary past; it is an essential part of any history which draws upon records and traditions from distinct peoples.   If the *Historia Brittonum* contained some synthetic history, synchronisms were part of its very structure, for it needed to weave the histories of the Romans, the Irish and the English into its account of the Britons.

In the early Middle Ages these forms of historical writing occur more often as elements in a larger whole than as self-contained entities.   The larger wholes are provided by two genres of history which interact: the history of a people and ecclesiastical history, *historia gentis* and *historia ecclesiastica*.   Jordanes's (and Cassiodorus's) *Historia Gothorum*, the *Liber Historiae Francorum* and Paul the Deacon's *Historia Langobardorum* were histories of a people, whereas Gregory of

Tours wrote ecclesiastical history.[22]   Gregory of Tours begins with the Creation, Paul the Deacon with the Scandinavian origins of the Lombards.   An *origo gentis* is thus a normal starting-point for the history of a people, whether it be in ancient Germania or in the city of Troy.

When ecclesiastical history was adapted for a readership ruled by barbarian kings, it became natural to begin on a broad scale, with the history of salvation, but to narrow the scope as the history developed.   Gregory of Tours might begin with the Creation and the Fall but he then proceeded via St Martin to Clovis and Frankish Gaul.   Bede began with the Roman conquest of Britain (the invasions of Julius Caesar and of Claudius straddled in time the Incarnation, Passion and Resurrection). However, he soon came to concentrate on the English people and so wrote an *Historia Ecclesiastica Gentis Anglorum*.   In Bede, therefore, there was a conscious interweaving of the two genres, the history of a people and ecclesiastical history. The same is true of the *Historia Brittonum*.   It begins with the Six Ages of the World, a theme appropriate to ecclesiastical history, but then turns to the origin of the British people, an *origo gentis* closely related to the *origo* of the Franks given in Fredegar's Chronicle and in the *Liber Historiae Francorum*.[23]   In the relationship between Gwrtheyrn, Germanus and Hengest the *Historia Brittonum* examines the fates of two peoples, the Britons and the English, and the progress of Christianity in Britain.   We may define the genre of the *Historia Brittonum*, therefore, as a fusion of *historia gentis* and *historia ecclesiastica*.   If such history is unhistorical, so also are all the major histories of the early Middle Ages.

Of the two elements in Dr Dumville's attack on the Heap interpretation of the *Historia Brittonum*, the one based on the history of the text is more securely founded than the historiographical argument.   Yet, even with the latter, while one may not give full assent to the labelling of the *Historia Brittonum* as synthetic history, there may yet be good reason to think that it has a unity of structure and outlook, and that it is therefore far more than a mere heap.   In spite of its relatively small scale, the *Historia Brittonum* is in the grand tradition of early medieval history.

The function of the account of Arthur's battles in c. 56 of the *Historia Brittonum* must now be judged in the light of our opinion of the structure and outlook of the whole work.   If we see the relationship between Germanus, Gwrtheyrn and Hengest as the central theme, between the origins of the British people and the history of Roman Britain, on the one hand, and the English genealogies and the Northern History on the other, the role of the Arthurian chapter becomes clear.   The author requires a link between two principal sections; since an essential element in much of his work is the relationship between holy man and the fate of nations, he finds a double link, first the story of Patrick and then the wars of Arthur.   Since he is fundamentally an ecclesiastical historian, he gives much more space to Patrick than to Arthur. Patrick gives the reader a sense of continuity from the central figure of Germanus; Arthur echoes the achievements of Gwrthefyr and so offers a further contrast with Gwrtheyrn; his victories also call forth another phase of migration from Germany leading to the establishment of Germanic kingdoms in Britain. The structure may thus be set out as follows:

Principal Themes	Linking Passages

Germanus, Gwrtheyrn and Hengest, cc. 31-49	
	Patrick (a link from Germanus), cc. 50-5
	Arthur (a link from Hengest and Gwrtheyrn to Ida and the Northern History), c. 56
The English royal genealogies and the Northern History, cc. 57-65	

The role of the Arthurian chapter is thus secondary but nevertheless important to the organization of the History as a whole.

Certain points of interpretation follow from this view of the form of the work. The chronological frame of the Arthurian chapter is provided by the two end-points, the death of Hengest and the establishment by Ida of an English kingdom in Bernicia; the death of Hengest looks back to the central theme of the *Historia*, while the accession of Ida brings us into the second half of the sixth century, to the wars of the North British kings against the English of Bernicia and eventually to the conversion of Northumbria by a Briton, Rhun ab Urien.

In geographical terms, however, there is a tension between the Kentish perspective implicit in the beginning of the Arthurian chapter and the wide spatial sweep of Arthur's battles.[24] The *Historia Brittonum* brings Octha down from the North to Kent and makes him the ancestor of its royal kindred. 'Then', so we are told, 'Arthur was fighting against them in those days with the kings of the Britons, but he himself was *dux bellorum.*' This introduces the list of twelve battles culminating in the battle 'in monte Badonis'; and, finally, the English are said to have turned in desperation to Germany from where they drew, not only fighting men, but kings 'that they might reign over them in Britain'. Mention of kings leads straight to Ida and Bernicia. Previously we have had the foundation of only one English kingdom, that of Kent. The implication, therefore, is that the kings of Kent alone derived their origin from a pre-Arthurian era; otherwise English kingship was imported from Germany as a reaction to Arthur's victories.

This conception is related to the movement from the theme of Germanus, Gwrtheyrn and Hengest to the material taken from the Anglian Collection of genealogies and regnal lists.[25] There the new English kingdoms are displayed in full. Again, however, there is no mere heap of borrowed material, for the author of the *Historia* knows how to link his various themes. In his source, the Anglian Collection, all the lines end with Woden Frealafing, 'Woden the son of Frealaf', except for the genealogy of the kings of Lindsey. This is taken back another four generations to Geat. In the *Historia* the lines are reversed so that they run from ancestor to descendant rather than the other way round; they thus begin, except for one, with Woden (not with his father Frealaf). The exception this time is Kent rather than Lindsey (which is omitted). In c. 58 the line begins, not with Woden, but with Hengest and descends to Ecgberht; in other words, the line is shorter than the others. The anomaly draws attention back to the genealogy of Hengest and Horsa in c. 31 where the anomaly works the other way, for the line here ascends back beyond Woden to Geat. The central position given to Lindsey in the Anglian Collection is now taken by the kings of Kent. Moreover the genealogy revolves around Hengest, descending from him in c. 58 and ascending from him in c. 31. Even in the section on the kings of the English, Hengest is given a pivotal position, and it is that position which provides structural unity.

The significance of all this is best understood by comparing the *Historia Brittonum* with Bede. Both were drawing on Kentish material for their account of the English settlement, which both see in terms of the supposed ancestors of the kings of Kent, Hengest, Oeric or Oisc and Octha or Ocga. In Bede it looks very much as though his Kentish source has combined two different accounts, one centred upon the heroic figure of Hengest, the other upon the eponymous ancestor of the kings of Kent, namely Oisc.[26] The same combination of Hengest and Oisc (Æsc) underlies the Kentish origin legend in the Anglo-Saxon Chronicle; but in Bede's account of Hengest there is the special feature, not found in the Chronicle, that Hengest came to England as the leader of a force made up of contingents from 'three of the more powerful peoples of Germany'. Hengest, in other words, was remembered as a *dux*, a warlord whose host was not confined within the limits of any one *gens*.[27]

The same conception may lie behind the *Historia*'s statement that Hengest invited so many ships from the islands off Germany that they were left empty of inhabitants (c. 38); he is perceived as the organizer of an army of settlement rather than as a mere ancestral king of a single people. The Arthurian chapter begins, therefore, with a reference to Hengest's function as the assembler of the English migration to Britain, but it also stresses the Kentish dimension of Hengest by saying that after his death Octha, his son, came from North Britain to Kent, 'and from him stem the kings of the Kentishmen'. We are then told that Arthur 'fought against them in those days with the kings of the Britons'. Although one might be forgiven for supposing that by 'them' the *Historia* meant the Kentishmen, the battles make it clear that this is not so: his enemies were the English as a whole.[28] Similarly Arthur fought 'together with the kings of the Britons, but he was their war-leader (*dux bellorum*)'. The role of Arthur as the leader of the Britons in a series of named battles is reminiscent of that assigned to Gwrthefyr, son of Gwrtheyrn, in cc. 43-4, where his leadership of the Britons introduces a list of battles with precise geographical specification. In that case the source appears to be ultimately Kentish and to be the same as that used, at one or more removes, by *The Anglo-Saxon Chronicle* in its account of the foundation of the kingdom of Kent.[29] Yet, with Arthur, although the introductory sentences in c. 56 are highly Kentish, the geography of the list of battles, as we have seen, is not. The Kentish starting-point of the Arthurian chapter is therefore necessitated by the balance between Hengest, the English *dux*, and Arthur, the British *dux*, and the way the battles of Arthur echo the battles of Gwrthefyr.

The scope and character of the authority assigned to Arthur in the *Historia Brittonum* is also closely comparable with that which it gives to Penda in the campaign leading to the battle of the Winwaed (the *Historia*'s 'Field of Gai'). The *reges Brittonum* are said to have 'gone out with Penda on an expedition as far as the fortress which is called Iudeu' (c. 64). It is now clear that this kind of war-leadership, embracing the contingents of a number of kings, was an essential element in the position of the so-called Bretwalda, although it is ascribed to rulers who were not mentioned by Bede in his famous list of kings who enjoyed an *imperium* either over the Southern English or, *maiore potentia*, over the whole, or almost the whole, of Britain.[30]

Our understanding of this position — one cannot go so far as to call it an office[31] — is hampered by the difficulty in balancing its English and British dimensions. On the one hand, it appears initially as an authority over the Southern English, those south of the Humber; on the other, the term Bretwalda, found in the Parker Chronicle, means 'British ruler', while the form found in the other versions of the Chronicle, Brytenwalda (Breotenwalda), means 'Ruler of Britain'. Even if the Parker Chronicle's version of the term is not a mere scribal error, there seems to be no genuine difference of meaning between them. The attempt of Mr E. John, following Kemble and others, to interpret Brytenwalda as 'wide ruler' rests on a straightforward philological error;[32] and the more general senses of the term found in poetry must therefore be secondary to its primary meaning, 'Ruler of Britain'. It is unlikely that the Chronicle's use of such a term is an innovation of the ninth century, for Adomnán in the late seventh describes Oswald as *totius Britanniae imperator*, and the Ismere charter of Æthelbald (AD 736) describes him in the witness-list as *rex Britanniae*.[33] The latter's apparent equation of 'king of the provinces of the Southern English' (in the proem of the charter) with 'king of Britain' (in the witness-list) may constitute a claim, not just that Æthelbald was in some sense the ruler of Britain, but also that the pre-eminent king of the Southern English should also be the ruler of Britain. Such an aspiration might not be acceptable to the Welsh — in spite of the much later acknowledgement that the 'crown of London' had passed to the English — but it would also be directed against the Northumbrians. The annal in the Continuation of Bede, *s.a.* 750, according to which 'Cuthred, king of the West Saxons, rebelled against King Æthelbald and Oingus', strongly suggests that some form of agreement had by then been made according to which Æthelbald was recognized as overlord of Southern Britain while Oingus was overlord of Northern Britain, including a claim to suzerainty over Northumbria.[34]

The uncertainty as to what kind of aspiration or claim such titles may have implied also hampers our interpretation of c. 56 of the *Historia Brittonum*. Its author plainly took much material from English as well as Irish sources. He appears to have favoured a reconciliation, based upon a common faith, between the Britons and the English: Oswald's death is portrayed in c. 65 as the killing of a saint by a pagan king, Penda, using treachery and also *diabolicam artem*; any participation of the Britons in the battle is passed over in silence. Gwrtheyrn, too, is depicted as a pagan, into whose heart 'Satan entered'. Arthur, however, in his eighth battle 'carried the image of the holy and perpetual Virgin Mary upon his shoulders and the pagans were turned to flight on that day', an act which is reminiscent of Bede's story that Oswald carried a Cross into battle against Cadwallon.[35] As Bede's story echoes the eastern cult of the Cross, so does the *Historia's* account remind us of the use of an icon of the Blessed Virgin in the defence of Constantinople.[36] The similarity to Bede's account of Oswald as bearer of the Cross is still clearer in the *Annales Cambriae*, of the tenth century, where Arthur's use of an icon of the Virgin is transmuted into the bearing of the Cross on his shoulders 'for three days and three nights', and it is applied to the Battle of Mount Badon (*s.a.* 516). This version appears to be later than that of the *Historia Brittonum* (because of the elaboration whereby the one day has become three days and nights) and is unlikely to be wholly independent of it. There is, as we shall see, no reason to suspect any earlier date for the other Arthurian annal in *Annales Cambriae* (*s.a.* 537): 'Gueith Camlann in qua Arthur et Medraut corruerunt'.[37]

The late Dr Kathleen Hughes, in her studies of the *Annales Cambriae* argued convincingly that the framework for the annals up to 613 was a version of the Chronicle of Ireland compiled in the early tenth century.[38] It has subsequently been argued by Dr Dumville that the source was a member of the Clonmacnoise group of annals deriving from the Chronicle of Ireland and that it continued at least as far as 888.[39] Dr Hughes also maintained that after 613 the *Annales Cambriae* drew upon a North British source which continued up to the late eighth century.[40] The problem with the Arthurian annals can now be seen more clearly: they derive from a period in which there is no secure evidence of any British annalistic source. It is conceivable that they belong to the same North British text which is more clearly detectible after 613, a text which Dr Hughes maintains was also used by the *Historia Brittonum*. It may be objected, however, that the distance between the annal on the Battle of Mount Badon and the *Historia*'s account of Arthur's battles is much greater than we should expect if both derived from the same North British source. A point of comparison is given by their accounts of the Battle of the Winwaed (the 'Field of Gai'), used by Hughes to argue, not only that the *Annales Cambriae* and the *Historia Brittonum* were using the same source, but that this source did not have an annalistic form.[41] If one pursues this objection, it is difficult to see how any reason could be given to show that the compiler of the *Annales Cambriae* in the mid-tenth century had a written source for his Arthurian material. Moreover, even if he did, there is no reason to suppose that it was ancient.

The problems may be seen even more clearly if we look at a suggestion made by Thomas Jones. He pointed out the oddity of the annal for 516: 'Bellum Badonis in quo Arthur portauit crucem Domini nostri Iesu Christi tribus diebus et tribus noctibus in humeros suos et Brittones uictores fuerunt.'[42] The bare style adopted by these annals would have led one to expect an entry consisting solely of the two words, 'Bellum Badonis'; and the rest may therefore be suspected of being later elaboration. This point may, however, be put in two forms. First, it may be an observation — as for Jones it was — about the style of the tenth-century A version of the *Annales Cambriae*; if so, the later elaboration might have occurred between the mid-tenth and the early twelfth century, the date of the MS. Or, secondly, it might be a point about the character of the source used by the *Annales Cambriae*. In that case the clear assumption would have been made that this source was annalistic. Only then would it be appropriate to expect the brevity associated with annals.

At this point further uncertainties come into view. Kathleen Hughes's view of the construction of the A version of the *Annales Cambriae* was that it was, so to speak, 'end-on': that is to say that the tenth-century compiler used the Chronicle of Ireland up to 613; he then switched to his North British source, following it until 777, after which he used St David's annals (at least from 796). There is some doubt about the date of the changeover from the northern source to the St David's annals, but in any case it seems that, for Hughes, the tenth-century annalist did not use two sources for the one period. This analysis leads directly to her view that the few Welsh annals for the period before 613 do not derive from the northern text and are not sufficient to give us grounds for positing a distinct source. They may, therefore, derive from tenth-century editing.

A different line is taken by Dr Dumville. He abandons the 'end-on' analysis, arguing that the *Annales Cambriae* used the Chronicle of Ireland after 613, and the North British source after 777.[43] Moreover, in his view the latter was a set of annals, whereas Hughes was quite clear that it was not annalistic.[44] On this analysis of the construction of *Annales Cambriae*, whereby the sources overlap, it becomes much easier to suppose that the sixth-century annals referring to Britain came from the North British source. This was also used by the *Historia Brittonum* and therefore cannot be later than the early ninth century. To return to Thomas Jones's suggestion, we seem to be, if we are prepared to follow Dr Dumville, in a position to posit an entry for the Battle of Badon already in existence in the North British annals, an entry which might have been expanded in the way Jones suggested.

Yet, at this point there is no escaping the serious difficulty already mentioned. The only grounds for supposing that the sixth-century British annals did come from the northern source are that there is evidently some kind of relationship between the annal on the Battle of Badon and the reference in the *Historia Brittonum* to that other battle, 'bellum in castello Guinnion, in quo Arthur portavit imaginem sanctae Mariae perpetuae virginis super humeros suos, et pagani versi sunt in fugam in illo die, et caedes magna fuit super illos per virtutem Domini nostri Jesu Christi et per virtutem sanctae Mariae virginis genetricis eius'. Yet the correspondence occurs in what, on Jones's view, is the elaboration upon the original bare annal (which was simply 'an. Bellum Badonis'). What points to a common source (in Dumville's view a set of annals), is precisely what, on Jones's view, is least annalistic. Moreover, we still have to explain why it is that different battles are in question, why in one case it is an icon of the Virgin and in the other a cross, why in one case Arthur carries the icon in a battle occurring on a single day, whereas in the other he carries the cross for three days and three nights. If both texts derive their information immediately from the same source, major rewriting has taken place. An easier conclusion is that divergent literary elaboration has led to two different versions, one in the *Historia Brittonum* and the other in the *Annales Cambriae*; such elaboration may have been within an oral rather than a written tradition, but even if it was in written form, it is unlikely that it was annalistic. There is, then, no need to suppose that the two versions of the story were taken into our historical texts before the dates of their final composition (829/30 and the 950s).

There is also the other Arthurian annal (*Annales Cambriae*, s.a. 537): 'Gueith Camlann in qua Arthur et Medraut corruerunt'. Here the form of the entry is entirely typical of annals. Unexceptionable form is, however, no guarantee of early date. There is nothing in the *Historia Brittonum* corresponding to this annal, and thus no reason to suppose that it came from the possible North British annals. On the evidence of the *Historia Brittonum*, especially c. 73 of the *mirabilia*, and the early poetry, interest in Arthur was amply sufficient by the tenth century for an annalist of that date to have composed such annals without any written source.[45]

The general position with c. 56 of the *Historia Brittonum* does not seem to be much more promising if one's interest is directed solely towards its demonstrable factual content. One cannot help suspecting that the account of Arthur's battles has in part been moulded by the concerns of the seventh and eighth centuries, in England as well as in Wales. The *dux bellorum* can hardly be entirely separated from the military *ducatus* exercised by such English kings as Edwin over other kingdoms. The significance of c. 56 for the *Historia Brittonum* itself is secondary, for its principal concern is with divine providence rather than with human heroism in war. By contrast with Vortigern, into whose heart the Devil had entered, and also by contrast with Vortigern's Britons, a people lacking in military capacity ruled by a king without vigour (c. 37), Gwrthefyr and Arthur fought victoriously against the invaders. Yet, in the end, their victories served only to reveal the more clearly that it was God who had determined that the Saxons should settle in Britain under their own kings. However Christian and however heroic Arthur's victories may have been, they, like Gwrthefyr's, only called forth a further wave of migration; moreover they brought into Britain kings, as well as warriors, out of Germany. The royal dynasties of the English therefore ruled their British lands by divine will. What was not just victorious in the short term but triumphant in the end was the missionary work of Patrick and Rhun ab Urien. Whether or not the author of the *Historia Brittonum* knew Bede's *Historia Ecclesiastica*, he had an answer to Bede's accusation (I. 22) that 'together with the other unspeakable crimes which their historian Gildas recounted in tearful prose, they were also adding this, that they never communicated the word of the Faith by preaching to the people of the Saxons or English who inhabited Britain with them'.

Although the use, in c. 56, of a Welsh battle-listing poem has been suspected,[46] perhaps rightly, no such source is likely for the list of Gwrthefyr's battles in c. 44.[47] And, if there was such a poem celebrating Arthur's battles, its date remains entirely uncertain. Such a theory about the source of c. 56 offers us no high road to the historical Arthur. Chapter 56 is very interesting for the student of the *Historia*

Brittonum; and it cannot be ruled out *a priori* that some useful information about the sixth century may, some day, be surmised on the basis of the text; but, at the moment, the prospects are poor. At this stage of the enquiry, one can only say that there may well have been an historical Arthur; that the historian can as yet say nothing of value about him, but that later conceptions of Arthur are likely to interest historians almost as much as they do students of medieval literature.

NOTES:

1. I am very grateful to the editors for their patience and to David Dumville and Morfydd Owen for reading drafts. I have greatly benefited from their suggestions. Previous studies of this question include the essay by K.H. Jackson, 'The Arthur of History', in ALMA 1-11; and the earlier part of T. Jones, 'The Early Evolution of the Legend of Arthur', *NMS*, 8 (1964), 3-21. Jones's article also embraces the earlier stages of Arthur's literary career; for a recent study which similarly includes both the historical and the literary Arthur, see R. Bromwich, 'Concepts of Arthur', *SC*, 10/11 (1975-6), 163-81.

2. *CA*, line 1242; A.O.H. Jarman, *Aneirin: Y Gododdin, Britain's Oldest Heroic Poem* (Llandysul, 1988), line 972, and the note *ad loc*. R. Bromwich, 'Concepts of Arthur', 176, sees Old Welsh orthography in this stanza and so considers it to date from the ninth century at the latest. This is unsafe: elements of Old Welsh orthography were still in use in the mid-thirteenth century, as in the Black Book of Chirk and Peniarth MS 28.

3. The poem on Geraint is ed. by B.F. Roberts in Ast. H., 286-96. John Morris's discussion is in his *The Age of Arthur* (London, 1973), 104-6. Early Welsh Arthurian poetry is surveyed by Thomas Jones, 'The Early Evolution of the Legend of Arthur', 13-18, and by K.H. Jackson, 'Arthur in Early Welsh Verse', ALMA 12-19. On the date of the *Historia Brittonum* see D.N. Dumville, 'Some Aspects of the Chronology of the *Historia Brittonum*', *B*, 25 (1974), 439-45.

4. One volume has appeared: *Historia Brittonum: iii. The 'Vatican' Recension*, ed. D.N. Dumville (Cambridge, 1985). For the early Harleian Recension, the text most commonly used is still the edition of Mommsen in his *Chronica Minora Saec. IV, V, VI, VII*, iii (MGH AA xiii). The Harleian text is to be found in E. Faral, LA iii, 1-62, from which it was printed, with some additions and a translation, by J. Morris, *Nennius, British History, and the Welsh Annals* (London and Chichester, 1980). My references to chapters are to those used by Mommsen and Morris.

5. D.N. Dumville, 'The Historical Value of the *Historia Brittonum*', *Arthurian Literature*, 6 (1986), 1-26.

6. Ed. Th. Mommsen, *Chronica Minora*, iii, 143; ed. Morris, p. 50.

7. Favourable: J. Morris (ed. and transl.) *Nennius, British History, and the Welsh Annals*, 8; unfavourable: see the collection of dismissive quotations assembled by Dumville, 'The Historical Value', 5.

8. D.N. Dumville, '"Nennius" and the *Historia Brittonum*', *SC*, 10/11 (1975-6), 78-95.

9. Cf. c. 15, 'sic mihi peritissimi Scottorum nuntiaverunt' and, e.g., the use of the Anglian Collection of genealogies and regnal lists in cc. 57-65.

10. *Collectio Canonum Hibernensis*, XXXI. 6; XXXII. 17. b (cf. 16. b); LXIII. 2. b (ed. F.W.H. Wasserschleben, *Die irische Kanonensammlung*, 2nd edn., Leipzig, 1885). Neither can very well be a generic reference to annals of the Jews or Romans. Material attributed to Origen seems to have been part of the *Annales Hebraeorum* (cf. XXXI. 6 with XXXII. 17. b), and the nature of the text following the phrase *In annalibus Romanorum* suggests that it is a quotation.

11. Dumville, 'The Historical Value', 5-8.

12. Cf. T.F. O'Rahilly, *Early Irish History and Mythology* (Dublin, 1946), 475-6.

13. O'Rahilly, *Early Irish History and Mythology*, 195-7.

14. For example, the sons of Niall of the Nine Hostages in Muirchú, I. 15-21, esp. 21 (2) and Tírechán, 8-10, 12 (ed. L. Bieler, *The Patrician Texts in the Book of Armagh*, Scriptores Latini Hiberniae, x (Dublin, 1979), 84-98, 130-2).

15. Dumville, 'The Historical Value', 7-8, 11.

16. Dr Dumville remarks very reasonably of the *Historia Brittonum* ('Sub-Roman Britain: History and Legend', *History*, N.S. 62 (1977), 177) 'that we must apply the same critical techniques to this text as we would to any other "historical" narrative', but the inverted commas around 'historical' are, to my mind, objectionable.

17. D.N. Dumville, 'Historical Archaeology and Northumbrian History', in *Coinage in Ninth-Century Northumbria: The Tenth Oxford Symposium on Coinage and Monetary History*, ed. D.M. Metcalf (Brit. Archaeol. Reports, British Ser., 180; Oxford, 1987), p. 55.

18. For example, in the *Annales Regni Francorum* (ed. F. Kurze, *MGH SRG in usum Schol.*, Hanover, 1895), *s.a.* 778, the disaster at Roncesvaux is only in the later version.

19. See above, n.12.

20. Paul the Deacon, *Historia Langobardorum*, I. 8 (ed. G. Waitz, *MGH, Scriptores Rerum Langobardicarum et Italicarum Saec. VI-IX*, 52) himself describes the tale as *risui digna*.

21. *Historia Brittonum*, cc. 40, 47. If the author of the *Historia Brittonum* had considered Gwrtheyrn to be a Christian, he should have used the phrase *ad Dominum*, not *ad Dominum suum*.

22. In the preface to Book II Gregory invokes the example of Eusebius and Orosius. The commonly used title *Historia Francorum* is not original: only MS *C1a* describes it as *ecclesiastica historia Francorum*. On Cassiodorus and Jordanes see P. Heather, 'Cassiodorus and the Rise of the Amals', *Journal of Roman Studies*, 79 (1989), 103-28, who cites earlier discussions.

23. R.A. Gerberding, *The Rise of the Carolingians and the Liber Historiae Francorum* (Oxford, 1987), ch.2.

24. K.H. Jackson, 'Once again Arthur's Battles', *Modern Philology*, 43 (1945-6), 57, points to Linnuis for Lindsey and Coit Celidon for Coed Celyddon in Scotland; he places Mons Badonis in southern Britain, but this is less certain (cf. K.H. Jackson, 'The Site of Mount Badon', *Journal of Celtic Studies*, 2 (1953-8), 152-5).

25. D.N. Dumville, 'The Anglian Collection of Royal Genealogies and Regnal Lists', *Anglo-Saxon England*, 5 (1976), 23-50.

26. P. Sims-Williams, 'The Settlement of England in Bede and the *Chronicle*', *Anglo-Saxon England*, 12 (1983), 22.

27. Cf. W. Schlesinger, 'Über germanisches Königtum', in *Das Königtum*, Vorträge und Forschungen, iii (1956), 103-41, esp. 116-31; J.M. Wallace-Hadrill, *Bede's Ecclesiastical History of the English People: A Historical Commentary* (Oxford Medieval Texts, 1988), 23-4 and 215.

28. See K.H. Jackson, 'Once again Arthur's Battles', n.24 above. It is likely that the author of the *Historia Brittonum* would himself have known, at least very approximately, the location of Linnuis and of Coed Celyddon, and perhaps also that of the *urbs legionis*.

29. N.P. Brooks, 'The Creation and Early Structure of the Kingdom of Kent', in *The Origins of Anglo-Saxon Kingdoms*, ed. S. Bassett, Studies in the Early History of Britain (London, 1989), 58-64.

30. Bede, *Historia Ecclesiastica*, II. 5; see the addendum on this chapter in J.M. Wallace-Hadrill, *Bede's Ecclesiastical History: A Historical Commentary*, 220-2.

31. P. Wormald, 'Bede, the Bretwaldas and the Origins of the *Gens Anglorum*', in *Ideal and Reality in Frankish and Anglo-Saxon Society*, ed. P. Wormald with D. Bullough and R. Collins (Oxford, 1983), 99-129.

32. E. John, *Orbis Britanniae and Other Studies* (Leicester, 1966), 7-8 (the Old Saxon *brēd* in *bredun giwald* corresponds to OE *brād*).

33. Adomnán, *Vita S. Columbae*, I. 1 (ed. A.O. and M.O. Anderson, *Adomnán's Life of Columba*, Edinburgh, 1961, 200); P.H. Sawyer, *Anglo-Saxon Charters: An Annotated List and Bibliography* (London, 1968), no. 89 (= Birch, *Cartularium Saxonicum*, no. 154).

34. C. Plummer (ed.), *Baedae Opera Historica* (Oxford, 1896), i, 362. Cf. *The Annals of Ulster*, i, ed. S. Mac Airt and G. Mac Niocaill (Dublin, 1983), *s.a.* 750, which records, after the killing of Óengus's brother by the Britons, 'aithbe flatho Oengussa', which is to be translated 'the ebbing of the power of Óengus', not, as by Mac Airt and Mac Niocaill, 'end of the reign of Aengus'.

35. Bede, *Historia Ecclesiastica*, III. 2.

36. D. Obolensky, *The Byzantine Commonwealth* (London, 1971), 54 (on the Avar siege of Constantinople in AD 626).

37. For the A Version of the *Annales Cambriae* see E. Phillimore, 'The "Annales Cambriae" and Old-Welsh Genealogies from "Harleian MS" 3859', *Cy.*, 9 (1888), 154.

38. K. Hughes, 'The A-text of *Annales Cambriae*', in her *Celtic Britain in the Early Middle Ages*, Studies in Celtic History 2 (Woodbridge, 1980), 88-92.

39. K. Grabowski and D. Dumville, *Chronicles and Annals of Mediaeval Ireland and Wales*, Studies in Celtic History 4 (Woodbridge, 1984), ch.4.

40. K. Hughes, 'The A-text of the *Annales Cambriae*', 92-8.

41. Cf. Hughes's discussion, ibid., 93.

42. T. Jones, 'The Early Evolution of the Legend of Arthur', *NMS*, 8 (1964), 5.

43. D.N. Dumville in K. Grabowski and D. Dumville, *Chronicles and Annals of Mediaeval Ireland and Wales*, 211-24.

44. 'North British annals', ibid., 209, and see also his review, *SC*, 12/13 (1977/8), 466-7, and K.H. Jackson, 'On the Northern British Section in Nennius', in N.K. Chadwick (ed.), *Celt and Saxon*

(Cambridge, 1963), 48-9, who calls it 'the Northern Chronicle'.

45. The other non-Irish entries before AD 600 in *Annales Cambriae* are not of a character to suggest early recording:

> (1) *AC*, *s.a.* 547, Maelgwn's obit, see D.N. Dumville, 'Gildas and Maelgwn: Problems of Dating', in M. Lapidge and D. Dumville (edd.), *Gildas: New Approaches*, Studies in Celtic History 5 (Woodbridge, 1984), 53.
>
> (2) There are two annals relating to the battle of Arfderydd and Gwrgi and Peredur (*s.aa.* 573 and 580): for their subsequent literary importance see R. Bromwich, *TYP*, Notes to Personal Names under Peredur m. Elif(f)er Gosgorduavr.
>
> (3) The burial of Daniel is recorded *s.a.* 584 and the death of Dunawt ap Pabo *s.a.* 595. Daniel may have been regarded as a son of Dunawt, who was himself an important literary figure: see Bromwich, *TYP*, Notes to Personal Names, under Dunavt m. Pabo Post Prydein.

46. This suggestion, made by H.M. and N.K. Chadwick, *The Growth of Literature*, i (Cambridge, 1932), 154-5, has been accepted by Jackson and by Thomas Jones among others; it is still maintained, most recently, by R. Bromwich, 'Concepts of Arthur', *SC*, 10/11 (1975-6), 169-72, and by Dumville, 'Sub-Roman Britain: History and Legend', *History*, 62 (1977), 188.

47. Gwrthefyr's four battles in c. 44 are unlike Arthur's twelve in c. 56 in the following respects:

> (1) the second battle is first given an English name and then provided with a Welsh equivalent; such a procedure does not suggest a Welsh poem as the source (see H.M. Chadwick, *The Origin of the English Nation* [Cambridge, 1907], 41-2);
>
> (2) *iuxta lapidem tituli* may be related to Bede's supposed Kentish inscription for Hors in *Historia Ecclesiastica* I. 15, itself presumably taken from a Kentish source; in any case it does not seem to be the kind of detail one would expect to come from a poem;
>
> (3) the four battles lead directly to the theme of the failure to bury Gwrthefyr in a position which would have enabled him to repel invasion; but that theme is suggestive of Welsh prose not verse: see T.M. Charles-Edwards, 'Boundaries in Irish Law', in *Medieval Settlement*, ed. P.H. Sawyer (London, 1976), 86-7.

2

THE EARLY WELSH ARTHURIAN POEMS

Patrick Sims-Williams

THIS chapter covers the same ground as Kenneth Jackson's 'Arthur in Early Welsh Verse' (1959), which has been one of the most useful and compact treatments of its subject.[1] No new poems have come to light in the intervening thirty years, but there are several good reasons for re-examining the poems which Jackson discussed. Many have now been edited, and advances in Welsh lexicography and literary prosopography have clarified the meaning and allusions of others. Our understanding of the stylistic demands of metre and genre in Welsh poetry has been sharpened,[2] and there is now more appreciation of the distinction between mere obscurity and allusiveness as a positive quality. Finally, studies in manuscripts and manuscript survival have enhanced our knowledge of how poems were, or were not, transmitted, and of the manuscript context in which they were enjoyed by later medieval readers and listeners.

On the other hand, the general 'character of early Welsh literature', with which Jackson began, now looks less clear than it did in 1959 — not that Jackson's account has been decisively superseded or disproved. Many scholars would now be more agnostic about the degree to which the extant poems are 'popular' oral compositions 'handed on mainly orally by professional entertainers called *cyfarwyddiaid* . . . of comparatively low standing in the literary hierarchy', who 'doubtless. . . could not read Latin' and whose 'training in their own vernacular tradition was such that Latin influences stood little chance of penetrating it'. Against these views, it can be argued that exclusively 'popular' compositions, in the sense of non-aristocratic or non-learned ones, would have stood little chance of being written down by churchmen, whether for themselves or for aristocratic patrons, and that, in any case, the literary interests of early medieval Welsh audiences may have been more homogeneous than the popular/non-popular dichotomy supposes. Types of literature which scholars once apportioned among different classes of *literati* (or *illiterati*) and different audiences have been reinterpreted in terms of different genres which coexisted and interacted, satisfying the universal preference for variety in literature.[3] It is not at all clear from the sources that terms such as *penceirddiaid* ('chief poets') and *cyfarwyddiaid* referred to distinct literary men, rather than different roles which one and the same poet might adopt on different occasions. There is less evidence from Wales than there is from Ireland for elaborate hierarchies of learned men; and, in any case, the point of such schemes was not that the classes of poet were mutually exclusive, but that an aspiring poet could work his way up the hierarchy until he had embraced all possible functions.[4]

It would be wrong to be misled by the way in which the medieval Welsh and, still more, Irish, writers themselves liked to contrast native with foreign (biblical and classical) learning. Such schematization was probably a way of reducing a more or less common body of knowledge into order, of constructing a workable epistemology; it is not an indication that in practice there were mutually exclusive classes of knowledge.[5] The similarity in tone between the early Welsh poems based on biblical or classical themes and those on native subjects suggests that any distinction between Latin and vernacular culture was a matter of language, genre and literary convention and did not preclude fruitful influence at the level of content. Moreover, even at the level of poetic language and convention, the gulf between Latin and vernacular practice may have been exaggerated by scholars who failed to consider the full range of Latin literature available in the early Middle Ages and the degree to which it may have been appreciated by non-classical norms. The poems in the Book of Taliesin which assert the archetypical bard Taliesin's superiority both over bookish clerics and over poets of lower rank reflect the sort of religious/secular tensions and professional jealousies that exist in all societies. They do not reflect a genuine conflict between Christian-Latin knowledge and surviving types of esoteric native knowledge; those conflicts must have been settled long before the period of the extant Welsh poems. Indeed, a considerable amount of the esoteric learning ascribed to Taliesin derives from medieval Latin encyclopaedic knowledge.[6]

By the period with which we shall be concerned — roughly the ninth to twelfth centuries — there was probably one indivisible body of knowledge in Wales, although presumably different people were expert in different parts of it and no one (unlike the exemplary Taliesin of legend) could hope to become expert in all of it. The word for 'experts' was *cyfarwyddiaid*. At its first occurrence in Old Welsh, this word refers to local people who know what rents are due on an estate — the sort of people that are called *periti* in Anglo-Saxon charters — but in other contexts other sorts of experts and expertise might be involved. The specialization of the word in the sense 'story-tellers' (these were not necessarily discrete from 'bards') reflects the high status of traditional narrative — both history and story — as an embodiment of knowledge. Such knowledge might (to use modern terms) include historical or mythic truth, or an uncertain mixture of both, as was the case with Arthur himself. We cannot and should not distinguish between a 'historical' Latin tradition represented by Gildas's *De Excidio Britanniae*, the *Historia Brittonum* and Geoffrey of Monmouth's *Historia Regum Britanniae* on the one hand and a 'mythic' or 'fictitious' vernacular tradition on the other. The Latin and Welsh texts share too many basic assumptions, such as the idea of the Island of Britain as a former and potential unity: from a functional point of view it mattered little whether this unity had been attacked by Anglo-Saxons or monsters, whether it had been defended by Aurelius Ambrosius or Arthur, or whether it would be restored by contemporary Britons and Dubliners or by heroes returning from the past. The world-picture is the same in either case.[7]

The difficulty of dating the Arthurian poems is still as severe as Jackson described it in 1959. There are several reasons why this is so. Twelve *englynion* in the margins of the Cambridge Juvencus are direct proof that secular and religious poems in Welsh were being written down at least as early as the first half of the tenth century, but the earliest extant poetic codex, the Black Book of Carmarthen, is no older than the thirteenth century. For some reason such as poor storage conditions, early codices, whether Latin or vernacular, survived badly in Wales, Ireland and Scotland, and most of the famous early Celtic manuscripts are extant because at an early stage they were taken to the Continent or, as in the case of the Juvencus and other surviving manuscripts from Wales, to England. Such manuscripts were preserved abroad for the sake of their Latin contents, rather than for any incidental vernacular glosses and marginalia; and completely vernacular manuscripts would not have warranted preservation. As a result, contemporary manuscript evidence for early Irish and Welsh texts consists almost exclusively of glosses and short prose notes; poems like the Juvencus *englynion* are rare.[8] Consequently early Welsh poems preserved in later poetic codices have to be dated partly by linguistic comparison with the Old Welsh glosses — a perilous exercise in view of the difference in genre and transmission — and partly on the basis of internal evidence of content and authorship.

The internal approach to dating is less fruitful in Wales than in Ireland. From the ninth- to early-twelfth-century period, the only securely datable poems in later manuscripts are: the prophetic *Armes Prydein*, which belongs in a tenth-century political context; an anonymous poem in praise of Hywel ap Goronwy, who flourished *c.* 1100; and two poems by Meilyr Brydydd *c.* 1137. The continuous stream of praise-poems by named poets only begins with Meilyr. Scholars have often taken *c.* 1150 as a linguistic watershed for the dating of Arthurian poems, as Jackson mentions.[9] This terminus has some validity — *c.* 1150 is also the approximate date for the demise of certain Old Welsh spelling conventions and Insular letter forms which appear to have been present in the exemplars of some poems, to judge by transcription errors — but insofar as it is based on comparison with the praise-poems, it may be misleading since the Arthurian poems may have followed different stylistic and metrical conventions, both in preserving certain archaisms (e.g. 'Irish' and *trwm ac ysgafn* rhymes) and in allowing innovations which the *penceirddiaid* eschewed, at least when composing praise-poetry.[10] One consequence of this uncertainty is that it is rarely possible to know whether an Arthurian poem, in its extant form, is earlier or later than Geoffrey of Monmouth (*c.* 1138). It is frustrating that 'pre-1150' leaves this important question unanswered. Such a dating should not, however, be misinterpreted as meaning 'shortly before 1150'; indeed, it is possible that many 'pre-1150' poems may be as old as the Juvencus *englynion* or even earlier. In this connection it must be stressed that already in the *Historia Brittonum* of 829/30 there is clear evidence for the existence of a vernacular poetic tradition and of a body of Arthurian stories — the two necessary preconditions for the Arthurian poems.[11]

Another uncertainty is the degree to which the extant poems were orally composed and transmitted.[12] Presumably they are 'oral' poems in the sense that they were composed aloud (rather than silently, pen in hand) and were intended for oral communication, either through recitation from memory or from reading out a manuscript; but were they written down at the time of composition and then transmitted primarily by manuscripts? We do not have the evidence to answer these questions, but at least some possible misunderstandings can be cleared away. First of all, the present lack of early manuscripts in no way indicates illiteracy; to give a *reductio ad absurdum*, on such negative evidence one could argue that the Latin liturgy of the early Welsh Church existed only orally, for no early liturgical manuscripts survive! Secondly, as we have seen, there are no grounds for supposing that there was a complete divide in early Wales between an oral, secular, vernacular culture and a literate, clerical, Latin culture: indeed, the secular Juvencus *englynion* are tangible proof that this was not the case. Thirdly, when the texts of poems found in more than one manuscript vary 'in a way natural to the oral tradition of the *cyfarwyddiaid*',[13] this can be taken as proof only of oral transmission (or, more narrowly, of writing down from memory), not of oral composition; one need only compare the extreme textual variation in certain Middle English romances which must originally have been composed by scribes translating French exemplars, and only subsequently came to be orally transmitted.[14] Fourthly, it is possible that the literary culture of Wales was indeed largely oral, but that what has survived in manuscript is untypical of what once existed orally: to put an extreme case, it is not impossible that poems now extant in single medieval manuscripts, such as the Juvencus *englynion* or *Preiddeu Annwn*, were never widely disseminated, either orally or in writing.

A final point on which there is now less scholarly agreement than in 1959 is the existence in early Wales of the 'prose-verse sagas' posited by Joseph Loth and Ifor Williams on the analogy of certain Irish tales. Although Jackson speaks of early Welsh verse 'having quite often taken the form of embellishments in a narrative which was chiefly in prose', there is no *direct* evidence for this form before the late medieval *chantefable* of Trystan and Esyllt; the handful of *englynion* scattered through *Culhwch ac Olwen* and the *Four Branches of the Mabinogi* are not really comparable. While it is possible that some extant Welsh poems were originally recited with a prose framework which was later lost, or was never written down, recent critics, such as Jenny Rowland, have been sceptical and have tended to treat each case on its merits.[15] Obviously the modern reader is at a disadvantage in knowing less about traditional characters, places and incidents than medieval audiences did; but to appreciate most of the poems only a limited amount of such general knowledge is necessary, not a detailed prose narrative. In many cases, the *essential* narrative context emerges obliquely while the poem is recited, as happens, for instance, with modern ballads and *Lieder*. Even if some important narrative element is apparently omitted, the resulting allusiveness or disjuncture can add an appropriate air of mystery or wonder; that this atmosphere was acceptable or desirable even in prose narrative is shown by the story of the mysterious claw in the *Four Branches of the Mabinogi*, where the audience is left to guess at the existence and actions of supernatural beings.[16] The Arthurian poems undoubtedly rely on some pre-existing knowledge about the identity of Arthur and his band, and some of them are related to narratives which were also told in prose form (e.g. the poems 'Pa gur?' and *Preiddeu Annwn* have analogues in *Culhwch ac Olwen*), but few of them demand the reconstruction of an elaborate prose framework. To a considerable extent the poets seem to have succeeded in creating free-standing evocations of an Arthurian world. The Norse Eddaic poems and the Old English 'elegies' may provide better comparisons than most Irish prose-verse tales or the *Four Branches*, where the poetry is only a minor adjunct to the prose.

The most important manuscript sources for early Welsh Arthurian poems are the Black Book of Carmarthen (mid-thirteenth century) and the Book of Taliesin (early fourteenth century); I shall discuss these in turn. Two other codices need be mentioned only in passing. The Book of Aneirin (late thirteenth century) contains only one Arthurian allusion, of uncertain antiquity, in the text of the *Gododdin*:[17] Gwawrddur, a warrior in the warband gathered by the sixth-century ruler of Edinburgh,[18] is praised highly 'although he was not Arthur'.[19] Arthur, then, was without peer according to the author of this line; but, alas, no one can say for certain when it was composed.[20] Another important compilation, the Red Book of Hergest (*c.* 1400), contains several allusions to Arthur, but all except one are in late court poetry and are only of secondary interest here.[21] The exception is the early poem in *englyn* metre on Geraint fab Erbin (discussed below), and this is known independently from the Black Book of Carmarthen and from a fragment in the White Book of Rhydderch (*c.* 1350). Arthur's absence from the other early 'saga *englynion*' in the White and Red Books[22] is striking; apparently he did not dominate the early narrative tradition in the way he dominates *Culhwch ac Olwen*, the *Three Romances* and the *Triads* (see below, chs.3, 6, 7, 8).

The Black Book of Carmarthen is the earliest extant volume containing Welsh Arthurian poems. It was compiled *c.* 1250 by a southern Welsh cleric, possibly at Carmarthen itself. The extant quires include about forty items, of which only the *Triads of the Horses* are in prose. The compiler seems to have been a man of moderately conservative tastes, favouring poems composed a few generations earlier, and admitting nothing recognizably contemporary. The datable praise-poems stretch from 1100 to 1160, and the identifiable allusions in the prophetic poems relate to the period 1151-1212.[23] The fourteen items relating to Welsh narrative tradition cannot be dated so precisely. Pre-1100 dates have been claimed for some of them, but while these are quite credible, the linguistic and metrical criteria by which they might be confirmed have still to be found. There is no *obvious* influence from Geoffrey of Monmouth and the French romances. On the other hand, since there may be one case where material deriving from Geoffrey (via the *Brut*) has been transmuted almost beyond recognition,[24] one suspects that there could be other *unobvious* borrowings.

The most substantial Arthurian poem in the Black Book is the dialogue beginning 'Pa gur yv y porthaur?' (no. 31: 'What man is the gatekeeper?').[25] While this dialogue is not necessarily a remnant of a saga, it echoes many stories. Most of these stories are now forgotten, yet the poem remains effective, because, far from providing a dry catalogue, the poet includes details which conjure up the heroes and localities he names. Just as a free-standing poem like the Old English *Widsith* conjures up the sombre world of Germanic legend, so 'Pa gur?' evokes, and indeed creates, the wonderful, irresponsible atmosphere of an Arthurian past. Like the lists in *Culhwch*, its recitation would remind an audience of half-forgotten stories and whet their appetites for new ones. For the most part, the tone is light (despite the heroic clichés), and the poet revels in his non-stop metre (a sort of Skeltonics), his word-play, and his obsessive numerology. On the other hand, the repeated use of the imperfect tense gives an elegiac colour to Arthur's boasting (note in particular lines 62-3); perhaps we should imagine an Arthur down on his luck, accompanied by Cai and only three other warriors ('the vultures of Eleï'), and living in the past. The poem seems to reflect the tension inherent in the Arthurian fable: while Arthur's time was a glorious high point, it doomed subsequent ages to mediocrity.[26]

In the extant portion of the poem, Bedwyr and Cai are Arthur's main henchmen. We may recall their similar role in *Culhwch* and in the *Triads*, and, more usefully for dating purposes, in the *Vita Sancti Cadoci*, composed by Lifris of Llancarfan *c.* 1100.[27] A similar date and south-eastern provenance would suit 'Pa gur?' very well: in particular, such a localization would make sense of the reference to Eléï, the River Ely near Llandaf.[28] This unusual topographical reference in line 11 is more valuable for localizing the poem than the more conventional references to Edinburgh and Anglesey further on.

The relationship between 'Pa gur?' and *Culhwch* is problematic. Besides Arthur, Cai, and Bedwyr, a number of characters reappear in *Culhwch*, such as Glewlwyd the gatekeeper, Mabon son of Modron and Mabon son of Mellt (perhaps the same person with matronymic and patronymic?),[29] Manawyd(an) son of Llŷr, and God himself (in a pious reference in line 74 that has parallels in *Culhwch*). Moreover, in line 33 there is a reference to *celli* ('grove'), which may be Arthur's court at Celli Wig in Cornwall, as *passim* in *Culhwch*.[30] On the other hand, a degree of overlap is not very surprising considering the length of *Culhwch* and its catalogues, and it is perhaps more striking that many persons and places in 'Pa gur?' are *not* gathered into *Culhwch*: Uthr Pendragon; Cys[t]aint fab Banon;[31] Afarnach (unless the same name as Wrnach); Pen Palach; Garwlwyd; Llachau; Palug; and, among the places: Eléï; Tryfrwyd; Eidin (except in the epithet of Clydno Eidin); Disethach; *Ystawingun*; and even Môn (Anglesey). Besides, there are various contradictions (or apparent contradictions) between the texts. In *Culhwch* Glewlwyd is Arthur's porter, although there is some hesitation;[32] in 'Pa gur?', however, he seems independent of Arthur (compare the late medieval *Araith Iolo Goch* where he is Taran's porter).[33] Again, in 'Pa gur?' Mabon is described as a servant of Uthr Pendragon (Arthur's father), whereas in *Culhwch* he has been incarcerated almost since the dawn of time!

It is unlikely, then, that the compilers of *Culhwch* drew on a written text of the poem as a main source (or vice versa). Nevertheless, three passages in *Culhwch* suggest that the compiler(s) of its catalogues may have had a vague memory of parts of 'Pa gur?'. First, the names 'Glewlwyt Gauaeluawr, a Lloch Llawwynnyawc, ac Anwas Edeinawc' in lines 192-3 of *Culhwch* seem to recall lines 2 and 25-6 of the poem. Llwch and Anwas may, however, have been linked in some lost story (about their defence of Edinburgh?) to which both texts refer independently. (Llwch's sons are mentioned in *Culhwch* line 291, and a Twrch son of Anwas in line 201.) Secondly, in lines 288-92, *Culhwch* invokes 'Gwynn Gotyuron', Arthur's four maternal uncles (all named Gwair!), and 'the sons of Llwch Llawwynnyawc from beyond Môr Terwyn'.[34] The otherwise unknown 'Gwynn Gotyuron' is clearly the same as *Guin Godybrion* in 'Pa gur?'; the *-b-* in the latter (like the *-gu-* in *Anguas*, line 25) is a trace of an exemplar in Old Welsh orthography. The epithet, which is perhaps a place-name, looks as if it contains OW *dubr* 'water' (cf. Old Irish *fodoborda(e)* 'underwater, aquatic'?). Thirdly, a few sentences further on in *Culhwch*, 'Kelli and Cuel' (variants *Keli* and *Cueli*) are named (297-8); these odd names are surely due to a faulty memory of lines 33-4 of 'Pa gur?', where *kelli* is a place-name (i.e. Celli Wig) and *cuelli* is a rare common-noun meaning 'fury'.[35]

'Pa gur?' begins as a dialogue between Arthur (one presumes) and the porter:

> 1 'What man is the gatekeeper?'
> 2 — 'Glewlwyd Great Grasp;
> 3 what man asks it?'
> 4 — 'Arthur and [*or* with] Cai the fair.'
> 5 — 'What [band] goes with you?'
> 6 — 'The best men in the world.'
> 7 — 'Into my house you will not come
> 8 unless you vouch for them.'
> 9 — 'I shall vouch for them,
> 10 and you will see them,
> 11 the vultures of Ely,
> 12 and all three of them wizards:
> 13 Mabon son of Mydron,
> 14 Uthr Pendragon's servant;
> 15 Cys[t]aint son of Banon;
> 16 and Gwyn Goddyfrion.

Such exchanges with recalcitrant porters were commonplace in medieval literature, and in real life, too, no doubt. Within Welsh literature one thinks immediately of Culhwch's dialogue with Glewlwyd at the gate of Arthur's court, and, further on in *Culhwch*, the dialogue with another porter at the gate of 'Wrnach's hall' (line 773, *neuad Vrnach/Wrnach*; cf. *neuat Awarnach* in line 39 of 'Pa gur?' ?). Because it is extremely effective, the porter-scene may well have been a stock narrative formula: there is already an example in the early-ninth-century *Historia Brittonum*, c.32 (cf. c.47), which probably echoes vernacular story-telling here.[36]

At line 17 Arthur goes off into the imperfect tense (as noted above), praising his warriors:

> 17 Stout were my servants
> 18 defending their rights.
> 19 Manawydan son of Llŷr,
> 20 whose counsel was weighty;
> 21 Manawyd brought
> 22 shattered spears (*or* shields) back from Tryfrwyd.
> 23 And Mabon son of Mellt,
> 24 he used to stain grass with blood.
> 25 And Anwas the Winged
> 26 and Llwch Windy(?) Hand:
> 27 they were accustomed to defend
> 28 at Edinburgh on the border.
> 29 A lord would give them refuge,

30 where he would avenge them. [*or* my nephew would avenge.]

It is unclear whether these people are present in Arthur's company; indeed they may all be dead. *Manawyd* is an attested variant of *Manawydan*, who is best known from the *Four Branches of the Mabinogi*, where his wise counsel is repeatedly stressed. His patronymic suggests that he had been equated with the Irish and Manx sea-god, Manannán *mac Lir*, but as he has nothing to do with the sea in Welsh sources the view that the equation was secondary is attractive.[37] Line 22, *eis tull o trywruid*, is ambiguous. *Eis* are 'ribs', metaphorically 'timbers' and hence arms of some kind; the point is that Manawyd or his weapons, being *tull* ('pierced'), bore the marks of brave fighting in the thick of the fray. *O trywruid* could be a misspelling of another adjective qualifying *eis*, that is *gotrywruid* 'speckled, bespattered [with blood]', which describes a shield elsewhere in the Black Book. On the other hand the verb in line 21 seems to require a place-name, and its tense (preterite) suggests that Arthur is referring to a particular incident rather than to Manawydan's habitual bravery. For these reasons *o trywruid* is best taken as an allusion to the 'battle on the bank of a river which is called *Tribruit*', the tenth in the list of Arthur's battles in the *Historia Brittonum*, c.56.[38] *Traeth Tryfrwyd* (the name means 'very speckled shore') is unfortunately unidentified.[39] It is mentioned again in line 48.

The following lines mark the start of a long sequence about Cai:

31 Cai would entreat them,
32 while he struck three at a time.
33 When Celli was lost,
34 there was fury.
35 Cai would entreat them
36 as he cut them down.

If these lines refer to Arthur's court at Celli Wig in Cornwall, they must relate to a period of adversity for Arthur.[40] Who are Cai's opponents here? If Arthur's afore-mentioned servants are meant, we have to imagine that for a period Cai turned against his own side; this would be why he pleads with them even as he strikes them. Indeed there is a dark hint in *Culhwch* that Cai did indeed turn against Arthur in his hour of need, when his men were being slain.[41]

The account of Cai is interrupted by some lines about Arthur himself:

37 Though Arthur laughed [*or* ?played],
38 he caused the/her blood to flow
39 in Afarnach's hall,
40 fighting with a witch.
41 He pierced Cudgel(?) Head
42 in the dwellings of Disethach.
43 On the mountain of Edinburgh
44 he fought with dogheads.
45 By the hundred they fell;

> 46 they fell by the hundred
> 47 before Bedwyr the Perfect [*or* Perfect-Sinew].
> 48 On the shores of Tryfrwyd,
> 49 fighting with Rough Grey,
> 50 furious was his nature
> 51 with sword and shield.

It is odd that Arthur should speak of himself in the third person. It has been suggested that these lines are spoken by Cai,[42] or that we should emend *Arthur* to *aruth(u)r* 'terrible', therefore translating: 'Terribly he (i.e. Cai) laughed. . .'[43] If Cai is meant, one might compare his murderous visit to the 'hall of Wrnach' in *Culhwch*; on the other hand, in *Culhwch* it is Arthur himself who attempts to fight with a witch (*gwidon*) 'in the uplands of Hell' in the 'North' with the object of obtaining her blood.[44]

Nothing else is known about Pen Palach ('Cudgel Head'?) and Disethach, but the termination *-ach* evokes their unpleasantness.[45] The term *cinbin* (i.e. *cynbyn* 'dogheads') is clearly a calque on the classical *Cynocephali*, mythical inhabitants of India. According to St Augustine's discussion of 'monstrous births', their 'dogs' heads and even barking show them to be beasts rather than men',[46] but other early medieval scholars regarded them as humans with souls;[47] they appear, for example, among the more exotic members of the human race in the twelfth-century tympanum at Vézelay. In Irish texts, dogheads (*conchinn*) appear both as saints and as monsters, in the latter aspect alongside catheads and goatheads.[48] Clearly the *cinbin* which Arthur (or Cai) fights are monsters. But what are they doing on the 'mountain of Edinburgh', seeing that Pliny (*Natural History*, VII.ii.23) placed them in the mountains of India? We should perhaps compare the way in which Old Irish scholars numbered *Conchind* among the prehistoric conquerors of Ireland. On the other hand, we might see here an instance of the tendency to transfer marvels from one periphery of the medieval world to another.[49]

Bedwyr seems to be named as an assistant in line 47, but seems to be the main focus by lines 48-51. Here we learn that the enemy at the battle of *traethev trywruid* was *garvluid* 'rough grey', presumably an ellipsis for Gwrgi Garwlwyd ('Gwrgi Rough Grey'), who is mentioned in the *Triads*. *Gwrgi* was a normal personal-name in Wales, but the train of thought in the poem becomes clear when we note that the transparent etymology of *Gwr-gi* is 'man-dog'. Quite likely, then, 'Rough Grey' in line 49 was imagined to be one of the dogheads of line 44. *Triad* 32 states that the killing of Gwrgi Garwlwyd by Diffydell son of Dysgyfdawd was one of the Three Fortunate Assassinations. Then, with curious deference to early medieval Sabbatarianism, the *Triad* adds: 'That Gwrgi used to make a corpse of one of the Cymry every day, and two on Saturday so as not to slay on a Sunday'![50] Since another triad (no. 10) names the poet-sons of Disgyfdawd as the Three Chieftains of Deira and Bernicia,[51] we should presumably place Gwrgi somewhere in the vicinity of Northumbria, and this suits the poem's reference to the 'mountain of Edinburgh' nicely.

Bedwyr's epithet *pedrydant* slightly resembles his patronymic in the *Triads* and *Geraint*, where he is the son of *Bedrawc* or *Pedrawt*,[52] but it is not necessary to suppose any corruption. There is more about Bedwyr in the following lines of 'Pa gur?', where an otherwise unknown *Bridlav* appears to be named along with him:

> 52 Vain was a host
> 53 compared with Cai in battle.
> 54 He was a sword in battle;
> 55 from [*or* into] his hand pledges were given.
> 56 He was a constant chief
> 57 over a host [*or* a defence] for the sake of a land.
> 58 Bedwyr and [*or* with] Bridlaw:
> 59 nine hundred listening,
> 60 [and] six hundred scattering,
> 61 was the worth (effect) of his incitement.

As Bridlaw seems out of place here, we could perhaps emend *Beduir. a Bridlav.* to *Beduir ab Bridlav*, or, better, *Beduir ab Ritlav* ('Bedwyr son of Rhyddlaw [i.e. 'Generous-Hand']'); either emendation would conflict, however, with the patronymic quoted above. The numerical exaggeration, using multiples of three, can be paralleled in more serious heroic poetry, and also in the statement in *Historia Brittonum*, c.56, which may be based on a vernacular poem, that Arthur slew 960 men in a single onrush at the Battle of Badon.[53]

In the following lines of the poem, Arthur is undoubtedly recalling the past (with what effect on the waiting porter we shall never know):

> 62 I used to have servants;
> 63 it was better when they were alive.
> 64 Before the lord [*or* lords] of Emrys [i.e. Gwynedd]
> 65 I saw Cai hastening.
> 66 Prince of plunder,
> 67 he was a warrior long (= unrelenting) as an enemy.
> 68 Heavy was his vengeance,
> 69 painful was his fury.
> 70 When he would drink from a horn
> 71 he would drink enough for four.
> 72 When he came into battle,
> 73 he would slay enough for a hundred.
> 74 Unless it were God who accomplished it,
> 75 Cai's death were unattainable.
> 76 Cai the fair and Llachau,
> 77 they performed battles
> 78 before the pain of blue spears (ended the conflict).

Emrys/Emreis is the Welsh derivative of *Ambrosius*. The reference may be to the historical Ambrosius Aurelianus, whose victories against the Saxons were mentioned by Gildas, or to the wonder-child Ambrosius of the *Historia Brittonum*. As the latter was associated with Snowdonia, the Welsh praise-poets often use *Emrys* as a periphrasis for Gwynedd,[54] and this gives the best sense in the above text. The formula *gweleis* ('I saw. . .') is common in praise-poems listing battles and exploits, and we can assume that Cai was hastening into conflict at the head of (rather than against) the lords of Gwynedd: thus Meilyr, lamenting Gruffudd ap Cynan of Gwynedd (d. 1137), remembers him *rac bytin Emreis* 'before/at the head of the host of Emreis'.[55] The literal meaning of line 67 is 'he was a warrior long/tall as an enemy', but there is probably a pun on Cai's epithet *hir* 'the tall', which appears in later medieval poetry.[56] The comment in lines 74-5 suggests that, in addition to Cai's other 'peculiarities' listed in *Culhwch*, he could only be killed in special circumstances; compare Lleu in the *Four Branches*, who says that 'Unless God kills me, it is not easy to kill me'.[57]

Llachau is presumably Arthur's son Llachau.[58] The text is usually assumed (especially as Arthur is speaking) to refer to Llachau battling on the same side as Cai, but the two could be opponents, fighting to the death.[59] That there may have been some such story is suggested by the fact that the Welsh translator of *Perlesvaus*, translating the story of Cai's treacherous murder of Arthur's son Loholt, replaced the name *Loholt* with *Llacheu*.[60] There are two earlier, but unfortunately vague, allusions to Llachau's death. The first is in the Black Book itself, where a speaker (Gwyddneu Garanhir?), using the formula *Mi a wum* ('I have been'), evokes the heroic past by cataloguing the 'warriors of Britain' at whose deaths he has been present:

> . . . I have been where Llachau was killed, son of Arthur, marvellous in songs, when the ravens croaked(?) over blood. . . I have been where the warriors of Britain were slain, from the east to the north; I am alive, they in the grave! . .[61]

This gives no clue as to how and where Llachau was slain, but Bleddyn Fardd, in an elegy on Dafydd ap Gruffudd ap Llywelyn, who was brutally executed at Shrewsbury in 1283 — having been betrayed, significantly, by his own kinsmen[62] — recalls how 'Llachau was slain below Llech Ysgar'. While the latter place is unidentified, it is known to have been the site of one of the courts of Madog ap Maredudd (d. 1160) of Powys.[63] There may have been a local legend there comparable to that already found further south in Ergyng when the *Historia Brittonum* was composed in the ninth century; that reported (c.73) the wonderful grave of Arthur's son Amr, whom Arthur himself slew and buried.[64]

The remaining lines of the poem recount further exploits by Cai:

> 79 On the top/upland of *Ystawingun*
> 80 Cai pierced nine witches.

81 Cai the fair went to Anglesey
82 to destroy lions [? wild-cats].
83 His shield was polished
84 against Palug's Cat.
85 When [or Why do?] people ask
86 'Who pierced Palug's Cat?':
87 (the story is that) nine score warriors [or greyheads]
88 used to fall as [or into] its food;
89 nine score champions
90 used to . . .

The nine witches here recall the Nine Witches of Gloucester in *Peredur*.[65] Nine is also the number of the maidens in *Preiddeu Annwn* and elsewhere, and was evidently a conventional figure (three threes) for supernatural females.[66] In particular, however, we can compare the nine witches in the seventh-century(?) Breton-Latin *Life of St Samson*, I.26-7. (A version of this *Vita* was available in Wales in the early-twelfth-century Book of Llandaf.) The episode shows close similarities with the *Peredur* episode, including the geographical area (south-east Wales or the border).[67] Can *Ystawingun* be localized in the same general area? So far it has defied identification,[68] but in view of the reference to Anglesey in line 81, it may be connected with Porth Ysgewin (Portskewett), in the extreme south-east of Wales, which is often contrasted with Anglesey in the extreme north-west.[69] An Old Welsh spelling of *Ysgewin* such as **Yscauguin* might easily be corrupted to *Ystawingun*.

Like Cai, St Samson was also said to have vanquished a lion (*Vita*, I.57), presumably another conventional heroic exploit transferred to the saint. The distinction between lions and wild-cats may have been vague, so Cath Palug ('Palug's Cat', but originally 'the clawing cat'?) may well have been one of the 'lions' of Anglesey of line 82. Certainly Cath Palug is associated with that island in *Triad* 26: the magic sow Henwen, after travelling across Wales from Aber Tarogi (near Porth Ysgewin) to Arfon, gave birth to a kitten, which Coll son of Collfrewy threw into the Menai, 'and she was afterwards Palug's Cat'. Later versions add that she was also 'one of the Three Oppressions of Anglesey', having been fostered by 'the sons of Palug . . . to their own harm'. She may be the same cat that is already referred to as 'the speckled cat' in a prophecy in the Book of Taliesin, dated 942-50(?) by Ifor Williams.[70] If this is the case, the monster cat had a long literary career, for she lived on in French romance as the *C(h)apalu* which fought, and according to some vanquished, Arthur himself. Fordun, too, reported an oral tradition about how Arthur's soldier Caius sought out and slew a gigantic cat (*cattus*).[71] A particularly close analogue, which explains the description of Cai's shield as *mynud* 'polished, smooth' (line 83), is preserved by a fifteenth-century English writer: Arthur destroyed some wild-cats, either in Cornwall or at Glastonbury, by using a glass shield, which tricked them into attacking their own reflections.[72]

Even in its incomplete state, 'Pa gur?' is by far the most substantial Arthurian poem in the Black Book. Otherwise, there are only brief allusions to Arthur in this manuscript. He is named as the father of Llachau in the poem quoted above. Cynddelw, in *englynion* to the warband of the above-mentioned Madog ap Maredudd (d. 1160), compares their shout to 'the shout of the host of Arthur's warband'.[73] Finally, he is mentioned in passing in *Gereint fil[ius] Erbin* and in the 'Stanzas of the Graves' (*Englynion y Beddau*).[74] These two poems deserve detailed treatment.

Geraint son of Erbin, as he appears in Welsh tales and genealogies, may be a composite figure, based on more than one person of the name: the British general Gerontius who rebelled against Constantine in the early fifth century; a sixth-century Geraint in the *Gododdin* (see below); a still later Geruntius, King of Domnonia (> English *Devon*, Welsh *Dyfnaint*), who corresponded with Aldhelm and fought against the West Saxons in 710; the Cornish saint Gerent (patron saint of Gerrans), who seems to have been regarded as a king by the eleventh century; and a Gerennius, King of Cornwall, in the Book of Llandaf's *Life of St Teilo*.[75] There is also the hero of *Gereint*, but this romance is clearly later than the poem, although the latter cannot be dated more precisely than to the early twelfth century or before.

It might be argued on the basis of their genealogical tracts that the Welsh became interested in Geraint on various counts: as an alleged grandson of Custennin of Cornwall (arguably the tyrant Constantine of *Damnonia* castigated by Gildas in the sixth century); as the alleged ancestor of Cornish saints known or culted in Wales; and as the ancestor of the south-eastern Welsh dynasty of Morgan ab Owain (d. 980). On the other hand, the relevant genealogical materials are late and they may have been inspired by Geraint's literary fame rather than the reverse. The earliest extant manuscript is BL Cotton Vespasian A.xiv (Monmouth, *c.* 1200), according to which St Cybi (the patron of Llangybi, Monmouthshire) was born in Cornwall to a *princeps miliciae* named Salomon, 'Erbin filius, filius Gereint, filius Lud'.[76] Geraint and his father have probably been inadvertently swapped here, but the absence of Custennin makes one suspect that in later genealogical manuscripts he may have been inserted in order to make Geraint and Arthur first cousins, both grandsons of Constantine (Arthur's grandfather in Geoffrey of Monmouth), as in the romance of *Gereint*.[77]

The structure of the Black Book poem is simple, and relies heavily on the stylistic and mnemonic device of 'incremental repetition',[78] which is varied three times in the course of the poem to give a triptych evoking three dynamic aspects of the hero. First come three *englynion* in the following form (the italicized words are the ones varied in the next two *englynion*):

> In front of Geraint, foe's *affliction*,
> I saw horses *white and red-fetlocked*(?),
> and, after the shout, a rough *grave*.

The shout of battle is an heroic commonplace (like the 'I saw' and 'after' formulas), but it may be no coincidence that a reference to a warrior Geraint in the *Gododdin* (line 1042) runs: *Gereint rac deheu gawr a dodet*, 'Geraint: *in front of* the (men of the) South a *shout* was raised'. Whether or not this line is authentic, and whether or not it refers to Geraint son of Erbin, it may have influenced the Black Book poem (or the influence may be vice versa, if line 1042 is an interpolation in the *Gododdin*).

In the second sequence the 'I saw' formula continues for five out of the six *englynion*, and a new initial element is introduced:

> In Llongborth [*or* In a sea-port] I saw *vultures* [*or rage*],
> *and biers beyond measure*,
> *and* men *red in front of Geraint's onrush*.

Llongborth may be a Cambricization of Langport, Somerset (OE *lang-port* 'long market-place'). This is a credible site for a real or legendary battle against the West Saxons; moreover, Sherborne Abbey nearby claimed to have been granted land on the Tamar by Gerontius himself.[79]   Alternatively, 'Llongborth' may be the rare common-noun *llongborth* 'sea-port' (< *longa* (*navis*) + *portus*), which also occurs in an early-twelfth-century poem in the Black Book. If the latter is the case, note that *Triad* no. 14 includes Geraint son of Erbin among the Three Seafarers of Britain, that Gerrans, St Gerent's parish in southern Cornwall, lay on the coast, and that the *Vita* of St Teilo includes a story about King Gerennius dying (of natural causes) in a *portus* called *Din Gerein*, presumably Gerrans itself.[80]   Could this be the *llongborth* of the poem?

The fifth and sixth *englynion* of the 'En llogborth. . .' sequence introduce Arthur — and a difficult textual problem. Literally translated, the Black Book text runs:

> In Llongborth [*or* In a sea-port] I saw to (*y*) Arthur
> brave men — (they) used to slay with steel —
> the emperor, the leader (in the) toil (of battle).

> In Llongborth [*or* In a sea-port] were slain to (*y*) Geraint
> brave men from the region of Dyfnaint;
> and though they might be slain, they slew.

Syntactically, the preposition *y* is tortuous, especially in the former stanza, and it has been doubted whether Jackson was right to translate 'belonging to Arthur'; instead, *y* could be deleted, making *Arthur* the direct object.[81]   This emendation has some support from the Red Book of Hergest text which, although it does have *y* in the Arthur stanza, lacks it in the Geraint stanza ('. . . Geraint was slain'). In consequence it then reads 'man' in the next line (in apposition to Geraint) rather than 'men'; but as this spoils the repetition of *men* and leaves the 'they' unspecified in the third line, it casts doubt on the omission of the *y*.   To complicate matters further, the verb 'was/were slain' occurs in *both* stanzas in the Red Book; this seems plausible, however, since the two *englynion* then form a pair (i.e. a further short sequence), whereas in the Black Book the change of verb in the Geraint stanza is isolated.   On balance, then, I would read 'were slain' in both stanzas,[82] but otherwise accept the Black Book text, understanding 'to Arthur/Geraint men. . .' as poetic inversion for 'men to (i.e. vassals of) Arthur/Geraint', an idiom which occurs a little earlier in the Red Book version of the poem (see below).[83]   The implication is that while many of Arthur's and Geraint's men were slain (indeed the passage verbally echoes the defeat of the Gododdin), the leaders themselves survived.   Arthur was presumably on the same side as Geraint, but this is not necessarily the case, and Jackson rightly points out that the (unemended) texts do not actually state that Arthur was present.   In any case, the mention of Arthur in the same context as Geraint and the men of Dyfnaint is further evidence for his association with the Dumnonian peninsula, which is undoubtedly older than Geoffrey of Monmouth.[84]   The description of him as 'emperor' (*ameraudur/amherawdur* < Latin *imperator*) could reflect Geoffrey's Arthur, but not necessarily so.

The next sequence begins with the following pattern:

> Swiftly there used to run(?) under Geraint's thigh
> long-shanked (horses), (fed on) grains of *wheat*,
> roans (with the) onrush of *speckled* eagles.

With slight variants on this pattern, the sequence runs through eight *englynion* and as many groups of horses. Perhaps the association between Geraint and horses here was one factor that led the Welsh author of *Gereint* to pick Geraint's name, in place of the unfamiliar *Erec/*Guerec*, for this chivalric hero, who assembled an impressive collection of horses in the course of his travels with his wife.[85]

The poem ends with a final extravagent stanza in praise of Geraint ('When Geraint was born, heaven's gates were open. . .'). This *englyn* stands first in the later version of the poem in the White Book (a fragment) and the Red Book. The two versions also differ on the order of stanzas within the sequences, and each includes stanzas lacking in the other. The variations between the texts strongly suggest oral transmission. Nevertheless, there is no reason to suspect that anything crucial has been lost; in either version the poem would probably have made sense to an audience that knew the bare gist of the story of the battle 'en llogporth'. There is only one *englyn* (missing in the Black Book text) that might suggest that the poem is a speech-poem from a saga, and here the imperative can equally well be understood as an intervention by the impersonal witness-narrator, momentarily caught up in the action of the past (as often in *chansons de geste*):

> In Llongborth [*or* In a sea-port] I saw confusion,
> men in battle and blood around feet;
> whosoever is vassal to Geraint, let him make haste![86]

The 'Stanzas of the Graves' (*Englynion y Beddau*) record, often with unexpected poetic power, the sites of the graves of once-famous heroes, testifying to the close association between heroes and places in early Welsh literature. This characteristic is already reflected by the inclusion of topographical lore in the *Historia Brittonum*, such as the wonderful grave of Arthur's son Amr in Ergyng (Herefordshire), which changed size by magic.[87] The Black Book of Carmarthen is the earliest of the manuscripts, but there can be no doubt that some of the *englynion* are much older than the thirteenth century, although some, such as the *englyn* on Myrddin, are probably late medieval.[88] On the whole, however, the general obscurity of the heroes suggests that the bulk of *Englynion y Beddau* are early. There are few allusions, for example, to the well-known Arthurian characters of *Culhwch* and the other tales. Out of seventy-three stanzas in the Black Book series, only three (sts. 8, 12 and 44) fall into this category.[89] The most important of these is the *englyn* naming Arthur himself (st. 44):

> [There is] a grave for March, a grave for Gwythur,
> a grave for Gwgawn Red-sword;
> the world's wonder (*anoeth*) [is] a grave for Arthur.

Since all these characters are well-known from the *Triads* and elsewhere, it might be suspected that this *englyn* is relatively late, although this is not at all certain. The word *anoeth* is, admittedly, archaic and rare, occurring in prose only in *Culhwch*, where it refers to the difficult or impossible tasks which Arthur's warriors undertake; however, the word may allude to the story of *Culhwch* itself.[90] March is, of course, drawn from the Trystan stories, Gwythur figures alongside Arthur in *Culhwch*, and Gwgawn Red-sword (possibly the king of Ceredigion drowned *c.* 871) appears as messenger to Arthur in *Breuddwyd Rhonabwy*.[91] The poet's implication is that the graves of these Arthurian heroes are all known, whereas that of Arthur himself cannot be found. This idea could be compared with the statement in the *Historia Brittonum*, c.55, that St Patrick is like Moses because 'no one knows his grave, but he was buried in secret, no one knowing'.[92] A more usual interpretation, however, is that Arthur's grave was unknown because he was never buried, but was still alive somewhere, biding his time to return and deliver the Britons.[93] The first positive testimony to such a belief in Arthur's survival, among the Cornish and Bretons, is in the account of the journey of the canons of Laon to Bodmin in 1113.[94] It is corroborated *c.* 1125 by William of Malmesbury; discussing the alleged discovery in

Wales of the grave of Arthur's nephew Walwen, in William the Conqueror's reign, William adds that 'Arthur's grave is nowhere to be seen, with the result that old songs say that he will come again'.[95] There may be some connection between William's statement and the grave-stanza, or both may reflect a common background of interest in this Arthurian problem. This possibility is slightly supported by the fact that the *Englynion·y Beddau* (st. 8) also refer to the grave of Gwalchmai (the name which in Welsh texts corresponds to Walwen/Gauvain/Gawain, etc.):

> The grave of Gwalchmai is in Peryddon (*periton*)
> as a reproach to men;
> at Llanbadarn is the grave of Cynon.[96]

The second line here could allude to the more disgraceful of the two stories of Walwen's death, reported by William, that 'he was killed by his fellow-citizens at a public banquet' (the alternative version being that he was shipwrecked). Peryddon appears elsewhere as an alternative name for the River Dee (Welsh *Dyfrdwy*), or part of it.[97] If the Dee is meant in the *englyn* it conflicts with William's assertion that Walwen's grave, 'fourteen feet in length', was found on the sea-shore in the province of Rhos (presumably the Rhos in Pembrokeshire, Dyfed). But there may well have been more than one River Peryddon. The tenth-century prophecy *Armes Prydein*, which reflects the southern Welsh interests of the churches dedicated to St David, alludes to English tax-collectors from Cirencester (*Caer Geri*) coming to *Aber Perydon*, presumably therefore somewhere in south Wales. This allusion can be reconciled with William and *Englynion y Beddau* by supposing that this southern Peryddon was in Rhos, and that the tax-collectors would be on their way to St David's itself.[98] *Peryddon* could perhaps be the old Welsh name for the Sandyhaven Pill in Rhos, which runs down to the sea from the significantly named Walwyn's Castle/Castell Gwalchmai.[99] If Peryddon is a river-name, the statement that Gwalchmai's grave is 'in' it could mean that the grave was actually in its flood plain,[100] and this would agree neatly with what William says about Walwen's grave being on the sea-shore.

St. 12 of the Black Book *Englynion y Beddau* has two points of Arthurian interest. Thomas Jones translated as follows (although line b could also be taken with line c):

> The grave of Osfran's son is at Camlan,
> after many a slaughter;
> the grave of Bedwyr is on Tryfan hill.

Bedwyr's death is not recorded in 'Pa gur?' or elsewhere. There may have been a native story about it to judge by Llywelyn ap y Moel's allusion *c.* 1425 to Cai breaking his heart after Bedwyr's death, but this could be a half-reminiscence of

Geoffrey of Monmouth's pathetic account of Bedevere and Kay's last stand against the Romans in Burgundy.[101] *Alld Tryvan*, 'the slope of Tryfan', probably refers to Tryfan in Snowdonia (grid ref. SH/6659).[102] Interestingly, this peak is close to Pen y Gwryd and Nant y Gwryd, which take their names from a medieval place-name *gwryt Kei* 'Cai's fathom' (already attested *c.* 1200); this would have been a pass across which the gigantic Cai could stretch his arms.[103]

Camlan is no doubt the site of Arthur's last defeat, his most famous battle in Welsh literature, mentioned already in *Annales Cambriae, s.a.* 537.[104] Modern scholarly tradition has favoured *Camboglanna* on Hadrian's Wall as the site, but the collocation with Tryfan in the *englyn* suggests that it was identified, rightly or wrongly, with the Camlan near Mallwyd, Merioneth (SH/8512). 'Osfran's son' has not been identified, but, significantly, a twelfth-century poet, praising St Cadfan and his church at Tywyn, Merioneth, about eighteen miles from Camlan, alludes (vaguely but favourably) to Osfran. The first element of this name looks like the Anglo-Saxon *Ōs-* (e.g. *Oswulf, Oswald*, etc.), but the second (*brân*) is clearly Welsh. One wonders whether Os*fran* was supposed to be related to a certain Mor*fran* son of Tegid; Morfran is often mentioned as one who escaped at the Battle of Camlan and is associated with Llyn Tegid (Bala Lake), only a dozen miles north of Camlan.[105]

The so-called Book of Taliesin is an early-fourteenth-century southern or eastern manuscript, of which 38 folios survive.[106] The name of Arthur appears in only five poems in the Book, all of them probably spoken in the persona of the legendary bard Taliesin. The most significant is *Preiddeu Annwn*. In the others Arthur is mentioned only incidentally. This is rather surprising considering his central role in texts such as *Culhwch ac Olwen* and considering that Taliesin was closely associated with many other legendary figures of various periods. It can hardly be the case that the Taliesin poems date from a period before Arthur became important, for Arthur is already prominent in the *Historia Brittonum*. Possibly the explanation is a matter of genre: that Arthur and Taliesin (like, say, Arthur and Charlemagne) were too important to share the same platform? Or is there a regional distinction: was Arthur chiefly a hero of south Wales and Cornwall, whereas the legendary Taliesin belonged in Gwynedd with the characters of the Fourth Branch of the *Mabinogi*?

The poems other than *Preiddeu Annwn* warrant only a brief mention.[107] In a boastful passage near the end of *Kat Godeu*, 'Taliesin' addresses certain druids of a 'wise one' (i.e. Arthur or Taliesin himself?):

> Derwydon doethur
> Darogenwch y Arthur.[108]

This is ambiguous. Taliesin's command to these 'druids of the wise one' may be:

'prophesy (impv.) [the coming of/return of] Arthur', implying that Arthur is absent, or alternatively 'prophesy *to* Arthur', implying that he is present and waiting to hear the druids (compare Arthur listening to the bards at the end of the *Breuddwyd Rhonabwy*). The latter possibility seems more likely, because the following lines refer to the Flood, Crucifixion and Doomsday, which could be the subjects of the (Christianized) druids' prophecies.[109] Unfortunately Arthur is not mentioned by name elsewhere in *Kat Godeu*, but it has been suggested that he may be the 'lord of Britain' (*Prydein wledic*) referred to in an earlier section of the poem. This describes a battle in which 'Taliesin' spurs on various magically animated trees and shrubs into battle:

> Keint yg kat godeu bric
> Rac Prydein wledic.
>
> (*I sang in the van of the tree-battalion* (or *in the battle
> of the branchy trees*) *before the lord of Britain.*)

As another poem in the Book of Taliesin places *Godeu* in the north of Britain, and as the triad of the Three Futile Battles groups 'the Battle of Goddeu' (*kat Godeu*) together with the Battles of Camlan (where Arthur fell) and Arfderydd (where Myrddin/Merlin went mad), Arthur may easily have come to be associated with *kat Godeu* too. Nevertheless, the poem's *Prydein wledic*, Taliesin's patron, may originally have been someone else, or indeed no particular ruler at all.[110]

Another boasting poem, *Kadeir Teyrnon* ('The chair of Teyrnon/of a prince') is even more obscure, but it seems to be uttered by Taliesin before releasing his patron Elffin from imprisonment. Taliesin begins by praising a certain *Teyrnon*; this is either the proper name Teyrnon or the common-noun *teyrnon* 'a prince' (perhaps Elffin or Arthur himself?). Then:

> Treded dofyn doethur
> Y vendigaw Arthur.
> Arthur vendigat [MS *vendigan*]
> Ar gerd gyfaena(n)t. [*punctum delens under* n]
> Arwyneb yg kat,
> Ar naw bystylat.

If the feminine forms of the adjectives are taken at face value, some word such as *cân* (f.) 'song' has to be understood:

> The third profound [song] of the sage [is] to bless Arthur, Arthur the blest,
> with harmonious art: the defender in battle, the trampler on nine [enemies].[111]

Such a triadic expression would fit in with what follows, where triads of the Three *cynweisiaid* ('guardians'), Three *cyfarwyddiaid*, and Three *caerau* ('fortresses') are mentioned; as a whole, however, the poem remains unintelligible.

The untitled, probably composite, poem generally called *Kanu y Meirch* ('Poem of the Horses') includes a long list of the horses of traditional heroes, including Arthur's horse which 'fearless[ly] used to cause hurt':

> A march Gwythur,
> A march Gwardur,
> A march Arthur,
> ehofyn rodi cur.[112]

This grouping of the heroes was obviously dictated by rhyme, but we may recall that a Gwythur and Gwawrddur (*sic*) occur alongside Arthur in *Englynion y Beddau* and the *Gododdin* respectively. Arthur's mare is named in *Culhwch* and elsewhere as Llamrei, and she is also mentioned (without owner's name) later in *Kanu y Meirch*.[113]

The manuscript title of the poem *Marwnat vthyr pen[dragon]* ('Uthr Pen[dragon]'s Elegy') may be a mistake — Arthur's father does not appear in the poem — but it can be accepted if we suppose that Uthr, rather than Taliesin, is the speaker, who refers to 'my elegy' towards the end. Admittedly, he sounds very like 'Taliesin'; however, judging by the *Triads* and Geoffrey of Monmouth, Uthr himself was a Taliesin-like figure, a magician and shape-changer.[114] In the *Marwnat* the speaker (Uthr?) mentions Arthur in the course of boasting about his own prowess in battle and poetry:

> Neu vi arannwys vy echlessur
> Nauetran yg gwrhyt Arthur.

This seems to mean 'I have shared my refuge, a ninth share in Arthur's valour',[115] but the import is unclear. Perhaps, if the speaker is Uthr, he means that he has passed on his kingdom or qualities to his famous son; further on he boasts *Nyt oed vyt ny bei vy eissillyd*, 'The world [or 'battle'] would not exist if it were not for my progeny'.[116] In the line preceding the couplet quoted above, the speaker refers to his attack on the 'sons of Cawrnur'; this recalls *Kadeir Teyrnon*, where someone is praised for rustling the horses of Cawrnur.[117] Presumably the fact that *Cawrnur* and *Arthur* rhyme partly explains their collocation, but both poems may allude to some lost Arthurian story. The name *Cawrnur* is perhaps that of a giant (Welsh *cawr*).

We have another reference to Uthr in a pair of apparently unrelated elegies on his son Madog and on the biblical Herod. These are entitled *mad. drut ac erof* ('Mad[awg] the fierce and Herod') in the marginal heading, which is by the main scribe.[118] The former poem is of seven lines only, and is probably an acephalous fragment since the first line does not rhyme:

> Madawc mur menwyt.
> Madawc kyn bu bed,
> Bu dinas edryssed

o gamp a chymwed.
Mab vthyr kyn lleas
Oe law dywystlas.[119]

(Madog, the rampart of rejoicing. Madog, before he was in the grave,
he was a fortress of generosity [consisting] of feat(s) and play.
The son of Uthr, before death [or 'before he was slain (llas)'],
he handed over pledges.)

Mab vthyr could mean 'terrible son/lad', but 'son of Uthr' is more likely, since
Arthur's nephew is called the 'son of Madog son of Uthr' (*mab madawc uab uthyr*) in
the *Dialogue of Arthur and the Eagle* (discussed below). Evidently there was some
story about Arthur's brother Madog. He is mentioned ironically in a list of former
worthies in a religious poem variously attributed to Prydydd y Moch (fl. 1173-1220)
and to Cynddelw (fl. 1155-1200):

Rybu gamwetawc madawc modur faw;
Rybut wu itaw dylaw dolur.[120]

(Madog, famous leader, was false; he had great profit: wretched sorrow!)

The epithet *camwetawc* 'false' here looks like a half-reminiscence of the sound of
camp a chymwed in the elegy.

The fifth Book of Taliesin poem which mentions Arthur is *Preiddeu Annwn* ('The
Spoils of Annwfn'). The title is a fourteenth-century addition in another hand, but it
is appropriate since *Annwfn* (the Otherworld) and *preideu* (Mod.W. *preiddiau*) occur
in the poem itself. The partial edition and translation by Loomis has been superseded
by the version of all sixty lines in Marged Haycock's '*"Preiddeu Annwn"* and the
Figure of Taliesin'.[121] As her title indicates, she argues that the unifying personality
in the poem is not Arthur, but the unnamed but distinctive voice of the speaker
Taliesin. Taliesin begins with sonorous, evocative lines boasting of his role in
Arthur's voyage to Annwfn. He ends more acerbically by asserting his superiority
over monks and bookmen who neither know such native lore (e.g. 'about the Brindled
Ox, stout his collar') nor understand the nature of the cosmos properly (e.g. 'when the
darkness and the light divide, or the wind, what is its course, what is its onrush'). By
contrast, it is implied, Taliesin 'knows all this because he has been there'.[122]
Through the persona of Taliesin, then, the poet strikes a playful blow for the secular
poets or *cyfarwyddiaid* against the vain pretensions of the Welsh clerical orders, with
their noses in the scientific works of Macrobius, Isidore and Bede. The date of
composition cannot easily be narrowed further than *c.* 850-1150.

We are not in a position to know how far the details of Taliesin's account of
Annwfn and Arthur's expedition were drawn from authentic Welsh tradition. The
poet may have invented some of them to enhance Taliesin's reputation for esoteric
knowledge. Some details, like the many alternative names for Annwfn, may have

been deliberately obscure from the first; others, like the description of the magic cauldron of the Head of Annwfn, 'indigo and pearls round its rim', may have been novel but readily intelligible; and others would be motifs well known from other stories, for example the attempt to rescue a prisoner, or the seven survivors of an ill-fated expedition.[123]

There are three close analogues to Arthur's expedition which enable us, as they may have enabled some of its original audience, to understand *Preiddeu Annwn's* allusive narrative.[124] The only one in which Arthur is also the protagonist is the story of his quest for Diwrnach the Irishman's cauldron in *Culhwch ac Olwen*.[125] One minor character in this episode in *Culhwch*, Llenlleog the Irishman, may owe his existence to a misunderstanding of a passage in *Preiddeu Annwn* itself.[126] Another link is established by the statement in the *Thirteen Treasures of the Island of Britain* (though not in *Culhwch* itself) that Dyrnwch the Giant's cauldron boiled for the brave, but not for cowards; *Preiddeu Annwn* claims the same for the cauldron of the Head of Annwfn (line 17).[127]

The second analogue is the story in *Branwen*, the Second Branch of *Pedeir Keinc y Mabinogi* (PKM), about Brân's expedition to Ireland to rescue his sister Branwen, who is effectively held prisoner there by her husband, the King of Ireland. The magic cauldron here plays a different role, helping the slain Irish warriors to revive and fight again. In *Branwen* Pryderi (also mentioned in *Preiddeu Annwn*) and Taliesin are named among the seven survivors. Taliesin's role in this expedition is confirmed in a boasting poem in the Book of Taliesin: 'I was with Brân in Ireland;/ I saw when *Morddwyd Tyllion* was struck.'[128]

The third and earliest analogue is in the early-ninth-century *Historia Brittonum*, c.13. This tells how the three sons of a Spanish soldier (*miles*, i.e. the character Míl of the Irish *Lebor Gabála Érenn*) settled in Ireland, with their thirty ships and thirty wives in each ship. After a year:

> They saw a glass tower in the middle of the sea, and they could see men on the tower, and they sought to speak with them. They never replied, and in that same year they hastened to attack the tower with all their ships and with all their women, except for one ship which was damaged by shipwreck, in which were thirty men and the same number of women. And the other ships voyaged to attack the tower, and, while they all disembarked on the shore around the tower, the sea engulfed them, and they were drowned and not one of them escaped. And from the household of that ship which was left behind because of damage, all Ireland was filled up to the present day. And afterwards they came over gradually from the parts of Spain and held many regions.

This episode probably came from an Irish text, presumably in Latin, about the legendary origins of the peoples of Ireland.[129] It is close to *Preiddeu Annwn*, lines 29-34:

> I do not deserve ?readers concerned with the literature of the Lord
> Who had not seen Arthur's valour beyond the Glass Fort.
> Six thousand men were standing on its wall;
> It was difficult [i.e. impossible] to converse with their watchman.
> Three full loads of Prydwen [Arthur's ship] went with Arthur;
> Apart from seven, none came back from the Fort of Impediment.

These lines echo the *Historia Brittonum* itself or some closely related source or analogue. The silence of the inhabitants, like the muteness of those revived by the cauldron of regeneration in *Branwen*, probably indicates that they are really dead.[130] The preposition 'beyond' (*tra*) in line 30 suggests that Annwfn was not identical with the Glass Fort but lay on the far side of it.

The four analogues differ, with varying protagonists, objectives and outcomes, but their structural similarity is clear:

> *Departure from*: Spain via Ireland (*HB*); Britain (*PA, CO, PKM*).
> *Protagonists*: the three sons of the *miles*, their wives, (and followers?)
> in ships (*HB*); Arthur and three shiploads of Prydwen (*PA*);
> Arthur and small host in *Prydwen* (*CO*);
> Brân (wading) and his host in ships (*PKM*).
> *Destination*: Glass tower in sea (*HB*);
> Annwfn via(?) glass fort (*PA*); Ireland (*CO, PKM*).
> *Objective*: ?territory or national security (*HB*);
> rescue of Gwair, capture/destruction of cauldron,
> and ?capture of Brindled Ox (*PA*); capture of cauldron (*CO*);
> rescue of Branwen, which depends upon destruction of cauldron (*PKM*).
> *Result*: all drowned by ?supernatural tide (*HB*);
> battle involving magic cauldron and sword of ?Lleog (*PA*);
> fight in hall involving sword of Llenlleog and defeat of Irish host (*CO*);
> fight in hall involving magic cauldron and the death of whole Irish host(*PKM*).
> *Escapers*: one shipload, shipwrecked earlier, which re-peoples Ireland (*HB*);
> seven survivors including Taliesin (*PA*);
> triumphant return with cauldron for Culhwch and Olwen's wedding (*CO*);
> seven survivors including Taliesin return to Britain, while five pregnant
> Irishwomen re-people Ireland (*PKM*).

While it is likely enough that the four versions influenced each other, it is more convincing to think of them as reworkings of a common story-pattern for different purposes than as texts to be related by a stemma. The main differences between the four versions are the result of the intersection of two dichotomies:

> 1. In *PA* and *CO* the genre is that of the heroic wonder tale; in *HB* and *PKM*, on the other hand, the genre is that of (or is close to that of) the origin legend.[131]
> 2. In *PA* and *HB* the destination is a magical Otherworld; in *CO* and *PKM* it is Ireland, perhaps as a result of euhemerization (although it is noteworthy that in many cultures the 'Otherworld' or land of the dead has an actual physical location).[132]

These dichotomies are not absolute. In particular, the ever-rich *Four Branches* does manage to include the Otherworld as well, immediately after the return from Ireland, when the survivors celebrate Otherwordly feasts with Brân's severed head, first in Harlech and then on the island of Gwales.[133]

There are many parallels to the themes of *Preiddeu Annwn* and its analogues in early Irish literature. These are best regarded as further analogues rather than sources. One of them, however, was certainly known in early Wales, since it is mentioned in the *Elegy on Cú Roí mac Dáiri* (*Marwnat Corröi m[ab] Dayry*) in the Book of Taliesin. This alludes to the Old Irish story about Cú Roí's expedition with Cú Chulainn to the land of the mysterious Fir Fhálgae (sometimes identified with the Isle of Man) to carry off a woman, magic cauldron and other spoils.[134] Another Old Irish parallel is provided by the stories of Bran mac Febail's encounter with the Otherworld, which is situated either under a spring or, in the *Voyage of Bran*, across the sea.[135] The similarities are rather vague, however, and Glyn E. Jones has argued convincingly against any close relationship between the *Voyage of Bran* and *Branwen*.[136] The only striking similarity is between the Welsh name *Brân* ('raven') and the (very common) name of the Irish hero *Bran* (and that of his saintly counterpart, St *Brendanus* or *Brandanus* — note here Brân's epithet *bendigeid* 'blessed'). Whether this should be explained by common origins or medieval contamination is unclear.[137] The only detail in *Preiddeu Annwn* that is clearly of Irish origin is *kaer sidi*, one of the names given to Annwfn; this derives from the Irish name for fairy-mounds and their inhabitants, *sídhe*.[138]

Two dialogues in *englyn* metre, only extant in fourteenth-century or later manuscripts, remain to be considered: the *Dialogue of Arthur and the Eagle* and the *Dialogue of Melwas and Gwenhwyfar*. These poems cannot be dated exactly, but may both be as early as the twelfth century. The second shows clear signs of oral transmission, and no doubt both were originally written (or orally composed) for oral performance. This could have been by pairs of performers as was done with the Early Modern Welsh Interludes, or by a single performer, impersonating the two characters in the dialogue, as was done (according to Walter Scott) with the Gaelic dialogues between St Patrick and Oisín.[139]

In the *Dialogue of Arthur and the Eagle*, Arthur represents a typical member of the secular aristocracy, as in the Welsh saints' Lives (see ch.3 below), and is the vehicle for some basic Christian instruction.[140] Like Oisín in some of the Irish dialogues with St Patrick, Arthur is a religiously uneducated, but sympathetic, pagan seeking enlightenment. This is provided by the eagle, whom Arthur sees in the very first *englyn*:

> I am amazed, since I am a poet,
> why, at the top of the fair-branched oak,
> the eagle stares, and why it laughs.

The choice of a bird can be paralleled in the *Englynion y Clywaid*, where thrush, raven, jay, and so on, appear alongside the Welsh saints to offer moral precepts.[141] One may recall, too, Geoffrey of Monmouth's tantalizing allusions to a book of the prophecies uttered by an eagle while Shaftesbury was being built.[142] In the *Dialogue* there is an added complication, however, in that the eagle reveals itself to be Arthur's deceased nephew, Eliwlod son of Madawg son of Uthr (on whom see above). This of course gives added authority to its religious instruction. The same motif of a dialogue with a revenant seems to occur in the *englynion* in the Red Book of Hergest between the hermits Llywelyn and Gwrnerth and in those in the Black Book of Carmarthen between the deceased sinner Ysgolan and someone who (to judge by Modern Breton versions) is probably his mother.[143] Perhaps the closest parallel, however, occurs in the Fourth Branch of the Mabinogi, where Gwydion addresses *englynion* to his nephew Lleu, who has been transformed into the form of an eagle after receiving a mortal wound, and, like Eliwlod, is espied at the top of an oak tree.[144]

The *Dialogue* is worked out with some psychological subtlety, but from an 'Arthurian' point of view the most interesting aspect of the poem is its incidental characterization of Arthur. We may be sure that the poet is not trying to represent a novel Arthur, but to recall a well-known figure. Arthur is not described as a king but as 'bear of the host' (*arth llu*), 'most strong in valour' (*gwryt gadarnaf*), and so on.[145] He is *penn kadoed Kernyw*, 'head of the battalions of Cornwall', and, as *cad* meant both 'battalion' and 'battle', the title recalls the *Historia Brittonum's dux bellorum*, which may be a calque on just such a vernacular title for Arthur.[146] Indeed, the dialogue seems to occur on the coast of Cornwall, for Arthur speaks 'beside the seas' (*o tu myr*) and addresses the eagle as one who 'roams the valley-woods of Cornwall' (*a dreigla glyncoet Kernyw*). The place-name element *glynn* is rare in Cornwall, so if a real place is intended, the large, wooded Glynn valley near Bodmin in central Cornwall may be meant.[147] Be this as it may, the Cornish setting is reminiscent of Arthur's association with 'Celli wig in Cornwall' in *Culhwch* and elsewhere. Another similarity is that Arthur describes himself as a poet (*bard*). We may recall the episode in *Culhwch* where Arthur utters a satirical *englyn milwr* about Cai's cowardly attack on the giant Dillus.[148]

The *Dialogue of Melwas and Gwenhwyfar* is extant principally in two manuscripts of the sixteenth and seventeenth centuries (A and B).[149] Both texts are defective and show signs of redaction from faulty memory, with some weak lines invented simply to keep the rhyme-scheme going. In the eighteenth century Lewis Morris gave B the queried title *Ymddiddan rhwng Arthur a Gwenhwyfar* ('Dialogue between A. and G.'),[150] but the dialogue is more likely to be between Arthur's queen

and her would-be lover, Melwas. Cai may speak too, towards the end. In A the
dialogue seems to begin at a feast, where Gwenhwyfar is waiting on the guests,
among them Melwas ('honey-youth', rather than 'prince-youth'):

> 'Who is the man who sits in the common part of the feast,
> without for him either its beginning or its end,
> sitting down there below the dais?'

> 'The Melwas from Ynys Wydrin (Isle of Glass);
> you, with the golden, gilded vessels,
> I have drunk none of your wine.'

> 'Wait a little . . .
> I do not pour out my wine
> for a man who cannot hold out and would not stand in battle
> [and] would not stand up to Cai in his wine.'

In the succeeding *englynion* (in A and B) Gwenhwyfar continues to taunt Melwas,
while he praises his warhorse (in B) and asserts his own valour, especially as
compared to Cai:

> 'Gwenhwyfar of the deer's glance,
> Do not despise me although I am young;
> I would stand up to Cai alone.'

Melwas then asks Gwenhwyfar 'Where have you seen me before this?'. Her reply in
A is corrupt:

> 'In a court of great privilege,
> drinking wine from Geraint [*or* from companions] ,
> a place . . . on the land of Devon.'

B's version of this is:

> 'I saw a man of moderate size
> on a long table . . . Devon,
> dispensing wine to his companions (*iw geraint*).'

B ends with Melwas agreeing that it was he. A, however, ends with two
(linguistically late) stanzas contrasting an old coward (Cai?) and a garrulous coward
(Melwas?), and implies that a combat between them is to ensue.

The story behind these *englynion* is clearly similar to Chrétien de Troyes's
Chevalier de la Charette, where Meleagant abducts Guenièvre from Arthur's court
(which has recently moved from Caerleon to Camelot), wounding Keu in the process,
and takes her to his otherwordly kingdom of Go(i)rre (cf. OFr. *voirre* 'glass', Welsh
gwydr 'glass'). The Welsh names, however, are closer to those in Chrétien's earlier
Erec, where the guests at Arthur's court include 'Maheloas, a great baron, lord of the
Isle of Glass (*Voirre*), an island where thunder is not heard, no lightning strikes or
tempest blows, no toads or snakes stay, and it is never too hot or too cold'.[151]

Behind Chrétien there probably lies a Welsh story about the rescue of Gwenhwyfar from an Otherworld Island of Glass, similar to *Preiddeu Annwn* and its analogues. The Welsh original does not survive, unless the *englynion* are remnants of it, but an adaptation appears already in the Latin *Life of St Gildas* which Caradog of Llancarfan wrote for the monks of Glastonbury in the 1120s or 1130s.[152] Caradog euhemerizes the idyllic Isle of Glass as Glastonbury, the Old English names of which really mean 'island, or fortress, of the Glastings'. This equation was made possible by Latinizing its name as *insula/urbs vitrea*, taking the first element to be OE *glæs* 'glass' or Old Celtic **glasto-* (Gaulish *glastum*) 'woad' (cf. Latin *vitrum* 'glass, woad'), and by deriving the name of Somerset from the English word *summer*. Probably both these etymologies were already current in Wales before Caradog wrote.[153] He was thus able to introduce the abbot of Glastonbury as peace-maker and (of course) as beneficiary:

> Gildas . . . embarked in a little boat and entered Glastonbury, . . . while King Melvas was reigning in the Summer Region. . . . Glastonbury, that is, the Glass City . . . was besieged by the tyrant Arthur with an innumerable multitude on account of his wife Guennuvar, who had been violated and carried off by the aforesaid iniquitous king, and had been brought there on account of the refuge of its inviolate position, which was due to the defences of its reeds, river and protecting marsh. The warring king had sought the queen for a year, and at last heard that she dwelt there. He moved there the armies of all Cornwall and Devon (*Dibnenia*); battle was made ready between the enemies. Seeing this, the abbot of Glastonbury, accompanied by his clergy and Gildas the Wise, went between the lines of battle, and peacefully advised his king Melvas that he should return the abducted woman. She who was to be returned was therefore returned in peace and goodwill. This done, the two kings granted the abbot many lands . . .[154]

It is interesting to note that Arthur is principally associated with the south-west here; one may compared the reference to *Dyfneint* in the *englynion* (and possibly the latter's reference to Geraint, though this probably represents the common-noun *ceraint* rather than the Dumnonian hero). Despite the ecclesiastical element, Caradog's version of the story is doubtless more primitive than Chrétien's in assigning a principal role in the quest to Arthur himself, rather than to his knights, but the Otherworld aspect is absent, owing to the localization at Glastonbury.

The *englynion* are too fragmentary to reveal whether or not Melwas was portrayed as an Otherworld character in them,[155] but some allusions by fourteenth- and fifteenth-century poets imply that he used both stealth and magic, and went to the 'end of the world' (*i eitha' byd*). Dafydd ap Gwilym speaks of Melwas, 'because of great love', getting through a window at Caerlleon 'near the house of Ogfran the Giant's daughter' (that is, Gwenhwyfar) — compare the reference to Caerleon in Chrétien, and the latter's subsequent episode in which Lancelot climbs through

Guenièvre's window (lines 4586ff.). Dafydd ab Edmwnd longs for 'the art of Melwas, the thief that by magic and enchantment took a girl to the end of the world: to the green wood the deceiver went, to walls of branches of tree-tops'. In another poem Dafydd ab Edmwnd complains, 'even if it were Melwas who were to seek you, he would be hated'; this seems to imply that Melwas's attentions, by contrast, were welcomed by Gwenhwyfar. These poets may well have known the full story behind the fragmentary *englynion*. Unfortunately, they may well have changed the emphasis for their own purposes, so reliance cannot be placed on details.[156]

Many Welsh Arthurian poems must have been lost. The few that survive display remarkable variety and vitality. They all happen to be anonymous, but we are not required to treat them as the work of pure tradition-bearers rather than as creations by individual court poets or clerics. They can be read as works of imaginative literature in their own right as well as reflections of possible 'sources' for Arthurian romance. None of them seems to owe much to Geoffrey of Monmouth's realism; indeed, many of them may have been composed before the *Historia Regum Britanniae* appeared. Their affinities are more with the native *Historia Brittonum*, the Welsh-Latin saints' Lives, and above all with the early heroic poetry. Yet whereas much of that early poetry displays a sombre, didactic view of the world, dominated by ideas of past defeat, present oppression, and prophesied revenge,[157] the Arthurian poems are literature of entertainment, closer in mood to the early prose tales. In them we find the poets and their audiences at play, escaping into a never-never land of idealized conflicts and magical quests. They help us understand how the Celtic peripheries became the focus for marvels and adventures in twelfth-century European literature.[158]

NOTES:

1. ALMA 12-19. Subsequent surveys include Thomas Jones, 'The Early Evolution of the Legend of Arthur', *NMS*, 8 (1964), 3-21; A. O. H. Jarman, 'The Delineation of Arthur in Early Welsh Verse', in *An Arthurian Tapestry: Essays in Memory of Lewis Thorpe*, edited by Kenneth Varty (Glasgow, 1981), 1-21; idem, 'The Arthurian Allusions in the Black Book of Carmarthen', in LAMA 99-112 and 240-2; and John K. Bollard, 'Arthur in the Early Welsh Tradition', in *The Romance of Arthur*, [I], edited by James J. Wilhelm and Laila Zamuelis Gross (New York, 1984), 13-25. Still useful for Rhŷs's pioneering translations is E. K. Chambers, *Arthur of Britain*, repr. with supplementary bibliography by B. F. Roberts (Cambridge, 1964).

2. Marged Haycock, 'Metrical Models for the Poems in the Book of Taliesin', in *Early Welsh Poetry: Studies in the Book of Aneirin*, edited by Brynley F. Roberts (Aberystwyth, 1988), 155-77; Jenny Rowland, 'Genres', ibid., 179-208.

3. Rowland, 'Genres'.

4. Cf. Proinsias Mac Cana, *The Learned Tales of Medieval Ireland* (Dublin, 1980), 132-41; *Uraicecht na Ríar: The Poetic Grades in Early Irish Law*, edited by Liam Breatnach (Dublin, 1987); Dafydd Jenkins, 'Pencerdd a Bardd Teilu [sic]', *YB*, 14 (1988), 19-46.

5. Cf. Proinsias Mac Cana, 'The Three Languages and the Three Laws', *SC*, 5 (1970), 62-78; Donnchadh Ó Corráin, 'Irish Origin Legends and Genealogy: Recurrent Aetiologies', in *History and Heroic Tale*, edited by Tore Nyberg and others (Odense, 1983), 51-96; Kim McCone, 'Zur Frage der Register im frühen Irischen', in *Early Irish Literature — Media and Communication: Mündlichkeit und Schriftlichkeit in der frühen irischen Literatur*, edited by Stephen N. Tranter and Hildegard L. C. Tristram, ScriptOralia, 10 (Tübingen, 1989), 57-97; John Carey, 'The Two Laws in Dubthach's Judgment', *CMCS*, 19 (1990), 1-18.

6. Marged Haycock, '"Preiddeu Annwn" and the Figure of Taliesin', *SC*, 18/19 (1983-4), 52-78; '"Some Talk of Alexander and Some of Hercules": Three Early Welsh Poems from the Book of Taliesin', *CMCS*, 13 (1987), 7-38; 'Taliesin's Lesser Song of the World', *Celtica* (forthcoming).

7. For the above see my 'Some Functions of Origin Stories in Early Medieval Wales', in *History and Heroic Tale*, edited by Nyberg and others, 97-131.

8. For more detailed discussion of transmission and preservation see my 'The Evidence for Vernacular Irish Literary Influence on Early Mediaeval Welsh Literature', in *Ireland in Early Mediaeval Europe: Studies in Memory of Kathleen Hughes*, edited by Dorothy Whitelock and others (Cambridge, 1982), 235-57; for Scotland, see my review of K. Hughes, *Celtic Britain in the Early Middle Ages* (Woodbridge, 1980) in *Journal of Ecclesiastical History*, 36 (1985), 306-7, and Ronald Black, 'The Gaelic Manuscripts of Scotland', in *Gaelic and Scotland: Alba agus a' Ghàidhlig*, edited by William Gillies (Edinburgh, 1989), 160-5.

9. ALMA 13. This suits the nature of the evidence better than 'c. 1100', a date sometimes given.

10. These points are well-known, but there is no convenient survey.

11. On the *Historia Brittonum* see T. M. Charles-Edwards above, ch.1, and Brynley F. Roberts below, pp.88-92.

12. Cf. Brynley F. Roberts, 'Oral Tradition and Welsh Literature: A Description and Survey', *Oral Tradition*, 3 (1988), 61-87.

13. Jackson, ALMA 13.

14. Albert C. Baugh, 'The Middle English Romance: Some Questions of Creation, Presentation, and Preservation', *Speculum*, 42 (1967), 1-31.

15. Jackson, ALMA 12. Cf. Mac Cana, *Learned Tales*, 132, n.2; 'Rhai o Gerddi Ymddiddan Llyfr Du Caerfyrddin', edited by Brynley F. Roberts, in Ast. H. 281-325; Jenny Rowland, 'The Prose Setting of the Early Welsh *Englynion Chwedlonol*', *Ériu*, 36 (1985), 29-43 (cf. n.22 below); Proinsias Mac Cana, 'Notes on the Combination of Prose and Verse in Early Irish Narrative', in *Early Irish Literature*, edited by Tranter and Tristram, 125-47; N. Jacobs, *ÉC*, 26 (1989), 95-142.

16. *Mab.* 18-21. Cf. J. K. Bollard, 'The Role of Myth and Tradition in the *Four Branches of the Mabinogi*', *CMCS*, 6 (1983), 74-5; Andrew Welsh, 'Traditional Tales and the Harmonizing of Story in *Pwyll Pendeuic Dyuet*', *CMCS*, 17 (1989), 36-9.

17. *CA*; Aneirin, *Y Gododdin*, edited and trans. by A. O. H. Jarman (Llandysul, 1988).

18. Cf. stanza XXXI (A-text).

19. Stanza CII (B-text).

20. Cf. Jarman, 'Delineation', 3-4, *SC*, 24/5 (1989-90), 15-25.

21. See G s.n. *Arthur*; *TYP* 277.

22. See Jenny Rowland's *Early Welsh Saga Poetry* (Cambridge, 1990). This appeared after this chapter was written. It also includes discussion of all the *englynion* covered here and an edition of the poem on Geraint (pp. 240-3, 273, 457-61, 504-7 and 636-9).

23. *LlDC*; A. O. H. Jarman, '*Llyfr Du Caerfyrddin*: The Black Book of Carmarthen', *PBA*, 71 (1985), 333-56.

24. *Enweu Meibon Llywarch Hen* [recte *Kynwarch*], *LlDC* no. 40. See Rachel Bromwich, 'CLlH. viii.3 (= BBC. 107, 10-12)', *B*, 17 (1956-8), 180-1; Brynley F. Roberts, 'The Treatment of Personal Names in the Early Welsh Versions of *Historia Regum Britanniae*', *B*, 25 (1972-4), 283-4. But P. C. Bartrum, 'Bonedd yr Arwyr', *B*, 18 (1958-60), 243, suggested that the tradition of Cynfarch's three sons might be 'anterior to the time of Geoffrey'.

25. Edited by Roberts, 'Rhai o Gerddi Ymddiddan', no. II. Earlier translations include Chambers, *Arthur of Britain*, 64-6; Gwyn Thomas, *Y Traddodiad Barddol* (Cardiff, 1976), 69-70; Rachel Bromwich, 'Celtic Elements in Arthurian Romance: A General Survey', in LAMA 41-55 and 230-3 (at pp. 45-6 and 231); Bollard, 'Arthur', 19-21. The metre is Class 1 of Haycock, 'Metrical Models'.

26. On this theme see Edgar M. Slotkin, 'The Fabula, Story, and Text of *Breuddwyd Rhonabwy*', *CMCS*, 18 (1989), 89-111.

27. *TYP* no. 21; *VSB* 26-9 and 68-73.

28. Cf. R. J. Thomas, *Enwau Afonydd a Nentydd Cymru* (Cardiff, 1938), 141-2; there is no need to hypothesize unattested personal names in the poem. *Vytheint* 'vultures' (line 11) is an emendation of the meaningless *vythneint* '?eight streams', a scribal error perhaps influenced by awareness that *Eleï* was the name of a stream, or by confusion with the word *gwyth*, pl. *gwytheint*, 'stream'.

29. Jarman, 'Allusions', 108.

30. Cf. O. J. Padel, below, pp.234-8. For references see indices of proper names in *CO*. Dr

Bromwich will argue in her forthcoming commentary on *Culhwch* with D. Simon Evans that 'Pa gur?' and *Culhwch* are closely related.

31. MS *Cysceint*, usually emended because *Cysteint* is an attested derivative of *Constantinus*; however, as Dr Bromwich points out to me, one might (with G 266) compare *Yscawin/Iscawin mab Panon* in *CO*(1) 225 and 1118. If the latter is the correct name, the character could be the eponym of Porth Ysgewin in Gwent, on which see below, comments on line 79.

32. He is only his porter on New Year's Day (*CO*   84); cf. *Geraint* (*Mab.* 229), also *Owain*, where Glewlwyd has the rank of porter although Arthur has no porter (*Mab.* 155).

33. *Yr Areithiau Pros*, edited by D. Gwenallt Jones (Cardiff, 1934), 14.

34. Despite the semicolon in the printed text, the uncles may be the sons of Llwch, so that the latter is Arthur's maternal grandfather.   On Llwch and Môr Terwyn, cf. John T. Koch, 'Mor Terwyn', *B*, 30 (1983), 296-303;   and Patrick Sims-Williams, 'The Irish Geography of *Culhwch and Olwen*', in *Sages, Saints and Storytellers: Celtic Studies in Honour of Professor James Carney*, edited by Donnchadh Ó Corráin and others (Maynooth, 1989), 418-20.

35. *Kelli* could be the common noun 'grove', and in his edition (p. 305) Roberts cites Thomas Jones's suggestion, **kelli* 'wisdom' from *call* 'wise'.

36. Cf. Ifor Williams, 'Hen Chwedlau', *THSC*, 1946-7, 55, on *usque ad caput anni, in medio urbis meae* (c.32) as Cambricisims, i.e. *hyd ben y flwyddyn, i mewn i'm dinas i*.   For a similar phenomenon in Hiberno-Latin see McCone, 'Zur Frage der Register', 73-4.

37. Cf. John T. Koch, 'A Welsh Window on the Iron Age: Manawydan, Mandubracios', *CMCS*, 14 (1987), 17-52.

38. '. . . which we call *Traht Treuroit*' in the Vatican Recension, c.27,   edited by David N. Dumville, *The Historia Brittonum*, iii, *The 'Vatican' Recension* (Cambridge, 1985), 104.

39. Ifor Williams, 'Vocabularium Cornicum II', *B*, 11 (1941-4), 95; Kenneth Jackson, 'The Arthur of History', ALMA 4 n.1, 6, and 8. *Trywruid/Tribruit/Treuroit* are merely spelling variants.

40. Possibly at the hands of Medrawd/Modred (on whom see *TYP* 454-5 and 558), perhaps 'my nephew' in line 30.   But for emendations of *mynei* see Gwyn Thomas, *Traddodiad Barddol*, 69, and Bromwich, LAMA, 231, n.36.

41. *CO*(1) 981-4.

42. Thomas, *Traddodiad Barddol*, 69; Bollard, 'Arthur', 19.

43. J. Lloyd-Jones, 'Welsh *palach*, etc.', *Ériu*, 16 (1952), 123-31; cf. G 43 for another scribe writing *Arthur* in error. On *Wrnach* and *Awarnach* see *CO*(1) xli and lxii.

44. The redactor seems to try to minimize this unseemly role for Arthur in lines 1219-21 (but note that he fights with the Witches of Gloucester in *Peredur*).   The parallel with *Culhwch* supports the view that the verb *gouerei* is transitive, rather than the intransitive 'the/his blood flowed'.   In medieval thought the Devil was associated with the North: see *The Poems of John Milton*, edited by John Carey and Alistair Fowler (London, 1968), 718-19.

45. Lloyd-Jones, 'Welsh *palach*'; Patrick Sims-Williams, 'The Significance of the Irish Personal Names in *Culhwch ac Olwen*', *B*, 29 (1980-2), 615-16.

46. *De Civitate Dei*, XVI.8.   Similarly Isidore, *Etymologiae*, XI.iii.15 and XII.ii.32.   Gerald of Wales

found this type of material current in Welsh folklore, e.g. ape-dogs in *Itinerarium Kambriae*, II.11. See in general *Métamorphose et bestiaire fantastique au moyen âge*, edited by Laurence Harf-Lancner (Paris, 1985).

47. *Epistolae Karolini Aevi*, iv, edited by E. Duemmler and E. Perels, Monumenta Germaniae Historica, Epistolae, 6 (Berlin, 1925), 155-7. On the other hand, they were a sort of Ethiopian monkey according to Solinus: *C. Iulii Solini Collectanea Rerum Memorabilium*, edited by T. Mommsen (Berlin, repr. 1958), 128 (c.27.58).

48. Myles Dillon, 'Notes on Irish Words', *Language*, 17 (1941), 249-51; *Serglige Con Culainn*, edited by Myles Dillon (Dublin, 1953), 38; Kathleen Hughes, 'On an Irish Litany of Pilgrim Saints', *Analecta Bollandiana*, 77 (1959), 328-31; W. B. Stanford, 'Monsters and Odyssean Echoes in the Early Hiberno-Latin and Irish Hymns', in *Latin Script and Letters A.D. 400-900: Festschrift presented to Ludwig Bieler*, edited by John J. O'Meara and Bernd Naumann (Leiden, 1976), 114-16; Donald E. Meek, 'The Banners of the Fian in Gaelic Ballad Tradition', *CMCS*, 11 (1986), 29-69.

49. See respectively Dillon, 'Notes', 250, and P. Sims-Williams, 'The Visionary Celt: The Construction of an Ethnic Preconception', *CMCS*, 11 (1986), 87-91.

50. In *TYP* 391 it is suggested that Gwrgi is the prototype of Urgan in Gottfried's *Tristan* — and we may add (*pace* Maurice Delbouille, 'Le témoignage de Wace sur la légende arthurienne', *Romania*, 74 (1953), 181-3) of Wace's Guergint of Hereford.

51. *TYP* 17 and 531.

52. *TYP* 279.

53. Cf. Jones, 'Early Evolution', 10-11; Rachel Bromwich, 'Concepts of Arthur', *SC*, 10/11 (1975-6), 170.

54. G 475.

55. *Hend.* 2; cf. *rac llu gwychryt*, p. 5. For *gweleis* see I. Ll. Foster, 'Rhai Sylwadau ar yr Hengerdd', *YB*, 5 (1970), 21-3.

56. *TYP* 306.

57. *PKM* 86; *Mab.* 70.

58. *TYP* 416 and 555.

59. Cf. the case of Cocholyn and Corroi in *Marwnat Corroi*: 'many their conflicts on either side of their borders' (edited by Sims-Williams, 'Evidence', 249-50).

60. *TYP* 219 and 417-18; Keith Busby, 'The Enigma of Loholt', in *Arthurian Tapestry*, edited by Varty, 28-36.

61. *LlDC* no. 34; 'Rhai o Gerddi Ymddiddan', edited by Roberts, no. IV; Rowland, *Saga Poetry*, 243-7, 299, 461-3, 506-7 and 639-40. Jarman, 'Delineation', 18, n.26, argues that 'marvellous in songs' refers to Llachau, not Arthur. The speaker is probably not a subsequent tourist, in view of the references to the carrion birds. For the *Mi a wum* formula, cf. Sims-Williams, 'Significance', 601-2.

62. *Nepotes* according to *Annales Cambriae*.

63. *Hend.* 25, 70, and 152; *TYP* 416; 'Poèmes de Bleddyn Vardd', edited and trans. by J. Vendryes,

RC, 49 (1932), 194, 231, and 234-5.

64. Cf. Jackson, 'Arthur of History', ALMA 1; Jones, 'Early Evolution', 12; and below p.91.

65. *Historia Peredur vab Efrawc*, edited by Glenys Witchard Goetinck (Cardiff, 1976), 29-30 and 70; *Mab.* 198 and 227.

66. Cf. Jarman, 'Delineation', 14; P. Sims-Williams, 'Some Celtic Otherworld Terms', in *Celtic Language, Celtic Culture: A Festschrift for Eric P. Hamp*, edited by A.T.E. Matonis and Daniel F. Melia (Van Nuys, 1990), p. 57-81.

67. *La Vie de saint Samson*, edited by Robert Fawtier (Paris, 1912), 124-6; *LL* 13-14. Strangely, this version was not noted by John Rhŷs, 'The Nine Witches of Gloucester', in *Anthropological Essays Presented to Edward Burnett Tylor* (Oxford, 1907), 285-93, but cf. *CO*(1) lxxiv.

68. G 624 notes that *yng ngwarthaf* is generally followed by a place-name. He suggests emending to *-eu*, but *proest* with *-on* is quite acceptable.

69. *TYP* 236-7. See also above, n.31. The reference might be to the barrow above Portskewett, or its hinterland in general.

70. *BT* 73; *PT* xxvi-xxviii; *TYP* 237 and 485. Unfortunately, however, the date and import of the line (which is hypermetrical) remain very uncertain.

71. *EAR* i, 41, n.2; *TYP* 486-7; *John of Fordun's Chronicle of the Scottish Nation*, ed. W.F. Skene, 2 vols. (Edinburgh, 1871-2), i, 166, and ii, 157-8 (Book IV.23) — I owe this reference to Dr Bromwich.

72. Lister M. Matheson, 'The Arthurian Stories of Lambeth Palace Library MS 84', *Arthurian Literature*, 5 (1985), 70-91. There is no need, then, to postulate **mynud* 'hacked small' < Latin *minutus*.

73. *LlDC* no. 37; cf. Jarman, 'Allusions', 102.

74. *LlDC* nos. 21 and 18. The former is edited by Roberts, 'Rhai o Gerddi Ymddiddan', no. I, and trans. in Gwyn Williams, *To Look for a Word: Collected Translations of Welsh Poetry* (Llandysul, 1976), 20-2, in *The Oxford Book of Welsh Verse in English*, edited by Gwyn Jones (Oxford, 1977), 14-16, and in Bollard, 'Arthur', 17-18. See also n.22 above. The latter is edited and trans. by Thomas Jones, 'The Black Book of Carmarthen "Stanzas of the Graves"', *PBA*, 53 (1967), 97-137.

75. See references in *TYP* 25-6, 355-60 and 551; G. H. Doble, *Lives of the Welsh Saints*, edited by D. Simon Evans (Cardiff, 1971), 185, n.60; B. Lynette Olsen and O. J. Padel, 'A Tenth-Century List of Cornish Parochial Saints', *CMCS*, 12 (1986), 45 and 48. Identification with the general was argued by N. Lukman, 'The British General Gerontius (†410) in Medieval Epics', *Classica et Mediaevalia*, 12 (1951), 215-35. His argument was highly speculative (cf. A. O. H. Jarman, 'Geraint: Gerontius', *LlC*, 2 (1952), 129), but it is conceivable that medieval Welsh scholarship was attracted by the collocation of the names Gerontius, Constans son of Constantinus, and Maximus in the accounts of him by Orosius, *Historiae Adversum Paganos*, VII.42.4, edited by C. Zangemeister (Leipzig, 1889), 297, and by Gregory of Tours, *Historia Francorum*, II.9.

76. *VSB* 234 (cf. pp. xii and n.1 and 321, n.2, and *EWGT* 27 and 132). For *princeps miliciae* see Claude Sterckx, '"Princeps Militiae" dans l'*Historia Regum Britanniae* de Geoffrey de Monmouth', *AB*, 76 (1969), 725-30.

77. *Mab.* 246. Note that in the Black Book version Erbin is only named as the father in the *title* of the poem *Gereint fil[ius] Erbin*.

78. Kenneth Jackson, 'Incremental Repetition in the Early Welsh *Englyn'*, *Speculum*, 16 (1941), 304-21; Roberts, 'Oral Tradition', 64-5. Jackson gives parallels from other cultures for varying the colour of animals; this also occurs in the Melwas dialogue discussed below.

79. *Charters of Sherborne*, edited by M. A. O'Donovan (London, 1988), xli, xlviii-xlix, and 81.

80. *LL* 114; cf. Doble, *Lives of the Welsh Saints*, 183 and 185.

81. ALMA 13; cf. Roberts, 'Rhai o Gerddi Ymddiddan', 294-5.

82. The Black Book's 'y gueleis e. y arthur' may be due to simple haplography (at the stop), for it skips over several 'gueleis' *englynion*, to judge by the evidence of the Red Book.

83. For *gwr y* 'vassal to' see T. M. Charles-Edwards, 'The Date of the Four Branches of the Mabinogi', *THSC*, 1970, 274-5.

84. O. J. Padel, 'Geoffrey of Monmouth and Cornwall', *CMCS*, 8 (1984), 1-28; *CO*(1) lxxix-lxxxi.

85. The prominence of horses in *Erec/Gereint* and the *englynion* was pointed out by O. J. Padel in an unpublished lecture.

86. Edited by Roberts, stanza 12.

87. See above, n.64. Compare the collocation of the name *Amhir* and a grave which is both 'narrow' and 'long' in *englyn* 19 (edited by Jones, p. 120); but this cannot refer to Amhir's own grave without emendation.

88. See on the latter my note, *'Anfab[2], "Illegitimate Child": A Ghost-Word'*, *B*, 28 (1978-80), 90-3. In general see Rowland, *Saga Poetry*, 294-8.

89. I leave out persons like Owain ab Urien (st.13), who were probably brought into Arthur's orbit at a late stage.

90. On *anoeth*, cf. Proinsias Mac Cana, 'C. anoeth: Gw. deccair', *B*, 23 (1968-70), 28-29; *CO*(1) xxi-xxii. Another possible sign of age is the rhyme of *-ur* and *-ut* (t = [ð]), but such rhymes do occur even in post-medieval informal verse.

91. *Mab.* 107, 128-9, and 150; *TYP* 389-90 and 403-4.

92. This derives from Irish sources; see Richard Sharpe, 'St Patrick and the See of Armagh', *CMCS*, 4 (1982), 42.

93. Jones, '"Stanzas of the Graves"', 108-9 and 'Early Evolution', 17-18; Bromwich, 'Concepts', 164; Jarman, 'Arthurian Allusions', 111-12 and 242, n.65. J. E. Lloyd, 'The Death of Arthur', *B*, 11 (1941-4), 158-60, argued that Geoffrey was deliberately ambiguous, balancing a Breton/Cornish belief in Arthur's survival with a Welsh belief that he was slain at Camlan.

94. Chambers, *Arthur of Britain*, 18 and 249. See J. E. C. Williams, ch.12 below, p.262.

95. *Willelmi Malmesbiriensis De Gestis Regum Anglorum*, edited by W. Stubbs, 2 vols., Rolls Ser. (London, 1887), ii, 342 (cf. p. lxxxix, n.1); Chambers, *Arthur of Britain*, 17-18 and 249-50.

96. It may be relevant that Gwalchmai and Cynon are both Arthur's courtiers in *Owain*. On the other hand, the latter was originally a non-Arthurian hero. See ch.13, n.27; *TYP* 323-4 and Rachel Bromwich, 'Cynon fab Clydno', Ast. H. 151-64.

97. Dafydd Huw Evans, 'An Incident on the Dee during the Glyn Dŵr Rebellion?', *Trans. Denbighshire Historical Soc.*, 1988, 19 and n.62; J. E. C. Williams, '*kyfedwynt y gynrein kywyn don* CT ii. 20', *B*, 21 (1964-6), 229-30.

98. For a different but equally speculative view, equating *Perydon* with a south-eastern *Periron*, see *AP* xxxiv-xl and lines 18 and 71.

99. This has often been identified as the grave site (see indices to *Archaeologia Cambrensis*, s.n. 'Walwyn's Castle'), which is impossible if William is correct in placing it on the 'sea-shore'. According to B. G. Charles, *Non-Celtic Place-Names in Wales* (London, 1938), 87-8, the name *Castle Galwan/Gaweyn*, etc., is first attested from the 1290s, but may reflect an earlier *Castell Gwalchmai*. On the other hand, the latter name may be a 'translation' of the English (or French or Flemish) name. See also G 609; *TYP* 371-2.

100. Like Penda's in st.10; see P. Sims-Williams, *Religion and Literature in Western England, 600-800* (Cambridge, 1990), 28, n.57.

101. *Cywyddau Iolo Goch ac Eraill*, edited by Henry Lewis and others, second edn. (Cardiff, 1937), 160, no. LIV.16; *TYP* 280; *HRB* c.171 (X.9); *BD* 178.

102. Cf. BWP 188 (there is another Tryfan near Llansannan, SH/9766). It is curious that, while Bedwyr is linked with Tryfrwyd and Tryfan in 'Pa gur?' and the above *englyn* respectively, *otryuruyd* and *otryuan* are linked in a quite different context in *LlDC* no. 1 (*YMTh*), line 4.

103. C. A. Gresham, 'The Aberconwy Charter', *Archaeologia Cambrensis*, 94 (1939), 152, and 'The Aberconwy Charter; Further Consideration', *B*, 30 (1982-3), 334; I. Williams, 'gwryd, gwrhyd', *B*, 8 (1935-7), 236; Melville Richards, 'Arthurian Onomastics', *THSC*, 1969, 262-3 (with other instances). Cai was also associated with Caer Gai near Bala: R. B. White, 'Caer Gai and the Giants of Penllyn', *Jnl Merioneth Hist. and Rec. Soc.*, 10 (1985-6), 31-5.

104. *TYP* 160-2.

105. For Osfran (a unique allusion) and Morfran see respectively *Hend.* 43 and *TYP* 161 and 463-5. On the problematic element *Os(s)*- see *CA* 103 and cf. *LL* 218 (*Osulf* = OE *Oswulf*).

106. Marged Haycock, 'Llyfr Taliesin', *National Library of Wales Journal*, 25 (1988), 357-86.

107. Cf. Chambers, *Arthur of Britain*, 61.

108. *BT* 27; cf. Marged Haycock, 'The Significance of the "Cad Goddau" Tree-List in the Book of Taliesin', in *Celtic Linguistics: Readings in the Brythonic Languages for T. Arwyn Watkins*, edited by Martin J. Ball and others (Amsterdam, 1990), 310, n.10.

109. Cf. Wace's statement that Taliesin prophesied the birth of Christ, a passage misinterpreted by Delbouille, 'Témoignage de Wace', 180-1.

110. Cf. Haycock, 'Significance of the Tree List'.

111. *BT* 34; Marged Haycock, 'Llyfr Taliesin: Astudiaethau ar Rai Agweddau', unpubl. Ph.D. diss. (University of Wales, Aberystwyth, 1983), 205.

112. *BT* 48; *TYP* xcviii-cvii.

113. *TYP* ci-cii; *CO*(1) 1016 and 1225. *Cafall* (< *caballus*) is the name of his dog (*CO*(1) 1015 etc.), as in the *Historia Brittonum*, c.73. This has been supposed, on etymological grounds, to have been the name of Arthur's horse (e.g. Jones, 'Early Evolution', 11-12; *CO*(1) lxiv-lxvi and ciii), but

the point may be that Arthur's dog was of horse-like proportions; compare, too, Leo and Tiger as modern cats' names. This is not to deny that *Carn cabal*, the name etymologized in the *Historia*, probably meant 'horse's hoof/cairn' originally. See R. J. Thomas, 'Cysylltiad Arthur â Gogledd Ceredigion', *B*, 8 (1935-7), 124-5; *The Description of Penbrokshire by George Owen of Henllys*, edited by Henry Owen, 4 parts (London, 1892-1906), ii, 344, and iv, 530, 680, and 707-8. See below pp.90-1.

114. On Uthr see *TYP* 56 (no. 28) and 520-3; Jackson, ALMA 14, n.2; A. O. H. Jarman, 'Emrys Wledig; Amlawdd Wledig; Uthr Bendragon', *LlC*, 2 (1952), 127-8.

115. *BT* 71; *TYP* 521.

116. *BT* 71; cf. Haycock, 'Astudiaethau', 270.

117. *BT* 34.

118. Information from M. Haycock.

119. *BT* 66; A. O. H. Jarman, 'Erof Greulawn', *LlC*, 7 (1962), 106-7.

120. *Hend.* 254 = *RBP* col. 1171; cf. *TYP* 521; Haycock, '"Some Talk of Alexander"', 22, n.81.

121. WAL 131-78; Haycock, '"Preiddeu Annwn"' (n.6 above). The metre is basically Class 2 of Haycock, 'Metrical Models' (see p. 172).

122. Haycock, '"Preiddeu Annwn"', 74.

123. Ibid., 65 and 68; *TYP* 141 and 161.

124. For references to earlier discussions see Haycock, '"Preiddeu Annwn"', and Jarman, 'Delineation', 11-14.

125. *CO*(1), lines 635-6, 1036-56.

126. Cf. Haycock, '"Preiddeu Annwn"', 70; Sims-Williams, 'Irish Geography', 418-20. Loomis implausibly saw forms of Lug and Lancelot here.

127. Cf. Sims-Williams, 'Significance', 604, and *CO*(1) lxii-lxiii on the names Diwrnach, Dyrnwch etc. For the *Thirteen Treasures*, see below pp.85-8.

128. *BT* 33; Haycock, '"Preiddeu Annwn"', 54 and n.27; *Mab.* xiii and 37.

129. Sims-Williams, 'Evidence', 246-7; cf. R. Mark Scowcroft, 'Leabhar Gabhála: Part II, The Growth of the Tradition', *Ériu*, 39 (1988), 53-7.

130. Kenneth Jackson, 'Some Popular Motifs in Early Welsh Tradition', *ÉC*, 11 (1964-5), 95-9.

131. Cf. Sims-Williams, 'Origin Stories'; this aspect is developed in *PKM* in an earlier passage linking Llasar, the cauldron, and the Irish settlements in Wales, and in a later passage about Llasar and the invention of *calch lassar*.

132. E.g. the Dilmun of the Sumerians, the Polynesians' island of Tuma, and the belief, recorded by Procopius, that Britain itself was an island of the dead; I hope to discuss these elsewhere.

133. Glyn E. Jones, 'Y Wledd yn Harlech ac yng Ngwales ym Mabinogi *Branwen*', *B*, 25 (1972-4), 380-6.

134. Sims-Williams, 'Evidence', pp. 248-55.

135. J. Carney, 'The Earliest Irish Brân Material', in *Latin Script and Letters*, edited by O'Meara and Naumann (see n.48 above), 174-93.

136. 'Astudiaeth ar Rai Agweddau ar Fabinogi *Branwen*', unpubl. MA Diss. (University of Wales, Cardiff, 1970), 300-12.

137. Common origins or Irish dependence on Britain would seem to follow from the argument of John T. Koch, 'Brân, Brennos', *CMCS*, 20 (1990), 1-20. The Irish names *Bran* and *Brénainn* (> *Brendanus*), etc., are listed as 'borrowed names' by M. A. O'Brien, 'Old Irish Personal Names', *Celtica*, 10 (1973), 231, but this seems unlikely in the case of *Bran* ('raven'); cf. Donnchadh Ó Corráin and Fidelma Maguire, *Gaelic Personal Names* (Dublin, 1981), 33-4.

138. Sims-Williams, 'Evidence', 243-8, and 'Some Celtic Otherworld Terms'.

139. A. Watkin-Jones, 'The Interludes of Wales in the Eighteenth Century', *B*, 4 (1927-9), 104; *Duanaire Finn*, iii, edited by Gerard Murphy, Irish Texts Soc. 43 (Dublin, 1953), 132. Cf. John MacInnes, 'Twentieth-Century Recordings of Scottish Gaelic Ballads', in *The Heroic Process*, edited by Bo Almqvist *et al*. (Dublin, 1987), 126.

140. 'Ymddiddan Arthur a'r Eryr', edited by Ifor Williams, *B*, 2 (1923-5), 269-86; also edited with trans. by Marged Haycock, *Blodeugerdd o Gerddi Crefyddol Cynnar* (forthcoming). Cf. Janem Mary Williams, 'Y Darlun o Arthur ym Mucheddau'r Saint ac yn Englynion Ymddiddan Arthur a'r Eryr', unpubl. MA Diss. (Univ. of Wales, Aberystwyth, 1967); Rowland, 'Genres', 198-9; Rowland, *Saga Poetry*, 285-6.

141. 'Englynion y Clyweit', edited by Ifor Williams and T. H. Parry-Williams, *B*, 3 (1926-7), 4-21; *Blodeugerdd*, edited and trans. by Haycock. Cf. Watkin-Jones, 'Interludes', 104, on a 'Dialogue between a Young Man and the Wren' and similar Interludes.

142. *HRB* cc.29 and 206 (II.9 and XII.18); cf. J. S. P. Tatlock, Leg. Hist., 44-5, who wrongly describes our *Dialogue* as 'evidently late'. For post-Galfridian attempts to supply the eagle's prophecy see Henry Lewis, 'Proffwydoliaeth yr Eryr', *B*, 9 (1937-9), 112-15.

143. 'The Colloquy of Llywelyn and Gwrnerth', edited by K. Jackson, *ZCP*, 21 (1940), 24-32; *LlDC* no. 25; Donatien Laurent, 'La gwerz de Skolan et la légende de Merlin', *Éthnologie française*, 1 (1971), 19-54; Rowland, *Saga Poetry*, 201-2 and 284-5.

144. *Mab*. 71-3. Cf. Williams, 'Ymddiddan', 286; Jackson, 'Popular Motifs', 89-91.

145. Cf. 'Y Gwr Cadarn' in the Interludes: Watkin-Jones, 'Interludes', 104, n.5.

146. Jones, 'Early Evolution', 10; Jarman, 'Delineation', 15.

147. Information from O. J. Padel; see his *Cornish Place-Name Elements* (Nottingham, 1985), 104-5.

148. *CO* 35; *Mab*. 128. For later instances of Arthur as a bard uttering *englynion* see *TYP* 21-2, 31-2, and 532; Rowland, *Saga Poetry*, 250-1, 254-6 and cf. 258-60.

149. Both printed and trans. by Mary Williams, 'An Early Ritual Poem in Welsh', *Speculum*, 13 (1938), 38-43; cf. ATC 197, n.9; Jackson, ALMA 18-19; *TYP* 383-4; Rowland, *Saga Poetry*, 256-8. Cf. below p.83.

150. Evan D. Jones, 'Melwas, Gwenhwyfar, a Chai', *B*, 8 (1935-7), 204.

151. *Erec*, lines 1946-51; trans. D. D. R. Owen, *Chrétien de Troyes: Arthurian Romances* (London, 1987), 26.

152. So dated by C. N. L. Brooke, *The Church and the Welsh Border in the Central Middle Ages* (Woodbridge, 1986), 42. Caradog has other vernacular material, about Huail and Arthur; cf. Elissa R. Henken, *Traditions of the Welsh Saints* (Cambridge, 1987), 136-7; *CO*(1) xcix-ci; Proinsias Mac Cana, 'Fianaigecht in the Pre-Norman Period', in *Heroic Process*, edited by Almqvist *et al.*, 96, n.45.

153. *Ineswitrin* appears already in William of Malmesbury, *De Gestis Regum Anglorum*, ed. Stubbs, i, 28-9 (cf. *The Early History of Glastonbury*, edited by John Scott (Woodbridge, 1981), 188, nn.24-5). See also Thomas, *Enwau Afonydd*, 180 and 198; H. P. R. Finberg, *Lucerna* (London, 1964), 83-94. For Welsh *Gwlat yr Haf* (Summer Country) see *CO* 1059; G 689.

154. *Chronica Minora*, iii, edited by T. Mommsen, Monumenta Germaniae Historica, Auctores Antiquissimi, 13 (Berlin, 1898), 109; cf. Chambers, *Arthur of Britain*, 84-5, 116-17, 121-3, and 263; ATC 214-15 and 219; ALMA 67; *TYP* 381-2 and 553. Some of the enormous literature on Glastonbury, Avalon, etc. is cited in *Llyfryddiaeth Llenyddiaeth Gymraeg*, edited by Thomas Parry and Merfyn Morgan (Cardiff, 1976), 52-3.

155. The motif of colour variation is simply a stylistic device; see n.78 above.

156. As Loomis does, ATC 215-18, in stressing the seasonal theme. Note also that the 'end(s) of the world' (*eithafoedd byd*) is a commonplace in *Owain* and elsewhere (G 465). For the above poems see *TYP* 382-3.

157. Sims-Williams, 'Functions of Origin Stories' (n.7 above).

158. See further Sims-Williams, 'The Visionary Celt' (n.49 above), 87-93. I am grateful to Drs Marged Haycock and Rachel Bromwich for comments on this chapter.

3

CULHWCH AC OLWEN, THE TRIADS, SAINTS' LIVES

Brynley F. Roberts

THE texts referred to in the title, in spite of differences between them in literary form, language, and authorial intention, constitute, together with some early poetry, the most important sources for our knowledge of native Welsh Arthurian legend. The evidence is partly in the form of extended narratives but partly consists of episodes and allusions, comprehensible in the full sense to the medieval audiences of these texts but for us the vestiges of a rich tradition, now fragmented, the characteristic features of which may nevertheless be recoverable.

Culhwch ac Olwen[1] is the longest and the earliest of the surviving native prose tales given written form in medieval Welsh. These stories, collectively termed *'mabinogion'* in modern usage, are generally assumed to derive from traditional oral narratives recited by professional story-tellers to audiences in courts, both lay and ecclesiastic, and aristocratic houses. In their manuscript versions, however, none can be regarded simply as written, almost verbatim, copies of an orally performed text, and in every case, though to different degrees, they are literary compositions based on antecedent traditional narratives and reflecting some of their conventions, but inevitably removed from the shared world of traditional literature towards the individual's use, manipulation and re-ordering of traditional material. The evidence which they present must be viewed, as far as is possible, in the context of their genre, motivation and intentions.[2]

Culhwch ac Olwen is found in the White Book of Rhydderch and in the Red Book of Hergest. In spite of a number of variant readings, these copies represent a single recension and there is evidence neither of a lengthy or complex textual tradition, nor of any other version of the tale. The loss of a number of folios from the White Book results in the loss of one third of the story but the Red Book text, which reveals considerable modernization, is complete. The former contains many linguistic and syntactic archaisms, and a comparison with Welsh saga *englynion* and early court poetry suggests that the final written version of the tale belongs to the same period as this poetry, c. 1100.[3] Crudity of tone and archaic social and legal customs may be further evidence of an early date as none of the other *mabinogion* stories lacks so completely conventional signs of civilized relationships. It is all the more remarkable, therefore, that almost the only explicit reference to an ideal standard of 'courtly' behaviour should be made with reference to Arthur himself. When the sullen Cai challenges Culhwch's right to enter the court he is chided by Arthur who reminds him that 'we are noblemen while people come to us. The greater the boon we grant, the greater will be our nobility, our praise and our honour.'

The story has no title in the manuscripts but the explicit, 'how Culhwch gained Olwen the daughter of Ysbaddaden Chief Giant', places the tale in the category of wooings, a recognized type in the Old Irish tale classifications. Culhwch's name, used as a standard of valour, appears in an *englyn* in a lament to Cynddylan, usually dated to the mid or late ninth century but apart from apparently confirming an acknowledged heroic role for him the allusion does not suggest any context for stories or traditions about him.[4] Rachel Bromwich, *CO*(1) p. lxxxv, regards this reference as a scribal error for some word such as *culwyd* and believes that Culhwch had no narrative told of him prior to his appearance in the tale, though the personal name was established.[5] Olwen occurs for the first time in this story. The proper name may be a feminine adjective 'beautiful', but it is given a fanciful etymology as though it were *ôl* 'track' and *gwen*, fem. 'white': 'Four white clover grew on her track where ever she went and thus was she called Olwen'. This motif ('Where e're you walk') is widespread and is not peculiarly Welsh or onomastic in origin.[6] Both names — Culhwch and Olwen — are transparent, affording an opportunity for the etymological word-play which was, and continues to be, a feature of popular Welsh onomastics. Culhwch's birth in a swine-run may have been intended as an etymological explanation of his name, but whatever its original significance may have been, its easy identification with *hwch*, 'sow', may have suggested bringing into the orbit of his tradition the unrelated story of the hunting of the boar Twrch Trwyth which had been one of Arthur's exploits at least since the ninth century when it was referred to in the *mirabilia* of the *Historia Brittonum* (see below pp.90-1). *Culhwch ac Olwen* may be a new composition which uses an international tale-type as a frame for a number of existing stories,[7] but even if an antecedent oral tale of the same type as the written story is assumed to be the source, this has surely been greatly elaborated. Though revealing clear evidence of its oral origins in features of its style and presentation, *Culhwch ac Olwen* bears many of the hallmarks of a literary composition, inconclusive though it may be in its fulfilment.

The story can be simply analysed. Culhwch, having rejected his step-mother's daughter, is prohibited from marrying any but the giant's daughter. He claims as his boon the help of his cousin Arthur who sends a group of his men to search out the giant and his court. Seemingly impossible tasks are imposed upon Culhwch by the giant but Arthur and his retinue accomplish these; the giant is slain and Culhwch claims his bride. Jackson[8] has identified the basic tale-type as Six go through the World (AT 513A), possibly revealing traces of conflation with the Magic Flight (AT 313), but the elaboration of a simple tale and the extended narrative pattern have so affected the structure of the story that to reduce it to a typological skeleton is misleading. The story is composed of an introductory passage, followed by three discrete sections, defined by the development of the narrative but bounded also by stylistic markers. The opening three columns of the White Book text (*CO*(1) lines 1-59) introduce Culhwch and provide a well-ordered and skilfully narrated motivation for the *tynged* (cf. Irish *geasa* 'taboos', p.129 below) laid upon him by his step-mother.[9] But the author firmly reminds his audience that the essence of the tale is the winning of a bride in the closing words of this introductory passage, that the boy shall never have a bride until he gets Olwen daughter of Ysbaddaden, and he moves forward to his central theme in the father's response, 'Arthur is your cousin. Go to Arthur to trim your hair and seek that [i.e. the winning of Olwen] as your boon'. A rhetorical passage describes Culhwch in conventional heroic terms setting out on his quest and his subsequent arrival at Arthur's court. This is followed by an equally traditional, and rhetorically structured, passage, in which the hero parleys with an unwilling porter and gains entry on account of his arrogant, but formulaic,[10] threats upon the king's honour and the well-being of his house. Arthur takes a golden comb and silver scissors, and as he trims the boy's hair, his heart warms towards him (in what appears to be a traditional ceremony acknowledging kinship) and he invites Culhwch to seek his boon. Culhwch claims the winning of Olwen for himself invoking a long list of Arthur's household to be his warranties for the fulfilling of his request,[11] a formal catalogue which closes the section. Arthur responds by sending out messengers to seek Olwen, and their unsuccessful search is followed, after Culhwch again threatens the king's honour, by a more formally constituted party — Cai, Bedwyr, Gwalchmai, together with a Guide, an Interpreter and a Sorcerer. They discover the giant's court and a second rhetorical passage, as skilfully crafted, though in a different pattern, as the first, describes the approach of Olwen. A three-day confrontation with the giant ensues during which Ysbaddaden's feeble efforts to delay a decision and his barbaric attempts to kill Culhwch are thwarted and rebound to his own discomfort but to the amusement of the audience, so that he is compelled to catalogue the tasks which must be accomplished before the suitor may marry his daughter.

These two sections follow a similar pattern. Both are quests — Culhwch seeks Arthur's court, Arthur's men seek Ysbaddaden's. The one contains a formal, finely wrought description of the hero, the other of the heroine, both of which are followed by extended conventional episodes which delay the presentation of his request by the hero. Both conclude with a formal catalogue, the closing words of which re-state the theme of the story, the winning of Olwen. These two parallel sections set the scene for what will become the kernel of the story, the accomplishing of tasks.

The giant lists some forty tasks, and had each one a story chronicling its fulfilment *Culhwch ac Olwen* would have been an enormous compilation. In fact there are only ten such stories (with a few references to the completion of others), and whether the author ever intended any more must be doubted. The majority of the tasks listed are merely components of a few central quests, most of which have to do with the winning of wondrous feeding vessels for the wedding feast, or with slaying the boars Ysgithrwyn, to obtain his tusks to shave the giant, and Twrch Trwyth, to snatch the comb, razor and shears which lie between his ears, to trim his hair. The tasks which are fulfilled appear to have been established folk-tales (the freeing of famous prisoners (two), the seizing of a giant's sword, the capture of a giant's beard, the hunting of some fierce boars (three), the winning of feeding vessels (two)), so that it seems that the author of *Culhwch ac Olwen* has tried to utilize existing stories,[12] giving them the unifying motivation provided by his basic tale-type. The remainder of the giant's tasks are part of the author's capacity for elaboration and their non-fulfilment is not a sign of structural weakness. The list functions quite separately from the fulfilment tales and there is no correlation in the sequence. Nevertheless the author appears to have attempted to ensure some degree of coherence in the progress of these narratives. They frequently open with Arthur's question 'What shall we seek next?', an implicit reference back to the list, and authorial glosses which confirm or contradict what the giant had specified, or which provide a temporal reference, serve a similar purpose. More subtly, one tale ends as the host returns to court, one by one, two by two: the next episodes relate the adventures of an individual, and then of a pair.

After some twelve episodes, some of which are briefly told thematic doublets of more fully narrated adventures, the author moves his story towards what he regards as his climax, the hunting of Twrch Trwyth. The scene shifts to Ireland, where a brief reconnaissance provides an opportunity for the achieving of another task. The hunting quest has conventional hero-tale introductory features — hostings, skirmishes, the slaying of minor characters, until the two protagonists, Arthur and the boar, challenge each other and enter upon a wild pursuit across south Wales and Cornwall. The boar is chased off the cliffs of Land's End (?) but not before Arthur's men have succeeded in snatching the razor, comb and shears. The hunt is the quest for these significant objects[13] (in some undefined way echoing the trimming of Culhwch's hair by Arthur) but the narration has a strong onomastic element which may or may not have been an essential feature of the story.[14] It is a breathless chase and it is a measure of the author's awareness of the impact of his narrative that the broad humour and farce of the closing adventures, as savagely comic as a modern cartoon, bring welcome release.

The similarity in structure of the parallel sections, the elaboration of the catalogue of tasks, the dislocation of the fulfilment from the setting of the tasks, all suggest a literate rather than an oral author. The tendency towards complexity and formalization appears to be a literary feature, and that we have here a self-confident author rather than an oral performer is suggested by some other features. The underlining of contradictions in details of the narrative, and the authorial interventions in the catalogue of Arthur's men, mark his objectivity which is made even more apparent by a sense of humour unmatched in any other Middle Welsh narrative. Sometimes it is broad burlesque, sometimes it revels in the comic characteristics of some of the characters, sometimes it is revealed in personal names which cannot be taken seriously. But the author's detachment is seen more frequently in his dry verbal comments which deflate a conventional rhetorical passage and which emphasize the exaggeration of a conventional situation. There are a few indications that the author has used written sources (Old Welsh — Gorbothu, Twrbliant — but more significantly Latin — *Glini Gliui* < *colonia Gleui*, Gwrgi Severi) but also perhaps in his borrowings from *vitae sanctorum*, and ecclesiastical traditions.[15] Nevertheless, other features reveal how close this author was to traditional modes of narration. He is the master of a variety of styles,[16] from the sharp staccato style which uses short sentences and verb-nouns to give clear uncomplicated movement and convey simplistic social mores, to the extended narrative and naturalistic dialogue which is the norm of Middle Welsh narrative prose. He is able to contrast his styles effectively so that the delightful, leisurely, Oldest Animals episode is immediately followed by a swiftly moving account of Mabon's release, the heroic Twrch Trwyth's pursuit by the Black Witch episode which uses a lower linguistic register appropriate to the comedy. The descriptions of Culhwch, of Olwen, and of the parley at the gate display fluent rhetorical skills.[17] The account of Culhwch's passage to and reception at the court moves from set-piece to set-piece, each in its appropriate style. The legal and ritualistic formulas in this section, as in the hair-trimming episode, reflect one of the deepest levels of Welsh narrative patterning, but in contrast, the arrival at Custennin's house and Ysbaddaden's court is clearly non-heroic and popular in ethos, comic in tone, with the result that the parallelism in the structure of the two sections is heightened by the stylistic contrast of the discourse. Throughout, the performance elements are apparent, in the dialogue, the dramatic sense, the tension of violent action and arrogance, the repetition of episodes, personal names, epithets, and in the comic elements. *Culhwch ac Olwen* is the work of a virtuoso, an author as knowledgeable in Welsh *cyfarwyddyd*[18] as he was skilful in its modes of narration.

It is a complex amalgam of stories, and although the theme of the winning of Olwen gives it a coherent structure, some of its elements are not fully integrated. Gorau son of Custennin displays the vestiges of another giant-killer (see below pp.80-1) but the major intrusive element, one which has affected the role of the nominal hero Culhwch, is Arthur himself. Arthur may have entered the tale when some of his traditional exploits, most especially perhaps the hunting of Twrch Trwyth, were utilized as fulfilment stories (alternatively the tale may have been composed specifically to bring together some Arthurian stories).[19]

Some of the Arthurian episodes in *Culhwch ac Olwen* are traditional in theme and may be compared with other Arthurian adventures in early Welsh poetry — the release of captives, the slaying of witches and giants, the hunting of oppressive beasts and the winning of precious otherworld objects. An Arthurian world, not yet chivalrous perhaps, but wondrous, dangerous and defended by the leader, is clearly established. Its characteristics can be recognized here as in the poems in the Black Book of Carmarthen and the Book of Taliesin, and in the *Vitae* especially, but it has also its specific frame of references. The hunting of the boar Twrch Trwyth by Arthur was noted in the ninth-century *mirabilia* of the *Historia Brittonum*, and though we cannot say whether the extended onomastic hunt was part of that version, it is clear that it included some firm topographic references, as is noted below. The cauldron of Diwrnach the Irishman which Arthur brings from Ireland is closely related to the vessel which he sought in the other world in the *Preiddeu Annwn* poem (p. 55 above), while his judgement in the abduction of Creiddylad by Gwynn ap Nudd bears the hallmarks of an established episode.[20] Arthur's pre-eminence, affirmed by his title Chief of the Kings of Britain, is confirmed by the central role of his court (at Celli Wig in *Culhwch ac Olwen*) to which Culhwch comes, as is obviously the custom, to seek help from one recognized as a magnanimous king. The catalogue of warriors and courtiers invoked by Culhwch is not to be taken as a traditional list of Arthur's men. It makes use of a far briefer catalogue found in the poem *Pa gur yw y porthaur* (Black Book of Carmarthen) tentatively dated to the tenth century.[21] Here Arthur seeks admission to a court but is prevented by the porter Glewlwyd Gafaelfawr until he can '? vouch for, reveal' his men. The relationship of the tale and the poem is not wholly clear but the catalogue episode at Arthur's court in *Culhwch ac Olwen* may be a comic reversal of the roles of those in the poem. The catalogue is more appropriate to the poem as a familiar device intended to enhance the hero's stature, than it is to the tale where it is used by Culhwch to compel Arthur to fulfil his promise and by the author as a structural marker while retaining its rhetorical function as an extended 'run'. The list is characteristically taken to extremes by the author of the tale.

That such a list, including as it does in the tale and the poem traditional figures who were not Arthurian in origin, was possible is, however, testimony to Arthur's increasing magnetism and to the strength of his legend in the medieval Welsh narrative tradition. Arthur is not the ill-defined figure he was later to become. He does not appear in every adventure in *Culhwch ac Olwen*, though he is throughout a leader whose presence permeates the whole, and becomes dominant as the tale reaches its climax in the boar hunt and the killing of the Black Witch, but it is significant that his closest companions, Cai, Bedwyr, and Gwalchmai,[22] comprise the warrior element in the group who search out Olwen; they invariably deputize for Arthur and they take part in almost every exploit, a clear sign that the Arthurian court is in being. Cai, the foremost champion, is heroic, brave, and possesses wondrous qualities, but he already betrays that cantankerous aspect of a mean spirit which is his characteristic feature in later romance. He takes umbrage at Arthur's teasing of him and drops out of *Culhwch ac Olwen* but the allusion to Arthur avenging his death is probably genuine. Bedwyr too is already well established enough to have his attributes and exploits formally listed by the author. Arthur has a firm context for his adventures. He has a wife (Gwenhwyfar), and a hero's accoutrements — ship, arms, steed, hound, magic cloak — and the story of his death by betrayal at Camlan is itself a developed theme in the narrative tradition, judging by the numerous substantive allusions in *Culhwch ac Olwen* and elsewhere. From his entry to Arthur's court up to the slaying of the giant, Culhwch's importance and role in the story decline and he all but disappears from the narrative (as the giant remarks when Olwen is won — 'and don't thank me for that, but thank Arthur who brought it about for you'). The Arthurian scene — king, companions, an acknowledged legend of exploits and death — was so well defined that Arthur could not be less than central in any narrative in which he appeared. His presence in any story was overpowering and could brook no competition.

The Arthurian tales which the author of *Culhwch ac Olwen* introduced into the story of how Culhwch won Olwen created an impossible tension between the two heroes — Culhwch and Arthur, a tension which leaves the final version of the tale not so much incomplete as unfulfilled. As Doris Edel has claimed,[23] the fusion of the Arthurian and wooing tales is not fully realized, and at a different level of analysis other critics find in *Culhwch ac Olwen* the dynamic tension of a work caught between two modes of literary creation, the oral tradition in which the tale is rooted, and the unrealized thematic purpose to which this literary composition could have been put. As we have seen, most critics would now place the manuscript version of the story closer to the concept of a literary composition than to a view of it as a 'monument . . . of the *cyvarwydd*'s art'.[24]   MacCana[25] and Radner[26] discover in the tale a high level of intellectual sophistication, detachment and irony but are less sure of any deep social or cultural message which may be found in a reading of the story.[27]

The Welsh Arthurian world underlies the allusions to legends of Arthur found in *Trioedd Ynys Prydein* (The Triads of the Island of Britain).[28]   The triads are a classification technique devised by the guardians of Welsh tradition to facilitate the recall of this material by systematizing it and associating three characters or episodes with one another on the basis of a feature common to all three: the triad would then have a formulaic title, 'the three [epithets, or adjectives] of the Island of Britain . . .' The triadic grouping of a body of information is fairly common, but the collection, The Triads of the Island of Britain, seems to have been put together in the eleventh or twelfth centuries.   In its Early Version (Aberystwyth NLW MS Peniarth 16, mid-thirteenth century) the collection is allusive and bereft of detail, but the Later Version (White Book of Rhydderch, Red Book of Hergest) gives brief synopses of episodes, an indication, perhaps, that the material was losing some of its traditional strength and that the index, now containing more information, was achieving independent textual status.

In the later version Arthur's court (at Celli Wig as in *Culhwch ac Olwen*) sometimes displaces the earlier formulaic 'Island of Britain' which gives contextual cohesion to the collection, but it is significant that the concept of Arthur's court is established even in the Early Version, as in Triad 9, 'The Three Chieftains of Arthur's Court'.   Arthur himself is sometimes added to a triad as a fourth and exceptional example of a particular feature.   These additions have, in essence, rhetorical force as the 'fourth generous lord', or the 'fourth red ravager' inevitably is given greater prominence than the three noted in the triad, but Triad 52, 'The Three Exalted Prisoners of the Island of Britain', contains an extended reference to 'one who was more exalted than the three of them', Arthur, a reference which may derive from the narrative tradition.   One of the three prisoners is Mabon son of Modron (who is released by Arthur, Cai and Bedwyr in *Culhwch ac Olwen*), and who had used a form of Triad 52 to complain that not even Lludd or Graid son of Eri had suffered worse imprisonment than he.   The author of *Culhwch ac Olwen* had an imprecise recollection of the triad (which names Llyr and Gwair son of Geirioedd) though he was not unaware of some tradition of the three captives.   The author of the triad, however, has added a further triadic reference, to Arthur, imprisoned three times (for three nights on each occasion) and rescued each time by Gorau, son of Custennin, his cousin.   *Culhwch ac Olwen* makes Arthur, Gorau and Culhwch cousins, but in the tale, though Culhwch is the titular hero and Arthur the main protagonist, Gorau is the one who kills the giant, as though he too had traditionally been a giant-killer. There is clearly some relationship between this triad and the tale, but it seems equally apparent that existing traditions have been confused, suggesting that the author of the tale was not intimately familiar with his material and that he had drawn together a number of strands in composing his story.

As in *Culhwch ac Olwen*, Arthur is chief lord (*Penn Teyrnedd*) of the Island, ruler in all three realms, Wales, Cornwall and the North (Triad 1). He is a generous lord but he has the hero's destructive energy as his ravaging devastates the land for seven years. His role as the hunter of fierce, supernatural boars has led to his displacing in the Later Version Coll son of Collfrewy, named in the Early Version as the pursuer of the sow Henwen; but more significantly in the same triad (26), 'The Three Powerful Swineherds', Arthur attempts unsuccessfully to obtain a pig by deceit or force from Drystan, the swineherd of March, while he went to seek Esyllt (in the Later Version Arthur is joined not only by March, but by Cai and Bedwyr also). Some five triads in the Later Version refer to Camlan, Arthur's last battle (nos.51, 53, 59, 84, 54). These show some evidence of Geoffrey of Monmouth's *Historia Regum Britanniae* and they are not wholly consistent one with another, but together they are evidence of a strong tradition of Arthur's last battle, a tradition reflected in, but not created, by the *Historia*. Even in the native tradition it would appear that the circumstances of Arthur's death, real or apparent, were the tragic consequences of plotting, dissension at court, and perhaps a nephew's betrayal. There may well have been a *chwedl* (saga) of Camlan, alluded to, not always seriously, in another triadic grouping in *Culhwch ac Olwen*, but which was, nevertheless, an integral part of the Welsh legend of Arthur.

Between the Early and Later Versions of the triads it would appear that Arthur, his companions, his court, his role, were growing in identity so that Arthur's name and person were a central feature in Welsh story and legend, strong enough to oust other characters from their proper stories, and to attract to himself other narrative traditions. The portrayal of Arthur, nevertheless, is not uniformly heroic. The author of *Culhwch ac Olwen* may occasionally view Arthur with an irreverent attitude, but he is never critical of him. The triads, however, sometimes suggest that a negative portrayal was part of the tradition. 'The Triad of the Three Unfortunate Disclosures' (no.37R) gives Arthur his legendary role as the defender of the Island, but notes that the talismanic burying of Bendigeidfran's head in the White Hill in London — an episode related in the *mabinogi* of Branwen — was rendered futile when Arthur revealed it 'because it did not seem right to him that this Island should be defended by the strength of anyone, but by his own'. There is no other evidence for this episode and it cannot be decided how well founded the reference may be, but though Arthur's role as leader and defender of his realm is central, criticism of his pride and arrogance as potential causes of downfall and deceit seems to be equally an aspect of his legend.

This inversion of Arthur's role is a characteristic element in saints' lives in which he appears. These Celtic 'saints' are the leaders of the anchorite and missionary activities of the Church in Celtic lands in the sixth and seventh centuries, and the majority of them are recalled in the names of the churches and monastic settlements directly associated with them or lying within the sphere of influence of the mother-churches. Their Latin Lives, although containing traditional elements and perhaps some historical features, are compositions of the eleventh and twelfth centuries and constitute a well-defined genre of semi-biographical writing. Their primary aim is the magnifying of the saint's name, both as a local hero and as the defender (or founder) of the privileges of his church, so that local elements — topographic especially — predominate. The *Vitae* are ecclesiastical hero-tales which reveal many of the same generic features as their secular counterparts.[29] As an established narrative genre one of the consistent elements is that these popular religious heroes should be brought into conflict with the secular power represented by local kings and lords. The conflict is often a struggle for land, privileges and authority, but it is commonly portrayed in terms of a battle of magical (or divine) powers and conventional force-at-arms. Inevitably the king is belittled in defeat and the saint, and his ecclesiastical successors, are seen to enjoy the divine favour which confirms their rights and privileges. The conflict may be unlocalized and the king unnamed, or it may use local legend as in the Life of St David where secular authority is represented by a tribal king, the Irish Boya. But not infrequently an established secular ruler of some stature in the legendary tradition is cast in this role, Maelgwn Gwynedd, or in some seven *Vitae* of Welsh and Breton origin, Arthur.[30]

In the Life of Illtud the saint visits the magnificent court of his cousin Arthur where he is dazzled by the generosity and splendour of all he sees. Nothing more is said of Arthur but the episode is reminiscent of Culhwch's visit to the court which is now portrayed in the terms of the post-Galfridian concept of Arthur. Illtud and Culhwch are Arthur's cousins by the same conventional device, that their mothers are daughters of Anlawdd Wledig,[31] but that Illtud's visit is unmotivated suggests that the hero's visit to Arthur's court was becoming a stereotyped feature. In the other 'Welsh' *Vitae*, all pre-Geoffrey, Arthur is a powerful king whose titles, *rex totius majoris Brittanie*, *rex illustrissimus Britannie*, *rex universale Brittanie*, are suggestive of the titles used in *Culhwch* and the Triads, *penn Teyrnedd yr ynys hon*, but in fact his actual role in most of these *Vitae* is better described by the more dismissive *quidam tirranus* which is also found. For the most part he is a foil for the saint, an arrogant, grasping tyrant who is humbled in ignominious defeat, not in any armed struggle but in his childish greed and even in his failure to fulfil his traditional role as giant or dragon-slayer (e.g. Lives of Padarn, Carantoc, Cadoc, Efflam). These may be exemplary, conventional episodes, but in other *Vitae* the Arthurian episodes appear to be genuine fragments of Arthurian legend, manipulated so that they may display Arthur in the worst possible light.

One of the clearest examples of the inversion of traditional Arthurian values occurs in the Life of Cadoc by Lifris of Llancarfan, *c.* 1090. Arthur is prevented from fulfilling his lustful desires upon a fleeing maiden by his two companions, Cai and Bedwyr, who remind him that they normally help the needy (*nos enim soliti sumus inopes anxiosque iuuare*), a comment which is reminiscent of Arthur's rebuke to Cai in *Culhwch ac Olwen*.[32] The most important of the lives for its Arthurian evidence is Caradoc of Llancarfan's Life of Gildas which has two fully narrated Arthurian episodes which can be corroborated by other sources. One is the long-standing enmity between Arthur and Huail, Gildas's brother, recorded by Giraldus Cambrensis and noted as a folk-tale in north Wales in the sixteenth century by Elis Gruffudd.[33] The other is the earliest extant narration of the abduction of Gwenhwyfar by Melwas, *rege regnante in aestiva region* (Somerset) and her imprisonment in *Urbs vitrea* (Glastonbury). Arthur (*rex rebellis, tyrannus*) is intent on attacking the city but Gildas mediates and brings peace to the two factions. The saint's wisdom and pacifying powers contrast with Arthur's belligerency and they are presented as the effective means of resolving disputes. Caradoc uses the tale to justify some of the privileges of Glastonbury Abbey, but judging from subsequent and variant versions of this adventure, for example in Continental romance, Chrétien de Troyes' *Chevalier de la Charette*, and in Welsh literature, Dafydd ap Gwilym, (Thomas Parry, *Gwaith Dafydd ap Gwilym*, no.64), where the abductor is still Melwas, and cf. the *Englynion Ymddiddan* discussed above, pp.58-61, it would appear that he found it a deeply entrenched story in the Arthurian complex of tales and that as an experienced hagiographer he was able to turn it to his own advantage. The portrayal of Arthur in the *Vitae* is consistent, though as a negative image, with that found in *Culhwch ac Olwen* and the Triads. Arthur is the required secular ruler thwarted by the saint, but his own unique stature is necessary to point to the saint's even greater achievement. The skill of the more experienced hagiographers lay in their ability to use specific Arthurian traditions for their own ends and to invert them for their own aims as writers. Close correspondences between *Culhwch ac Olwen* and some *Vitae* suggest that such adaptation was a conscious process. Reference has already been made to Illtud's visit to the court and to Cai's comment in the Life of

Cadoc which mirrors that of Arthur in *Culhwch*; to these may be added the description of Huail in *Culhwch* (*CO*(1) lines 212-13), *nyd asswynwys eiroet yn llaw arglwyd*, 'he never sought the hand of a lord', and in the life of Gildas, *Hueil . . . nulli regi obedivit*. The Dialogue of Arthur and the Eagle (see pp.57-8) is based on this inversion of the Arthurian ethos and though its theme of 'trust not in chariots' is biblical (e.g. Isaiah, 31. 1, Jerem. 9. 23, Psalm 20. 7), the verbal correspondence between the poem's negative *ai gwiw ymladd am danad?* and the tale's positive *Y gymeint ohonof i a gaffer, a geffir drwy ymlad* is striking.[34]   This negative portrayal of Arthur may have been made easier if there existed an anti-heroic, or unfavourable, tradition of Arthur's character which clerical authors could use.   The tone of some of the Triads, the ironic, less than serious, treatment of, for example Arthur's relationships with Cai in *Culhwch ac Olwen*, the mockery of *Breuddwyd Rhonabwy*, together with the clerical portrayal of Arthur may suggest that the Arthur of Welsh tradition was not the uniformly heroic character which is suggested by most of the evidence.

It is almost impossible to recreate the mixed ethos of this tradition — even more so since the texts which convey the evidence stand at several removes from any popular tradition.   The author of *Culhwch ac Olwen* is a compiler rather than a reciter, a scholarly man who uses literary sources and who is a manipulator rather than a bearer of tradition; the Triads, it seems, have moved away from their original practical purpose, and the hagiographers were consciously expressing the persona of Arthur in anti-heroic terms.   Nevertheless, and granting such distillation, the tenor of the tradition emerges fairly clearly.   In pre-Galfridian Welsh story-telling Arthur was a king of pre-eminent stature, described as Chief of all the Kings of the Island of Britain.   The title is never explained or justified and in spite of references to Arthur in Welsh chronicles, the legendary tradition is not historical; his court attracts suitors who are magnanimously received and whose boons are granted; there is an Arthurian entourage constantly drawing to itself new characters, but there is a group of close companions — Cai, Bedwyr, Gwalchmai — who already have well-defined attributes and are themselves established characters in their own sub-tales, and there is a typical Arthurian adventure — an encounter with giant, witch or monster, an Otherworld raid, a hunt — as Arthur is seen as the defender of the land.   But the legend is not simply a frame of reference, for it has some fixed points which permit us, even at this early period, to conceive of a cycle.   For Arthur's court has an established location (at Celli Wig in Cornwall), his stories, in the hunting of Twrch Trwyth, and in the *Vitae*, are located in south-east Wales and south-west Britain; he has a wife, a range of remarkable possessions, he has not only a close group of companions but named enemies or rivals, chief of whom is the abductor of his wife; and though the details are unclear it would seem that in this episode lies the germ of his final defeat and death at Camlan, a battle the trauma of which is reflected in the cycle of traditions which are associated with it and give it a semi-independent role. Camlan became the symbol of irreversible, calamitous defeat, so that when the last native prince of Wales was killed in 1282 the poet Gruffudd ab yr Ynad Coch saw the event in terms of Arthur's downfall — *Llawer llef druan fal ban fu Gamlan* ('Many a wretched cry as at Camlan').

By the late eleventh and early twelfth centuries when his legend achieves extensive written form in Welsh as narrative and allusions, Arthur is an imposing figure, too strong and clearly established to be other than central in any context in which he appears and thus an irresistible attraction for the figures and episodes of unrelated story-cycles. In this lay the seeds of decline as the story becomes the setting, the hero a story-telling device, and the Arthurian scene an opportunity for parody. Arthur, not integral in any foreign story-telling context, never achieves, in Continental romance, the active central role which he has in the earliest Welsh evidence, and even the later Welsh texts fail to maintain his real pre-eminence.

'The Thirteen Treasures of the Island of Britain'
(*Tri Thlws ar Ddeg Ynys Brydain*)

The forty tasks laid upon Culhwch by Ysbaddaden fall into two groups as was shown above, p.76. Those in the first are necessary to provide food and entertainment for the wedding feast. These involve the obtaining of specific pairs of oxen to till the land, and of certain mythological beings to be ploughman and husbandman, but more especially Culhwch is required to win five wondrous feeding vessels and a magic harp, all of which are the property of (or at least associated with) particular persons and which have remarkable powers: the cup (*cib*) of Llwyr son of Llwyryon to hold the strong bragget which the giant orders (in it is the best drink in the world); the hamper (*mwys*) of Gwyddno Garanhir to hold the food (even if thrice nine men at a time came, everyone would get the meat he wished for from it), the horn (*corn*) of Gwlgawd Gododdin to pour the drink, the cauldron (*pair*) of Diwrnach the Irishman to boil the food, the bottles (*botheu*) of Rhynnon Rhyn Barfawd to hold milk (in them no liquid ever turns sour), and the harp (*telyn*) of Teirtu (which plays of itself or is silent, as one desires). The second group of tasks centres on the hunting of the two boars, Ysgithrwyn and Twrch Trwyth, so that the tusks, shears and comb may be won which will allow the giant to be groomed for his daughter's wedding. Named huntsmen and hounds must be sought and also a particular leash, collar and chain to hold Drudwyn, the whelp of Graid son of Eri, namely the leash (*cynllafan*) of Cors Cant Ewin, the collar (*torch*) of Canhastyr Canllaw to hold the leash, and the chain

(*cadwyn*) of Cilydd Canhastyr to hold the collar. The blood of the Black Witch which
is to soften the giant's beard must be kept warm in the bottles (*botheu*) of
Gwyddolwyn Gor (in which any liquid retains its heat from the time it is put into
them in the east until one reaches the west). It was suggested above, p.76, that the
author of *Culhwch ac Olwen* has made use of established folk-tales in creating his
fulfilment stories and it was noted in n. 12 that two of the feeding vessels in the
giant's list — *mwys* and *pair* — appear in the text *Tri Thlws ar Ddeg Ynys
Brydain*.[35]

This list of the Thirteen Treasures of the Island of Britain, or 'of the North' in
some copies including the earliest, NLW MS Peniarth 51 (*c.* 1460), is found in over
forty manuscripts, the earliest of which belong to the fifteenth and sixteenth
centuries. Fifteen treasures are named in all, though each list contains thirteen.
Some are feeding vessels of wondrous abundant powers: *mwys Gwyddno Garanhir*,
the hamper in which the food of one man became food for a hundred; *corn Bran
Galed*, the horn which supplied any wished-for drink; *gren a dysgl Rhagennydd
Ysgolhaig*, the pot and dish which supplied their owner's wished-for meals; *cyllell
Llawfrodedd*, a knife which would serve twenty-four men at table. Some grant their
owner a magical advantage: *llen Arthur*, his cloak of invisibility; *car Morgan
Mwynfawr*, the vehicle which transported its owner wherever he wished to be;
cebystr Clydno Eidyn, the horse he might wish would be found in this halter. Others
are testing talismans: *pair Diwrnach Gawr* (the giant), the cauldron which would boil
food only for a brave man; *agalen Tudwal Tudclyd*, the whetstone which would
sharpen the weapon of a brave man but blunt that of a coward; *pais Padarn
Peisrudd*, the coat which fitted only a nobleman; *mantell Tegau Eurfron*, the mantle
which fitted only a faithful wife. The remainder are peculiar to their owner: *cleddyf*
(the sword) of Rhydderch Hael which would burst into flames if anyone but its owner
drew it. Or they have marvellous properties: *gwyddbwyll* (chess-set) of Gwenddolau,
in which the pieces played by themselves; *cwlltwr* (the coulter) of Rhun Gawr (or
alternatively of Tringer son of Nuddnod) which, if the borrowed article were placed
in a plough, would plough until asked to stop. The stone and ring of Luned found in
some copies derive from the Welsh story of *Owain*.

Where the possessors of these magic objects can be identified from references
elsewhere in Welsh tradition, they frequently have associations with the Old North of
the British Heroic Age (e.g. Brân, Morgan, Clydno, Tudwal, Gwenddolau, Padarn,
Rhydderch) and the list is further testimony to the mythologizing of the legendary
heroes of that period. The material, both in its nature and reference, is ancient and it
is part of the lost traditional literature of medieval Wales. The manuscript copies of
the fifteenth and sixteenth centuries are but one aspect of the attempt to transmit and

to preserve traditional learning in the period of the decline of the bardic order and the growth of humanist antiquarianism. As R.S. Loomis stressed:

> The importance of the list of the Thirteen Treasures of the Island of Britain should not be minimized by students of Welsh and Arthurian legend merely because our earliest manuscript authority is of the fifteenth century.[36]

Irish parallels suggest that the origins of these talismans are to be sought 'in stories concerning magic objects which had either been won from the Otherworld or bestowed on mortals by its inhabitants'.[37] The Cauldron of the Dagda, which is one of the 'Four Treasures of the Tuatha Dé Danann' (the family of the gods in Irish mythology), has the power that 'no company ever went away from it unthankful'. This is one clear parallel to the characteristics of some of the Welsh treasures, but the value of the Irish evidence lies not only in the individual analogues but in its character as reliable source material for information about Celtic mythology. Several early Irish sources testify to the ancient mythological context of objects such as these, for example the other three treasures of the Tuatha Dé Danann, the Stone of Fál, Lug's Spear, Nuadu's Sword; the Cup and Branch brought from the Otherworld by Cormac mac Airt; and the chariot, 'chess-board', and mantle given to Crimthann Nía Nar by a fairy-woman. The Otherworld visit was an adventure told of several Irish heroes and the gaining of divine objects was one feature of such tales. The cauldron of Diwrnach Wyddel brought back from Ireland by Arthur in *Culhwch ac Olwen* is paralleled by that of Diwrnach Gawr in the list of Treasures, the properties of which are similar to the cauldron of Pen Annwfn won by Arthur from the Otherworld in the poem *Preiddeu Annwn*, above p. 55.[38] This may be but one example of a number of similar Otherworld adventures related of Arthur and other heroes. The adaptation of tales about objects won from the Otherworld to a new context or motivation as tasks set by the giant and undertaken by the hero is a not unnatural development, given that there may have been a corpus of material relating to the winning of magical talismans of the types described in lists of 'The Thirteen Treasures'. A late attempt to impose a semblance of unity upon such stories is to be found in a marginal note in NLW MS Peniarth 147 (c. 1566), p. 14:

> Corn Bran galed oedd vn or tri thylws ar ddeg o vrenin-dlysse ynys Brydain, ag yno dayth Myrddin y erchi y tlysse hyny at bawb lle ydd oyddynt. Ag y cytynoedd pawb, os efe gaffe gorn Bran galed, y cae gantyn hwyntey, dan dybieid na chae ef ddim or corn. Ag er hyny fo gafas Myrddin y corn ag wedy hyny vo gafas y cwbwl ag aeth ag hwy yr Tû Gwydyr, ag yn hwy byth mwy.
>
> (*The horn of Bran galed was one of the thirteen royal treasures of the Island of Britain, and Myrddin came there to request those treasures from everyone where they were. And everyone agreed that if he would get the horn of Bran galed he would get theirs from them, supposing that he would not get the horn. Nevertheless Myrddin got the horn and then he got them all and he took them*

to the Glass House and there they remain for ever.)[39]

Lists, none of which might have been comprehensive, of these objects could be drawn up at any time. Such a list may underlie the references in Ysbaddaden's catalogue of tasks, or more properly of *anoetheu*, 'wonders', as they are termed in the text, and this would not have been identical with the extant list of 'Thirteen Treasures'. The differences between copies of this text show how variable the items in the list might be. It is not possible to say when the present list of thirteen treasures was compiled. The fifteenth-century poet Tudur Aled would appear to have known of it as he refers in the space of some six lines to *rhen a dysgl Rhagennydd, mwys Gwyddno Garanhir, Corn Bran Galed*, and *Pair Tyrnog* (a variant form of Dyrnwch) as vessels like those found at the table of his patron (*TYP* 246), and other poets from the same period also refer to Tegau's mantle and Brân's horn as standards of comparison with gifts which they request or generosity which they have enjoyed. The reference by Guto'r Glyn to Brân's horn suggests that he knew of a version of the story already quoted which named Taliesin rather than Myrddin but which nevertheless emphasized the niggardly character of its owner (Brân *galed*) (*TYP* 286, *MLR* 35 (1940), 403). Similar systematizations of categories of *cyfarwyddyd* could have occurred much earlier. The Triads are themselves evidence of a similar approach to a corpus of learning and catalogues of various kinds are common in oral literature.[40]

Culhwch ac Olwen also refers to Arthur's cloak of invisibility as one of his precious possessions. Though this is one of the 'Thirteen Treasures', the author of *Culhwch ac Olwen* may not have found it in the list which he knew and which included feeding vessels, hunting accoutrements and a harp. Such talismans must have been known within their own contexts independently of any list. Arthur's cloak (*Gwen*) is found in *Breuddwyd Rhonabwy*, and other objects have analogues in other stories. The chessboard with its moving chessmen occurs in *Peredur* and Continental romance,[41] but the most fully discussed parallel to the wondrous feeding vessels is the grail, according to the origins proposed for it by R. S. Loomis and others.[42]

Mirabilia

The final portions of the *Historia Brittonum* are catalogues of geographical and topographical names. As has been shown, lists are characteristic features of the systematizing methods of the learned classes (*cyfarwyddiaid*) responsible for preserving antiquarian and traditional material,[43] and much of this kind of information is extant in Welsh in triadic groupings, for example the Triads of the Island of Britain, the Triads of the Horses, legal triads, or in simple listings, with or without notes, either in prose or in verse. The catalogues of personal names in

Culhwch ac Olwen show occasional indications of triadic groupings and contain a few annotations but in the lists of the Thirteen Treasures of the Island of Britain, described above, the names have been given their narrative contexts as is done in some of the Triads. With these contextual notes may be compared the more literary listings which are the basis of the poem 'Pa gur' (see above pp. 38-46) and of the metrical Stanzas of the Graves (*Englynion y Beddau*) in the Black Book of Carmarthen.[44]   *Enwau Ynys Brydain* (The Names of the Island of Britain, *TYP* 228-9) is another example of an extended list, of geographical divisions and features perceived as having particular significance in traditional British history and geography. As found in the White Book of Rhydderch the text refers, but without any identification, to the thirty-three chief cities and the thirty-four chief marvels of the Island, but the version in the Red Book of Hergest lists thirty-two cities by name and also describes twenty-seven marvels (not the thirty-four intended according to the introductory statement). Later manuscripts contain different catalogues of cities and marvels. The treatise on the names of the Island of Britain in its various medieval and later forms appears to be derived from an old and well-established tradition of British city-lists which were associated with more fluid enumerations of marvellous physical features. Gildas's reference in his *De Excidio Britanniae*, chapter 3, to the twenty-eight cities of Britain is the earliest evidence for the tradition, but the two final sections of the *Historia Brittonum* are the first extant example of the combining of two lists[45] each containing specific names, and they are facets of that body of traditional lore, or *cyfarwyddyd*, which is a central component of the whole work.

The cataloguing and description of natural wonders was an old established literary activity. Solinus's *Collectanea* was well known throughout the medieval period, and Welsh scribes continued to list *mirabilia* after the compilation of the Red Book text. The Welsh lists show a great deal of variation both in content and nature and they are derived from a number of different sources, including Higden's *Polychronicon*, with the result that while some of the wonders are part of native Welsh tradition, many are examples of common medieval learning.

The list of *mirabilia* in the *Historia Brittonum*, which first appears in the Harleian text, derived from an original redacted in 829/830, has twenty marvels. The first four, which are not in Wales, are numbered in the text. Those in the following group are not numbered but are introduced simply *aliud miraculum* (or the like). Marvels 5 to 14 are located in Wales, and with the exception of the last of them, Crug Mawr in Ceredigion (west Wales), they are all situated in the south-east of the country and along the English border. A section on the Marvels of Anglesey follows, comprising four numbered marvels, and a section on the Marvels of Ireland — two in number — concludes the list. The author of the *Historia* seems to have drawn on existing groups of *mirabilia* in compiling his list and his first four marvels, the Anglesey and the Irish items, may have already been available to him, probably in separate sources.

The central group, 5 to 14, are markedly different from the others in their presentation. They are are short narratives in their own right, rather than an annotated list; they are lively and detailed descriptions of natural marvels, the physical features of some of which, however, have been elaborated by their association with a number of common folklore motifs. It seems clear that these Welsh marvels have a more popular context for the editor than the others in his list. The extended, and indeed exuberant, accounts of these wonders, the wealth of detail and the appeal to his own experience (*in hodiernum diem, nam et ego probavi et vidi, et ego solus probavi*) all suggest that the author is personally acquainted with these. In most cases he is able to give Welsh descriptive names to the physical features and in one example he records a local aetiological legend (*dou rig Habren*, the two kings of the Severn, whose conflict is seen in the Severn bore). These *mirabilia* are located in Gwent, Buellt, Erging (Archenfield), the upper Wye valley, the Severn valley, and Gower, and it would appear that this border country is the native area of the ninth-century redactor of the *Historia Brittonum*, a man as well-versed in his local legends and folklore as in the broader Welsh historical tradition.

Two of the *mirabilia* are associated with Arthur, numbers 12 and 13.

> Est aliud mirabile in regione quae dicitur Buelt. Est ibi cumulus lapidum et unus lapis superpositus super congestum cum vestigio canis in eo. Quando venatus est porcum Troynt, impressit Cabal, qui erat canis Arthuri militis, vestigium in lapide, et Arthur postea congregavit congestum lapidum sub lapide, in quo erat vestigium canis sui, et vocatur Carn Cabal. Et veniunt homines, et tollunt lapidem in manibus suis per spatium diei et noctis, et in crastino die invenitur super congestum suum.

> (*There is another wonder in the country called Builth. There is a heap of stones there, and one of the stones placed on top of the pile has the footprint of a dog on it. When he hunted Twrch Trwyth Cafal, the warrior Arthur's hound, impressed his footprint on the stone, and Arthur later brought together the pile of stones, under the stone in which was his dog's footprint, and it is called Carn Cafal. Men come and take the stone in their hands for the space of a day and a night, and on the morrow it is found upon the stone pile.*)

Carn Cabal is a cairn which gives its name now to Corn Gaffallt, a hill some 1,530 ft. above the upper Wye in north Brecknockshire, between Rhaeadr and Builth Wells. *Carn*, fem., is 'cairn, tumulus', and masc. 'hoof'; *cabal* is Old Welsh for *cafall*, Latin *caballus*, 'horse'. The Welsh word is attested in early verse (*CA* line 1203, *CLlH* 184) and in *Culhwch ac Olwen* (*CO*(1) 337, 739). If the original significance of the place-name was 'the cairn of the horse', it may be compared with Carn Gaffon (*CA* line 1344), 'the cairn of horses', but it has obviously been more imaginatively understood as 'the hoof of a horse' and the motif of the returning stone associated with what was regarded as a peculiarly marked rock.   Cafall, however, appears as the name of Arthur's hound, here *qui erat canis Arthuri militis*, as in *Culhwch ac Olwen*, presumably on account of its huge size, and the unmarked place-name Carn Cabal was reinterpreted as the cairn of Arthur's hound who left his imprint on the stone during the hunting of *porcum Troy(n)t*, the Twrch Trwyth of *Culhwch ac Olwen*.   Cafall the hound appears in *Culhwch ac Olwen* only in the narrative of the boar hunt, but is also referred to in *Geraint (Mab.* p.241) as Arthur's favourite dog (*annwylgi*), the only one named in the hunting of the white stag.   The author of *Geraint* used a number of personal names found in *Culhwch ac Olwen* and the older tale may have been the source of his reference.

If the development proposed here is correct, then the Arthurian associations of Carn Cabal are secondary.   It is interesting to observe that Rhos y Gaffallt, a moorland tract, lies some fourteen miles west of Corn Gaffallt and that the coincidence of names may reflect the story of the stone taken from its site for the space of a day and night but returning to its location on the morrow.[46]   The hunting of Twrch Trwyth, whatever may have been its original motivation, was a developed part of Arthurian folklore by the first half of the ninth century but in *Culhwch ac Olwen* onomastic elements have changed much of the significance of the episode which seems to have been relocated to accommodate a series of place-names containing elements understood as 'pig, swine, sow' extending over a wide area of south Wales.[47]

The second Arthurian *mirabilium* contains the familiar motif of the unmeasurable grave or tumulus.

> Est aliud miraculum in regione quae vocatur Ercing.   Habetur sepulcrum juxta fontem, qui cognominatur Licat Amr, et viri nomen qui sepultus est in tumulo, sic vocabatur Amr; filius Arthuri militis erat, et ipse occidit eum ibidem et sepelivit.   Et veniunt homines ad mensurandum tumulum in longitudine aliquando sex pedes, aliquando novem, aliquando duodecim, aliquando quindecim.   In qua mensura metieris eum in ista vice, iterum non invenies eum in una mensura, et ego solus probavi.
>
> (*There is another wonder in the country called Ergyng.   There is a tomb there by a spring, called Llygad Amr; the name of the man who is buried in the tomb was Amr.   He was a son of the warrior Arthur, and he killed him there and buried him.   Men come to measure the tomb, and it is sometimes six feet long, sometimes nine, sometimes twelve, sometimes fifteen.   At whatever measure you measure it on one occasion, you never find it again of the same measure, and I have tried it myself.*)

Licat Amr; *licat*, Mod. Welsh *llygad*, 'eye', is commonly used for the source of a stream: Amr, attested in *LL* 174, 200, 201, 226, Amhyr, Amir, Amyr, is the Gamber in Herefordshire, and its source Gamber Head in Llanwarne.[48]   The tumulus, which is near the spring, becomes the grave of an eponymous figure who is said to have been buried there, but he is further claimed to be Arthur's son, slain by his father. Amr, however, is not known in later Arthurian legend apart from a reference to Arthur's son Amhar, one of his chamberlains in *Geraint* (*Mab.* 231): another son, Llachau, seems to have been more integral to the tradition.[49]

These two *mirabilia* raise similar questions. Both accounts are in origin folkloric explanations of topographical features and the specific Arthurian elements appear to be later accretions.[50] They are evidence that by the ninth century Arthur had become a popular hero inasmuch that folklore motifs were being attached to his name and that he was a figure of sufficient fame to attract local legends into his orbit. This is, of course, a feature of the later development of the Arthurian legend and examples of Arthurian topography are widespread, but these *mirabilia* are the earliest examples which can be securely dated. How far these Arthurian allusions are due to the redactor of the *Historia Brittonum* cannot be known, but the south-east Wales and Wye and Severn valleys orientation of the most fully developed items on the list probably reflects his local knowledge. On their own the two *mirabilia* are not evidence that a special place should be assigned to this area in a study of Arthurian legendary origins though they may achieve greater significance when considered with other evidence.[51]

Reference is made, below p. 108, to the use which Geoffrey of Monmouth made of three of the *mirabilia* in his account (IX.6-7, *HRB*(T), 219-20) of the early years of Arthur's reign. The young king wages war in Scotland, forcing his enemies to seek refuge on the islands of Loch Lomond, *stagnum Lumonoi*. The description of the forty (*recte* sixty) islands, streams, rocks and eagles which is taken from the first *mirabilium* of the *Historia Brittonum* (*stagnum Lumonoy*, apparently identified as Loch Leven, as the one river which flows out from it is called *Lemn*), is well integrated into the account of the campaign, but the reference to the vaticinatory powers of the eagles is not found in the *Historia*. When the victory has been accomplished descriptions of two further marvellous lakes are introduced in a rather laboured fashion as comments by some of Arthur's company as they admire Loch Lomond. The method by which a narrative is elaborated by the adaptation and inclusion of unrelated material is typical of Geoffrey. The first of these, the square pool 'in the same neighbourhood', which has a different kind of fish in each of its corners, seems to have been developed from *Finnaun Guur Helic* in Cynllibiwg in Wales. The other, *Lin Liguua* near the Severn, the tidal ebb and flow of which has a powerful effect on bystanders, is derived from *Oper Linn Liuan*, *aber* (estuary) of

Llyn Lliwan, the lake referred to, without comment on its marvellous properties, in *Culhwch ac Olwen*, and also, in the same tale, as the home of one of the oldest animals, the salmon of Llyn Lliw (Llyw).

NOTES:

1. Edited by Rachel Bromwich and D. Simon Evans, *CO*(1). English translations: *Mab.*; Jeffrey Ganz, *The Mabinogion* (Penguin, 1976); P.K. Ford, *The Mabinogi* (Los Angeles, 1977); Richard Loomis in *The Romance of Arthur*, edd. James J. Wilhelm and Laila Z. Gross (New York, 1984), 31-55. Studies (in addition to *CO*(1)): ALMA 31-43; Doris Edel, *Helden und Freiersfussen: 'Tochmarc Emire' und 'Mal y kavas Kulhwch Olwen'* (Amsterdam, 1980).

2. B.F. Roberts, 'From Traditional Tale to Literary Story: Middle Welsh Prose Narratives', in *The Craft of Fiction*, ed. Leigh Arathoon (Rochester, 1984), 211-30. *Breuddwyd Rhonabwy* appears to be an exception to the thesis that the written tales derive ultimately from oral narratives (see below p. 184), and a similar view of the composition of *Culhwch ac Olwen* has been given; see pp. 79-80.

3. *CO*(1) xx-xxvii, *YB*, 13 (1985), 101-13. J.S.P. Tatlock's views, Leg. Hist. 195-8, ignore the linguistic evidence and are untenable.

4. *CLIH* xi, 10, 34. On this allusion see now J. Rowland, *Early Welsh Saga Poetry* (Cambridge, 1990), 580.

5. For the composition of the name Culhwch, *cul+hwch*, 'lean swine, pig' (cf. Irish Coelchéis), see *CO*(1) lxix: Hamp, *ZCP*, 41 (1986), 257-8, regards the two elements as being synonymous and proposes that originally 'Culhwch literally was a pig'. ALMA 33 proposes 'burrow of swine', though *cul* in this sense appears to be borrowed from English *kill*, kiln, GPC 629.

6. *YB*, 7 (1972), 57-71.

7. As is proposed in *CO*(1) lxxxvi.

8. IPT 71-5, and cf. *Cy.*, 42 (1931), 129-47.

9. For the linking of the motif of the jealous stepmother's 'destiny' with the giant's daughter theme cf. the Irish tale 'The daughter of the king of the glen of loneliness', as noted in ALMA 32, J.E. Caerwyn Williams, *Y Storïwr Gwyddeleg a'i Chwedlau* (Caerdydd, 1972), 229-36 (Welsh trans.), 253, *CO*(1) xxxv. Irish analogues are noted by Douglas Hyde in the *Trans. of the Celtic Congress*, 1921, 46-56, and Jackson, *ÉC*, 11 (1964-5), 92-4.

10. Cf. the formulaic response to the striking of the challenge pole noted by Kevin O'Nolan, in *The Heroic Process*, ed. Bo Almqvist *et al.* (Glendale, 1987), 476.

11. P.K. Ford, 'Welsh *asswynaw* and Celtic Legal Idiom', *B*, 26 (1975), 147-53. It is not strictly correct to see these as Culhwch's helpers, as they are sometimes described.

12. For analyses of individual episodes see *CO*(1) xl-lxxv. Wondrous feeding vessels, some of which are reflected in the giant's list, e.g. Mwys Gwyddno Garanhir, Pair Dyrnwch Gawr, are listed among The Thirteen Treasures of the Island of Britain. See below pp. 85-6.

13. The recurrence of references throughout the tale to combs, shears, hair and beards is remarked

upon by Stephen Knight, *Arthurian Literature and Society* (London, 1983), 25-6.

14. For the geography see Sir John Rhŷs, *THSC*, 1894-5, 1-34, 146-8, and for an evaluation of the significance of the hunt see Knight, op.cit., 26-34.

15. Patrick Sims-Williams, 'The Significance of the Irish Personal Names in *Culhwch ac Olwen'*, *B*, 29 (1982), 600-20, now shows that the Irish personal names which appear in the story are not evidence for any real knowledge of Irish literature but are used by the author to impress and entertain. For his use of ecclesiastical tradition see *CO*(1) xcix-cii.

16. P.L. Henry, *'Culhwch ac Olwen:* Some Aspects of Style and Structure', *SC*, 3 (1968), 30-8.

17. B.F. Roberts, 'Yr India Fawr a'r India Fechan', *LIC*, 13 (1980-1), 278-89.

18. *Cyfarwyddyd* is a compendious term for traditional lore, most especially narratives. Cf. Irish *seanchas*. Cf. ch.2, pp. 34-5 above.

19. The suggestion is made in *CO*(1) lxxxvii that as the giant-slayer *par excellence* Arthur attracted to himself a variety of giant tales, including the most familiar of all, a Welsh version of the international popular tale, 'The giant's daughter', in a form similar to *Culhwch ac Olwen*.

20. *CO*(1) lxxxvii-lxxxviii.

21. Text and discussion in Ast. H. 296-309: see also *TYP* 362, and pp. 38-46 above.

22. Cai and Bedwyr are central characters in the 'Pa gur' poem also.

23. 'The Arthur of *Culhwch ac Olwen* as a Figure of Epic Heroic Tradition', *Reading Medieval Studies*, 9 (1983), 3-15.

24. W.J. Gruffydd, 'Mabon fab Modron', *Cy.*, 42 (1931), 131.

25. *The Mabinogi* (Cardiff, 1977), 62-77.

26. 'Interpreting Irony in Mediaeval Celtic Narrative: the Case of *Culhwch ac Olwen'*, *CMCS*, 16 (1988), 41-59.

27. For suggestions of deeper meanings see Knight, op. cit., 1-37, Richard M. Loomis in *The Romance of Arthur*, 27-30, John Layard, *A Celtic Quest* (Zurich, 1975).

28. *TYP* is the fullest study of the collection in all its aspects. See also Eric P. Hamp, 'On the Justification of Ordering in *TYP'*, *SC*, 10/17 (1981-2), 104-9.

29. See Elissa R. Henken, *Traditions of the Welsh Saints* (Cambridge, 1987); idem, 'The Saint as Folk Hero', in *Celtic Folklore and Christianity*, ed. P.K. Ford (Santa Barbara, 1983), 58-74; idem, 'The Saint as a Secular Ruler', *Folklore*, 98, 226-32.

30. *CO*(1) xcvi-cii. Texts in *VSB* and see J.S.P. Tatlock, *Speculum*, 14 (1939), 345-65 for the dates, and Leg. Hist. 184-94, for his discussion.

31. Anlawdd Wledig seems to be a function rather than a person. He is an 'empty' character who is never given a narrative context but who exists merely so that his daughters may be the mothers of heroes who are all, therefore, cousins to Arthur. The Life of Illtud and *Culhwch ac Olwen* both use this convention to relate their heroes (Illtud, Culhwch, Gorau) to Arthur.

32. See above p. 74. For other comparisons with the Life of Cadoc see *CO*(1) lxxx, xcviii.

33. Thomas Jones, 'Chwedl Huail fab Caw ac Arthur' in *Astudiaethau Amrywiol* (Caerdydd, 1968), 48-66. *TYP* 408-10, 554-5.

34. 'Is it right to fight for you?' naïvely asks Arthur of the eagle in the poem, *c.* 1150, in contrast with the more heroic 'whatever of me may be won will be won by fighting' of the tale. *CO*(1) xci-cii discusses the relationship of the tale and the *Vitae* and would appear to see similarities as borrowings from ecclesiastical learning. The suggestion is made that *Culhwch ac Olwen* was composed in an ecclesiastical milieu, perhaps St David's, Carmarthen or Llanbadarn Fawr.

35. For the texts see Eurys I. Rowlands, 'Y Tri Thlws ar Ddeg', *LlC*, 5 (1958), 33-69, 145-7; P.C. Bartrum, 'Tri Thlws ar Ddeg Ynys Brydain', *ÉC*, 10 (1963), 434-77; *TYP* 240-9. Discussions are WAL 46, 156-61; *TYP* cxxx-xxxv, 529; Graham C. Thomas, 'Llen Arthur a Maen a Modrwy Luned', unpublished MA diss. (University of Wales, 1976).

36. WAL 161.

37. *TYP* cxxxv: see the discussion, cxxxiii-vi.

38. WAL 165-7, *CO*(1) lxi-xiii.

39. *ÉC*, 10 (1963), 455-6.

40. Cf. Doris Edel, 'The Catalogues in *Culhwch ac Olwen* and Insular Celtic Learning', *B*, 30 (1983), 253-67, esp. 263-6.

41. *TYP* 246-7.

42. ALMA 280-94.

43. See H.M. and N.K. Chadwick, *The Growth of Literature* (Cambridge, 1940), iii, 746-7, 804-7, Doris Edel, n.40 above.

44. Discussed by Thomas Jones, 'The Black Book of Carmarthen "Stanzas of the Graves"', *PBA*, 53, 97-138. See above pp. 49-51.

45. For a study of the city names in the *Historia Brittonum* and the Red Book of Hergest and later versions, see Ifor Williams, 'Enwau ac Anryfeddodau Ynys Prydain', *B*, 5 (1929), 19-25, Kenneth Jackson, 'Nennius and the Twenty-eight Cities of Britain', *Antiquity*, 12 (1938), 44-55, *TYP* cxxiii-iv.

46. This was suggested by R.J. Thomas, 'Cysylltiad Arthur â Gogledd Ceredigion', *B*, 8 (1936), 124-5, who also notes the names Llys Arthur (Arthur's court) and Maen Arthur (Arthur's stone) in the same area. Cf. ch.2, n.113 above.

47. Ruth Eliose Roberts, 'Welsh Place-names in the Earliest Arthurian Texts', Ph.D. diss. (Columbia University, 1957), p. 36-8, has, however, proposed that Carn Cabal originally figured in the narrative of the hunt and she draws attention to other Arthurian place-names in the Wye valley. See above p. 76 for the hunt.

48. A.T. Bannister, *The Place-names of Herefordshire* (Cambridge, 1916), 79.

49. See *TYP* 416-18.

50. Cf. Richard Barber, *The Figure of Arthur* (London, 1972), 109-10; David Dumville, 'The Historical Value of the *Historia Brittonum*', *Arthurian Literature*, 6 (1986), 21-2.

51. Cf. ch.2, pp. 39, 44 above.

4

GEOFFREY OF MONMOUTH, *HISTORIA REGUM BRITANNIAE* AND *BRUT Y BRENHINEDD*

Brynley F. Roberts

THE early history of the Britons appears to have been Geoffrey of Monmouth's sole literary or 'scholarly' interest, inasmuch that the two, perhaps three, works associated with his name are narratives of pre-Saxon Britain and of the English conquest. His earliest book was probably the *Prophetiae Merlini* which seems to have been issued a few years before his major work, *Historia Regum Britanniae*. The *Prophetiae* are incorporated into the *Historia* as Book VII, but as this section retains its own dedication to Alexander, Bishop of Lincoln, to whom no copies of the complete *Historia* are dedicated, it would appear to have had its own separate identity. The *Prophetiae* do not refer to the death of Henry I in 1135 but that the text was known about that date is shown by Ordericus Vitalis's quotations from it, referred to as a certain 'libellus Merlini', in his *Historia Ecclesiastica*, *c.* 1135-6. Nevertheless, it is clear that the *Prophetiae*, which Geoffrey claimed to have translated from the British tongue, were intended to be part of the complete *Historia*. This section has its own development and refers to events in the *Historia*, but the way in which it is placed at the central point in Geoffrey's narrative suggests strongly that it was part of his original literary conception (see below p. 103). Geoffrey says as much in his Preface and Dedication, for after describing Vortigern's flight to Wales and Merlin Ambrosius's explanation of the sinking foundations of his new fortress, he claims that he had not yet reached this point in his narrative when he realized that the prophet Merlin was the object of a great deal of general curiosity and a number of acquaintances, including Bishop Alexander, urged him to interrrupt his work to prepare a Latin translation of the *Prophecies*. This 'libellus Merlini' was in circulation *c.* 1135 but it is such an integral part of the *Historia* that there is little doubt that the latter had been well mapped-out and was in the process of being written by then. *Historia Regum Britanniae*[1] had appeared by January 1139, for in his *Epistola ad Warinum* Henry of Huntingdon says that Robert of Torigni showed him a copy at the Abbey of Bec at that time.[2] Henry's evident surprise and his unexpected pleasure at coming across 'librum grandem Gaufridi Arturi' which gave

him the information on the pre-Roman British kings which he had sought, suggest
that the book had been newly published, sometime late in 1138.[3] Geoffrey's last
work, *c.* 1150, was a hexameter poem *Vita Merlini* which claims to continue the
story of Merlin and to relate some of his other prophecies. In spite of Geoffrey's
attempts to harmonize the portraits of the two Merlins — that of the *Historia* and
the later figure of the *Vita* — what becomes clear is that the latter corresponds most
closely to the Welsh Myrddin[4] and that the former, while owing much to Ambrosius,
the fatherless boy of the *Historia Brittonum*, is largely Geoffrey's creation.

Geoffrey's work, in its overt subject matter and orientation, can be claimed to be
Welsh, but there is little or no evidence that he himself is to be regarded as Welsh or
Cambro-Norman, in contrast with, for example, Giraldus Cambrensis whom one may
regard as being Welsh not simply by domicile but also partly by descent. Geoffrey
was known to his contemporaries as Galfridus Artur(us), two names said to be more
common amongst Bretons than Welsh in the twelfth century.[5] In the *Historia* he
refers to himself as Galfridus Monemutensis, 'of Monmouth'.

The castle and lordship of Monmouth had been established in 1067 by William
FitzOsbern, Earl of Hereford. In 1075 they passed to Wihenoc, from Dol in
Brittany, who left the castle to his nephew William FitzBaderon while he established
at Monmouth a priory under the jurisdiction of the Abbey of St Florent de Saumur.[6]
Geoffrey shows some familiarity in his work with the topography of this part of the
March, and the role of Caerleon both as an episcopal seat and as Arthur's court in the
Historia may be the fruits of a lively historical imagination playing upon the visible
remains of an imposing Roman city. It is possible that Geoffrey's family were
among those Bretons who had been such a significant element in William I's forces,
many of whom settled in south-east Wales.[7] Geoffrey's subject was the early history
of the Britons who were the ancestors not only of the Welsh but also of Cornishmen
and Bretons. But the later history of the Welsh, though the essential theme of the
Historia, was held in scant respect by him. For when Maximianus and his noble
troops had emigrated to Armorica, there to establish Little Britain, there was left in
Britain a mere remnant of frightened, ineffectual soldiery, so despised that the crown
of Britain could be refused by the Breton king even when offered as a gift. The
greatest of all the kings of Britain has a Breton ancestry and Arthur's most glorious
soldiers are the Bretons. Hoelus, King of Brittany, alone comes to Arthur's Whitsun
crown-wearing ceremony with his own sub-kings and throughout the latter part of the
Historia Brittany is portrayed as a refuge where is to be found the true essence of
Britain's former glory. Geoffrey's 'racial sympathies'[8] may be inferred from his work,
but nevertheless there is no direct evidence of his Breton antecedents. The place
given to south-west Britain and Brittany in the *Historia* may reflect the orientation of

some of Geoffrey's source material rather than a personal predilection;[9] nor must it be forgotten that contemporary political considerations would have made it difficult for any author to present a favourable view of Welsh skill-at-arms and nobility to a Norman audience and to patrons at court. That branch of the ancient Britons who had aligned themselves so firmly with the Normans were better placed to express old British virtues. To what degree these Breton families might have been channels of Breton culture and traditions is open to question. From the tenth century the Breton aristocracy, even in Basse-Bretagne, had been strongly influenced by French culture and were bilingual French-Breton, or even monolingual French.[10] The bearing of a Breton name might frequently cloak a Normanized family.

Nothing is known of Geoffrey's early career. He signed as a witness in six charters in Oxford between 1129 and 1151. Some of these suggest an association with the secular College of St George and as Geoffrey twice uses the title *magister* he may have been a canon of the college and a teacher there. Three of these charters also name Walter, Archdeacon of Oxford, who was Provost of the college, and it is significant that the last of these charters also names Robert de Chesney, Bishop of Lincoln, a former canon of St George's to whom Geoffrey dedicated his *Vita Merlini*. The College of St George came to an end in 1148. In February 1152 Geoffrey was ordained priest at Westminster and consecrated Bishop of St Asaph a week later. There is no evidence that he ever visited his diocese. In 1153 he was a witness to the agreement between Stephen and Henry and the Welsh Chronicle of the Princes records his death in 1154, *recte* 1155.[11] It would appear, therefore, that he was born towards the end of the eleventh century, presumably in Monmouth, that the greater part of his life was spent at Oxford, and that preferment came to him only late in life.

At Oxford Geoffrey would have been in the mainstream of the intellectual and cultural life of the day. The university had not yet developed but colleges like St George's were already centres of learning and education and the city itself was an important crossroads which attracted learned visitors and political figures. Oxford was a centre of historical enquiry and writing, in the life of which Geoffrey would have shared. Alexander, Bishop of Lincoln (Oxford lay within his diocese) had already proved himself an intelligent and active patron of Henry of Huntingdon, and he was later to request from Geoffrey a version of the *Prophecies of Merlin*. Another of Geoffrey's patrons was Robert, Earl of Gloucester, who had supported William of Malmesbury and would continue to do so. Geoffrey dedicated his *Historia* to men who were both politically powerful and proven patrons of historical works, and there is little doubt that Oxford was an important element in his literary development.[12] Geoffrey's awareness of the gaps in British history which previous historians had failed to fill is one element in the motivation for the writing of the *Historia*, as he himself suggests in his epilogue where he leaves the kings of the Saxons to Henry and to William but warns them to say nothing of the later princes of Wales (a task which he leaves to Caradog of Llancarfan) as they did not have his unique source. By the twelfth century the Anglo-Normans, no longer conquerors in a strange land, had acquired an interest in the history of their new country and they had become conscious of the gap in their knowledge of the inheritance into which they were beginning to enter. Their claim to an English inheritance had from the first been given historical justification, but it was generally accepted that Angles and Saxons were themselves comparatively recent — and indeed pagan — newcomers to Britain whose claim to sovereignty was that of conquest.[13] The period of British, pre-Saxon rule was truly a dark age as far as historical evidence was in the question. Henry of Huntingdon's explanation in the letter to Warinus of the reason that he begins his account with Julius Caesar omitting what may have lain before,

> Respondeo igitur tibi quod nec voce nec scripto hortum temporum saepissime notitiam quaerens invenire potui
>
> (*My reply is therefore that in spite of very frequent enquiries I have not been able to obtain any information on these times either orally or in writing*)

is echoed by Geoffrey in his Preface

> in mirum contuli quod . . . nichil de regibus qui ante incarnationem Christi inhabitauerant, nichil etiam de Arturo ceterisque compluribus qui post incarnationem successerunt repperissem.
>
> (*It seems remarkable to me that I have not found anything about the kings who dwelt here before the Incarnation of Christ, nor anything even about Arthur and the many others who succeeded him after the Incarnation.*)

The lack of historical evidence for pre-Saxon Britain was an old problem which had been addressed in the ninth-century *Historia Brittonum* and by twelfth-century writers, and Geoffrey of Monmouth, cogitating on a possible theme which would be attractive to patrons, may have resolved, with an audacity too blatant to be doubted, to overcome the problem by claiming for himself a unique source which made good the deficiencies in the narratives of Gildas, Bede, and 'Nennius' of the early history of the Island of Britain. Geoffrey provided the book which his audience, lay and learned, had long wished to read. At the root of the popularity of the *Historia* is not only its lively narration of events but Geoffrey's recognition of the demands of his contemporaries and compatriots.[14]

He claimed for the *Historia* a privileged status in that his source which he had simply translated, he said in his Preface, was a certain

Britannici sermonis librum uetustissimum qui a Bruto primo rege Britonum usque ad Cadualadrum filium Caduallonis actus omnium continue et ex ordine perpulcris orationibus proponebat.

(*very ancient book in the British language which set out in a consecutive and orderly fashion the acts of all (the kings) from Brutus, the first king of the Britons, down to Cadwaladrus, the son of Cadwallo, in a style of great beauty.*)

In his epilogue he referred again to this book presented to him by Walter, Archdeacon of Oxford, and which had been brought by him *ex Britannia*.

The *Historia*, however, cannot be a mere translation, even in the extended medieval sense. Almost every study of the work reveals its imaginative and creative use of a range of literary sources, the majority of which are in Latin, and it becomes increasingly clear that one of Geoffrey's most fruitful talents was his ability to create episodes and characters from a variety of disparate and unconnected elements. The firm narrative structure of the *Historia* and a developed authorial view of British history further mark this as an individually composed narrative.[15] The reference to the authoritative source may, therefore, be regarded as an example of the 'old book' topos, but Walter, Archdeacon of Oxford, Provost of St George's, the *uir in oratoria arte atque in exoticis historiis eruditus*, and *in multis historiis peritissimo uiro* described by Geoffrey, whose words recall those of Henry of Huntingdon, *superlative rethoricus*, was real enough. Stripped of its status as the sole source and of the description of its style as *perpulcris orationibus*, there is nothing inherently impossible in the suggestion that Walter should have brought from Brittany a manuscript which contained native historical material relating to Brittany and south-west Britain. Genealogies and traditional history were the common stock of Breton and south-west British culture[16] and king-lists, annals, genealogies and the like may be what is intended by Geoffrey's *actus omnium [regum] continue et ex ordine*. The *liber uetustissimus* may have had a real existence as a source used by Geoffrey, not perhaps a major one in terms of its contribution to the complete *Historia* but significant, nevertheless, as a source of information on British traditional history and as one of the seeds from which sprang the concept of an *Historia Regum Brittaniae*.[17]

British traditional history, however, involved more than knowledge of a collection of 'facts', names and documents. The learned classes of medieval Wales, responsible for the organization and transmission of traditional learning in all its varied aspects, seem to have developed a coherent historiography of the Britons, the major themes of which are central to the *Historia Regum Britanniae*. These are the myths (properly so-called) of the unity of the Island of Britain, symbolized by the Crown of London, the sign of a single kingship, of the loss of sovereignty to the English, and of national renewal and the restoration of British hegemony, expressed in prophetic terms. The concept of a succession of single kings, sovereigns of Britain, is at the root of Geoffrey's view of the path of British history. He accepted both the unity of Britain and the traditional divisions of the whole. The first king is Brutus and his sons are the eponymous founders of the three realms of Britain, England, Wales, Scotland (Locrinus of *Lloegr*, Kamber of *Cymru* and Albanactus of *yr Alban*), but there is also a suggestion that Cornwall was a recognized province, as in the older division found in the native tract *The Names of the Island of Britain*,[18] and it is given its own founder, Corineus. He also makes it clear that though there are three regions, there is only one kingdom. The eldest son Locrinus is the chief ruler (II.1), and the supremacy of the Crown of London is formally expressed later (II.1) when the elder Belinus is crowned King of the Island and rules England, Wales and Cornwall, leaving the North to the younger Brennius. Cassibellanus rules the whole island, though he has subordinate kings and powerful regional earls. Geoffrey stresses the unity and single kingship of Britain. In his first three books he presents pictures of the anarchy which stems from the denial of this concept. The jealousy of Ferreux and Porrex leads to civil war which is ended only by Dunuallo's accession, but history begins to repeat itself when his sons fall into the same snare and civil war is averted only by their mother's appeal. Geoffrey returns to this theme at the end of the *Historia*, for the final irrevocable breach between English and Welsh occurs when Edwin seeks permission to wear a crown in his own region. Caduallo's advisers are indignant: 'it was contrary to law and to the customs of their ancestors that an Island with one crown should be placed under the sway of two crowned heads' (XII.3). It is the upholding of this principle which leads to the final catastrophe, for the crown passes to Athelstan 'who was the first among them to be crowned King' (XII.19).

The idea of unity is implicit in the theme of loss and cannot be separated from it. This theme pervades the whole of the *Historia*, which is an account of the rise to greatness of a favoured people and their decline and loss of sovereignty. However glowing specific reigns may be, in Welsh eyes it is a rather sombre book in its final effect. The book opens with this statement: 'The Britons once occupied the land from sea to sea, before the others came. Then the vengeance of God overtook them because of their arrogance and they submitted to the Picts and Saxons' (I.2); the reader is allowed to view the working out of this vengeance but Geoffrey again states his theme clearly (XI.9, XII.6-7, 10, 12, 15, 17) as the book draws to an end. The theme of loss is deepened by the place Geoffrey gives to prophecy, which is used carefully to introduce significant characters and to point to the idea of greatness and loss. The representatives of the nation are introduced by prophecies, Brutus before his birth by Ascanius's magi, the greatness of his line by Diana. Arthur is first mentioned in Merlin's Prophecies and the final stages of the history are revealed by the Angelic Voice. *Prophetiae Merlini*, therefore, is not simply a virtuoso performance of abstruse nonsense. It is placed exactly in the centre of the book, immediately after that most significant event, the arrival of the Saxons who are the instruments of God's vengeance. History stands still for a moment while we seek its significance. We look ahead past Arthur, beyond the end of the *Historia*, to the very end of time. Merlin prophesies the greatness of Arthur, his victories against the Saxons and Romans. The spectre of civil war is revealed as the Red Dragon tears itself and the Saxons win sovereignty. The new conquerors are themselves bound in everlasting captivity by people in wood and iron suits, and so on to contemporary history. But the tone changes. Britons will arise, and Cadualadrus shall call Conanus; Welsh, Cornish, Bretons will drive out the foreigners and 'The Island shall be called by the name of Brutus'. Geoffrey derived this from Welsh prophecies, and here he has the themes of British unity and restitution at their simplest, the British alliance which even for the author of the tenth-century Welsh political prophecy, the poem *Armes Prydein*, had been 'long prophesied',[19] and which Geoffrey was to use again in *Vita Merlini*. The *Prophetiae* change their tone again and from here to the end they make use of animal symbolism and celestial portents, but it seems significant that the last clear, intelligible reference in these *Prophetiae* which set out the meaning of history, is to the restoration of British rule, sometime in an undefined future.[20]

The interweaving of these strands gives the narrative its thematic structure and confirms how integral to that structure is the section *Prophetiae Merlini* which must therefore have been conceived as part of the *Historia* though published earlier. The work achieves its cohesion in these themes, and through them Geoffrey invites his readers to discover the pattern of history and its significance for them. In this lies the paradox of the composition, for where contemporary historians had regretted the loss of material which would enable them to write the early history of Britain, Geoffrey resolved the problem by creating a spurious body of evidence but in so doing put on the mantle of a real historian. He learned to adopt (rather than to parody[21]) the methods of his contemporaries and he manipulated his sources effectively, but at a deeper level he perceived that history narrated and unfolded the fate of nations and that the historian laid before the people warnings from the past which they should heed. What binds the chronicle of events into a history is the moral principle that a nation reaps what is sown in past ages. Sometimes Geoffrey regards the righteous king and the rule of justice as the basis of national prosperity; in other sections he sees history in humanist terms as a progress of natural causes and consequences. The Britons are ruined by a combination of natural disasters and innate degeneracy, while the English, living more prudently, inevitably flourish.

Geoffrey's final verdict (XII.19) is:

> Supradicta namque moralitas et fames atque consuetudinarium discidium in
> tantum coegerat populum superbum degenare quod hostes longius arcere
> nequiuerant . . . At Saxones sapientius agentes, pacem et concordiam inter se
> habentes, agros colentes, ciuitates et opida aedificantes et sic abiecto dominio
> Britonum, iam toti Loegriae imperauerant duce Adelstano qui primus inter eos
> diadema portauit.
>
> (*Indeed, the plague about which I have told you, the famine and their own
> inveterate habit of civil discord had caused this proud people to degenerate so
> much that they were no longer able to keep their foes at bay. The Saxons, on
> the other hand, behaved more wisely. They kept peace and concord among
> themselves, they cultivated the fields, and they rebuilt the cities and castles.
> They threw off completely the dominion of the Britons and under their leader
> Adelstan, who was the first among them to be crowned King, they ruled over
> the whole of Loegria.*)

Discordia, treachery, plague and famine are all governed by Providence, and although
Geoffrey reflects views of the civic virtues of the just ruler and the practical value of
sensible husbandry, his underlying theme is that history is providential and that its
pattern is part of God's purpose.[22]   The Britons were called to high favour but they
retain their position only to the extent that they are faithful to their calling.   When
they reject moral law and follow the paths of jealousy, arrogance and laxity, they
suffer defeat and loss; and if they continue on this path they must forgo their
lordship of the Island of Britain.   This is the note struck in I.2 where the loss of
British sovereignty is attributed to *ultione diuina propter ipsorum superuentiente
superbiam*.   It recurs constantly, it is stated explicitly as the interpretation of history
in XI.9, and is proven consistently for the reader in a series of examples throughout
Book XII.

Geoffrey has planned his *Historia* on a broad canvas.   He is equally attentive to
the detail of the structure of his narrative.   Crucial episodes are used to point towards
later developments and significant characters are introduced unobtrusively but
insistently.   Modredus and Guenhuuara are casually named for the first time in the
same paragraph in IX.9, linked in X.2, and their unfaithfulness to Arthur is reported
immediately before the Battle of Camlan in X.12.   Gorlois, the respected warrior,
appears in VIII.6, he is a wise leader in VIII.18, and in the following chapter as the
husband of Igerna he is the crucial figure, already established in a sympathetic light,
in the account of the begetting of Arthur.   The clearest example of the preparing of
the ground before the significant appearance of an important character is Arthur
himself.   He is consistently introduced in a prophetic context — the Boar of Cornwall
in Merlin's Prophecies, the shaft of light over Gaul (VIII.15), and named at his
strange begetting as a future hero (VIII.19).   Throughout the latter part of the
Historia Geoffrey provides summaries of the history in a series of speeches or

monologues (Ambrosius VIII.2, Eldol VIII.5, Brianus XII.2, Salomon and Caduallo XII.5-6) which serve to tighten the narrative and to summarize the meaning of the history.

Geoffrey sets out in the Preface the parameters of his history which will run from Brutus, the first king, who gave his name to the Island and to his descendants, to Cadualadrus, son of Caduallo, that is he will trace the history of this people from their origins to what he regards as the crucial change in their status, the loss of sovereignty to Athelstan which is reflected in the change of the name of the Britons to Welsh (XII.19). The *Historia* has seven chronological sections: 1. Origins and the journey to Albion. 2. The settlement in Britain. 3. The Romans in Britain. 4. The decline of the Britons and the Breton deliverance. 5. Vortigern and the advent of the Saxons (the section includes Merlin's Prophecies). 6. King Arthur. 7. The Saxon supremacy. The 'plot' narrative, however, is thematically constructed around three characters who represent three peaks in British history viewed as the relationship of Britain and Rome, one of the most meaningful themes of traditional British historiography.[23] Following an introduction describing the Trojan descent of Brutus, section I narrates the history of the kings of the Britons which ends in periods of civil strife until Belinus and his brother Brennius attack Rome: II, Julius Caesar formally sets out the relationship of the two nations in IV.1. The moral superiority of the Britons is made clear in Cassibellanus's response that his people have ever sought the dignity of freedom in preference to the imposition of the yoke of servitude upon others, and the Roman conquest is achieved not by force of arms but by British discord and then by agreement. Periods of civil war again ensue until Constantinus returns to conquer Rome. In III the years of Roman rule are seen to have had a debilitating effect on the British character for their native love of freedom and their moral strength are now to be found in Brittany. Britain faces a new threat in the *adventus Saxonum* and Arthur emerges as the new hero. But though he succeeds in defeating the Saxons and establishing long periods of peace, the culmination of his reign is his meeting of the Emperor's challenge and his march upon Rome. He sees himself as the heir of Belinus and of Constantinus, but the measure of the decline of the Britons is that he fails where his predecessors had succeeded, a failure which symbolizes and foreshadows the end of British sovereignty. Characteristically it is brought about by treachery, disloyalty and civil war. Following Arthur's return from Rome and the Battle of Camlan there is little to relate and the *Historia* moves quickly to its close.

Arthur's role is central to the *Historia*. Geoffrey's theme is the loss of sovereignty. The change of orientation from Troy and Rome with their connotations of *British* dignity and status in the classical world to the contemporary reality of

Saxon and Norman domination over the *Welsh* required a powerful focus, while, equally, the vaticination of renewal which Geoffrey regarded as an important element in his view of British history also needed a strong emotional symbol.[24] Arthur is the final flicker of the flame of British sovereignty but in his ambiguous passing he becomes the hope for renewal. Arthur is a personification of British history. He is the king of all Britain, who fails the hero's quest but who is nevertheless the king who will return. Arthur's centrality in Geoffrey's structure is reflected in the space given to his antecedents and to his reign. About a quarter of the *Historia* (a little more than a quarter if the *Prophetiae* are included) deals with the House of Constantine and the wars of Aurelius and Uther Pendragon against the Saxons up to the birth of Arthur: just under another quarter of the book is taken up with the account of Arthur's reign and final defeat. When these proportions are considered in the context of the careful structuring of the complete narrative, then the significance of Arthurian Britain for Geoffrey becomes even more marked. This preoccupation with the figure of Arthur may have given rise, over the long period of the gestation of the *Historia*, to the nickname Galfridus *Artur(us)*.[25] The Arthurian section dominates the structure of the *Historia*. The long introduction to Arthur's appearance is necessary as a bridge from the end of Roman Britain to the beginnings of Saxon supremacy, but it is also a means of reintroducing from Brittany the old British virtues which give credence to the revival under Arthur. The king, even before his first appearance, is established in a genealogical and dynastic context which justifies his throne while at the same time distancing him from the Britons.[26]

It is clear that Geoffrey has designed his narrative of Arthur's reign so that it can achieve a dramatic epic quality which makes it an entity in its own right, separate from the rest of the book. Taking the historical context from 'Nennius' he makes Arthur come to the throne at a time of Saxon advance and the young king's first campaigns are structured around the battle-list of the *Historia Brittonum*. Douglas, (York), Kaerluidcoit i.e. Lincoln, Caledon Wood, culminate in the Battle of Badon (Bath), obviously a significant landmark as is shown by the description of the ritualistic arming of the hero with his personal weapons — the shield Pridwen, the spear Ron, and the sword forged in Avalon, Caliburnus. Arthur then turns against the Scots and the Picts, at Alclud, Moray and Loch Lomond (Geoffrey uses some of the Nennian *mirabilia* for his locations), with such ferocity that 'all the bishops of this pitiful country with all the clergy under their command, their feet bare and in their hands the relics of their saints and the treasures of their churches, assembled to beg pity', an episode reminiscent of the appeal of the Irish saints to Arthur in *Culhwch ac Olwen*. This second group of victories is necessary to justify his claim to be king of all Britain, Arthur's traditional title in *Culhwch ac Olwen* and the *Vitae* and a symbol of the unity of British sovereignty, so important in the historical myth.   Arthur exercises his kingship at York, where he re-establishes the privileges of the princes, the brothers Urianus and Anguselus, and Loth of Lodonesia, who had married Arthur's sister Anna and was the father of Gualguanus and Modredus.   He himself marries Guenhuuara.   The conquest of the neighbouring countries and islands follows and during the ensuing twelve years Arthur's court becomes the model of courtly behaviour.   The king's ambitions grow broader and the scene is set for his development over the next nine years into the world (i.e. European) emperor and the acknowledgement of his court as the epitome of chivalry.   Geoffrey is attempting to give historical expression to ideas which were already fruitful in Welsh tradition. The speech of the legendary figure of Glewlwyd Gafaelfawr and the court and Arthurian entourage at Celli Wig are the seeds from which grew the Galfridian account of the Whitsun crown-wearing at Caerleon with which Arthur celebrates his conquest of Europe from Ireland and Norway to Gaul and the borders of Rome and to which come all his subject kings and nobles.   The chivalric connotations of Caerleon were to be more potent than the heroic features of Celli Wig and one of Geoffrey's most enduring gifts to Arthurian literature was to be this transformed court and its central regal figure.

To this great celebration come, uninvited, the envoys of Lucius Hiberius, procurator, who accuse Arthur of offering an insult to Rome in the presumption which he displayed in his conquests and they call upon him to make amends before the Senate.   Though his nobles gladly accept the challenge, Arthur immediately sees it in historical terms comparing himself with Belinus, Maximianus and Constantinus. The scene soon acquires an epic quality as each noble pledges loyalty to the king in long formal speeches.   The reader is being prepared for a climax as the roll-call of kings and allies, the exchange of letters, of charge and counter-charge, lead to the battle preparations.   The defence of Britain is left to Modredus and Guenhuuara, and Arthur sets sail for Normandy.   Though the unexpected scene in which Arthur fights with the giant of Mont St Michel intervenes, the narrative of the campaign is soon taken up again and the reader is left in no doubt that he is approaching the end of the reign.   Skirmishes develop into the final battle, preceded by rhetorical speeches, and the king's closest companions are slain.   Arthur is victorious in his efforts, but as he sets out to subdue Rome the news reaches him of his betrayal by his nephew and his wife.   Geoffrey will not pursue the story of the betrayal, he says, but will describe the Battle of Camlan as he has read of it in his source and heard of it from Walter.   Modredus allies himself with the Saxons (Geoffrey has been careful to underline the fact that both the Roman and Saxon conquests owe more to British treachery than foreign superiority of arms) but this is the greatest civil war of all.

Having established Arthur as the most favoured of kings, his fall cannot but be final. He is mortally wounded and taken to the (unlocated) Isle of Avalon where his sword had been forged, for the healing of his wounds. His crown passes to his cousin Constantinus of Cornwall, but Arthur's end is uncertain.

Geoffrey aspired to present Arthur as a credible historical figure, acceptable in contemporary terms, both literary and realistic. He is the epic, *chanson de geste*, hero who engages in single combat, who leads by personal example, has personal arms and who wages his wars in real geographical areas. He is the Norman king ambitious to extend his realms, rewarding his most faithful companions with important dukedoms — Kaius of Anjou who is buried at Chinon, Beduerus of Normandy who is buried at Bayeux, and asserting his authority in crown-wearing ceremonies.[27]   Geoffrey was not above using some of the Nennian *mirabilia* to provide Arthurian locations or to supply interesting comments on the wonders of natural history, but it is significant that he rejects the Arthurian wonder-tales found in the same source, the hunt of *porcum Troy(n)t*, the Twrch Trwyth of *Culhwch ac Olwen*, and the account of the grave of Arthur's son. Traditional material is transmuted by Geoffrey into contemporary literary terms, but the historical realism comes closest to slipping in the episode of the giant of Mont St Michel which may be a traditional onomastic story given a new Arthurian context.[28]   Though this helps to prepare the reader for Arthur's later personal heroic exploits in the battles with the Romans and at Camlan, the source of the role fulfilled here is reflected in the comment that men crowded around to gape at the head of the giant 'and to praise the man who had freed the country from such a voracious monster', for freeing the land from giants and monsters was a characteristic Arthurian exploit in Welsh tradition.[29] Geoffrey uses this episode as a peg upon which to hang another giant story which appears to be a genuine and unadapted piece of Welsh tradition. This is the account of the fight between Arthur and Ritho *in Arauio monte*; Ritho had demanded Arthur's beard so that it might be given pride of place on the cloak which he had made of kings' beards. It is difficult to judge how independent of the story in the *Historia* later recordings of 'Ritta gawr' may be, but it has clear affinities with stories like that of Dillus Farfawg in *Culhwch ac Olwen*.[30]

The Arthurian section is Geoffrey's literary creation and it owes nothing to a prior narrative, but elements here as throughout the book appear to be drawn from Welsh — or British — tradition. In the *Historia* Geoffrey had access to some written Welsh sources. In Books II and III he has a series of king-lists in which names are reproduced with a minimum of comment. These lists derive from a collection of Welsh genealogies which have been manipulated and combined to produce chronological lists, while in Book IX.12 a similar type of source is employed to create a list of guests at Arthur's court.[31]   Other personal names, betraying their origin in the Old Welsh (or early Middle Welsh) orthography in which they appear, are taken at random and applied to new characters who are Geoffrey's creations, or are back formations derived from collections of city names similar to that which appears in the *Historia Brittonum*.[32]   Other place-names, cities, rivers, are also in Welsh orthography.   More important, however, were oral sources, by whatever means these may have been made available to Geoffrey.   His knowledge of Welsh cannot be assumed to have been extensive[33] and the *Historia* seems to have been largely composed while he was in Oxford.   Nevertheless he may well have retained some connection with Wales, and that he was cognizant with work, not unlike his own in character, being undertaken in south Wales during these years is suggested by the similarity of some of the features of the ecclesiastical pseudo-history of the 'archbishoprics' of Llandaf and of Caerleon and the accounts of saints Dubricius, Teilo and Samson given in the Book of Llandaf and the *Historia*.[34]

Some episodes and statements found in the *Historia* reflect extant Welsh traditional legend and story.   Geoffrey knows of the triadic geographical division of Britain and uses it to create the eponymous sons of Brutus.   His Dunuallo Molmutius owes something to the Dyfnwal Moel Mut of medieval Welsh legal legend, and Geoffrey has heard of the fame in battle of Owain ab Urien, *Hiwenus filius Uriani*, the hero of poems by the sixth-century poet Taliesin.   At times Geoffrey gives a version of a narrative which is similar to, but not identical with, that found in native (vernacular or Latin) sources and these are best regarded as cognate versions deriving from the same body of tradition.   His account of the relationship of Edwinus and Caduallo (Edwin and Cadwallawn) and the Battle of Chester is one example, while the more extended narrative of Maximianus, his British wife and the settlement of Brittany offers a number of points of comparison with the Welsh *Dream of Maxen* and with Breton Latin texts.[35]   Geoffrey's knowledge of Welsh (and possibly Breton) legendary and historical tradition is not insignificant but although he has understood the nature of the myth, in the developed narrative history which he produced from a multiplicity of sources — classical, Biblical, British, contemporary — the native material is one, but not a predominant, feature.   Geoffrey appears to have restricted his use of Welsh/Breton material to what might be regarded as historical, rather than folkloric, but the manipulation of his sources, which is his most characteristic literary skill, makes retrieving that material a hazardous task.

This is equally true of the Arthurian section.   Geoffrey has learned the names and the roles of the king's closest companions, Kaius and Beduerus (Cai, Bedwyr), the nephew Gualguanus (Gwalchmai), the queen Guenhuuara (Gwenhwyfar); he knows of three of Arthur's possessions (but *Prydwen* is his ship in the poem *Preiddeu Annwn* and in *Culhwch ac Olwen*, and his lance Ron is Rongomynyat, his sword Caliburnus is Caletuwlch in *Culhwch ac Olwen*). Utherpendragon may have been Arthur's father, or if not, could have been deduced to be so, but Arthur has no genealogy in early Welsh tradition (though he has sons and uncles not mentioned by Geoffrey), nor is there a tale of his birth; though Geoffrey's narrative has folkloric features there is nothing to show whether it is his creation or not. *Culhwch ac Olwen*, the *Vitae* and early Arthurian poetry portray an Arthur who is a great king, whose court is a centre for suitors seeking a boon, and who frees the land from the terror of monsters. Geoffrey gives this portrait a historical context and composes around the king a structured narrative, transforming into his own terms the image of Arthur and his court found in the Welsh tradition. But the account of Arthur's end appears to have a progression which may derive from an established coherent narrative. It is significant that Geoffrey's sole explicit reference to an oral source is made in connection with this part of his account of Arthur's reign (XI.1):

> . . . nuntiatur ei Modredum nepotem suum cuius tutele permiserat Britanniam eiusdem diademate per tyrannidem et proditionem insignitum esse reginamque Ganhumeram uiolato iure priorum nuptiarum eidem nephanda uenere copulatam fuisse.
> Nec hoc quidem, consul auguste, Galfridus Monemutensis tacebit sed, ut in prefato Britannico sermone inuenit et a Gwaltero Oxenefordensi in multis historiis peritissimo uiro audiuit, uili licet stilo breuiter propalabit que prelia inclitus ille rex post uictoriam istam in Britanniam reuersus cum nepote suo commiserit.

> *(the news was brought to him that his nephew Mordred, in whose care he had left Britain, had placed the crown upon his own head. What is more, this treacherous tyrant was living adulterously and out of wedlock with Queen Guinevere, who had broken the vows of her earlier marriage.*
> *About this particular matter, most noble Duke, Geoffrey of Monmouth prefers to say nothing. He will, however, in his own poor style and without wasting words, describe the battle which our most famous King fought against his nephew, once he had returned to Britain after his victory; for that he found in the British treatise already referred to. He heard it, too, from Walter of Oxford, a man most learned in all branches of history).*

To some degree, that these are episodes in an established narrative is confirmed by the existence of an account in *Vita Gildae* of the abduction of the queen by Melwas and also by a number of references to Camlan in the Triads and elsewhere which suggest that the account of this last battle was a focus for the development of associated minor episodes.36 The significance of the passing of the king to *Auallonis insula* is not developed by Geoffrey but the very ambiguity of his account suggests strongly that he was aware of it and chose to ignore it for political reasons.37 In the *Vita Merlini*, however, the story is recounted far more clearly, lines 929-40, 954-7.

Geoffrey's knowledge of Welsh tradition was sometimes confused, although he invariably made the best possible use of what he had. The example of Merlin is familiar (see below p. 135), and what he has on Beli and two of his sons, Lludd and Caswallawn (Heli, Lud, Cassibellanus) and their part in a saga of the Roman conquest is obviously incomplete,[38] but such was the authority which the *Historia* swiftly gained in medieval Wales that the translators and guardians of native tradition were more ready to attempt to adapt and harmonize than to correct inconsistencies between the Galfridian history and their own version. The *Historia* was translated into Welsh more than once (in texts often known as *Brut y Brenhinedd*, 'the *Brut* of the Kings') and some three versions of the *Prophetiae Merlini* were also produced. Three translations of the *Historia* appeared in the thirteenth century, two, possibly the three, of them from the same environment. Two other translations were made in the fourteenth century and amalgams of versions or combinations of texts were made up to the eighteenth century so that these Welsh *brutiau*, some sixty in number, are, with the Welsh laws, the most frequently copied texts in Welsh manuscript literature.[39]

These are for the most part translations, more in the modern than in the common medieval sense. They do not alter the shape of the narrative nor do they change its nature, though they normally omit Geoffrey's dedications. In general they are content to relate specific statements in the *Historia* to Welsh tradition or to confirm the identity of certain characters when this could be accomplished with minimum effort or change. The Cleopatra *Brut* (*CBB*) is the most individual of all the translations but the borrowings and harmonization here reflect the translator's knowledge not only of Welsh tradition but also of other texts in Latin and perhaps Wace (or Laymon). Most of the Welsh translators recognized the names of Geoffrey's characters and gave them their Welsh equivalents or restored the Old Welsh names more or less successfully to their contemporary Middle Welsh forms. In a few cases the Welsh texts add patronymics or epithets which are found in native sources. Eygyr (Eigr), a name apparently not attested in a pre-Galfridian source, is used for Igerna, Arthur's mother. She is claimed, in the Dingestow *Brut*, to be a daughter of Amlawdd Wledig, a shadowy figure whose daughters are the mothers of heroes, his only role in extant Welsh texts and a device which allows heroes like Culhwch, Gorau and St Illtud to be Arthur's cousins.[40] Whether Eygyr daughter of Amlawdd is traditional is, however, not clear. The Breton *Hoelus . . . filius sororis Arthuri ex Budicio rege Armoricae* consistently appears as Howel son of Emhyr Llydav. *Emyr* is a common noun, 'leader, prince', and *emyr Llydaw* must originally have been a description, 'king of Brittany'. In the *brutiau* it becomes a personal name, displacing Budicius, and as an Arthurian character he finds his way into the lists in *Breuddwyd Rhonabwy* and *Geraint*, but not that in *Culhwch ac Olwen*.

Where Geoffrey was dealing with characters established and familiar in Welsh tradition, the translators naturally used native forms of names and occasionally attempted a synthesis of the *Historia* and their own knowledge.[41]   At its simplest this might involve no more than the use of a Welsh name or a traditional epithet, but in other cases even a simple substitution might reveal inconsistencies between the *Historia* and traditions associated with the 'restored' characters. One such example is Heli son of Cligueillus, father of Lud. Lud was an established figure in Welsh tradition and the names could easily be 'corrected' to Beli Mawr son of Manogan, father of Lludd. But having made the substitution, the Llanstephan I translator (followed by all later writers of the Welsh *brutiau*) felt obliged to insert into his version the tale of Lludd and his brother Llefelys, which he prefaced (III.20), 'Beli had three sons, Lludd, Caswallawn and Nynnyav, *and as some of the story-tellers say, he had a fourth son, Llefelys'.*[42]

Geoffrey refers in V.6 to Coel's daughter Helena, who married Constantius, the Roman senator, and who was the mother of Constantinus. He obviously has in mind St Helena, mother of Constantine the Great, and the discoverer of the Cross. The translators duly rendered the passage, using the names of Coel, Constans, and Cystennyn. Both the Dingestow *Brut* and Llanstephan I identified her with an already existing figure in Welsh tradition, Elen Luyddawg, using this epithet for Helen daughter of Coel. Elen Luyddawg, however, appears in a different context in the tale *The Dream of Maxen Wledig*, where she is the daughter of Eudaf and is the British princess whom the Emperor Maxen (Maximianus) had seen in his dream. Geoffrey has a variant form of this tradition in V.9. Octavius, ruling in Britain, is persuaded to give his daughter (unnamed), with the crown, to Maximianus senator, to the chagrin of her cousin Conanus Meriadocus (named as her brother in the *Dream*). The translators follow the tradition of the *Dream* in the names, changing Octavius (which might have been suggested by the Old Welsh form, Oudam) to Eudaf, Maximianus to Maxen and call the unnamed daughter 'Helen', but they were unable to use the epithet *Luyddawg* as it had already been applied to (St) Helena.

The names of the chief figures in the Arthurian section were traditional, and Utherpendragon, Guenhuuara, Beduerus, Kaius, caused no difficulty as there was identification here of character and name. Modredus was, apparently, a little different. The form may be Cornish and the translators substituted for it the cognate Welsh name Medrawt. This led to a change in the latter's status in Welsh, for traditionally Gwenhwyfar's abductor had been Melwas, and Medrawd who fell with Arthur at the Battle of Camlan according to the annal, was an acceptable heroic character, though not claimed to be Arthur's nephew, in the poetic tradition.[43] By the fifteenth century, however, Geoffrey's identification had been accepted together with a deterioration in the character's role. 'Gualguanus filius Loth' also caused some difficulty.   Loth had been rendered Llev vap Kynvarch by the translators, and Gwalchmai and Gualguanus had already been accepted as equivalents.   Gwalchmei vap Llev, therefore, was acceptable.   But Geoffrey, having to explain the relationship with Arthur, claims that Arthur's sister Anna was the mother of Gualguanus and Modreduṣ, in Welsh, Anna mother of Gwalchmai and Medrawd.   But Gwalchmai was already firmly known in Welsh tradition as Gwalchmei vap Gwyar, and the two statements regarding his mother had to be reconciled.   Llanstephan I did not attempt to reconcile them but the translator, nevertheless, seems aware of the difficulty when he refers to 'Anna, and she was the mother of Gwalchmey and Medrawt and was wife to Llev vap Kynvarch, *according to the truth of the Historia*', which may be taken as an indication of his uncertainty.   Peniarth 44 resolved the difficulty quite simply by claiming for Anna that 'she was also called Gwyar and was the mother of Gwalchmey and Medravt', though there were no grounds for connecting Gwyar and Medrawd.   The Dingestow *Brut* accepted Geoffrey's account and refers to Gwalchmai son of Lleu and Anna in IX.9, 11, but when this character begins to play a prominent role (X.4 etc.), the earlier statments are ignored and he appears consistently as Gwalchmei vap Gwyar.

There are comparatively few examples of inconsistencies of this kind between Geoffrey and his Welsh translators.   The *Historia* seems to use existing Welsh tradition directly in only a few sections and consequently these were the only opportunities for differences between the two to arise.   By replacing the proper names by genuine Welsh forms, sometimes related to the Latin forms, frequently not, they made the *Historia* even more acceptable to a Welsh audience.   The scribes did occasionally note discrepancies between their own knowledge and statements in the *Historia*, and they sometimes refer to Welsh or other traditions,[44] but viewed as a whole, the *Historia* and the Welsh versions were quickly accepted in Wales as the authoritative account of the early history of Britain.   The 'traditional history' was to remain a potent element in Welsh national consciousness until the end of the eighteenth century, such was the pride engendered by Geoffrey in a glorious past and the hope sustained in a restored future.   If the most surprising gloss in the medieval Welsh translations is the explanation in the Peniarth 44 text that the translator omits Merlin's Prophecies because 'they are difficult for people to believe', the most intriguing is the comment made by the translator of the Dingestow *Brut* after he has translated Geoffrey's ambiguous description of the passing of Arthur: 'And the book does not say anything more certain or clearer than that about him.'

NOTES:

1. This is the usual title given to the work since it was first used in the Commelin edition of 1587. It does not have MS authority but it is now too well established to be replaced. Commelin too is responsible for the division of the text into twelve books which I have followed here.

2. For the text see E.K. Chambers, *Arthur of Britain* (Cambridge, 1964), 251-2, and cf. *HRB* xii.

3. See further *HRB*(T) x-xxi. The *Historia* is found in a 'vulgate' version but a number of variant versions also exist. The most important of these is edited in *HRB*(V) where it is shown to be an abbreviated revision of Geoffrey's text.

4. See A.O.H. Jarman, below pp. 131-2, and *VM*.

5. J.E. Lloyd, 'Geoffrey of Monmouth', *EHR*, 57 (1942), 460-8.

6. Silas M. Harries, 'The Kalendar of the *Vitae Sanctorum Wallensium*', *Journal of the Historical Society of the Church in Wales*, 3 (1953), 3-25, 10-16.

7. See, e.g. F.M. Stenton, *The First Century of English Feudalism* (Oxford, 1961), 25-9. Cf. p. 259 below.

8. This is Tatlock's phrase: see ch.16 of Leg. Hist.

9. The fullest discussion of this matter is O.J. Padel, 'Geoffrey of Monmouth and Cornwall', *CMCS*, 8 (1984), 1-27.

10. Roparz Hemon, *La langue bretonne et ses combats* (La Baule, 1947), 46; Henri Waquet, *Histoire de la Bretagne* (Paris, 1958), 33-4; J Loth, 'Les langues romane et bretonne en Armorique', *RC*, 28 (1907), 378-403. See J.E.C. Williams below, p. 259.

11. For accounts of Geoffrey's life and interpretations of the evidence, see Lloyd, art. cit., E. Faral, 'Geoffroy de Monmouth, les faits et les dates de sa biographie', *Romania*, 53 (1927), 1-42; *VM* 26-35, *HRB* ix-xi; *HRB*(T) 10-14.

12. See further M. Dominica Legge, 'L'influence littéraire de la cour d'Henri Beauclerc', in *Mélanges offerts à Rita Lejeune* (Gembloux, 1969), 679-87; H.E. Salter, *Medieval Oxford*, Oxford Hist. Soc., 100 (1935), 90-2. For Geoffrey's dedications see A. Griscom, 'The Date of Composition of Geoffrey of Monmouth's *Historia*: New Manuscript Evidence', *Speculum*, 1 (1926), 129-56; *HRB* xii-xvi.

13. See comments by R.W. Southern, 'The Place of England in the Twelfth Century Renaissance', *History*, 45 (1960), 201-16, 208; H.V. Galbraith, *Historical Research in Medieval England* (London, 1951).

14. For comparisons of the *Historia* with the works of contemporary historians see LA, ii, 386-401, Leg. Hist. 428-30, Myra J. Rosenhaus, 'Britain between Myth and Reality', (unpublished Ph.D. dissertation, University of Indiana, 1983), Nancy F. Partner, *Serious Entertainments: the Writing of History in Twelfth Century England* (Chicago, 1977). For Geoffrey's influence on British historiography see Robert W. Hanning, *The Vision of History in Early Britain from Gildas to Geoffrey of Monmouth* (New York, 1966), R. William Leckie, Jr., *The Passage of Dominion: Geoffrey of Monmouth and the Periodization of Insular History in the Twelfth Century* (Toronto, 1981). See also references in TRh 280-2.

15. Studies are LA, Leg. Hist., W.F. Schirmer, *Die frühen Darstellungen der Arthurstoffes* (Köln, 1958), 7-40, *HRB*, ALMA ch.8, B.F. Roberts, 'Sylwadau ar Sieffre o Fynwy a'r *Historia Regum Britanniae*', *LlC*, 12 (1973), 127-45.

16. For such common material see Susan Pearce, 'The Traditions of the Royal King-list of Dumnonia', *THSC*, 1971, 128-39; Léon Fleuriot, 'Old Breton Genealogies and Early British Traditions', *B*, 26 (1974), 1-6; Gwenael Le Duc, 'L'Historia Brittanica avant Geoffrey de Monmouth', *AB*, 79 (1972), 819-35; HLCB 98-102, 116-18; Caroline Brett, 'Breton Latin Literature as Evidence for Literature in the Vernacular, AD 800-1300', *CMCS*, 18 (1989), 1-26, discusses the fragmented nature of Breton historiography and reviews the extant texts.

17. Most modern scholarship is sceptical of Geoffrey's claim, but cf. R.W. Southern, 'Aspects of the European Tradition of Historical Writing, 1 The Classical Tradition from Einhard to Geoffrey of Monmouth', *Trans. Royal. Hist. Soc.*, 5S, 20 (1970), 173-96, p. 194: 'Personally I am convinced that the source which he claimed to have received from Walter, archdeacon of Oxford, really existed.'

18. For the text and discussion see *TYP* 228-37, cxxiii-vii.

19. *AP* 1. 13. Cf. p. 136 below.

20. See further 'Geoffrey of Monmouth and Welsh historical tradition', *NMS*, 20 (1976), 29-40. I am grateful to the editor for permission to reproduce here portions of my article.

21. V.I.J. Flint, 'The *Historia Regum Brittaniae* of Geoffrey of Monmouth: Parody and its Purpose. A suggestion', *Speculum*, 54 (1979), 447-68. See also C.N.L. Brooke, 'Geoffrey of Monmouth as a Historian' in C.N.L. Brooke *et al.*, *Church and Government in the Middle Ages* (Cambridge, 1976), 77-91 (repr. in C.N.L. Brooke, *The Church and the Welsh Border in the Central Middle Ages*, ch.9), and n.14 above.

22. This moral view of history is, of course, not unique to Geoffrey nor is it specifically Welsh. Deriving from the Old Testament prophets and St Augustine it is a common medieval interpretation. For a study of Geoffrey in this context see S.M. Schwartz, 'The Founding and Self-betrayal of Britain: an Augustinian Approach to Geoffrey of Monmouth's *Historia Regum Britanniae*', *Medievalia et Humanistica*, 10 (1981), 33-58.

23. For this theme see *NMS*, 20 (1976), 33-4 and references cited there; also G. Goetinck, 'The Blessed Heroes', *SC*, 20/21 (1985-6), 87-109.

24. Geoffrey refers to the hope of Arthur's return obliquely in XI.2, 'letaliter uulneratus est; qui illinc ad sananda uulnera sua in insulam Auallonis euectus'.

25. For the suggestion that this is a nickname see Padel, art. cit., 2. William of Newburgh claimed that 'Gaufridus . . . agnomen habens Arturi, pro eo quod fabulas de Arturo, ex priscis Britonum figmentis sumptas et ex proprio auctas, per superductum Latini sermonis colorem honesto historiae nomine palliavit', E.K. Chambers, *Arthur of Britain*, 274-5.

26. For an ideological interpretation of Geoffrey's Arthurian section see Stephen Knight, *Arthurian Literature and Society* (London, 1983), ch.2.

27. Cai is referred to as *swyddwr* in *Culhwch ac Olwen*, with which compare *BD* 156, *pen swyddwr*, 'dapifer'. For the Whitsun crown-wearing see Leg. Hist. p. 271-4.

28. See LA ii, 284-9. For a view which ascribes the episode to Geoffrey see Lewis Thorpe, 'Le Mont Saint-Michel et Geoffrei de Monmouth', in *Millénaire du Mont Saint Michel*, ii (Paris, 1967), 377-82.

29. *CO*(1) lxxxvi-vii, and cf. above p. 84.

30. *CO*(1) lvi-viii.

31. S. Piggott, 'The Sources of Geoffrey of Monmouth: I The "pre-Roman" King-list', *Antiquity*, 15 (1941), 269-86. The text of the genealogies from London, British Library MS Harleian 3859, a text very similar to, or identical with, that used by Geoffrey, is given in *EWGT* 9-13. See also P.C. Bartrum, 'Was there a British Book of Conquests?', *B*, 23 (1968), 2-5.

32. *Historia Brittonum* was one of the sources for Geoffrey's account of Merlin and his story of Vortigern and the *adventus Saxonum*. For lists of city names see above, ch.3, n.45.

33. Views differ on the extent of Geoffrey's knowledge of Welsh. Tatlock, Leg. Hist. 445, believed that his ability to translate some epithets and his use of some place and personal names revealed some real knowledge and T.D. Crawford, 'On the Linguistic Competence of Geoffrey of Monmouth', *Medium Aevum*, 51 (1982), 152-62, suggests that Geoffrey had a better knowledge of spoken than of written Welsh. The evidence remains inconclusive. Geoffrey's derivation of 'loquela gentis que prius Troiana siue curum Grecum nuncupabatur dicta fuit Britannica' (I:16) is academic folk etymology which explains *Cymraeg* as *cam-roeg*, and which is repeated by Giraldus Cambrensis, *Descriptio Kambriae* I.7.

34. Christopher Brooke, 'The Archbishops of St David's, Llandaff and Caerleon-on-Usk', *SEBC* 201-42 (rev. version in ch. 2, *The Church and the Welsh Border*).

35. For these examples see *TYP* cxxv-vi, xcv-viii, 480-1; CS 150-1; SEBH 107-9, 126-8; *LlC*, 12, 138. For Breton narrative material similar to Geoffrey's accounts see n.16 above, J.E.C. Williams below p. 265, *HRB* xvii-viii; C Sterckx and G. Le Duc, 'Les fragments inédits de la Vie de saint Goëznou', *AB*, 78 (1971), 277-85, C. Brett, *CMCS*, 18 (1989), 15-17.

36. See above pp. 81, 85.

37. See J.E. Lloyd, 'The Death of Arthur', *B*, 11 (1941), 158-60.

38. *CLILl* xiii-xv.

39. The three thirteenth-century translations are, referring only to the oldest MS in each group, Aberystwyth NLW MS Llanstephan I, NLW MS Peniarth 44, and the Dingestow *Brut* (*BD*), the two former are in the same hand. Fourteenth-century versions are NLW MSS Peniarth 21 and 23, and the Cleopatra *Brut* (*CBB*). For fuller discussions on the Welsh *brutiau* see Edmund Reis, 'The Welsh Versions of Geoffrey of Monmouth's *Historia*', *WHR*, 4 (1968), 97-127; *BB* xxiv-xxxvi; Brynley F. Roberts, 'Testunau Hanes Cymraeg Canol'; TRh 274-301, 'Historical Writing', Guide, 244-7. For the so-called *Brut Tysilio* see Brynley F. Roberts, *Brut Tysilio* (Abertawe, 1980); and for Geoffrey's influence in Wales see *BB*, Appendix, 55-74; 'Ymagweddau at *Brut y Brenhinedd* hyd 1890', *B*, 24 (1971), 122-38.

40. *TYP* 365-7. See also p. 82, and ch.3, n.31 above.

41. On the Welsh personal names see Brynley F. Roberts, 'The Treatment of Personal Names in the Early Welsh Versions of *Historia Regum Britanniae*', *B*, 25 (1973), 274-90.

42. Cf. *CLILl* 1.

43. *TYP* 454.

44. Examples are the circumstances of the death of Malgo, quotations from triads, Dubricius's exile in Bardsey, and the name 'given by the poets' to Severus's wall. See also TRh 291-2, *BB* xxxiii-iv.

5

THE MERLIN LEGEND AND THE WELSH TRADITION OF PROPHECY

A. O. H. Jarman

THOUGH linked together in the Middle Ages, the legend of Merlin and the Welsh prophetic tradition were originally distinct and separate. Similarly, despite the inclusion of the legend in the Arthurian complex in the twelfth century, no such association existed at any earlier period. It was in his *Historia Regum Britanniae*, completed *c.* 1138, that Geoffrey of Monmouth transformed the legendary Welsh seer Myrddin into the internationally famous Merlin, wizard as well as vaticinator, who played a crucial role in bringing about the conception of Arthur and was prominent in later Arthurian story. Thus, both the Merlin legend and its associated prophecies may be divided into pre-Geoffrey and post-Geoffrey phases, with the proviso that manifestations of the first phase often continued after Geoffrey's lifetime and uninfluenced by him.

The legend of Myrddin, as found in early Welsh verse, embodied the primitive motif of the Wild Man of the Woods. The roots of the theme extended back in time as far as the Babylonian Epic of Gilgamesh and the Indian tale of Rishyasninga, which included legends of hairy anchorites or hermits leading solitary lives in the desert.[1] A notable example of a Wild Man was Nebuchadnezzar who, driven from the society of men as a punishment for his arrogance and pride, 'did eat grass as oxen, and his body was wet with the dew of heaven, till his hairs were grown like eagles' feathers, and his nails like birds' claws'.[2] A religious or penitential ingredient was usually present in the early Asiatic as well as the later European tales embodying the theme, and this was also a feature of the legends of wild men found in Wales, Scotland and Ireland. There was, however, no direct link between the tales preserved in Celtic sources and those found in eastern or Asiatic countries.

We do not possess a prose version of the Myrddin legend in Middle Welsh, but a general idea of its content may be deduced from a number of allusions found in half a dozen medieval poems. Combined with supplementary material from the Scottish and Irish versions of the tale these make possible a feasible reconstruction both of its main outline and probable development, though many details remain obscure. The poems are (1) *Yr Afallennau* ('The Apple-trees'); (2) *Yr Oianau* ('The Greetings'); (3)

Ymddiddan Myrddin a Thaliesin ('The Dialogue of Myrddin and Taliesin'); (4)
Cyfoesi Myrddin a Gwenddydd ei Chwaer ('The Conversation of Myrddin and his
Sister Gwenddydd'); (5) *Gwasgargerdd Fyrddin yn y Bedd* ('The Diffused Song of
Myrddin in the Grave'); and (6) *Peirian Faban* ('Commanding Youth'). Texts of the
first three are found in the Black Book of Carmarthen, written *c.* 1250, and of the
remaining three in manuscripts dating from the two succeeding centuries. All the
poems contain matter which is older, and in many cases considerably older, than the
dates of the written texts.[3]

The content of these poems may be divided into (a) passages of a legendary
character, and (b) prophecies. Though purporting to be almost entirely uttered by
Myrddin himself, the legendary matter which they include is undoubtedly older than
the prophetic. The proportion of legend and prophecy, respectively, found in each
stanza and each poem is variable. Thus, in *Yr Afallennau* some 50 lines are devoted
to the legend and 38 to prophecy, while in *Yr Oianau* only about 80 out of 230 lines
contain legendary matter. In *Yr Afallennau* three consecutive stanzas, totalling 31
lines, are completely free of vaticination and may legitimately be regarded as the
oldest existing document of the Myrddin legend. The Black Book text of the poem
consists of ten stanzas, each commencing with an address to the 'sweet-apple tree'
which Myrddin describes as growing 'in a glade', or 'on a river-bank' or 'hidden in the
forest of Celyddon'. He declares that, after the fall of his former suzerain
Gwenddolau in the Battle of Arfderydd, he has suffered hardship for fifty years,
'wandering with madness and madmen' in the Caledonian wilds. We gather that he
himself lost his reason in the battle and joined the company of the *gwyllon* or 'wild
men', but that previously he had been a warrior of note, wearing a torque of gold. In
one stanza, after stating that the apple-tree's 'peculiar power hides it from the lords
of Rhydderch', he appears to be living in fear of persecution from that quarter. He
then mentions a certain Gwasawg, describing him as a 'supporter of Rhydderch', who
had been 'angered' by some obscure event and to whom he (i.e. Myrddin) is 'hateful'.
Gwasawg's function in the story is unclear, but it seems permissible to speculate that
Rhydderch had been the enemy leader who defeated both Gwenddolau and Myrddin
at the Battle of Arfderydd. A further complication is added by Myrddin's expression
of regret that his end had not come before he became guilty of the death of the son
of Gwenddydd. He further complains that Gwenddydd, whom the *Cyfoesi* names as
his sister, 'does not now love or greet' him. In *Yr Afallennau* a moral dimension is
thus present, perhaps associated with the cause of the fateful battle and Myrddin's
subsequent and possibly retributive suffering. At the end of the three exclusively
legendary stanzas he utters the prayer of the penitent that, 'having endured sickness
and grief in the Forest of Celyddon', he be 'received into bliss by the Lord of Hosts'.[4]

Yr Oianau is probably a later poem than *Yr Afallennau*. Each of its twenty-five stanzas commences with a greeting to the 'little pig' which was Myrddin's companion in the forest. A similar greeting occurring in a stanza of *Yr Afallennau* may initially have suggested a formulaic model for the later poem. Myrddin seeks to imbue the pigling with his own feelings, uttering dire warnings that in their wild state both face the same perils. Thus, the pigling is advised to burrow its lair 'in a hidden place in the woodlands' and to avoid morning drowsiness lest it be obliged to flee before the trained hunting-dogs of Rhydderch. The latter, to whose name the epithet *Hael* (the 'Generous') is here, as elsewhere, attached, was clearly considered to be the oppressor of both wild man and wild beast. A touch of humour is sometimes apparent, as when Myrddin avers that his companion is 'a rude bed-fellow' with 'sharp claws'. A bitter reference to Rhydderch, however, contrasts his life of opulent feasting with the hardships endured by Myrddin among the snows and forest wolves. A stanza mourning Myrddin's former overlord Gwenddolau, now lying 'still beneath the brown earth', declares that in his day he was the 'chief of the kings of the North, the greatest in generosity'.

The *Cyfoesi* is a poem of some hundred and thirty stanzas composed mainly in the three-line *englyn* metre. It consists principally of a series of consecutive prophecies, uttered by Myrddin in alternate stanzas responding to questions by his sister Gwenddydd, which span British and Welsh history for a period of six or seven hundred years from the late sixth century onwards. Various sections of the poem are probably of varying dates, but no part of it can be older than the commencement of the *englyn* tradition, which first comes to light in the ninth century. A number of allusions to the matter of the Myrddin legend and its background occur among the prophecies. The early northern kings Rhydderch Hael, Morgant Fawr and Urien are mentioned, and two stanzas refer to the 'slaying of Gwenddolau in the blood-shedding of Arfderydd'. Myrddin describes himself as 'bitter' or 'wrathful' in consequence of that battle, and asserts that his 'reason has gone with the wild men of the mountain'. In some particulars the legendary content of the poem differs from that of *Yr Afallennau* and *Yr Oianau*. Although Gwenddydd appears to refer to an estrangement between herself and her brother, she now shows concern for his well-being, both physical and spiritual, and addresses him in terms of respect and honour. In the third stanza she describes him as 'my *Llallogan Fyrddin*, sage, prophet', and a little later as 'my renowned *Llallawg*, noble in the hosts'.[5] One stanza refers to Myrddin as the 'son of Morfryn', while another mentions the 'whelps' (i.e. sons, progeny) of Morfryn. Two stanzas appear to contain the names of these whelps, who must be presumed to have been Myrddin's brothers: Morgenau, Morial, Morien, Mordaf. The possible significance of these names is considered below.

The bulk of the *Gwasgargerdd* consists of prophecies but at its commencement Myrddin, purporting to speak 'in the grave' and again described as the 'son of Morfryn', asserts that formerly he drank wine in the presence of 'lords powerful in war'. There are also obscure references to Gwasawg, Gwenddydd and 'the wild men of the mountain'. As Myrddin's death had been contemplated at the end of *Y Cyfoesi*, the *Gwasgargerdd* may be regarded as a sequel to that poem, particularly as it immediately succeeds it in the Red Book of Hergest. *Peirian Faban* is a vaticinatory poem found in a fifteenth-century copy and gives prominence to the name of the Scottish Dalriadic king Aedán Mac Gabráin (Aeddan ap Gafran), who was a contemporary of Rhydderch Hael and is believed to have enjoyed close relations with the British kingdom of Strathclyde. It also mentions Myrddin ap Morfryn, Gwenddolau, Rhydderch, Gwasawg, and Gwenddydd.

The contents of the *Ymddiddan* set it somewhat apart from the other five poems. It may be conjecturally dated *c.* 1100, if not earlier, and contains two distinct parts. Of its total of thirty-eight lines the first twenty-two treat of a subject unconnected with the Myrddin legend, namely a tradition of a battle fought by the men of Dyfed against an invading host led by Maelgwn (presumably Maelgwn Gwynedd, though this is not stated) at some time during the first half of the sixth century. In their alternate comments on the battle Myrddin seems to be speaking for the men of Dyfed and Taliesin for Maelgwn and his followers. Myrddin names heroes, attested in Dyfed tradition, with whom Maelgwn, who is believed to have died *c.* 547, was probably contemporary. In its twenty-third line, however, the poem turns from the affairs of Dyfed to those of northern Britain and refers to the Battle of Arfderydd, recorded in the *Annales Cambriae* under 573. Lines 23-34 appear to envisage the event as occurring in the future and mention traditional north-British figures such as Cynfelyn and the 'sons of Eliffer'. We thus have the incongruity that Myrddin, speaking in Dyfed before 547, is made to utter a prophetic description of the northern battle, fought a generation later, at which according to his legend he himself became mad and acquired prophetic powers. He does not, however, refer to his own mental state or mention Rhydderch, Gwenddolau, Gwenddydd, Gwasawg, the apple-tree or the pigling. The legendary content of the poem is thus tenuous, but in its two final couplets Myrddin asserts that at the Battle of Arfderydd sevenscore men of rank 'lapsed into madness' and perished in the forest of Celyddon. Here he uses a verb in the past tense to record the event.[6]

Though we lack a medieval prose version of the Myrddin legend, there are indications in the Welsh Triads that the Battle of Arfderydd was the subject of a saga, whether oral or written, in which Myrddin's overlord Gwenddolau figured prominently. The Triads contain brief synopses, albeit sometimes quite detailed and circumstantial, of episodes in tales which have not been preserved in a more expanded form. Thus, the triad of the *Three Faithful War-bands* tells us that the war-band of Gwenddolau 'continued the struggle at Arfderydd for a fortnight and a month after their lord was slain'. This statement is clearly sympathetic towards Gwenddolau but another triad, that of the *Three Men who Performed the Three Fortunate Assassinations*, is hostile. It asserts that 'Gall son of Dysgyfdawd slew the two birds of Gwenddolau, and there was a yoke of gold on them; they ate two corpses of the Cymry for their dinner, and two for their supper.' The significance of the reference to the 'Cymry' in this triad is difficult to assess, particularly as Gwenddolau's protégé, Myrddin, had by the Middle Ages come to be regarded as the prophet of the Cymry. Whether or not Gwenddolau was originally an historical person, the triad shows him as a central figure in a bizarre tale which has been lost. Another event connected with the Battle of Arfderydd is recounted in some detail in the triad of the *Three Horses which Carried the Three Horse-Burdens*. This states that 'Cornan (or Corvan), horse of the sons of Eliffer, bore Gwrgi and Peredur on its back, and Dunawd the Stout and Cynfelyn the Leprous to look upon the battle-fog (of the host of) Gwenddolau (in) Arfderydd; and no one overtook it save Dinogad son of Cynan Garwyn upon Swift Eager Roan, and he incurred dishonour on account of that until today.' The narrative background of this scenario eludes us, but all the characters named belonged to northern Britain with the exception of Dinogad son of Cynan, ruler of Powys. Yet another triad lists the Battle of Arfderydd as one of the *Three Futile Battles* owing to its having been fought 'on account of the lark's nest'; it adds the explanation that the description 'futile' referred to the 'barren' or 'worthless' causes of the battles. It has been conjectured that the reference to the 'lark's nest' reflected a tradition of a sixth-century dispute concerning the possession of Caerlaverock ('Lark's Fort') some twenty miles west of the probable site of Arfderydd to the north of Carlisle (cf. below, p. 125). It is to be noted, however, that the tale of Myrddin and his madness in the Caledonian forest is nowhere mentioned in the Triads. There can be no doubt that at one time there existed a considerable saga concerning the Battle of Arfderydd, in which Myrddin can be presumed to have participated. At some stage the material associated with him must have separated from the main body of the saga and developed as an independent tale which, however, was not recorded in the Triads.[7]

The Scottish versions of the tale of the wild man dovetail well with that of Myrddin and add considerably to our knowledge of the legend. A passage in the twelfth-century *Life of St Kentigern* by Joceline of Furness records the presence at the court of King 'Rederech' (Rhydderch) of a certain *homo fatuus* named Laloecen or Laloicen who, on the death of the saint, correctly prophesied the deaths within the year of the king himself as well as another of the great ones of the land. This Laloecen appears again in two longer tales preserved in a fifteenth-century copy which probably derived from an earlier twelfth-century *Life* of St Kentigern than that by Joceline. Here Laloecen's name takes the form *Lailoken* (or *Lailochen*) and the tales may be called respectively *Lailoken and Kentigern* and *Lailoken and Meldred*. In the first, and longer, of the two Lailoken is portrayed not as a court fool or jester, as in Joceline's *Life*, but as a naked, hairy madman whom Kentigern met while praying in a lonely wood. Though completely destitute, the madman was said by some to have been Merlin (*Merlynus*), 'an extraordinary prophet of the British', but this, the narrator adds, 'is not certain'. On being questioned by Kentigern, Lailoken accepted responsibility for his sad condition, stating that he had been 'the cause of the slaughter of all the dead who fell in the battle . . . which took place in the plain lying between Lidel and Carwannok'. At that battle the heavens above him opened and a voice from above spoke to him thus: 'Lailoken, Lailoken, because you alone are responsible for the blood of all these dead men, you alone will bear the punishment for the misdeeds of all. For you will be given over to the angels of Satan, and until the day of your death you will have communion with the creatures of the wood.' He then beheld a vision in the sky, amid 'a brightness too great for human senses to endure', consisting of 'numberless martial battalions in the heaven like flashing lightning, holding in their hands fiery lances and glittering spears which they shook most fiercely' at him. Thereupon he was seized by an evil spirit and driven to the forest. Having told his story to the saint, Lailoken leapt from his presence and fled to the deepest woods. He later appeared again on several occasions uttering obscure prophecies, to which however little or no credence was given. Then one day he interrupted the celebration of mass by Kentigern demanding that he be given the viaticum, as on that day he was destined to die a threefold death. On being questioned, he explained that this would come about through cudgelling, piercing, and drowning. After some hesitation the saint acceded to his demand and gave him the Sacrament. Later that day he was attacked by certain shepherds of King Meldred, who beat him to death. Simultaneously his body fell into the River Tweed, where it was pierced by a sharp stake and his head was immersed in the water. Thus the prophecy of a threefold death was fulfilled. After receiving the Sacrament Lailoken had also prophesied the deaths within the year of 'the most outstanding king of Britain, and the most holy of bishops, and the most noble of lords'. This corresponds closely, though not in every particular, to Laloecen's prophecy in Joceline's *Life* of the saint.[8]

Lailoken and Meldred is a tale about an event which antedated the madman's final meeting with the saint by several years. Lailoken had been captured by King

Meldred and held in his fort of Dunmeller. One day, seeing the queen entering the court with a leaf on her head, he laughed loudly, but refused to explain his laughter unless promised his freedom. He also prophesied that he would die a threefold death and requested burial 'not far from the spot where Pausayl burn falls into the River Tweed', adding that when the confluence of the two rivers came up to his tomb at that spot 'the marshal of the British race will defeat the foreign race'. After receiving a promise of liberty he informed the king that the queen had committed adultery in the garden and that the leaf, caught up by her shawl, had betrayed her. The murder of Lailoken, described in detail in the other tale, is here presented as an act of revenge plotted by the queen. The mad prophet was buried at the place of his choice 'some thirty miles from the city of Glasgow'.

The statement at the beginning of *Lailoken and Kentigern* that Lailoken was said by some to be Merlin was no doubt associated with the activities of Geoffrey of Monmouth, as will be seen below. It has been argued that the Lailoken tales had at one time been a part of the 'Herbertian' *Life* of St Kentigern, so called owing to its having been written at the instance of Herbert, Bishop of Glasgow (1147-64). The reference to Merlin was probably added to the text at a later date, though the composition of the *Life* may be presumed to have post-dated the publication of Geoffrey's *Historia* (c. 1138) by a brief period. Joceline's new *Life*, which is dated c. 1180, is without the reference.[9] It has, however, been shown that Joceline 'watered down' the legendary material concerning Lailoken and used it in a much truncated form, shorn of its primitive 'wildness', and somewhat mutilated the prophecy of the threefold death by making Laloecen utter it after, and not before, the death of Kentigern.[10] There can be no doubt of the ultimate identity of the Lailoken of the Scottish sources and the Myrddin of the Welsh poems. It is equally clear that each had existed separately and independently in Scottish and Welsh tradition respectively for several centuries before their relationship was perceived in the post-Geoffrey period. The historical and geographical setting of the Welsh legends of Arfderydd and Myrddin was exclusively northern and it must be assumed that these tales migrated to Wales together with much other early material at some time between the sixth century and the Middle Ages. During these centuries the tales also continued to be transmitted and to develop in the territory of their origin.

The Welsh poems admittedly lack some of the features of the Scottish legend. These include the heavenly vision, the voice which spoke to Lailoken, the association with a saint, the tale of the queen's adultery and the prophecy of the threefold death. King Meldred's name does not occur in the poems (or in any other known source). On the other hand, Gwenddolau, Gwasawg and Gwenddydd are absent from the Scottish legend and, unlike Myrddin, Lailoken does not address the apple-tree or the pigling, nor does he contrast his abject condition in the forest with his former status as a warrior of note.   However, both Myrddin and Lailoken are wild men of the woods who belong to the same historical and geographical milieu, and suffer loss of reason in battle.   Both are burdened with moral guilt and both Laloecen in Joceline's narrative and Myrddin in the poems have associations, albeit greatly differing, with Rhydderch, the sixth-century ruler of Strathclyde whose historicity is confirmed by an allusion to him in the near-contemporary *Life of St Columba* by Adomnán.[11]   The name Lailoken has a parallel Welsh form *Llallogan* which, as we have seen, is coupled in the *Cyfoesi* with the name 'Myrddin' and must have migrated to Wales with the tale from the North.   And as a consequence of their mental derangement both Lailoken and Myrddin possess the power of prophecy.

In his *Itinerarium Kambriae* Giraldus Cambrensis (*c.* 1146-1223) stated that Merlin lost his reason when, having taken up his position in battle, he saw a monstrous sight in the heavens above him and fled to spend the rest of his life in the forest.[12]   In part this compensates for the absence of the heavenly vision from the other Welsh sources, but it must be remembered that Giraldus was a man of wide-ranging cultural contacts and we cannot be sure that a Welsh source lay behind the statement.   It certainly did not derive from the Welsh poems as we know them. The identity of the Welsh Arfderydd with the site of the battle at which Lailoken was said to have lost his reason was convincingly demonstrated by W.F. Skene in 1865/6, when he was able to show that Arfderydd could safely be located at Arthuret, near Longtown, some eight miles north of Carlisle in the 'plain lying between Lidel and Carwannok'.   The second of these two names, alternatively Carwanolow, he identified with the modern Carwinley, which he very plausibly derived from *Caer Wenddolau*, 'Gwenddolau's fort'.[13]   The causes of the Battle of Arfderydd, so famous in later Welsh tradition, can only be a matter of speculation. Skene regarded it as an encounter between 'advancing Christianity and the departing paganism', represented respectively by Rhydderch and Gwenddolau, but this view is not now thought to be well based.   It is, however, undeniable that both Joceline's *Life of St Kentigern* and the very much earlier *Life of St Columba* depict Rhydderch as a ruler well disposed to the Church and the saints, and that the first stanza of *Yr Oianau* refers to 'Rhydderch Hael protector of the Faith'.   This last description may well reflect an early tradition preserved in Wales. The Welsh poems do not at any point specifically state that Rhydderch fought at the Battle of Arfderydd, but they certainly give the impression that he was the victor by registering Myrddin's subsequent fear of him and his men.   Skene's argument that the pagan interest in the battle was represented by Gwenddolau was based mainly on allusions in the Triads, particularly that to his man-devouring birds.[14]

A thirteenth-century copy of the *Annales Cambriae* states that the Battle of Arfderydd was fought 'between the sons of Eliffer and Gwenddolau son of Ceidio; in which battle Gwenddolau fell [and] Merlin became mad'.[15] These statements, however, are later additions to the original entry, which merely read *bellum armterid* ('the Battle of Arfderydd') under the year 573. The references to Gwenddolau and Merlin are confirmed by the Welsh poems *Yr Afallennau*, *Yr Oianau* and the *Cyfoesi*, but these sources do not mention the 'sons of Eliffer'. According to early genealogies the 'sons' bore the names Gwrgi and Peredur, and the oldest text of the *Annales Cambriae* records their deaths in 580. As we have seen, the triad of the *Three Horse-burdens* tells us that both were borne on their horse's back to witness the battle-fog (or 'steaming') of Gwenddolau's host at Arfderydd, and *Ymddiddan Myrddin a Thaliesin* asserts in a rhetorical passage that, not two, but 'the seven sons of Eliffer . . . will not avoid seven spears in their seven battle-sections' during the encounter. These may be the sources of the entry in the late text of the *Annales Cambriae* concerning the Battle of Arfderydd, but as historical evidence they must be disregarded. In 1975 Dr Molly Miller interpreted the situation leading to the battle as a conflict among members of the Coeling (i.e. descendants of Coel Hen), resulting in the overthrow of Gwenddolau by his enemies, who included Gwrgi and Peredur.[16] It is unfortunate, however, that the interpretation leans heavily on sources such as the Triads, which are legendary rather than historical in character. The allusions to Rhydderch in the poems are also saga material, but as he was a descendant of Dyfnwal Hen, and thus not a member of the Coeling, he has no place in Dr Miller's scenario. Dr Miller was not prepared to accept the Welsh Myrddin poems as a continuation of the Lailoken tradition, but her argument must fail in view of the indisputable correspondence between the forms *Lailoken* and *Llallogan* and Skene's success in locating Arfderydd at Arthuret. Modern lexicographers have assigned meanings such as 'friend' or 'twin brother' to *llallogan* and *llallawg*, supposing them to be based on *llall*, 'other'. Basil Clarke, however, has suggested that a clue to the meaning of 'Lailoken' may possibly be found in the name of a Gaulish village known as *Laliacensis* after the family of Lollius Urbicus, for three years Governor of Britain (139-42), who was associated in particular with the 'pacification' of the North and the building of the Antonine Wall. A Romano-British estate settlement perpetuating his name could have provided the basis for the Cumbric form *Lailoken*, and the Welsh *Llallogan*. It is conceivable, Clarke argues, that a person bearing this name fled from the field of Arfderydd and was therefore the 'Merlin-original'. Such a person might even have been a follower or retainer of Gwenddolau (if we accept the latter's historicity), and in due course his memory could have attracted to itself the additional legendary matter found in the Lailoken tales and the Welsh poems. All these possibilities are, of course, purely speculative.[17]

Versions of the Wild Man legend in medieval Irish literature offer numerous parallels to those in the Welsh and Scottish sources. The Irish wild man was known as *gelt* and his condition as *geltacht*. These words correspond in meaning to *gwyllt*, 'wild; mad', in Myrddin *Wyllt* and *gwylleith*, 'madness', in *Yr Afallennau*. An account of the *gelt* is found in the Irish *Mirabilia* in the thirteenth-century Old Norse text, *Kongs Skuggsjo* or *Speculum Regale*. This states that when battle is joined between two hosts

> It happens . . . that cowardly men run wild and lose their wits from the dread and fear which seize them. And then they run into a wood away from other men, and live there like wild beasts, and shun the meeting of men like wild beasts. And it is said of these men that when they have lived in the woods in that condition for twenty years, then feathers grow on their bodies as on birds, whereby their bodies are protected against frost and cold, but the feathers are not so large that they may fly like birds. Yet their swiftness is said to be so great that other men cannot approach them, and greyhounds just as little as men. For these men run along the trees almost as swiftly as monkeys or squirrels.[18]

It will be noted that the passage gives cowardice or fear in battle as the cause of the *gelt*'s flight to the forest, rather than a heavenly vision and an imputation of guilt, as in the tale of Lailoken. The Welsh poems do not specify the cause of Myrddin's madness, though they make him admit his responsibility for the death of the son of Gwenddydd and dwell on his distress at the fall of his former lord Gwenddolau. Swiftness of movement is not attributed to Myrddin, but that it was originally a feature of the Welsh tradition is suggested by a passage in the *Gorchan* of Cynfelyn, a poem preserved in the Book of Aneirin, which states that 'long-striding horses galloped . . . swift as the movement of the wild men (*gwyllion*) over the grassy plain'.[19] Lailoken also, after he had received the blessing of Kentigern, is said to have 'rushed away like a wild goat breaking out of the hunter's noose and happily seeking the undergrowth of the wilderness'.[20] Myrddin and Lailoken have no feathers to protect them against the cold. Admittedly, Lailoken is 'hairy', but Myrddin, enduring snow up to his hips and icicles in his hair, complains that his cloak is thin and insufficient.[21]

The outstanding *gelt* in Irish literature was Suibhne, son of Colman Cuar, a legendary Ulster kinglet whose story is found as part of a cycle of tales concerning Domnall son of Aed, High King of Ireland. Two tales, 'The Feast of Dún na nGéd' and 'The Battle of Moira' (*Mag Rath*), give us a fictional account of the causes and events of the historical Battle of Moira, fought in 637 near Lurgan in Co. Down.[22] These tales relate that Congal Claen, King of Ulster, had rebelled against the High King but was defeated by him, and that Suibhne, a vassal of Congal, became mad during the battle and fled to the forest. A separate tale, 'The Frenzy of Suibhne' (*Buile Shuibhne*) tells in circumstantial detail of this occurrence and Suibhne's subsequent career.[23] The Battle of Moira clearly corresponds to that of Arfderydd in the Welsh legend, and the relationship of Suibhne to Congal and Domnall, respectively, resembles that of Myrddin to Gwenddolau and Rhydderch in the Welsh poems. The story of Suibhne was not originally a part of the saga of Moira, but an added subsidiary theme which later developed as a separate tale. It has already been suggested that a similar relationship existed between the legend of Myrddin and the more widely-embracing saga of Arfderydd. Originally separate, the legend was probably incorporated in the saga before hiving off again as a distinct tale (cf. p. 121).

At a feast given by Domnall, Congal Claen considered himself to have been grossly insulted when a silver dish and goose-egg placed before him suddenly changed into a wooden dish and a hen-egg. The incident was one of the contributory causes of the Battle of Moira (*Mag Ráth*) and recalls the Welsh triad of the *Three Futile Battles*, thus designated owing to the 'futile' causes for which they were fought (cf. p. 121). The text of the *Buile Shuibhne*, in its present form, has been dated to the twelfth century, but references to the tradition of Suibhne occur in the ninth, if not earlier.[24] The tale records that before the Battle of Moira, having thrown St Ronán's psalter into a lake, Suibhne had slain one of the saint's clerics and cast a spear against the saint himself. In response to these outrages Ronán uttered a curse against Suibhne, predicting that he would die by a spear. The incident of the psalter invites comparison with a poem in the Black Book of Carmarthen in which a certain Ysgolan asserts that he has 'drowned a gift book', presumably Church property, for which he has been condemned to severe penance.[25] The slaying of the cleric is closely paralleled by the deeds of homicide admitted by Lailoken and Myrddin.

The *Buile Shuibhne* gives a colourful account of Suibhne's derangement, which it attributes ultimately to 'Ronán's curse'. As its immediate cause, however, it mentions 'three mighty shouts' uttered by the opposing armies:

> Now, when Suibhne heard these great cries together with their sounds and reverberations in the clouds of Heaven and in the vault of the firmament, he looked up, whereupon turbulence, and darkness, and fury, and giddiness, and frenzy, and flight, unsteadiness, restlessness, and unquiet filled him, likewise disgust with every place in which he used to be and desire for every place which he had not reached. His fingers were palsied, his feet trembled, his heart beat quick, his senses were overcome, his sight was distorted, his weapons fell naked from his hands, so that through Ronan's curse he went, like any bird of the air, in madness and imbecility.[26]

Though Suibhne is said to have 'looked up', it will be noted that there is no mention here of a heavenly vision. The omission may, or may not, be attributable to a lacuna in the text. A much expanded fourteenth-century version of the 'Battle of Moira', however, asserts that

> huge flickering horrible aerial phantoms rose up, so that they were in cursed, commingled crowds tormenting him; and in dense, rustling, clamorous, left-turning hordes, without ceasing; and in dismal, regular, aerial, storm-shrieking, hovering, fiend-like hosts constantly in motion, shrieking and howling as they hovered about them [i.e. about both armies] in every direction . . . so that from the uproar of the battle, the frantic pranks of the demons and the clashing of arms, . . . the noble Suibhne was filled and intoxicated with tremor, horror, panic, dismay, fickleness, unsteadiness, fear, flightiness, giddiness, terror and imbecility; so that there was not a joint of a member of him from head to foot which was not converted into a confused, shaking mass, from the effect of fear, and the panic of dismay.[27]

It is further stated that Suibhne's 'very soul fluttered with hallucination and with many and various phantasms'. Whether these spectres, or 'demons', are to be understood as emanating from Suibhne's inner self, or were external to him as in the Lailoken legend, is not completely clear. This recension of the tale is described by Dillon as 'a late romance composed from earlier sources', but it must remain doubtful whether Suibhne's 'phantasms' were the product of the fourteenth-century writer's imagination, or had their basis in earlier tradition.

In his madness Suibhne acquired the power of levitation and, having fled from the battle, settled on the branches of a yew-tree. Subsequently he wandered throughout Ireland, but spent much of his time thus perched on trees. When in this position on one occasion, he was surrounded by Domnall and his men, the victors of Moira, who endeavoured to persuade him to descend. Not wishing, however, to be captured by his former enemy, he 'ascended from the tree towards the rainclouds of the firmament' and fled. The incident may be used to elucidate the passage in the fifth stanza of *Yr Afallennau*, which asserts that the 'peculiar power' of Myrddin's apple-tree 'hides it from the men of Rhydderch' and adds that there was 'a crowd by its trunk, a host around it', for whom 'it would be a treasure'.[28] As other references in the poem describe the apple-tree as 'hidden in the forest of Celyddon', we may reasonably conclude that it possessed a quality of invisibility which it was able to impart to Myrddin. There are no indications that the Welsh wild men were capable of levitation, apart perhaps from the implied suggestion in the reference to the swiftness of their movement in the *Gorchan* of Cynfelyn (p. 126). Invisibility, as an attribute of the apple-tree, and a protection for Myrddin, could have replaced the power of levitation, if the latter had existed as an early feature of the legend but had afterwards been lost. It is clear, however, that the correspondence in detail between Suibhne on his yew-tree and Myrddin on his apple-tree, both encircled by their former enemies, is an indication of a close relationship between the Irish and Welsh forms of the legend at a not too early date.

Suibhne spent many years wandering throughout Ireland and uttering nature poems, which comprise much of the *Buile Shuibhne*. Once or twice he was captured, regained his sanity, and re-established relations with his wife Eorann, who had been cohabiting with Guaire, a successor to Suibhne in his former kingdom. His mental powers failed him again, however, and he returned to the wilds. Later he received the protection of St Moling, who gave him the Sacrament, and whose role at the end of the story resembles that of Kentigern in the tale of Lailoken. Then, following on Ronán's curse and fulfilling his prediction, Moling's herdsman, suspecting Suibhne of adultery with his wife, speared him to death.

A curious episode in Suibhne's career of wandering was a visit which he made to the 'land of the Britons'.[29] After passing the king's fortress he came to a great wood, where he encountered another madman, similar to himself, lamenting and wailing. The British madman explained that he was known as Fer Caille ('Man of the Woods') but added that his name was Alladhán. He also expressed fear of being seized by men of the king's household and enquired whether Suibhne was one of them. After receiving a reassurance on this score he described himself as 'the son of a landholder' and stated that he had lost his reason in a battle when 'two kings were contending for the sovereignty of this country'. He attributed his derangement to his own action in putting *geasa* ('taboos') on each member of his side prohibiting them from coming to the battle 'except they were clothed in silk, so that they might be conspicuous beyond all for pomp and pride'. The hosts, however, gave 'three shouts of malediction' against Alladhán, which sent him fleeing. Suibhne related how the curse of Ronán had driven him to madness at the Battle of Moira, and the two became friends and lived together for a year. Then Alladhán announced that the end of his life had come and foretold his imminent death by drowning. Suibhne also prophesied the manner of his own death, whereupon he returned to Ireland and Alladhán was drowned as he had predicted.

It would be a plausible comment that this is the record of a meeting between Suibhne and Lailoken, particularly if the length of the period separating the reputed dates of the Battles of Arfderydd (573) and Moira (637) be disregarded. According to Clarke Suibhne met Alladhán near Dumbarton.[30] This was the site of the fortress of Rhydderch Hael, and the fear expressed by Alladhán of his capture by men of the king's household closely resembles Myrddin's reference in *Yr Afallennau* to the followers of Rhydderch who have encircled his apple-tree. The name *Alladhán* has been explained as 'possibly a derivative of *allaidh*, wild', and therefore roughly equivalent in meaning to *ge(i)lt* and *gwyllt*, but Professor Carney has expressed the view that 'the name rests ultimately upon that of *Lailoken (Llallogan)'.*[31]   This suggestion is also made by Clarke, with the further point that Alladhán's description of himself as 'the son of a landholder' may be linked to the possible connection between Lailoken and Lollius Urbicus.[32]   The reason given by Alladhán for his flight from the battle differs from the causes of madness in the cases of Suibhne, Lailoken and Myrddin, and lacks both the heavenly vision and the moral dimension.   Alladhán prophesies the time and manner of his own death, as does Lailoken, and the element of drowning is common to the deaths of both.   There can be little doubt that the Alladhán episode in the *Buile Shuibhne* is a reflex of the tale of the north-British wild man.   According to Carney the entire theme of Suibhne's madness was borrowed by the Irish from northern Britain in the eighth century,[33] but Jackson has favoured the contrary view that the borrowing was by the British from the Goidels of Scottish Dál Riada.[34]   The theme of the wild man may have existed independently in both Irish and British/Welsh tradition from early times but, as has been noted, the similarities between the various tales are evidence of a close relationship in the historical period rather than of totally separate development in each individual country at a remoter date.   On balance, the correspondences between the Alladhán incident and the north-British and Welsh forms of the legend would appear to weigh in favour of the view that the Irish were the borrowers.

We come now to the intervention of Geoffrey of Monmouth in the development of the Merlin legend. Geoffrey (1090/1100-1155), who lived through the entire first half of the twelfth century,[35] is believed to have belonged to a Norman/Breton community settled at Monmouth, but by 1129 was in Oxford where he composed his *Historia.*[36]   It has also been conjectured that he spent some time in south-eastern Wales in association with the see of Llandaf.[37]   In 1152 he was consecrated Bishop of St Asaph but probably did not visit his bishopric, which at that time was subject to Welsh rather than Norman domination.   In his *Historia* he purported to give an account of the history of the Britons from the time of Brutus, over a thousand years BC, to that of the last 'British' king, Cadwaladr, in the seventh century AD.   A section towards the end of the work on the reign and conquests of Arthur in the early sixth century brings the history to a climax and constitutes one of the fundamental documents of the Arthurian legend.

Shortly before the Arthurian section Geoffrey told the story of Vortigern, the mid-fifth-century British king who, having fled from the Saxons to the fastness of Snowdon, gave orders for the building of a fortress or tower. Whatever the masons built during one day, however, disappeared into the earth by the next. Vortigern's magicians advised him that the tower's foundations could only be rendered secure if a fatherless youth were found and slain, and his blood sprinkled on the stones. Such a youth, named Merlin (*Merlinus*), was discovered at Carmarthen (*Kaermerdin*). His mother was the daughter of a king of Dyfed (*Demetia*) who, living with the nuns at a local convent, had been impregnated by an incubus demon. He was thus a 'fatherless' youth who qualified for the role of sacrificial victim demanded by the magicians. He was also a 'wonder-child', the offspring of an earthly mother and a superhuman father, and his powers were manifested when he was brought to Vortigern's court. There he confounded the magicians by showing that the subsidence was caused by an underground pool at the bottom of which were two stone vessels, each containing a dragon, one white and one red. The two fought each other with varying fortunes and Merlin, whose name is here given as *Ambrosius Merlinus*, explained that they respectively represented the Saxon and British peoples. He then uttered a long series of obscure prophecies which, under the title *Prophetiae Merlini*, enjoyed a considerable vogue as a work of literature in its own right during the later centuries of the Middle Ages, and which had been separately circulated some three years before the publication of the *Historia*.[38]

This tale was not the product of Geoffrey's own imagination but had been lifted bodily by him from the ninth-century collection of early British and Welsh saga material and semi-historical traditions known as the *Historia Brittonum*.[39] Geoffrey reproduced the essentials of the tale but told it in his own words, with contractions and expansions of his source-material here and there, including the prophecies added at the end. He made two changes in the story itself, however, which gave it a completely new orientation. According to the *Historia Brittonum* the fatherless youth was called Ambrosius, a name which recalls that of Ambrosius Aurelianus, a British ruler contemporary with Vortigern. It has been argued that the two were respectively leaders of pro-Roman and anti-Roman factions among the Britons and that the story of the confounding of the king's magicians by the youth preserves a memory of the conflict between them.[40] Geoffrey, however, twice referred to the youth as *Ambrosius Merlinus*, and once as *Merlinus qui et Ambrosius dicebatur*,[41] but more usually simply as *Merlinus*. There was no warrant for this in his source, but henceforth the central figure in the story of Vortigern's tower would invariably be known as 'Merlin', albeit with the addition of 'Ambrosius' on occasions. The second change made by Geoffrey concerned the place where the youth was found. According to the *Historia Brittonum* this occurred in Glywysing, that is Glamorgan, but in Geoffrey's narrative the discovery was made in the town 'called Carmarthen' (*Caer Merddin*, 'Merddin's Fort'). Geoffrey no doubt intended the link between the town's name and that of the youth to be understood in an onomastic sense: that is the town's name commemorated its most famous erstwhile inhabitant.[42] As will be argued below, the linkage between the fort of Carmarthen and a certain

Merddin/Myrddin, celebrated locally as a sage or vaticinator, had probably existed since early times, but to Geoffrey belongs the credit of creating a new literary character by identifying the youth Ambrosius of the *Historia Brittonum* with the reputed eponym of Carmarthen, whose name he wrote in the Latin form *Merlin(us)*.[43] Through the incident of the white and red dragons Ambrosius was also associated with the genesis of the Welsh tradition of political prophecy. Before the end of the tale he drove Vortigern from the site of his fortress and possessed it for himself; his memory is still perpetuated at Dinas Emrys ('Ambrosius's Fort'), near Beddgelert in Eryri (Snowdonia), where these events were supposed to have taken place. In Geoffrey's 'History', also, Merlin foretold that Vortigern would be destroyed by his enemies, and this came to pass. He later removed the stones of Stonehenge from Ireland to Salisbury Plain, interpreted the appearance of a comet as heralding the coming of King Arthur, and played a leading part in bringing about the king's conception. These events were additions by Geoffrey to the content of the Merlin legend and bore no relation to the tale of Myrddin the wild man. Merlin played no further part in Geoffrey's story, but the *Historia* provided a framework for the development of the legend in French romance, culminating in the seer's infatuation for Viviane and his imprisonment in the Forest of Brocéliande.[44]

Geoffrey's interest in Merlin continued after the completion of his *Historia*, as was made manifest in his second work, entitled *Vita Merlini*, a poem of 1529 lines in Latin hexameters, which may be dated *c.* 1150.[45] This presented a portrait of Merlin which was totally at variance with that in the *Historia*. Geoffrey, however, insisted on the identity of the Merlin of both works, claiming that in the *Vita* the prophet lived on to another age. Critics have generally treated the portrait as light and fanciful in character, though an American scholar has recently described the poem as 'profoundly religious'.[46] Neil Wright also sees it as 'more complex and difficult' than the *Historia*, in that it 'adds elements of Latin astronomical and philosophical learning . . . to a rich blend of Celtic legend and pseudo-history'.[47] Basically, however, Geoffrey portrayed Merlin in the *Vita*, not as the wonder-child who possessed himself of Vortigern's court, but according to Welsh tradition as a *silvester homo* or 'man of the woods'.

The poem opens with the statement that Merlin was renowned both as a prophet and as King of the Demetae or southern Welsh. Together with Peredurus, King of the northern Welsh, and Rodarchus, King of the Cumbrians, he engaged in war against Guennolous, King of Scotland. During the fighting three of his brothers were killed and in his grief he became mad and fled to the forest. There, with a wolf for a companion, he subsisted on roots, grass and fruits, and was sustained by nineteen apple-trees. When winter with its hardships came he was discovered by an emissary of his sister Ganieda, who was married to King Rodarchus. The emissary sang to him of the sadness of Ganieda as well as of his beautiful wife Guendoloena at his absence, and succeeded in bringing his mind back to normality and leading him to Rodarchus's court.

At court Merlin expressed a desire to return to the forest of 'Calidon' but he was kept chained in order to prevent him from doing so. One day, when Queen Ganieda appeared in the hall with a leaf hanging from her hair, Merlin laughed but refused to give the reason for his laughter unless granted his liberty. Ultimately he revealed that the queen had lain with a lover in the undergrowth where a leaf had been caught in her loosened hair. Denying the accusation, Ganieda was able to discredit her brother by the ruse of inducing him to prophesy three apparently different deaths for a youth brought before him in various disguises. Merlin, however, was now allowed to leave the court, and before going he intimated to his wife that in his absence she would be free to remarry, provided her new spouse kept far away from him. He also promised to attend the wedding in person and when, years later, a marriage ceremony was arranged, he made his appearance sitting astride a stag. But on seeing the new bridegroom he wrenched the stag's horns from its head and hurled them at his rival, killing him instantly. He then attempted to escape but was captured and brought again to the court. Later, however, he was permitted to return to the woods and provided with a house for his use in the winter, as well as a hall with seventy doors and seventy windows and as many secretaries to record his prophecies. There his sister would often visit him and see to his needs. When Rodarchus died she resolved to leave the court and live in the forest with her brother.

At this point Merlin was visited by Telgesinus (Taliesin) who delivered a long discourse concerning the Creation, the World and various natural phenomena. This included the first account in literature of the bearing of the wounded Arthur to the Celtic Otherworld to be healed by Morgen. Telgesinus further suggested that Arthur should now be invited to return to lead the Britons to victory and peace, but Merlin replied that the time for the restoration of the ancient liberties was not yet. This would come about after many years through an alliance of the Scots and Welsh, Cornishmen and Bretons led by Conanus of Brittany and Cadwaladrus of Wales. When it was announced that a fountain of pure water had burst forth at the foot of a nearby mountain Merlin drank of it, and his reason was restored. Reviewing his mental condition during his madness, he described it as follows: 'I was taken out of my true self, I was as a spirit and knew the history of people long past and could foretell the future. I knew then the secrets of nature, bird flight, star wanderings and the way fish glide.'[48] Another madman suddenly appeared, and he too was cured by drinking of the pure spring. Merlin recognized him as Maeldinus, a companion of his youth, who had suffered mental derangement through eating poisoned apples which had been intended for Merlin himself by a former mistress. The four, Merlin, Telgesinus, Maeldinus and Ganieda, then decided to spend the rest of their lives together in the forest. There is no further mention of Guendoloena.

The Merlin of this poem is clearly the same person as the Myrddin of the Welsh texts. Both are wild men of the woods who have lost their reason in a battle fought in northern Britain and live subsequently in the forest of Calidon or Celyddon. Both converse with the famous poet and reputed vaticinator Taliesin. Themes connected with apples and apple-trees occur in both the Welsh poems and the *Vita*, and Myrddin's pigling is matched by Merlin's wolf companion. The names Guennolous, Rodarchus and Ganieda are plainly Latinizations of Gwenddolau, Rhydderch and Gwenddydd. Ganieda is sister to the wild man in the *Vita* as is Gwenddydd in the *Cyfoesi*, and the close relationship between brother and sister described in the *Vita* may be presumed, judging from references in *Yr Afallennau*, to resemble that existing in earlier and happier days between Myrddin and Gwenddydd. Merlin's three brothers, who fell in battle, may well be derived from the 'three men of note' who, according to the *Ymddiddan*, were slain in the battle fought in Dyfed. In *Yr Afallennau* Myrddin is fearful of Rhydderch and his 'lords', while in the *Vita* Merlin is held captive by Rodarchus. In *Yr Afallennau*, too, Myrddin recalls that when he was 'in his right mind' he was accompanied at the foot of the apple-tree by 'a fair wanton maiden, one slender and queenly', who with some plausibility may be identified with Merlin's erstwhile but discarded mistress. Peredur is not named in the Welsh poems, but in the *Vita* Peredurus is Prince of northern Wales. He was, however, one of the sons of Eliffer, who are mentioned in the *Ymddiddan*. And, as we have seen, one of the Triads names him in connection with the Battle of Arfderydd which, according to a text of the *Annales Cambriae*, was fought between the sons of Eliffer and Gwenddolau son of Ceidio.

The points of contact between the *Vita* and the Lailoken tales are less numerous. They consist of the common portraits of Merlin and Lailoken as wild men, the motif of the threefold death, and the incident of the leaf in the queen's hair. In the two tales the motif of the threefold death refers to Lailoken's own demise, whereas in the *Vita* it is used in the story of the boy brought before Merlin in various disguises.[49] There are also two similarities between the *Vita* and the *Buile Shuibhne*. Both Merlin and Suibhne are induced to return to the life of the court, whence however they flee again to the wilds; both are married, and each of their wives acquires another partner or spouse after her husband's loss of sanity.

There are, of course, many differences. In the Welsh poems Myrddin claims to have been a vassal of Gwenddolau, but in the *Vita* Merlinus is King of the Demetae and engages in hostilities against Guennolous. Rodarchus is not his enemy but his ally. The original roles of Myrddin, Gwenddolau and Rhydderch have therefore been reversed in the *Vita*. In the Latin poem, too, Ganieda is Rodarchus's wife, but there is no suggestion of such a relationship between Gwenddydd and Rhydderch in the Welsh poems. Merlin's wife Guendoloena is found only in the *Vita*. The tales of the wild man's capture and return to the forest and of the queen's adultery, as well as the theme of the threefold death, do not occur in the poems. The slaying of the new bridegroom at Guendoloena's wedding and the house built for Merlin in the forest are only found in the *Vita*, while the subjects discussed at great length by Merlinus and Telgesinus bear no relation to those briefly mentioned by Myrddin and Taliesin in the *Ymddiddan*. The name Maeldinus (which may be based on the Irish *Mael Duin*[50]) is absent from the other sources. Myrddin and Lailoken do not regain their sanity, as does Merlin, but the appearance of another madman at the end of the *Vita* recalls the *gwyllon* mentioned in the Welsh poems as Myrddin's companions in the forest.

It is, however, in the difference between Geoffrey's two portraits of Merlin, respectively those in the *Historia* and the *Vita Merlini*, that we must look for the crux in the development of the legend. Though the *Vita* was written about a dozen years after the *Historia*, it was the Merlin of the earlier work that became the famous wizard and seer of international romance. When he was working on the *Historia*, in the years preceding its publication *c.* 1138, Geoffrey's acquaintance with the legend was clearly slight and merely amounted to an awareness of a belief at Carmarthen in an eponymous founder-figure named Merddin/Myrddin who was credited with being the author of prophecies relating to the future of the Brythonic and Welsh peoples. At this stage he probably did not know of any narrative told of Myrddin. He was using the earlier *Historia Brittonum* as a source for the 'history' which he was writing, and in retelling the story of Vortigern's tower took the liberty, for reasons best known to himself, of making the two changes in the narrative which we have noted. It would probably be safe to surmise that Myrddin's local fame at Carmarthen as a vaticinator fired his imagination and suggested to him the possibility of enriching the tale of Vortigern's tower by identifying the prophet with the boy Ambrosius. At some time subsequent to 1138, however, Geoffrey must have learnt more about the Myrddin of legend and realized that the account given of him in the *Historia* was contrary to popular tradition. His interest in the vaticinator was in no way diminished, but apparently enhanced, by the new information which he acquired, for he set about composing a new 'life' of Merlin which shows indebtedness both to the Welsh poems and the Lailoken tales. In the *Vita*, rather than admit to any previous error, Geoffrey presented Merlin's career as one which had lasted from his childhood in the reign of Vortigern in the mid fifth century to the age of the

'Men of the North', Rhydderch, Gwenddolau and Peredur, in the late sixth.   This strained even medieval credulity, however, and the view developed that there had in fact been two Merlins.   In his *Itinerarium Kambriae*, the record of his journey through Wales in 1188, Giraldus Cambrensis distinguished clearly between Merlinus Ambrosius and Merlinus Celidonius or Silvester.   The first was the Merlin of Geoffrey's *Historia* and became known to the Welsh as *Myrddin Emrys*.   The other, Giraldus averred, was called *Celidonius*, from the *Celidonia silua* in which he prophesied, and *Silvester* owing to the forest life (*siluestrem uitam*) which he led. The latter title is no doubt an approximate rendering of the Welsh *Myrddin Wyllt*. We do not know whether Giraldus knew the *Vita Merlini* but his mention of the heavenly vision shows that a source other than the Welsh poems (as we possess them) was available to him.   It is probable that he knew of the contents of the poems for both in his *Itinerarium* and in his incomplete work on prophecies, *De Vaticiniis*, he referred to his discovery at Nefyn in Llŷn in 1188 of an old and revered manuscript of the prophecies of Merlinus Silvester, adding that men conversant with the 'British' tongue helped him to translate them.[51]

The medieval Welsh tradition of prophecy sprang from memories of the struggle of the Britons and the English for supremacy in the fifth and sixth centuries. Gildas, writing of the coming of the Saxons sustained by favourable 'omens and auguries', cited a prophecy that 'they would live for three hundred years in the land towards which their prows were directed'.[52]   More specifically, however, the roots of later Welsh prophecy are to be associated with the tradition of the struggle of the red and white dragons recorded in the *Historia Brittonum*.   In that work the boy Ambrosius tells Vortigern that the white dragon represents 'the people who have seized many peoples and countries in Britain, and will reach almost from sea to sea; but later our people will arise, and valiantly throw the English people across the sea'.[53]   For centuries this aspiration persisted among the Welsh, although its fulfilment could hardly have seemed feasible after the failure of the attempts to reconquer parts of the North by Cadwallon in 634 and Cadafael in 655.   The creation of a confederacy of the Welsh and Irish, the men of Strathclyde, Cornwall and Brittany and the Norsemen of Dublin, with the aim of driving the invaders from Britain, was both advocated and prophesied in the poem *Armes Prydein* ('The Prophecy of Britain'), composed *c.* 930 which refers twice to Vortigern, though not to the tale of the fatherless boy, and in one line mentions Myrddin.[54]   The names Cynan and Cadwaladr (Geoffrey's Conanus and Cadualadrus) figure in it as those of the expected leaders of the resistance to the Saxons.   The return as deliverers of these two shadowy princes from early times was frequently foretold in vaticinatory poems, and they are linked together in *Yr Afallennau* and *Yr Oianau*.   Geoffrey was clearly aware of this ingredient in the

Welsh tradition, and a reference made by him to *fluuium Perironis* in the *Prophetiae Merlini* suggests that he knew of the prophecy relating to *Aber Peryddon* ascribed to Myrddin in *Armes Prydein*.[55]   On the whole, however, what Geoffrey received from Welsh tradition was a general concept of the nature and purpose of vaticination, rather than specific prophecies related to particular events.   He then deployed the concept with the aid of the inexhaustible resources of his imagination, and thus made his vast individual contribution to this curious genre of medieval literature.[56]

One feature of the Merlin legend, which may have puzzled Geoffrey himself, was the duality in the prevailing concepts of Merlin.   At times he was a prophet, at others a wild man of the woods, and frequently both simultaneously.   Rooted in 'Caerfyrddin', the 'fortress of Myrddin', and of local royal ancestry according to Geoffrey, he later functioned both as a wild man and a prophet in the Caledonian forest of northern Britain.   Though Geoffrey's *Historia* places the commencement of his career in the reign of Vortigern, in the *Vita Merlini* he is made to survive the death of Rhydderch, which a late source (Joceline's *Life* of St Kentigern, cf. p. 121) records as having occurred in 612.[57]   Giraldus resolved the difficulty with the aid of the doctrine of the two Merlins, and this view prevailed for many centuries.   The problem, however, was too complex for such a comparatively simple explanation to be adequate, and it was not until 1868 that a hypothesis capable of leading to a credible elucidation was proposed.

In that year the French Celtic scholar D'Arbois de Jubainville explained *Merddin/Myrddin* as a personal name evolved from the place-name *Caer-fyrddin*.[58] An identical view, independently arrived at, was expressed with more corroborative etymological detail, by Egerton Phillimore in 1890.[59]   De Jubainville's derivation of the name *Merddin/Myrddin* from the Brythonic *Moridunon* (for which he gave the Latinate forms *Maridunum*, *Moridunum*), meaning 'Sea-fort', was sound and is endorsed by later philologists.[60]   For speakers of Brythonic, he further argued, the meanings of the two elements in the name were clear, but after *Mori-dunon* had become the Welsh *Mer-ddin* or *Myr-ddin* this ceased to be the case, and the word *Caer*, identical in meaning with *-ddin*, was then prefixed to the name.   This was a pleonasm and de Jubainville compared the French habit of referring to 'la ville de Verdun'.   Once the name *Caer-fyrddin* had been established the etymologists of the time began asking the question 'Who was this Myrddin?', and in due course folk imagination fashioned an eponymous founder-figure out of the place-name.   The development was probably facilitated by the existence of a number of early place-names such as *Caer Aranrhod*, *Caer Gai*, *Caer Garadog*, *Caer Dathal*, etc., in which *Caer* was combined with a personal name, often legendary or mythical.   As a parallel instance of a personal name derived from a place-name de Jubainville cited

Port from *Portus*, described by Plummer in 1899 as 'a mere abstraction from Portsmouth, which really means the mouth of the Port *or* harbour'.[61] This instance is perhaps not certain,[62] but there can be no doubt, as was pointed out by Phillimore, that the personal names *Efrawg* and *Lleon* in the Welsh versions of Geoffrey's *Historia* were abstracted from the place-names *Caer Efrawg* (York) and *Caer Lleon* (Chester), which were respectively based on *Eburacum* ('place of the cow-parsnip') and *(Castra) Legionum* ('Fort of the Legions').[63] In the Welsh romance of *Peredur*, Efrawg is the name of the hero's father. A comparable Anglo-Saxon example was the creation of the personal name *Hrof* from the common noun *hrof*, 'roof', to explain the place-name *Hrofaescaestrae* (Rochester).[64]

It is therefore reasonable to conclude that by the end of the sixth century, but possibly later, popular speculation at Carmarthen had created an eponym who, however, would at first have been an obscure figure with no legend attached to his name. In that age such a person would inevitably have been credited with prophetic powers and we have seen that the tenth-century *Armes Prydein* ascribes a prophecy to Myrddin. The *Armes* was probably a Dyfed poem, and in the somewhat later *Ymddiddan* Myrddin speaks for Dyfed. In the latter poem also there is a reference to the Battle of Arfderydd and Myrddin mentions the *gwyllon* of Coed Celyddon. This indicates the attachment of saga material concerned with the northern wild man to the prophet of Dyfed. At some time between the sixth century and the eleventh the legend of Lailoken must have migrated to Wales, where it took root in Dyfed, and the name 'Myrddin' replaced that of 'Lailoken'. The details of the process of transmission are hidden from us, but the name-substitution was doubtless facilitated by the fact that both Lailoken and Myrddin were credited with prophetic powers. We can only guess at the date of the migration of the legend but the ninth century is generally considered to have been the period when the saga of Llywarch Hen and his sons came from the North to Powys, where it took verse form in the *englyn* metre. We have seen that in the *Cyfoesi*, which also is a series of *englynion*, Gwenddydd applies the name *Llallogan Fyrddin* to her brother. *Llallogan* and *Llallawg* were the Welsh forms of the Cumbric *Lailoken*, (or *Laloecen*) and *Lailak*, and the linking of the name with that of Myrddin is the clearest evidence of the identification of the northern wild man with the eponymous seer of Carmarthen. The names *Llallogan* and *Myrddin* do not appear in *Yr Afallennau* or *Yr Oianau*, which are in any case speeches in the first person, but in these poems the northern background has been firmly wedded to prophecies which are mostly concerned with places and events in Wales. In the *Ymddiddan*, on the other hand, the fusion of the northern and Welsh traditions is uneasy and incomplete. Here, as has already been noted, Myrddin is made to foretell the battle at which he himself would lose his reason and acquire the ability to prophesy.

Saga concerning Lailoken/Llallogan probably came to Wales in two stages. The first, perhaps oral, may be conjecturally dated in the ninth or tenth century. It would have provided material for the central core of *Yr Afallennau* and the earliest section of the *Cyfoesi*, and various prophecies were subsequently added to the original nuclei of these poems.[65] The second stage perhaps coincided with the first half of the twelfth century, when written Latin sources linking Lailoken with St Kentigern reached Wales from the North, and it has been suggested that they came to Geoffrey's notice during the, possibly protracted, preliminaries to his elevation to the see of St Asaph.[66] While scholars are unanimous in rejecting Joceline's claim that Kentigern was the founder of the see, it is possible that a story to this effect may have existed there in the twelfth century.[67] Geoffrey could therefore have learnt of Lailoken shortly after, if not simultaneously with, his acquirement of fuller knowledge of the Welsh legend of Myrddin. He drew on both sources to write the *Vita Merlini*.

In conclusion, we may here note two other derivations which have been proposed for the name *Myrddin*. Nikolai Tolstoy has given some qualified support to Rhŷs's suggestion that it could be based on **Moridunios*, meaning 'man of the sea-fort', understanding *-dunios* as possibly a dual reflection of both **dunon*, 'fort', and **donios*, 'man'.[68] Even granting such a possibility, if the sea-fort in question was Carmarthen the personal name would have been assimilated easily to that of the fort. Professor Eric Hamp has explained the name as a reflex of British **moriji:n-* (? meaning 'one of the sea').[69] Here again, assimilation to the place-name would probably have occurred. If either of these derivations is correct, however, the existence of the personal name could well have contributed to the creation of an eponymous founder-figure associated with the town. The possibility becomes the more intriguing if we consider it in conjunction with the references in the *Cyfoesi* to Myrddin's father Morfryn, and his 'brothers' Morgenau, Morial, Mordaf and Morien. In three, if not four, of these names, the syllable *Mor-* represents *mawr*, 'great', but in *Morien* it is from *môr*, 'sea'. This Morien is named in a probably interpolated passage in *Y Gododdin*, which credits him with having 'defended the fair song of Myrddin'.[70] These tantalizingly brief allusions bristle with problems. Do the names reflect an early association, perhaps mythological, with the sea? The poet of the *Cyfoesi* may have understood *Mor-* in all these names as *môr*, 'sea', and may even have divined that this was the significance of *Myr-* in *Myrddin*. Would it be profitable to ask why the 'Sea-born' (Morien) should have defended the fair song of 'Sea-fort' or 'Sea-man' (Myrddin) the son of 'Sea-hill' (Morfryn)? We would doubtless be on firmer ground pondering Jackson's suggestion that the phrase 'Myrddin's fair song' simply meant the tradition of Welsh poetry.[71]   More particularly, this should perhaps be understood as the tradition of prophetic poetry rooted in the legend which has been the subject of this chapter.

Throughout this discussion Myrddin/Merlin has been treated as a legendary character, but it may be noted that since the Middle Ages there has existed a widespread belief that in fact he was an historical poet contemporary with Taliesin, Aneirin and Llywarch Hen.   During the present century a number of Welsh scholars have upheld the view that he was either a panegyrist or a vaticinator, though admitting that not one of his poems has survived.   However, Sir Ifor Williams, who made significant contributions to our understanding of the legend, was uncertain and in 1933 his verdict was that 'for the moment, we will just fail Myrddin' as a 'candidate for sixth-century honours'.   The case for the historical Myrddin is based on the apparent strength of the medieval tradition concerning him, according to which he was almost the co-equal of Taliesin as a vaticinator.   Arguments against his historicity include the absence of his name both from the list of early Welsh poets added to the *Historia Brittonum* (which mentions Taliesin and Aneirin), and from northern and Scottish tradition in general (apart from post-Geoffrey forms such as *Merlynus*, cf. pp. 122-3).   Moreover, unlike Taliesin and Aneirin, no known works are now ascribed to Myrddin.   Due weight should also be attached to the clear connection between the name *Myrddin* and the place-name *Caerfyrddin*, and to the feasibility of the hypothetical reconstruction of the development of the legend outlined above.[72]

NOTES:

1. N.K. Sandars, *The Epic of Gilgamesh* (Harmondsworth, 1960); C.A. Williams, 'Oriental Affinities of the Legend of the Hairy Anchorite', *University of Illinois Studies in Language and Literature*, 10 (1925), 189-242; 11 (1926), 429-510; cf. idem, 'The German Legends of the Hairy Anchorite', ibid., 18 (1935), 429-510. Cf. also D.A. Wells, *The Wild Man from the Epic of Gilgamesh to Hartmann von Aue's Iwein. An Inaugural Lecture*, The Queen's University, Belfast, 1925.

2. Daniel 4. 31-3.

3. For the texts see L*l*DC 1-2 (*Ymddiddan*), 26-8 (*Afallennau*), 29-35 (*Oianau*); *RBP*, 1-4 (*Cyfoesi*), 5 (*Gwasgargerdd*); *Cy.*, 7 (1885), 151-4 (*Gwasgargerdd*); *B*, 4 (1928), 114-21 (*Cyfoesi*) and see now J. Rowland, *Early Welsh Saga Poetry* (Cambridge, 1990), 291-4, 121-5 (*Afallennau*), 125-9 (*Oianau*); ibid., 14 (1951), 104-6 (*Peirian Faban*).

4. For my translation of the legendary passages in the *Ymddiddan*, *Afallennau* and *Oianau* see Nikolai Tolstoy, *The Quest for Merlin* (London, 1985), 251-5. Cf. also *VM* 235; ALMA 21-2, 28.

5. For *Llallogan*, *Llallawg* see below, pp. 125-6.

6. See my edition of the poem, *YMTh*, for further details of its contents.

7. See *TYP* nos. 29, 44, 84 for the texts of the triads cited, and for further details see Ast.H 338-9. The question of Caerlaverock and the 'lark's nest' is discussed by N.K. Chadwick, *The British Heroic Age* (Cardiff, 1976), 99; K.H. Jackson, 'O achaws Nyth yr Ychedydd', *YB*, 10 (1977), 45-50; *VM* 160.

8. The *Life* of St Kentigern was edited by A.P. Forbes in *Lives of S. Ninian and S. Kentigern* (Edinburgh, 1874). For a detailed analysis of its probable sources see K.H. Jackson, 'The Sources for the Life of St Kentigern', in N.K. Chadwick (ed.), *Studies in the Early British Church* (Cambridge, 1958), 273-357. The Latin texts of the two Lailoken tales were printed by H.L.D. Ward in 'Lailoken (or Merlin Silvester)', *Romania*, 22 (1893), 504-26, and English translations published in *VM* 227-34.

9. Forbes, op. cit., 118, 241. For the date of composition see Jackson, 'Sources', 274.

10. Jackson, 'Sources', 329-30.

11. A.O. and M.O. Anderson, *Adomnan's Life of Columba* (Edinburgh, 1961), 238-9; *VM* 213.

12. J.F. Dimock, *Giraldi Cambrensis Opera* (London, 1868), vi, 133. Cf. also Lewis Thorpe, *The Journey through Wales and the Description of Wales* (Harmondsworth, 1978), 192; H.M. and N.K. Chadwick, *The Growth of Literature*, i (Cambridge, 1932; 1968), 112; *VM* 38.

13. 'Notice of the Site of the Battle of Arddderyd or Arderyth', *Proceedings of the Society of Antiquaries of Scotland*, 6 (1866), 91-8; also quoted extensively in Forbes, op. cit., 360-6, and Nikolai Tolstoy, op. cit., 50-2. Skene's *Ardderyd* is a misreading of the medieval *Arderydd*, earlier *Arfderydd*. In the twelfth to fourteenth centuries the name Arthuret appears as *Artureth*, *Arturet*, *Artured*, and medieval forms of Carwinley are *Karwindelhou*, *Karwendelowe*, *Kaerwyndlo*, *Carwendlow*, etc. Cf. ALMA 27.

14. Skene also mistakenly took *mygedorth* in the triad of the *Three Horse-burdens* to mean 'sacred fire', a pagan concept.

15. *Bellum armterid (inter filios Elifer et Guendoleu filium Keidiau; in quo bello Guendoleu cecidit: Merlinus insanus effectus est)*, J. Williams (Ab Ithel), *Annales Cambriae* (Rolls, 1860), 5; J. Morris, *Nennius: British History and the Welsh Annals* (London and Chichester, 1980), 85.

16. See M. Miller, 'The Commanders at Arthuret', *Transactions of the Cumberland and Westmorland Antiquarian & Archaeological Society*, 75 (1975), 96-118.

17. See *VM* 160, 195. The short form *Lailok* occurs in *Lailoken and Meldred*, see *VM* 232. For Lollius Urbicus see Peter Salway, *Roman Britain* (Oxford, 1984), 193-4, and cf. the reference in ibid., 513, to the third-century legionary Tiberius Flavius Virilis who acquired a British wife, Lollia Bodecca. Salway comments that her 'first name suggests that she came from a native family that first received the Roman citizenship during Lollius Urbicus' governership'.

18. *Ériu*, 4 (1910), 11.

19. A.O.H. Jarman, *Aneirin: Y Gododdin* (The Welsh Classics, Llandysul, 1988), 72.

20. *VM* 231.

21. *LlDC* 17.87-8, 213; Tolstoy, op. cit., 254-5.

22. Edited and translated by J. O'Donovan, *The Banquet of Dún na nGédh and the Battle of Mag Rath* (Dublin, 1848). For further editions of the texts see ALMA 27. In *The Cycles of the Kings* (Oxford, 1946), Myles Dillon published comprehensive summaries of the tales.

23. Edited and translated by J.G. O'Keeffe, *Buile Shuibhne (The Frenzy of Suibhne) Being The Adventures of Suibhne Geilt, A Middle-Irish Romance* (London, 1913). For a summary see Dillon, op. cit., 68-74, and idem, *Early Irish Literature* (Chicago, 1948), 94-100. Further bibliographical references are given in R. Bromwich, *Medieval Celtic Literature, A Select Bibliography* (Toronto, 1974), 44; and *TYP* 469-74.

24. Dillon, *The Cycles of the Kings*, 68; O'Keeffe, op. cit., xvi-xviii.

25. *LlDC* 25.8-9; *YB*, 10 (1977), 55, 73. In his article, 'La gwerz de Skolan et la légende de Merlin', *Ethnologie française*, 1, 3-4, 19-54, Donatien Laurent treats the Ysgolan poem as a part of, or as closely related to, the Merlin cycle of poems.

26. *Buile Shuibhne*, 15.

27. O'Donovan, op. cit., 231-3; *B*, 9 (1937), 12-13.

28. *LlDC* 16.36-8; Tolstoy, op. cit., 252.

29. *Buile Shuibhne*, 100-5.

30. *VM* 24.

31. *Éigse*, 6 (1950), 101.

32. *VM* 195. Clarke, however, thinks that *Lailoken* was assimilated to *allaidh* by the Irish writer of the *Buile Shuibhne c.* 1200, who may have seen both Geoffrey's *Vita Merlini* and the Lailoken material at Glasgow.

33. *Éigse*, 6 (1950), 100. Reprinted as ch.4 of James Carney, *Studies in Irish Literature and History* (DIAS 1955), 129-164.

34. 'The Motive of the Threefold Death in the Story of Suibhne Geilt' in J. Ryan (ed.), *Essays and Studies presented to Eoin Macneill* (Dublin, 1940), 550.

35. *VM* 26; Meic Stephens (ed.), *The Oxford Companion to the Literature of Wales* (Oxford, 1986), 212.

36. After a detailed examination of the evidence, Neil Wright concludes in his edition of the Bern Burgerbibliothek MS 568, *HRB* xvi, that 'Geoffrey began work on the *Historia* at some time before 1135 and that it was completed in 1138'. It appears that the title by which the work is now known was first used in the edition of Commelin (Heidelberg, 1587), see ibid., xii.

37. *VM* 31-2.

38. *HRB* xi; *VM* 19. For the text of the tale of Vortigern's tower see Wright, 71-3; translation in *HRB*(T) 166-9.

39. For the ascription of the *Historia Brittonum* to 'Nennius', until recently 'taken for granted', see the article by David N. Dumville, '"Nennius" and the *Historia Brittonum*', *SC*, 10/11 (1975/1976), 78-95, which concludes with the statement that 'we must admit to ignorance of the name of its ninth-century author'.

40. See N. Lukman in *Classica et Mediaevalia, Revue Danoise de Philologie et d'Histoire*, 6 (1944), 98-9; *LIC*, 2 (1952-3), 126. Cf. Salway, *Roman Britain*, 468, where it is stated that Ambrosius 'may or may not be the same as' Ambrosius Aurelianus, for whom also see ibid., 483.

41. *HRB* 73.

42. For Geoffrey's words see *HRB* 71, *cum in urbem que Kaermerdin uocata fuit uenissent*, cf. the medieval Welsh translation in *BD*, 101, *A guedy dyuot deu o'r kennadeu hynny hyt y dinas a elwit guedy hynny Caer Uyrdin*, and *HRB*(T) 167, 'They came to a town which was afterwards called Kaermerdin'.

43. Geoffrey rendered the *dd* sound in *Merddin* (i.e. the *th* sound in English *the*) as *l* rather than *d*, possibly in order to avoid an association with the French *merde*.

44. For summaries see ALMA 319-24; A.O.H. Jarman, *The Legend of Merlin* (Cardiff, 1976), 6-8; idem, 'The Legend of Merlin and its Association with Carmarthen', *The Carmarthenshire Antiquary*, 22 (1986), 16.

45. For the text with facing translation see *VM* 52-135, and for earlier editions see ibid., 45-7. On Geoffrey's authorship of the poem, on which doubts have been cast in the past, and its probable date, see ibid., 36-42, and cf. *HRB* xx.

46. Penelope B.R. Doob, *Nebuchadnezzar's Children, Conventions of Madness in Middle English Literature* (Yale and London, 1974), 153.

47. *HRB* xx.

48. *VM* 115.

49. For this motif cf. K.H. Jackson, 'The Motive of the Threefold Death in the Story of Suibhne Geilt', in J. Ryan (ed.), op. cit., 535-50.

50. *VM* 197.

51. For Geoffrey's two portraits of Merlin see H.M. and N.K. Chadwick, *The Growth of Literature*,

i, 123-32, 'Merlin in the Works of Geoffrey of Monmouth'. Cf. the suggestion by Clarke, *VM* 31-2, that the fuller knowledge of Welsh tradition displayed by Geoffrey in the *Vita Merlini* may be derived from residence in south-eastern Wales after 1139. For the references by Giraldus to Merlin see the Chadwicks, op. cit., 111-12, 129-30, and Thorpe, *The Journey through Wales*, 183, 192-3, 280, and index 319.

52. Michael Winterbottom, *Gildas: The Ruin of Britain and Other Works* (London and Chichester, 1978), 26; Hugh Williams, *Gildas, Part I* (Cymmrodorion Record Series, No 3, 1899), 55.

53. Morris, *Nennius*, 31; David N. Dumville, *The Historia Brittonum, 3. The Vatican Recension* (Cambridge, 1985), 94. The latter text adds the words *unde antea uenerant*.

54. See *AP*.

55. *AP* xxxiv-xl; *HRB* 77.

56. The Welsh tradition of prophecy is a large subject into which much critical and interpretative research is still required, and considerations of space have inevitably reduced the above discussion to the merest sketch. For comprehensive general surveys see M.E. Griffiths, *Early Vaticinatory Material in Welsh with English Parallels* (Cardiff, 1937); R. Wallis Evans, 'Prophetic Poetry', ch.13, 278-97, in *A Guide to Welsh Literature*, ii, ed. by A.O.H. Jarman and Gwilym Rees Hughes (Swansea, 1979); Glanmor Williams, *Religion, Language and Nationality in Wales* (Cardiff, 1979), ch.3, 71-86, 'Prophecy, Poetry, and Politics in Medieval and Tudor Wales'. The vaticinations in *Yr Afallennau* and *Yr Oianau* are discussed on pp. 346-51 of A.O.H. Jarman, 'Llyfr Du Caerfyrddin; The Black Book of Carmarthen', *PBA*, 71 (1985), 333-56. For the *Prophetia Merlini* of John of Cornwall, composed *c.* 1143-4, see Michael J. Curley, 'A New Edition of John of Cornwall's "Prophetia Merlini"', *Speculum*, 57 (1982), 217-49; idem, 'Gerallt Gymro a Siôn o Gernyw fel Cyfieithwyr Proffwydoliaethau Myrddin', *LlC*, 15 (1984-6), 23-33. See also P. Zumthor, *Merlin le Prophète* (Lausanne, 1943) for Merlin's prophecies in medieval literature in general.

57. *TYP* 320, 504.

58. 'Merlin Est-il un Personnage Réel?, ou Les Origines de la Légende de Merlin', *Revue des questions historiques*, (1868), 559-68. De Jubainville attributed 'l'idée première du présent travail' to Paulin Paris; the phrase is probably to be understood as meaning that the idea was suggested to him verbally or in written (but not printed) form.

59. *Cy.*, 11 (1890), 46-8.

60. J. Morris Jones, *A Welsh Grammar, Historical and Comparative* (Oxford, 1913), 189; Ifor Williams, *Breuddwyd Maxen* (Bangor, 1922), 27. Cf. Jackson, LHEB 225, and D. Ellis Evans, *Gaulish Personal Names* (Oxford, 1967), 232 for *Moridunon*.

61. C. Plummer, *Two of the Saxon Chronicles Parallel* (Oxford, 1899), ii, 13.

62. See Stenton, *Anglo-Saxon England* (Oxford, 1971), 20; cf. *SC*, 10/11 (1975/6), 196; ibid., 18/19 (1983/4), 17, 27.

63. Geoffrey is here referring to Carlisle. For *Lleon* he gives *Leil*, but has *Ebraucus* for *Efrawg*, stating that the latter 'condidit urbem quam de nomine suo uocauit Kaer Ebrauc, id est ciuitas Ebrauci'. See *HRB* 17-18; Brynley F. Roberts in *B*, 25 (1973), 282; H. Lewis, *BD* 24, 25, 216; Glenys Goetinck, *Historia Peredur vab Efrawc* (Cardiff, 1976), 71; I. Williams, *Enwau Lleoedd* (Lerpwl, 1945), 50; Jackson, LHEB 39.

64. L. Alcock, *Arthur's Britain, History and Archaeology AD 367-634* (London, 1971), 194.

65. For the dates of the latest prophecies in the Black Book of Carmarthen poems see *LlDC* xxix-xxxiii.

66. *VM* 42, 193.

67. Jackson, 'Sources', 317.

68. *SC*, 18/19 (1983/4), 17.

69. Hamp's words are: 'If we make allowance for confusion with the place name *Caer Fyrddin* (Carmarthen) perhaps we may see in *Morydd, Merddin* the pair **morij-: *moriji:n-'*, see Werner Winter (ed.), *Evidence for Laryngeals* (The Hague, 1965), 229, n.7.

70. Jarman, *Aneirin: Y Gododdin*, 30.

71. K.H. Jackson, *The Gododdin: The Oldest Scottish Poem* (Edinburgh, 1969; reprinted 1978), 133. Jackson makes the equation 'Welsh poetry = Celtic civilization'.

72. The case for the historical Merlin is argued by Nikolai Tolstoy, *The Quest for Merlin*; idem, 'Merlinus Redivivus', *SC*, 18/19 (1983/4), 11-29; R. Bromwich, 'Y Cynfeirdd a'r Traddodiad Cymraeg', *B*, 22 (1966), 30-7, cf. also the 2nd ed. of *TYP*, 559-60. I have discussed the arguments in some detail in 'A Oedd Myrddin yn Fardd Hanesyddol?', *SC*, 10/11 (1975/6), 182-97. For Sir Ifor William's views see BWP 123, 125.

6

CHWEDL GERAINT AB ERBIN

Roger Middleton

THE text of *Geraint ab Erbin* is preserved in three main manuscripts, plus two detached folios from a fourth. It is found complete in cols. 385-451 of the White Book of Rhydderch and is virtually identical in cols. 769-809 of the closely related Red Book of Hergest. The third manuscript is imperfect, lacking the first gathering of three; this is MS Peniarth 6, part iv. The detached folios are in MS Peniarth 6, part iii. Textual differences are limited to spelling and matters of detail; there are no major variations in the narrative.[1]

The ancestor of these manuscripts was probably written in the thirteenth century, but it is difficult to be more precise. The scribes of the extant manuscripts have occasionally preserved archaic spellings characteristic of the Black Book of Carmarthen, which was at one time thought to be *c.* 1200. However, now that the Black Book has been redated to *c.* 1250 and after, the archaic forms need no longer imply a date at the turn of the century. The added difficulty of knowing how long such orthography might have survived in the practice of individual scribes means that even a date as late as 1300 could not be definitely excluded, though one nearer the middle of the century is more likely.[2]

The story as such is certainly older, for there is a version of it in Old French, the romance of *Erec et Enide* by Chrétien de Troyes, written at some time between 1170 and 1185. With few exceptions Chrétien's narrative corresponds to *Geraint* episode by episode, and it is not unusual to find close resemblances or even phrases that would serve as exact translations. The precise relationship between *Geraint* and Chrétien's poem has long been a thorny problem, and will be rigorously excluded from the present discussion.[3]

The hero Geraint ab Erbin appears in earlier tradition, and the name at least is likely to be historical. Mentioned in the Latin *Lives* of several saints, and recorded in the Welsh *Bonedd y Saint*, he was apparently a king of Dumnonia in the sixth century. The Triads name him as one of three 'Seafarers' (*TYP* no. 14), and the poem *Gereint filius Erbin* (*LlDC* no. 21) portrays him as a hero who fought at 'Llongborth'. The suggestion that the surviving story derives from exploits of the fifth-century Roman general Gerontius is unconvincing, but we could not exclude the possibility that various historical figures contributed to the final composite.[4]

The name of the hero in the French poem implies an entirely different origin. The form *Erec* seems to be associated with the Breton name *Guerec* (from earlier *Weroc*), borne most notably by the ruler who gave his name to the territory around Vannes (*Bro Weroc*, meaning 'land of *(G)weroc'*). By the twelfth century phonetic developments had modified this to Broerec from which anyone unfamiliar with the principles of lenition might extract the new name *Erec* instead of the correct *Guerec*. An added attraction of this suggestion is that the name *Enid* (French *Enide*) can be obtained in similar fashion from the alternative name of this same territory (*Bro Wened*, 'land of the Veneti', becoming *Broened*). This coincidence of personal and territorial names is reminiscent of the Celtic myth of Sovereignty in which a king marries the female goddess who personifies his kingdom. The hunt of the white stag and the winning of Enid include several features that are characteristic of Sovereignty tales, and it is tempting to see these episodes as a much modified version of the myth (originating therefore in Bro Weroc/Bro Wened itself).[5]

If this explanation is correct, the phonological changes required imply that the story remained Breton until the twelfth century and only then found its way into French and Welsh. The traditional name Geraint (MSS *Gereint*) could have been introduced at this stage as an approximation for either Guerec or Erec. There is no need to prefer *Guerec*; the lenition of Welsh initial consonants makes it second nature to add or subtract *G-* as required. *Gereint* itself is regularly lenited to *Ereint*, and *Erec* invites the equivalent change in the opposite direction.[6] It is quite possible that the story was not known in Wales until the composition of the tale that we now read; it is certainly noteworthy that there are no allusions to it in the Triads or early poetry. References before 1300 are to Geraint alone and belong to an independent tradition, with only a single reference in an *awdl* by Prydydd y Moch to suggest otherwise (see *TYP* 360). This poem refers to the 'anger' of Geraint, and the prose tale uses the same word or its cognate (*llid, llidiawc*) to describe Geraint's reaction to Enid (*WM* 419.18, 424.5, 429.40, 430.14; *Mab.* 252.24, 255.25, 259.18, 259.27). However, the poet presumably meant the 'anger' (i.e. ferocity) of the warrior in battle. This meaning also appears in the prose tale (*WM* 398.13 and 15, 435.7 and 9, 450.23; *Mab.* 238.17 and 18, 263.4 and 5, 273.8), but the quality is common to all heroes and is already implied by the poem *Gereint filius Erbin*. Only when we find references to Enid can we be reasonably sure that a poet had our story in mind, but these do not appear until the fourteenth century (listed in *TYP* 348).

The most likely period for the composition of the surviving text is the first half of the thirteenth century, but the date implied by certain narrative details depends upon how far we expect literature to reflect conditions within the knowledge and experience of its prospective audience. Some of the living conditions depicted were not a reality in Wales until the thirteenth century, but if the author was borrowing from literature or from experience in Europe a date in the later twelfth century becomes possible.

The numerous French loan-words indicate that the language is later than the Norman Conquest, and the freedom with which they are used suggests that they are already well established. (Note the use of *twrneimeint* beginning at *WM* 395.17; *Mab.* 236.13. The contest for the sparrowhawk is not a tournament, and the lack of precision is likely to originate in Welsh usage; neither Chrétien nor Hartmann von Aue use *tornoiemant* or its equivalent in this episode.) The society depicted owes much to twelfth-century developments in European culture, and this too is treated as normal for the time, not some exotic intrusion. Features such as the personal combats, the quest for adventures (see especially *WM* 428.26, 436.40; *Mab.* 258.23, 264.12) and the assumption that each knight has an *amie* (repeatedly either *gorderch*, 'lady-love', or *gwreic uwyhaf a garo*, 'lady he loves best') are typical of the chivalric romances that did not begin to appear in France until the late twelfth century. The description of Edern (*WM* 390.22; *Mab.* 232.29) may imply the wearing of a closed helm (introduced about 1180), and there is repeated mention of armour on horses (not in common use until the thirteenth century).[7] The 'ystauell wydrin' (*WM* 416.30; *Mab.* 251.1: 'chamber of glass') would be possible before 1200, but glazed windows were extremely rare in secular buildings at this time.[8] Knowledge of the Welsh laws might have become more widespread after their codification in the later twelfth century, but we must allow for the fact that the laws themselves are much older. The influence of Geoffrey of Monmouth's *Historia* (see below and *TYP* 358) requires a date after 1136 if the author knew this text in Latin, after 1155 if he knew Wace's *Roman de Brut*, after about 1200 if he used one of the Welsh translations (as appears from a reference to Hywel mab Emyr Llydaw).

The use of French loan-words and the portrayal of a chivalric society simply reflect the linguistic and social conditions of the time, but other details specifically suggest a narrative source in French (though not necessarily the poem by Chrétien de Troyes). Best known are the names Gwiffret Petit (*WM* 433.19 and after; *Mab.* 261.32 and after) and Earl Limwris (*WM* 442.14, with variant spelling *lymwrs* in MS Peniarth 6, part iv; *Mab.* 267.33). The form *petit* is surely the French adjective meaning small, corresponding to Chrétien's *Guivret le petit* (first mentioned at line 3868 in the subject case, but see line 4940 for the oblique). The spelling *Limwris/Lymwrs* with the inital *L-* rather than *Ll-* is undoubtedly foreign, and Chrétien offers *Limors*, but as the name of the castle rather than the earl (lines 4717,

4947, 5065-70). Also worth considering is the 'twel' used for carrying food (*WM* 425.8; *Mab.* 256.15). The word itself is a borrowing from Old French *toaille*, meaning cloth, but the evidence suggests that *twel* was already restricted to meaning towel. Food can certainly be carried in a cloth and even in a towel, but unless some particular point is being made about the nature of the cloth, why should an author say 'towel' rather than 'cloth'? This discrepancy between the French form and the Welsh borrowing becomes apparent when *Y Seint Greal* either fails to translate *toaille* meaning cloth (*Queste* 82.10; *SG* 54.4/471.6: *Queste* 269.5; *SG* 163.6/541.40), or else uses *twel* but adds a gloss that would be redundant if the word had its French breadth of meaning (*Queste* 269.12; *SG* 163.10/541.44).[9] The appropriate word for the cloth in *Geraint* would be *lliein*, as is shown by two passages in *Owain* that juxtapose *twel* and *lliein* with a clear distinction of meaning (*WM* 226.37ff, 238.30ff; *Mab.* 157.19ff, 165.21ff). Chrétien's poem or some other French source with *toaille* would be an obvious explanation for the unexpected *twel* (compare *Erec et Enide*, lines 3154 and 3174).

Despite these hints of foreign origin, the story-telling is unmistakably Welsh. The tale is in prose, proceeds without significant deviation, and is written in a style common to other Welsh texts.[10] Also to be noted is the influence of the laws and other traditions. Several of the twenty-four 'Officers of the Court' are mentioned, and many of the personal names can be found in other Welsh texts; most notable is Glewlwyd the porter (see *TYP* 361-3). The marriage of Geraint and Enid, without a religious ceremony (*WM* 408.16 and 34; *Mab.* 245.16 and 27), can be compared with similar arrangements in *Culhwch* (*WM* 507.10; *Mab.* 136.27), *Branwen* (*WM* 41.5; *Mab.* 26.34), *Manawydan* (*WM* 63.15-23; *Mab.* 42.11-16) and *Macsen* (*WM* 187.10; *Mab.* 85.3).

The location of Arthur's court at Caerleon indicates the influence of Geoffrey of Monmouth, for in earlier Welsh tradition it is located at Celli Wig in Cornwall (see *TYP* 3-4). The description of the court at the beginning of *Geraint* may even draw specifically upon *HRB* IX.12-13 (caps 156-7). Note that the festival is Whitsun, that Caerleon is recommended as the most accessible place in the kingdom by sea and by land, that special mention is made of churches (surprisingly rare in medieval literature), and that there is an apparent segregation of the sexes in the churches.

In any event, the author of *Geraint* also had independent knowledge of the local geography. He knows that the road from Caerleon crosses the Usk on its way to the Forest of Dean (where the hunt of the white stag takes place) and that it is necessary to return and recross the Usk at Caerleon in order to reach Cardiff (the walled town in which the contest for the sparrowhawk is held).[11] This geographical knowledge does not necessarily mean that he knew the region at first hand, and the reference to crossing the Usk by means of a ford (*WM* 392.7; *Mab*. 233.35) suggests that he did not. If he read Latin, he could have obtained all that he required from Giraldus Cambrensis, but this major route to and from England may well have been known throughout Wales.[12] Even so, one wonders whether *Geraint* may have been written for an audience with local interests. The reference to Cardiff in particular would benefit from some such explanation because the name is withheld whilst the town features in the narrative, only to be revealed precisely when it is no longer relevant (*WM* 405.5; *Mab*. 243.7). Someone who knew the region would be able to guess the identity of the town in advance and derive satisfaction from being proved correct.

One of the most intriguing features of the text is the relatively large number of inconsistencies. Some look like unsuccessful attempts to explain unexpected circumstances, such as why the queen rides into the forest accompanied by just one of her maidens, and why Geraint does not take part in the hunt. Gwenhwyfar and all the maidens had overslept so that by the time they awoke there were only two horses left in the stable (*WM* 388.7 and 36; *Mab*. 231.7 and 24); likewise Geraint, who did not know when Arthur had set out (*WM* 389.25; *Mab*. 232.7). This certainly explains why the three are alone in the forest, but at a price. Do all the women of the court sleep through the noisy preparations for the hunt (*WM* 388.15; *Mab*. 231.11)? Why does Arthur refuse to let the men wake them (*WM* 388.10; *Mab*. 231.9), when he knows that Gwenhwyfar wanted to watch the hunt (*WM* 387.12; *Mab*. 230.23)? Why does Arthur have so few horses? How can Geraint have been unprepared when Arthur had entrusted the steward with making sure that everyone was ready (*WM* 387.29; *Mab*. 230.31)? If the explanations are taken seriously we are led to envisage a court that is ill-equipped and badly organized, but it is most unlikely that such an unfavourable impression was intended.

Other minor discrepancies have no apparent motivation. It is said that Edern will be called 'Marchawc y Llamysten' (Knight of the Sparrowhawk) if he wins the contest for the third year (*WM* 395.30; *Mab*. 236.21). Yet the author begins to call him by this title almost immediately (*WM* 396.22; *Mab*. 237.6), and continues to do so until his true name is revealed. The sparrowhawk itself is entirely forgotten once Edern is defeated; neither Geraint nor Enid ever claims the prize.

After the marriage of Geraint and Enid it is said (*WM* 408.38; *Mab*. 245.29): 'A cheneuinaw a oruc y uorwyn a'r llys, a dwyn kydymdeithon iti o wyr a gwraged hyd na dywedit am un uorwyn yn Ynys Brydein uwy noc ymdanei' (And the maiden acquainted herself with the court, and companions were brought to her of men and women till there was better report of no maiden in the Island of Britain than of her).

Only then does Gwenhwyfar raise the question of the stag's head. Taken at face value this would imply that the presentation was delayed for the time it took Enid to establish her reputation, but this can hardly be what is meant. The author has introduced what he knows about Enid in a place that fits the mood but not the fictional chronology.

When Geraint meets Arthur in the forest it is said that he stays with him 'agos y uis' (close on a month) until his wounds are healed, and Arthur specifically asks the physicians to confirm that he is fully fit (WM 440.9-22; Mab. 266.19-26). Yet as soon as Geraint fights the giants his wounds reopen and on returning to Enid he falls from his horse in a faint (WM 441.36-442.8; Mab. 267.22-9). The situation is further confused by the reaction of Earl Limwris when told by Enid that Geraint is dead. The other maiden says the same of the anonymous knight who really is dead, and the text continues (WM 442.36; Mab. 268.9): 'Y iarll a beris cladu y marchawc a edewssit yn uarw, ynteu a dybygei uot peth o'r eneit y mywn Gereint etwa ac a beris y dwyn gyt ac ef, y ydrych a uei uyw . . .' (The knight that had been left dead the earl had buried, but he thought there was still some life in Gereint and had him brought along with him . . . to see whether he would live). The author needs to explain why Limwris treats these two dead bodies differently, and he very reasonably seizes upon the real difference that exists between them. In the end, however, this produces more difficulties because neither Enid nor Limwris act in accordance with the expressed belief that Geraint might still be alive; there is no attempt to tend his wounds or to revive him. When Geraint regains consciousness and kills Limwris, the earl's retainers are terrified by 'y gwr marw yn kyuodi og eu llad' (WM 444.22; Mab. 269.15: 'the dead man rising up to slay them'). This is surprising, for they had brought Geraint to the castle precisely because they had thought he was still alive.

In all these cases the version of events given by Erec et Enide is free from these particular inconsistencies (although it sometimes offers problems of its own). It must be emphasized, however, that there is nothing here that would tell us which version (if either) is the 'original'. Even if it were agreed that the French text is preferable in these instances (which is not necessarily self-evident) there is still no satisfactory way of deciding whether the Welsh author made a confused attempt to deal with a source that he found mysterious, or whether Chrétien deliberately avoided what he found unsuitable.

Inconsistencies of this kind are less disturbing when a story is told rather than read, and it may be that their frequency in Geraint results from a background of oral performance. Not that Geraint is an oral tale in its raw state; its preservation in manuscripts already argues against that, and phrases such as 'dywedassam ni uchod' (we have mentioned above) and 'a dywetpwyt vchot' (which was spoken of above) could be taken as decisive (*WM* 385.34, 422.28; *Mab.* 229.20, 254.27). Nevertheless, certain characteristics suggest that the author learnt his craft in an environment where oral story-telling still flourished.[13]

Indeed, one of the most noticeable features of *Geraint* is the use of a technique that is known to be typical of oral compositions. Phrases, sentences, even whole passages of ten or a dozen lines are repeated either in exactly the same words or with only minor variation. Repetitions of this kind can be found in other Welsh texts and some of the phrases that appear in *Geraint* occur in identical form elsewhere. To give the most obvious example, the widely attested formulas for greeting and welcome conform to the pattern discussed by T.M. Charles-Edwards with reference to *Pwyll*, the first of the *Four Branches of the Mabinogi*.[14]

Some of the repeated phrases are entirely trivial, but others are combined into extended and often quite elaborate sequences. The sheer number of them makes it inconceivable that they should be accidental; more than two-fifths of the text consist of phrases that can be matched word for word either elsewhere in *Geraint* itself or in other Welsh texts.[15] Equally interesting is that very few of the phrases have direct alternatives; variety is possible through different combinations, but there is normally only one set phrase to fit each recurrent circumstance.

Thus a blow from a sword is always delivered to the crown of the head. If the opponent is wearing armour (Edern, Gwiffret Petit) there are phrases that describe the sword cutting through the layers of armour to reach the skull (*WM* 398.39, 435.11; *Mab.* 238.33, 263.6); without armour, the giant and Earl Limwris are cut in two (*WM* 441.40, 444.14; *Mab.* 267.24, 269.10). Note also that even the giant who is supposed to be bigger than three men is still struck on the top of the head. In the case of prolonged combats there are phrases to describe the effect of the blows, but not the blows themselves. Only the decisive stroke is clearly defined, and the author never describes swords being wielded in any other way.

In the combats with lances lesser opponents are run through at the first attempt; the lance always remains intact and is always instantly available for the next combat (*WM* 419-21 and 432.10; *Mab.* 252-4 and 261.1). More formidable adversaries succeed in breaking a few lances before being unhorsed (*WM* 397.12, 432.18, 450.18; *Mab.* 237.26, 261.6, 273.6). In the combat for the sparrowhawk the lances are handed to both knights by their supporters, but the reference to Geraint's own lances (*WM* 397.32; *Mab.* 238.3) is not well judged. The reason why he could not fight Edern in the forest was that he had left Caerleon unarmed, without even one lance, let alone several. On one occasion (*WM* 434.26; *Mab.* 262.28) a squire appears from nowhere to provide Gwiffret with lances, but there is no word of how Geraint can obtain his. Other combats take place in situations where a supply of lances is quite impossible. All of this implies that the pattern fixed in the author's mind takes precedence over any attempt to envisage the incident in realistic terms.

Similarly, the standardized description of 'the noble youth', assembled from traditional phrases that can be found in other texts, takes no account of social standing. That Geraint should wear brocaded silk and carry a sword with a gold hilt is in keeping with his rank (*WM* 389.5; *Mab.* 231.30), but this hardly seems appropriate for a forester (*WM* 386.11; *Mab.* 229.31). The two descriptions are not taken ready-made from any surviving text, for although most of the individual phrases can be matched from elsewhere, their combination is unique to *Geraint*.[16] There is enough variation between the two passages (including an unnecessary change of order) to show that the author did not copy blindly from one occasion to the next, but they still resemble each other more than anything found in the other texts. In particular, they are alone in having the phrase 'eskid issel' (low boots) where the expected word is *gwintas*, meaning high boots (translated 'buskins').[17] There is one other description with 'esgit' (translated 'shoes') in *Rhonabwy* (*WM* 215.8; *Mab.* 147.5), but no occurrence of the complete phrase 'eskid issel'. The author of *Geraint* never uses *gwintas*, whereas the author of *Owain* steadfastly retains it even when describing Luned or the Lady of the Fountain (*WM* 237.16 and 240.13; *Mab.* 164.22 and 166.28). There is no obvious reason for women to wear high boots, and a second possible contradiction arises when these descriptions follow the usual convention of claiming to reveal to the audience something that is actually seen by the character concerned (despite the fact that high boots would be concealed by the dress).

Even at the surface level the repetitions are an important feature of the author's style, but the failure to modify the set expressions to suit particular circumstances has a further special significance. It suggests that the repeated phrases belong to a system of formulas that is already well established, and this possibility is also supported by the number of the repetitions, by the occurrence of the same phrases in other Welsh texts, by their varied combination in longer descriptions, and by the virtual absence of duplication.

If the repeated phrases really do constitute a formulaic system there are a number of implications that would affect our understanding of *Geraint*. Presumably what we see in the written texts reflects what must have existed amongst oral story-tellers, who are the natural creators and users of such systems. A possible confirmation of this can be found in *Rhonabwy* where the oral technique seems to be the subject of a literary parody to which the author draws attention in his colophon. What he refers to as the 'colours that were on the horses . . . on the arms and their trappings, and on the precious mantles' look like traditional formulas, but closer examination reveals that they are far from being fixed expressions. The deliberate variation that distorts the formulaic pattern is surely a literary device, and we then understand why 'no one, neither bard nor story-teller, knows the Dream without a book' (*WM* 222.36; *Mab.* 152.17).

There are crucial differences between literary repetitions that exist in specific texts and a system of formulas that is part of a living tradition. Literary authors can borrow from other texts or invent new expressions at will, whereas the conditions of oral composition require a system that is essentially stable. True formulas are independent of narrative, for the system is part of the story-teller's craft; the formulas belong to him, and not to the tale he happens to be telling. Such a story-teller will use the same formulas throughout his repertoire and will introduce them as a matter of course into any new tale that he learns.

Most important of all is the fact that the system must be Welsh. It is not necessary for each individual formula to be exclusively Welsh, but there is no serious possibility that the system as a whole could be a ready-made foreign product. Even in cases that can be paralleled in other languages the exact form of words is still necessarily Welsh. Thus descriptions of jousts that give details of how Geraint struck the decisive blow always include the phrase 'dros bedrein y uarch y'r llawr'. This can be matched almost word for word by Old French 'par desus la crope del cheval a terre', such that both versions may be translated 'over the crupper of the horse to the ground'.[18] Now, it is perfectly possible that the Welsh phrase has been taken from French (given that the mode of combat itself was not native to Wales), but what creates a formula is the consistent use of one particular sequence of words to the exclusion of all others. In the French prose romances there are variants in the wording and several other more common endings for a joust. In *Geraint* there is no variation in wording and no alternative ending. The phrase may or may not be French in origin, but the formula is Welsh.[19]

The claim that the system is Welsh carries with it the implication that the formulas in *Geraint* will not have been transmitted by any version of the story that was in some other language. If the present redaction is the result of a lengthy Welsh tradition this observation is of limited value, but if there has been translation from Breton or French the effect is considerable. Any narrative not already in Welsh will have required the systematic introduction of the formulas to produce the text that we now read, and such a radical procedure would certainly obscure the relationship between *Geraint* and its source. In particular it would be pointless to require any such source to contain details that could be supplied by the formulas; only the outline of the narrative need be the same. We could also assume that any author who employed such a formulaic technique to tell the story in his own way would also have the requisite skills to convert the narrative to a suitable Welsh form in other respects.

The use of established names (Geraint, Erbin, Gwalchmai), the local geography, and the introduction of material from the laws, from Geoffrey of Monmouth and from Welsh tradition could easily fall within his professional competence.

This distinction between the narrative itself and the procedures that give it shape is of fundamental importance. The form in which the story is now cast, the words in which it is told and the elements from Welsh tradition can all be seen as part of an established technique by which an author transforms an existing tale into a new creation. The decisive factor in such a process is not the form in which he encounters the original story, but the means by which he is able to make it his own irrespective of what has gone before.

NOTES:

1. The Red Book text is available in *RM*; all the others are in *WM*. References will be to *WM* (cited by column and line) with translations from *Mab.* (cited by page and line). The manuscripts were described by Gwenogvryn Evans in *RWM*, and the complete ones discussed palaeographically by N. Denholm-Young, *Handwriting in England and Wales* (Cardiff, 1954), 40-5 and 78-9, but see now Introduction, pp. 10-12 above. According to Evans, MS Peniarth 6, part iv is in the same hand as the Book of Taliesin, which Denholm-Young (p. 44) dates as 'fourteenth century (? second quarter)'.

2. For the dating of the Black Book see the contribution by E.D. Jones to the Introduction of *LlDC*; compare also A.O.H. Jarman, 'The Arthurian Allusions in the Black Book of Carmarthen', in LAMA 99-112 (especially 99-100).

3. This question is treated in detail in my unpublished D.Phil. thesis, 'Studies in the Textual Relationships of the Erec/Gereint Stories' (University of Oxford, 1976). References to *Erec et Enide* will be to the critical edition by Wendelin Foerster (Halle, 1890).

4. Detailed references, with an important discussion of their significance, are in *TYP* 355-60 (supplemented by p. 551 in the second edition). On the poem in the Black Book see ch.2 above.

5. The suggestion was first made by Rachel Bromwich, *B*, 17 (1956-8), 181-2, and elaborated by her in 'Celtic Dynastic Themes and the Breton Lays', *EC*, 9 (1961), 439-74 (especially 464-6). The phonology of *Broerec* is confirmed by Kenneth Hurlstone Jackson, *A Historical Phonology of Breton* (Dublin, 1967), §§ 213, 375.1, 687, 1005. The form **Broened* is conjectural, as is the possible transition from **Ened* to *Enid/Enide*.

6. For the addition of G- to produce a false 'unlenited' form of a French name see *Cân Rolant: The Medieval Welsh Version of the Song of Roland*, edited by Annalee C. Rejhon (Berkeley and Los Angeles, 1984), 91 n.81.

7. See Claude Blair, *European Armour* (London, 1958), 29-30 and 184-5.

8. For early examples in literature see Chrétien de Troyes, *Le Roman de Perceval*, edited by William Roach (Geneva, 1959), lines 7720, 7783, and the close parallel to *Geraint* in Hartmann von

Aue, *Erec*, edited by Albert Leitzmann (Tübingen, 1939, revised in 1963, and much improved in 1985), line 3019; compare also *Perlesvaus*, edited by William A. Nitze and T. Atkinson Jenkins, 2 vols. (Chicago, 1932-7), line 593.

9. *La Queste del Saint Graal* [*Queste*], edited by Albert Pauphilet (Paris, CFMA, 1923), cited by page and line; *Selections from the Hengwrt MSS, Vol. 1, Y Seint Greal* [*SG*], edited and translated by the Revd Robert Williams (London, 1876), cited by page and line for text and translation.

10. See in particular Brynley F. Roberts, 'From Traditional Tale to Literary Story: Middle Welsh Prose Narratives', in *The Craft of Fiction*, edited by L.A. Arrathoon (Rochester, 1984), 211-30.

11. *WM* 388.21 and 39, 386.28, 392.7, 405.5; *Mab.* 231.15 and 25, 230.7, 233.35, 243.7.

12. See pp. 55-62 of *Itinerarium Kambrie* in *Giraldi Cambrensis Opera*, vi, edited by James F. Dimock (London, Rolls Series, 1868), or pp. 114-21 of *The Journey through Wales and The Description of Wales*, translated by Lewis Thorpe (Harmondsworth, 1978).

13. See Brynley F. Roberts, op. cit.

14. 'Honour and Status in some Irish and Welsh Prose Tales', *Ériu*, 29 (1978), 123-41 (esp. 124-8).

15. These repetitions are all marked in the edition of *Geraint* prepared for Vol. II of my D.Phil. thesis, where they represent the equivalent of 1,214 lines out of the total of 2,787 found in the White Book (43.6%).

16. Compare *WM* (*Culhwch*) 455.9; (*Pwyll*) 20.6; (*Macsen*) 181.6; (*Owain*) 225.13 and 29, 237.13, 243.38; (*Rhonabwy*) 212-19; *Mab.* 97.9; 13.1; 80.28; 156.17 and 27, 164.19, 169.11; 145-50.

17. *WM* (*Macsen*) 181.11; (*Owain*) 225.16, 225.33, 237.16, 240.13, 244.3; (*Rhonabwy*) 213.5, 214.10; *Mab.* 81.1; 156.20, 156.31, 164.22, 166.28, 169.13; 145.25, 146.17.

18. *WM* (*Geraint*) 398.11, 419.39, 421.35, 432.25, 450.30; (*Pwyll*) 7.31; (*Owain*) 248.19; (*Peredur*) 126.12, 136.18, 141.5; *Mab.* 238.16, 252.35, 254.8, 261.10, 273.12; 6.32; 172.20; 189.18, 196.29, 200.5. Representative French examples can be found in *Lancelot do Lac*, edited by Elspeth Kennedy, 2 vols. (Oxford, 1980), 176.35, 185.14, 231.1 etc. and, with a variation in word order, 189.37. Note that the usual dating of *Pwyll* (c. 1100) places it a full century earlier than any surviving French prose romances.

19. Even a translation like *Y Seint Greal* uses some of the established formulas; the author introduces oaths and greetings without reference to his French originals, and he uses 'dros bedrein y varch y'r llawr' in its fixed Welsh form regardless of the variants in his source (*SG* 253.10/601.32, 254.38/602.36, 416.34/709.39; *Perlesvaus* 2691, 2745, 9023). Even a plural version of this restores the standard word order (*SG* 101.19/501.42; *Queste* 173.22); the only other variant is independent of the French (*SG* 337.29/657.1; *Perlesvaus* 6136).

7

OWAIN: CHWEDL IARLLES Y FFYNNON

R. L. Thomson

THE text of *Owain* is preserved in whole or in part in three medieval and seven later manuscripts. The medieval sources are the White Book, Oxford, Jesus College MS 20,[1] and the Red Book. The complete text is to be found only in the Red Book; the White Book has lost a few lines at the beginning and the end and a long passage in the middle; Jesus 20 supplies only lines 1-148.[2]

The differences between these three texts are of the usual kind found in the transmission of Medieval Welsh prose: spelling, mutation, arrangement of words, substitution of synonyms, omission or addition of words that are grammatically optional, and accidental omission between two occurrences of a similar word or phrase. In no case does the frequency or scale of these differences give any ground for supposing that the starting point of all three manuscripts is other than a single version, though the different readings of Jesus 20, albeit of the usual kind, are more frequent than usual.

Unlike the other romances *Owain* is also extant in several later copies, which perhaps points to a special degree or duration of popularity, which would agree with the evidence cited in *TYP* 482-3. Only four of these are independent.[3] It is remarkable that three of them, while otherwise representing the same tradition as the medieval copies, entirely omit the episodes in which the lion plays a part. Llanstephan 58, on the other hand, is a very free modernization and re-telling of the story.[4]

The date of composition, as is the case with most anonymous medieval texts, is hard to determine. It must be earlier than the White Book, for that manuscript (and the Red Book) are collections of texts, and from the differing orthographic style of each of the romances it can be seen that they were culled from separate sources or at least had different histories of transmission. How long that transmission had been can only be guessed at in the light of style and content, but it would not be unreasonable to put the origin of the present text back to the end of the twelfth century.[5] How far back into that century it might go depends very much on the view that is taken of the relationship — for there must be some relationship — between this text and the verse romance of Chrétien de Troyes composed about 1177.

Nor do we know whether our *Owain* was the first version of the story, a new invention of the story-teller. Almost by accident we know that the hunting of Twrch Trwyth which is recounted in *Culhwch ac Olwen*, perhaps in the eleventh century, was already known in some version to 'Nennius' (c.73) early in the ninth, and the same historical miscellany contains stories about St Germanus (c.32), transparently latinized from a vernacular Welsh *chwedl*,[6] which are very much in the narrative style of the *Four Branches*, a style continued in the Romances. The raw material of the *Owain* story is therefore of unknown age, especially the first (perhaps once the only) part of it (lines 1-454, *Mab.* pp. 155-70),[7] the quest to overcome the defender of the storm-raising spring, which has very much the appearance of being mythological in origin.

The romance of *Owain* is conveniently so called for brevity's sake from the name of the leading male character, parallel to the method of naming its two companions, *Geraint* and *Peredur*. The Red Book, however, names it in the colophon *Chwedyl iarlles y ffynnawn* 'The tale of the lady (or countess) of the spring (or fountain, or well)' and so gives the leading place to one of the female characters, possibly one of the highest rank though not the one with the biggest part to play in the narrative, and in fact one whose personal name is never given. Llanstephan 58, in the title and colophon, calls Owain *Iarll y Kawg* 'Earl of the Basin', presumably from the place in the story where he, like Cynon before him and Arthur after him, throws the basinful of water on the slab by the spring (l.264) to provoke the hailstorm and challenge the defender (*Mab.* 163).

Though these three narratives are usually referred to now as *rhamantau* ('romances') the term has been objected to as misleading and inaccurate, in that it implies a similarity to the Continental literary form so called, whereas in fact these are narratives of a different kind. *Owain* is explicitly called *chwedl* ('tale') in the colophon (though the later manuscripts all term it *ystori*), perhaps implying something rather less factual than *ystoria* ('history'), which is the term applied to *Peredur*. The classification of these romances by genre has been discussed by Dr Tony Hunt who, without wishing to imply that *Owain* as we have it is a transcription of an oral folk-tale, maintains that the narrative method, structure and characterization in these stories is most immediately comparable with that of the European *Volkmärchen*.[8]

Like the other two, *Owain* takes the name of its hero from a genuine historical character of the British heroic age, Owain son of Urien of the northern British kingdom of Rheged about the end of the sixth century.[9] In view of that date there is no possibility of the historical Owain having ever met the historical Arthur, if the latter fell at the Battle of Camlan in 539 (according to the *Annales Cambriae*, or 542 according to Geoffrey of Monmouth — and both dates are probably too late rather than too early). Neither is there any probability that the connection between the events in the romance and the historical Owain goes back to so remote a period. The two items mentioned at the very end of the tale (1.819-21, *Mab.* 182), the three hundred swords of the descendants of Cynfarch (Owain's grandfather), and the flight of ravens (which appears also in *Breuddwyd Rhonabwy* and plays an active role there), may well belong to genuine tradition but they have no part in this tale; nor does the unfavourable tradition about Owain, that he fathered St Kentigern by deception and promptly deserted his paramour.[10]

Owain has a good claim to be counted an Arthurian romance for Arthur plays a reasonably active part in it, though he is less prominent than in *Culhwch ac Olwen* or *Breuddwyd Rhonabwy*. The opening scene is set in Arthur's court, located at Caerleon-on-Usk as in *Historia Regum Britanniae*, rather than in Cornwall as in *Culhwch ac Olwen* and, by implication, in *Breuddwyd Rhonabwy*.[11] Arthur himself is described as *amherawdyr* 'emperor', which may also reflect, though perhaps it need not, the status claimed for him in *Historia Regum Britanniae*. Yet the court is far less grand than Geoffrey depicts it, and the emperor is found seated on a heap of green rushes, not some splendid throne such as we might expect after Geoffrey's assertion that in Arthur's day Britain had reached such a pitch of excellence that *copia diuitiarum, luxu ornamentorum, facetia incolarum cetera regna excellebat* (*HRB* 156 = IX.13). The description in fact accords better with the realities of Welsh life in the twelfth century as related by Giraldus Cambrensis (*Descriptio Kambriae* I.10), and the usage of the court, with Glewlwyd Gafaelfawr filling the office of porter (which according to *Geraint*, he did only at the three chief festivals), corresponds with the enumeration of the officers of the court in the Welsh laws and his part in *Culhwch ac Olwen*. Cai similarly fulfils the duties of steward, but goes in person to the kitchen and mead-cellar to fetch refreshments for the company, in contrast with his splendour — *Kaius dapifer herminio ornatus, mille uero nobilibus comitatus qui omnes herminio induti fercula cum ipso ministrabant* — at Arthur's great feast in *HRB* (ibid.); and Owain himself as a character owes nothing to Geoffrey's single mention of him, *Hiwenus filius Uriani* (*HRB* 177 = XI.1). The setting is modest, domestic, and realistic.

Either this informality or an assumption that Arthur is no longer in the first flush of youth may account for the curious opening of the dialogue: 'Sirs, if you would not make game of me, I would sleep while I wait for my meat' (1.13-14). The thought of anyone, even one of his intimates, making fun of Arthur would hardly occur in courtly circles; this is not Geoffrey's conqueror of western Europe but the local chieftain in relaxed mood on his home ground. It is Arthur's tender-heartedness that sets the second part of the action in motion. After three years of Owain's absence Gwalchmai draws from him the confession: 'There is longing upon me for Owain, who has been lost to me the space of three years, and if I be the fourth year without sight of him my life will not stay in my body' (l.459-62, *Mab*. 170). In public the author makes him a more impressive figure for we read that the men of his household numbered 3,000, not counting hangers-on, and that was ten times the size of a normal chief's household band. After tracking Owain to the spring Arthur is himself prepared to fight the unknown defender but Gwalchmai relieves him of that task (l.514-15, *Mab*. 172); and it is Arthur, too, who begs permission for Owain to take the three months' leave at his court which begins the action of the second part of the story (*Mab*. 173). His two final appearances are more in accordance with the formal role assigned to him in the Continental romances: he receives Owain and his wife as permanent residents at his court after their reconciliation (l.780, *Mab*. 180-1); and he appoints Owain as his *pennteulu* or commander of his household band of warriors (l.818, *Mab*. 182).

The other traditional Arthurian characters in the story are Cai and Gwalchmai. Here Cai is portrayed in a fashion more like that of the Continental romances than of *Culhwch ac Olwen* or *Breuddwyd Rhonabwy*. He insists on the performance of the promise to entertain the companions with good conversation (l.25, *Mab*. 155); when Owain expresses interest in going in search of the site of Cynon's adventure Cai calls his courage in question, and when rebuked by the queen makes at best a qualified apology (l.219-25, *Mab*. 162); when Arthur reaches the spring Cai demands to be allowed to be the first to fight its defender, and when worsted in that encounter complains that it was unfair and demands a second chance (l.486-509, *Mab*. 171). His second defeat is Owain's retribution for his earlier insult, and was no doubt intended to give pleasure to the reader. Whether this characterization of Cai is a development of his quarrel with Arthur, recorded in *Culhwch ac Olwen* (l.981-2, *Mab*. 128), is uncertain.

Gwalchmai plays only a small part in the story: he appears in connection with Arthur's expedition to the spring where his three-day drawn battle with its defender helps to establish Owain's reputation as a fighter (l.518-42, *Mab*. 172); his courtesy appears in the contest of politeness at the end of the battle when neither he nor Owain will allow himself to be the victor; of his activity·as a lover the only hint is in the same episode, the fact that his disguising *cwnsallt* was the gift of the daughter of the Earl of Anjou (Cornwall, according to Llanstephan 58). He thus plays a much smaller part in *Owain* than in Chrétien's *Yvain*, or in its English version, entitled *Ywain and Gawain*.

Cynon fab Clydno belongs, like Owain, to the men of the North in the heroic age of late sixth-century Britain. He is mentioned in the *Gododdin* among those who took part in the expedition from Edinburgh that ended in the Battle of Catraeth *c.* 600, and probably did not survive it (*CA* 409, 416). A much later tradition makes him the lover of Owain's twin sister, though in the tale (l.27) he is represented as younger than Owain (*TYP* 323-4). At all events they were contemporaries and belonged to the same area so they may have been associated in tradition before *Owain* brought them together.[12] The role of Cynon is taken in *Yvain* by Calogrenant, whose name was interpreted by Loomis (ATC 480) as a doublet of Cai, 'Kay the Grumbler', though there is nothing in common between the two characters and the epithet does not suit Cynon.

Owain is the central character of the tale and his rise, fall and rehabilitation are its theme, paralleling, though with different motivation and under different circumstances, the story of *Geraint*. In both the hero is drawn into a preliminary adventure which ends in his marriage; an estrangement follows (in *Owain* as a result of his neglect of his wife, in *Geraint* indirectly from an excess of devotion to her); a further series of adventures leads to a re-establishment of the relationship on securer foundations.

In *Owain* the narrative falls into three unequal sections (l.1-563, 564-80, 581-821, *Mab.* 155-73, 173-4, 174-82). The first section consists of the three expeditions to the spring: that of Cynon, told in retrospect as a mortifying adventure of his early youth, which had helped to moderate his superabundant self-confidence; that of Owain, which, with the unlooked-for assistance of Luned, turned out more happily; and that of Arthur, in search of Owain, which also had an unexpectedly happy outcome. The story could have ended at the close of any one of these three episodes but in each case there is a stimulus to repeat the experience, first in Owain's curiosity about the site of Cynon's adventure, and secondly in Arthur's desire to find and rescue or avenge Owain.

Three accounts of the same journey could easily have been the recipe for boring repetition, either in exactly the same words or with the account growing steadily more circumstantial. Even more so when we notice that in each part of the sequence each event is first described in advance and then encountered in person by the hero of that episode, Cynon describing his own reactions and the story-teller describing those of Owain and Arthur's company. The narrator, however, knows how to avoid trying his audience's patience: the accounts grow progressively shorter with the biggest difference between the first and second, which follow one another almost immediately, while there is not much difference between the second and third, which are separated by the account of Owain's courtship and marriage. Precise figures are difficult to calculate because the three accounts are not set in exactly parallel circumstances, but the proportion is approximately 33 : 9 : 7.

Cynon sketches briefly the initial stages of his journey, gives a very full description of the castle at which he spent the night, of its inhabitants and all that happened to him there, and the guidance he was given for the next stage; the next morning he proceeds along his way and finds the dark man and his animals more wonderful than he had imagined from the account given him, hears about the next stage and goes forward again, carries out the prescribed actions at the spring, suffers the storm (more terrible than he had been led to expect), and finally encounters the defender of the spring who deals with him most expeditiously. His humiliating return and tactful reception by his hosts do not, of course, recur in the parallels.

When Owain retraces Cynon's journey the account can be severely abbreviated and the reader is continually referred back to the earlier account — nine instances in l.235-66, *Mab*. 162-3. On the third occasion the abbreviation is slightly different: the account of the journey takes only three lines and adds that Cynon acted as Arthur's guide; the young men, *y gwr melyn*, and the maidens are mentioned without any details, but the excellence of the hospitality is mentioned in new terms; the table conversation of the first two accounts is entirely omitted — the guests know what to expect and Cynon knows the way; it may even be hinted at that their hosts were not told where the expedition was heading (cf. *Owein* 475n.), though this seems improbable. There is no conversation with the dark man, for they have no need of his assistance. When they reach the spring the account of the provoking of the storm is almost as long as on the first occasion, but with the different detail necessitated by Cai's insistence on being the first challenger.

There is thus skilful variation in the three accounts while it is part of the story that the scenes, personages and events remain exactly the same, as if their existence was suspended in immobility except when an adventurer arrived to reactivate them. It is also part of the narrative style that the reality always exceeds the expectation aroused by hearing it described or knowing about it in advance, and this feature continues to be present in even the shortest versions. For comparison, the proportion of the whole text devoted to Cynon's narrative is 23% in *Owain*, 6.3% in *Yvain*, with the two repetitions in proportion. The much greater prominence given to this whole section in *Owain* is shown by its engrossing 68.5% of the entire text as against 39% in *Yvain* (as in T.B.W. Reid (ed.), *Yvain: Le Chevalier au Lion* (Manchester, 1942)).

After a three-year absence Owain returns to Arthur's court for three months' rest and recreation and stays for three years, forgetful of his wife's claim on him. The account of his fall is brief (l.561-73, *Mab*. 173-4), and even briefer is the space given to his wild conduct under the influence of remorse.[13] Found delirious in the park of a widowed countess he is rescued by her and a second time awakens affection in a female breast at the mere sight of him, despite his shaggy state, so that the handmaid disregards her mistress's instructions and lavishes the whole of the precious healing ointment on him (*Mab.* 174). Recovering his strength over three months he repays his hostess for her care by rescuing her from a persecuting suitor and placing him in her power. This he does without making any promise and without even declaring his intention.

His second adventure is the rescue of the lion and its consequent attachment to him (1.661-81, *Mab.* 177), including its supplying him with food, a story going back to classical times.[14] Its function in *Owain* is not altogether clear, except that it subsequently provides him with a formidable ally in his fights with various foes. As noted above, some later manuscripts lack these episodes entirely, parallel perhaps to the way in which, in Peniarth 7, *Peredur* appears to end at *Mab.* 217.

Now Owain encounters Luned again, apparently in the dark and in the peculiar circumstances of her imprisonment. Although he finds out who she is he does not reveal himself or make any promise. The better to raise suspense as to the outcome, a further adventure (1.711-55, *Mab.* 178-80) is inserted before her rescue.[15] The two sons of his host of the next night have been captured by a giant who will kill them unless their father gives him his only daughter. Owain shows sympathy but gives no undertaking to assist. Next morning the lion takes the field with its master but proves a more effective fighter than Owain; though sent off, the lion breaks out and delivers the *coup de grâce*. Owain arrives incognito to rescue Luned, offering to take her champion's place, saying he is sure that if Owain knew of her plight he would have come to her aid. The lion is again protested against and shut up, but escapes and quickly disposes of Luned's accusers (1.756-77, *Mab.* 180).

It is no doubt to be understood that Owain reveals himself, that Luned out of her affection for him and recognizing his repentance, took him to her mistress and a second time made his peace with her. All that is said is that they went together to the domain of the Lady of the Spring, and from there to Arthur's court.[16]

At this point the story seems effectively to have come to an end, but comparison with *Yvain* shows two further episodes in the rehabilitation process: one is the story of the quarrelling sisters (*Yvain* 4703-5106, 5808-6509). For this the Welsh tale has no need, for its battle between Owain and Gwalchmai is already over (1.515-42, *Mab.* 172-3), and in a different context, that of Arthur's search for the lost Owain. That the episode is unnecessary and would involve a repetition is perhaps a better reason for its absence than that the legal point at issue was alien to Welsh law.[17]

The second episode, the Pesme Avanture of *Yvain*, inserted within the quarrelling sisters' tale, is in *Owain* placed after the reconciliation with his wife. This seems to be its original position, because in it the lion plays no part,[18] and it is perhaps

Owain's final adventure before settling down to the responsibilities of kingship.[19]

The difference in position, and some differences in detail, appear to be an argument (among others) against dependence of the Welsh tale upon knowledge of Chrétien's text, for it is difficult to see why, when it was already incorporated within another episode, any adapter into another language should wish to extract it and move it to such a doubtful position as it now occupies. Furthermore, the narrative lacks the contemporizing social comment on sweated labour in the garment industry, which can hardly be other than Chrétien's addition, and the word-play on *yspeilty*, 'house of plunder', and *yspytty*, 'hospice', (1.808, 810) seems to demonstrate an originality unlikely in a mere adapter.[20]

Another argument lies in the timetable of the two tales. *Owain*, like the undoubtedly native stories, is leisurely, whereas in *Yvain* pressure of time plays an important part and is most naturally seen as Chrétien's contribution to the increase of dramatic tension. Arthur, on hearing Calogrenant's tale, resolves to mount an expedition to the spring within a fortnight, in order to arrive there on the eve of St John the Baptist, that is on 23 June. This is spoken at Whitsuntide for which the median date is 27 May. Hence Yvain's need to hurry away if he is to steal a march on the rest. The same dates impose pressure on Lunete in forwarding and Laudine in accepting the match with Yvain, for the Dameisele Sauvage has written that Arthur is due to arrive the following week. At first it would take five days to fetch Yvain from Arthur's court, but under pressure from Laudine's impatience Lunete promises that he will arrive on the third day. On arrival he is admitted immediately (in *Owain* he has to wait till noon the next day), their reconciliation is quickly effected, the approval of her counsellors obtained, and they are married the same day. The celebrations are not over when Arthur reaches the spring. This urgency creates excitement and exerts emotional pressure, but it also entails a loss of plausibility in Gauvain's insistence that Yvain must not be lost to martial activities but return immediately to the tournament circuit — he is, after all, permanently on call to defend the spring. After three years of marriage, as in *Owain*, the argument might have some force.

A further argument lies in the treatment of the mysterious and irrational. The tableau of young men shooting outside the castle (*Mab.* 156, 162, 170) is absent from *Yvain*. Owain's mysterious effect on women is explained away: Lunete had met Yvain before at Arthur's court; and the countess recognized his real identity from a scar. In *Owain*, however, the hero's charm is taken for granted and he plays a part like that of the Irish Diarmaid, 'the single best lover of women and maidens in the whole of Ireland.'[21] Only the ring of invisibility and the storm at the spring, both essential to the action, are left unrationalized.

Detailed comparison of all the versions[22] can establish two points: that all except the Welsh version are directly dependent on Chrétien's *Yvain* and that the relationship of *Owain* is different, in proportion, in the order of the two episodes (as noted above), and in the extent to which it echoes the characteristic features of Welsh prose narrative. If there is anything alien about *Owain* it is the matter, not the manner of its telling. The nature of this relationship constitutes the celebrated *Mabinogionfrage*, and the question has been variously answered. At one extreme the idea of direct derivation from *Yvain* seemed to have been given up. At the other the belief that *Owain* as we have it is the source, through some interpreter, has not found much favour. Most critics are to be found somewhere in the middle ground. Since Continental Arthurian texts exhibit place-names and personal names of British origin, sometimes even with their original patronymics,[23] it seems likely that some of the earliest stories share that same origin. On the Continent such stories survive only in a form adjusted to a different society with different interests and values; in Britain there is no record of the stories in their 'original' form but only in versions coloured by the influence of the Norman presence in south-east Wales. In effect, the conclusion is that *Owain* and *Yvain* share a common source, but there is room for endless argument over which is nearer to that source, and in what respects, and in what form each received it, and what factors modified it in each case. Personally, I think that *Owain*, shorn of its Norman trappings, is as near as we shall ever get to the version which came as raw material to Chrétien or his predecessors, the sort of thing of which he spoke so slightingly and ungratefully in his *Erec*, stories *Que devant rois et devant contes/ Depicier et corronpre suelent / Cil qui de conter vivre vuelent*. There is enough evidence to give a variety of answers to the *Mabinogionfrage*, but not enough to give a decisive one.

Nevertheless, the question will not go away. Professor Brynley Roberts wrote at the end of a long essay on *Owain* in 1977:[24] 'Throughout these observations I have not ventured to refer to the work of Chrétien de Troyes because my intention was simply to try to convey the pleasure the Welsh tale gives me, and that on its own terms. *Owain* is valuable whatever its relationship to *Yvain*.' That is true and needs to be said, though it is not an isolated opinion.[25] It is the price that has to be paid for Arthur's European celebrity that the literature connected with him is likewise an international one and so part of comparative literature rather than of individual national literatures, and that sources, diffusion and influences predominate in its study. Whenever an Arthurian work is outstanding in its own national and linguistic context, it deserves to be assessed and valued in that context irrespective of any elements from elsewhere. And so it is with the three Welsh romances.

Yet Professor Roberts cannot end his essay without a glance at the alternative approach: 'I think it likely that if a Welsh writer were trying to create or imitate or retell a "French romance" in the Welsh prose tradition the result would be something very like Owain.' And in a later article he discusses briefly 'the process by which a text or literary genre is transmitted from one culture and linguistic environment to another' and 'the choice of texts judged to be relevant to the receiving culture and the modification they undergo to become acceptable.'[26] This would provide an answer to the question why only three of Chrétien's romances have Welsh parallels, and why and how the three romances differ from the undoubtedly native prose narratives in technique and thematic significance. Here, of course, we are back to the oldest answer to the *Mabinogionfrage*, that Chrétien is the source of the Welsh romances, but with the proviso that, unlike the versions in the other languages, they are not translated but transmuted and naturalized.

NOTES:

1. First half of the fourteenth century; text in *B*, 15 (1953), 114-16.

2. References to line numbers here and below are to *Owein*.

3. Llanstephan 171 and Llanover B17 (both late sixteenth century), Llanstephan 58 (early seventeenth century), and Cwrtmawr 20 (mid-eighteenth century). All are National Library of Wales MSS.

4. Text and translation in *SC*, 6 (1971), 57-89.

5. Cf. R.M. Jones, *LlC*, 4 (1957), 225 for an early twelfth-century dating; R. Bromwich, *TRh* 154-5, late twelfth or early thirteenth century; A.H. Diverres, *SC*, 16/17 (1981-2), 162, late thirteenth century.

6. Ifor Williams, 'Hen Chwedlau', *THSC* (1946), 28-58.

7. Page references throughout are to *Mab*. This is the best translation though its style is somewhat idiosyncratic.

8. *SC*, 8/9 (1973-4),107-20, and again by Professor Diverres, *SC*, 16/17 (1981-2), 145-6.

9. *TYP* 479-83; here the romances differ from the Four Branches, the leading characters of which are euhemerized divinities, cf. Rachel Bromwich in *TRh* 161-3.

10. Anonymous *Life of Kentigern*, chs.1, 2 (*Historians of Scotland*, V, 245-7); named *Ewen filius Erwegende*, or *filius Ulien*. Cf. the unfavourable view of Arthur in some of the Welsh saints' lives; see above pp. 82-4.

11. R.M. Jones, *Y Tair Rhamant* (Aberystwyth, 1960), xiv, argues that this and other place-names reflect the area of composition.

12. See Rachel Bromwich in Ast.H., ch.6, 'Cynon fab Clydno'.

13. The similarity in some details to the conduct of Nebuchadnezzar (Daniel 4.29, 30, 5.21) may suggest that the author had in mind the punishment of pride and self-sufficiency.

14. Aulus Gellius, *Noctes Atticae,* V.14, 5-30, especially 24-5.

15. On the novelty of this device cf. *SC,* 16/17 (1981-2), 153-4; but any cleric would remember it from Mark 5.21-43 and parallels.

16. B.F. Roberts, 'The Welsh Romance of the "Lady of the Fountain", *Owein'* in LAMA 178, comments: 'A detailed description of the scene would be superflous as the whole "romance" has been progressing to this point and we have observed Owain's maturity developing.'

17. But cf. *SC,* 16/17 (1981-2), 155-7 for a fuller discussion.

18. Though it did not leave Owain until he overcame *y Du Traws* (783), but without its assistance!

19. B.F. Roberts, in Guide, I.229, compares the mist-hedge episode in *Geraint,* which is similarly 'irrelevant' after the reconciliation of husband and wife.

20. The word-play *nyt. . . anhygar. . . hagyr* (l.112) is of the same kind.

21. Cf. T.P. Cross and C.H. Slover, *Ancient Irish Tales* (rev. ed., Dublin, 1969), 373, 375.

22. For the details see *Owein,* xxix-lvi; T. Hunt, *ZCP,* 33 (1974), 95-113.

23. R. Bromwich in TRh 163.

24. *YB,* 10 (1977), 124-43 (my translation).

25. *SC,* 8/9 (1973-4), 108-11.

26. B.F. Roberts, in LAMA 181-2.

8

HISTORIA PEREDUR AB EFRAWG

Ian Lovecy

HISTORIA *Peredur vab Efrawg* (hereafter *Peredur*)[1] is a microcosm of almost all the problems which can be found in early Welsh prose literature. It is virtually impossible to unravel the manuscript tradition, and because of this it is difficult to settle upon an 'authoritative' text; the narrative structure has been analysed in different ways, and widely differing suggestions have been advanced as to the underlying structure which unifies the romance; and the relationship of the story to other versions, notably Chrétien's *Conte du graal* and its continuations, appears less than straightforward. It is clear that what we have here is a text (or texts) which has been subjected to revisions, the extent of which it is difficult to establish. The problems raised would not, in all probability, have received such attention were it not that Chrétien appears to have taken at least some of the elements of his Grail Castle from *a* version of *Peredur*, and the romance has therefore been seen as a key element in the interpretation of the Grail legends and in particular in the debate over their possible pagan origins and significance.

The manuscript tradition has received extensive treatment in the critical literature.[2] There are four early versions of the tale: (a) the White Book of Rhydderch (MS Peniarth 4), mid-fourteenth century (*WM* col.117-78); (b) MS Peniarth 7, no later than the beginning of the fourteenth century (*WM* col.5-48); (c) MS Peniarth 14, from the second quarter of the fourteenth century (*WM* col.180-90); (d) Red Book of Hergest, from the end of the fourteenth century (*RM* col.655-97). The longest version is found in (a) and (d), which are very close; (d) has sometimes been regarded as a copy of (a). However, the Red Book text contains traces of twelfth-century orthography not found in MS Peniarth 4, which suggests rather that both are copies of an earlier original. The relationship is further confused by the fact that the majority of differences occur in the first section, before the beginning of the story of Angharad Law Eurawg. This has been seen as indicating that the Jesus College MS was the work of two scribes,[3] or alternatively that the first part of the tale was better-known, and that therefore the scribe was not following his original as carefully as in the second part.[4]

The other two manuscripts equally appear to go together, although almost certainly MS Peniarth 14 is not a copy of MS Peniarth 7; there are too many variations in wording and even the order of events within episodes to make this reasonable.[5] In both, however, Gwalchmai takes the role of friend and helper which in the other MSS is played by Owain. Peniarth 14 is only a fragment, but although Peniarth 7 lacks the opening it seems to end very definitely with the fourteen-year reign of Peredur with the Empress: 'Ac velly y t'vyna kynnyd paredur ap efrawc' (and thus ends the progress of Peredur ap Efrawg). The whole episode of the Fortress of Marvels would seem therefore not to be a part of this tradition; and there are signs that this tradition is at least as early as the other. There are traces of the orthography of the Black Book of Carmarthen in Peniarth 7 (*e* for *y, u* or *w* for *f, t* or *th* for *dd*; Sir Edward Anwyl suggested that this results from the later survival of early orthography in the area in which this was written[6]); and Cai is referred to as 'Cei Wynn' (632.7) and 'Cei vap Kynyr' (631.28). Neither is found in Peniarth 4, and the former is certainly part of early tradition not found in the later tales.[7] It is also worth noting that the style of MS Peniarth 7 is very lively, and may therefore represent the oral tradition of story-telling.

With no certainty as to the extent of the basic text, it is not surprising that there have been several different views of the structure of the tale. Thurneysen divided *Peredur* into four sections,[8] namely:

I(a)   From the beginning to the close of the incident of the drops of blood on the snow (*WM* 117-145.8; *Mab.* 183-202).

I(b)   The story of Peredur and Angharad Law Eurawg (*WM* 145.9-152.2; *Mab.* 203-4).

II   The rest of the story up to Peredur's fourteen-year reign with the Empress (*WM* 152.3-165.26; *Mab.* 207-17).

III   The remainder of the tale (*WM* 165.26-178; *Mab.* 217-27).

This division follows the capitalization in Peniarth 4, except that the first section has been split because the story of Angharad seemed decidedly independent. Section I(a) Thurneysen regarded as a loose retelling of Chrétien's *Conte du graal*, while section III he thought to be a later addition which followed Chrétien much more closely, but which led to a conclusion produced by the Welsh redactor and influenced by I(a). The intervening sections he saw as independent inventions of Welsh story-tellers, influenced by I(a) but not dependent upon it.

Other critics have used variations on this analysis, both before and after Thurneysen. Professor Mary Williams felt that the story fell into three parts, combining Thurneysen's I(b) and II; this second section she felt was the closest to

Celtic tradition: 'Si pour ce trait nous comparons le récit de Peredur avec les quatre Branches des Mabinogion qui sont de véritables contes celtiques et parmi les plus anciens de la littérature galloise, nous voyons que c'est la partie B de notre récit qui leur rassemble le plus.' She also saw the final section as an addition to the original story.[9] Muhlhausen regarded sections I(b) and II as inessential to the narrative,[10] and Jean Marx equally felt that the final section was essential;[11] I shall return to this point later. In an earlier article[12] I also suggested that the story was basically to be found in sections I(a) and III, although at that time I believed that there was a degree of unity in II, and sufficient parallels with I(a) in particular to make me wonder whether it had once been an independent version of the same tale.

These are attempts to find narrative unity. Others have suggested that there is, in fact, narrative *dis*unity resulting from the failure of successive redactors to understand the myth which underlies the story. If properly understood, they argue, this myth gives thematic unity to *Peredur*. Their aim is therefore to reconstruct the 'original' form of the tale. This approach can be seen in the work of A.C.L. Brown, W.A. Nitze, and R.S. Loomis;[13] but it has been most recently and fully propounded by Dr Glenys Goetinck.[14]

Dr Goetinck sees *Peredur* as yet another example of the stories based on the personification of a country as a goddess with whom the rightful king has to mate. Explicit examples of this theme can be found in Irish literature,[15] and there is evidence from the recurrence of the motifs in Welsh- and Breton-based literature that the myth was known in both those countries.[16] One recurring motif in such tales is the recognition of the rightful ruler by his preparedness to love an apparently ugly lady — who rewards him by becoming a beautiful maiden. Dr Goetinck argues that the two forms taken by the Sovereignty goddess become rationalized as two separate characters, the ugly form giving rise to the ugly characters in *Peredur* (for example the Black Maiden, the *Addanc*). However, these figures in *Peredur* are also verbally or physically antagonistic to the hero, whereas in Irish tradition the Sovereignty is invariably polite. (Indeed, Dr Goetinck adds Peredur's half-sister to the derivatives of the ugly form on the basis of her attitude to the hero rather than her appearance.)

In her analysis of the structure of *Peredur* Dr Goetinck, too, splits the tale into four parts, but with a rather different arrangement up to the end of Thurneysen's part II:

(i) The story of the hero's birth and youth, ending with an event which causes him to go out into the world.

(ii) He visits the court of the king where the opposition he encounters serves as an introduction to the enmity and opposition of the world.

(iii) Adventures in which the hero is tested and trained by the powers of the Otherworld, culminating in his marriage. During this time he is shown, in symbolic form, the purpose of his coming into the world, to regain sovereignty and avenge the one from whom it was taken.

(iv)   The loss of his wife and a further series of tests and trials, culminating in his final success and the regaining of his wife and domain.[17]

To make this into a unified story, the series of adventures which make up the bulk of the tale have to be grouped under the heading of 'testing and training' of the hero. If they are really fulfilling this role in a coherent tale, there should be some signs of progress, some indication of what is being tested. Testing undoubtedly takes place in the courts of Peredur's uncles: testing of Peredur's ability at fighting in the first, and a more symbolic test in the second. It should be noted that the hero fails at the end of the latter, and one may well assume that it is because of this that the second uncle makes no attempt to countermand the first uncle's prohibition on asking questions. Training is subsequently given by the hags; all this is completed before Peredur's second appearance at Arthur's court, and his achievement of vengeance for the dwarfs.

Thereafter there is little that can be seen as adding to the hero's abilities, although much that may be said to demonstrate them. The only occasion which could in any way refer back to the first section is the story of the Black Oppressor, where again the asking of a question has major consequences. In this instance Peredur *does* ask; as the result is to rid the land of a tyrant, his action is presumably correct. There is, however, no explicit reference back. More importantly, at this point in the story there is no suggestion that Peredur *should* have asked anything at his second uncle's court, except by analogy with the *Conte du graal*; all that his foster-sister has laid to his charge is the death of his mother and the injuries to the dwarfs. It is therefore not possible to see the Black Oppressor episode as indicating any significant progress on Peredur's part.

The lack of actual development in either the physical prowess or the attitude and the approach of the hero seems to be the main problem also with the discussion by Dr Ceridwen Lloyd-Morgan.[18] Her concern, unlike Dr Goetinck's, is with the actual narrative structure of the story which survives, rather than of its possible origins. Her analysis of the tale is excellent, but we differ in the conclusions to be drawn from it.

Dr Lloyd-Morgan, too, makes use of generalizations when she divides the tale into five sections: introduction, training and education, first vengeance themes, further adventures, and main vengeance quest and conclusion. She insists, however, that the redactor is attempting to make a 'coherent' story, and she finds evidence of this in the hero's 'development':

When the focus returns to Peredur, the journey motif and the hero's arrival at a castle introduce the episode of the besieged maiden, which marks the beginning of a new thread, not apparently connected with the preceding adventures. Nevertheless, this is the first major adventure that Peredur has undertaken and so it marks a further step in his development as a knight. The hero's courteous treatment of the distressed girl, contrasting sharply with his rough and ready behaviour towards the girl in the tent, shows how far he has benefited from his training in 'moes a mynut'. [p.205]

I cannot easily see this 'development': the hero behaves one way in one situation, and differently in another, and there is little happening between that would account for the difference.

The story described by Dr Goetinck varies substantially from that of our manuscripts. This is clearly seen in her treatment of the end of the tale: in our version Peredur avenges his *cousin*, not his father (as Dr Goetinck suggests); the hero is never said to have lost the Empress (in this tale the parallel to the castigation Owain receives for deserting his wife in *Iarlles y Ffynnon* is the denunciation of Peredur for failing to ask the question); and in none of the versions does he regain a wife, or take up rule anywhere. Discussing an 'original' tale so significantly different from the extant versions helps us little in the understanding of the structure of these. Dr Lloyd-Morgan treats of the tale we have (or one version of it) but imposes a structure retrospectively, rather than demonstrating that it actually arises from the tale. She hints at this in her reference to Sartre's principle in *La Nausée* that all events are arbitrary and shape and pattern are imposed only with hindsight. Some of this shaping appears at the end in the speech of Peredur's cousin; the rest, however, must be deduction by the reader.

Some insight into the structure of *Peredur* may be gained from consideration of its relationship to the French versions, especially that of Chrétien de Troyes and his Continuators.[19] The first thing to note in this context is that *Peredur* is quite clearly a Celtic story. The name of the hero is significant here; whichever way the influence went the name was not carried across. 'Peredur' is a native name attested in the genealogies;[20] the two most relevant are those in Oxford, Jesus College MS 20 and BL Harleian MS 3859. The first — a fourteenth-century manuscript — links the name with an Arthur: 'Gwrgi a Pheredur ac Arthur penuchel',[21] while the second, a twelfth-century manuscript with signs of tenth-century orthography, gives the descent of Peredur thus:

[G]urci ha Peretur mepion Eleuther cascord maur map [Gurgust] letlum map ceneu map Coel hen.[22]

This would give Peredur a *floruit* in the sixth century, and a place in the old British North, a region from which a number of Arthurian heroes seem to have come;

it would also be consistent with the connection with York implied by giving him the patronymic 'uab Efrawg'.[23]

The procession in *Peredur* is very different from that in the French poem: specifically, there is no Grail, but rather a head. This is a point to which I shall return. Other features of *Peredur* which are clearly from Celtic tradition include: the Witches of Gloucester, who can be compared to those in the Life of St Samson,[24] and perhaps to Scathach who trains Cú Chulainn in arms,[25] and who are suggestive of the witches mentioned in the dialogue between Arthur and the Porter in the Black Book of Carmarthen;[26] the hunt for a magic beast (here a unicorn, more usually a stag) which is a common Celtic motif;[27] and the magic *gwyddbwyll* board in the Fortress of Marvels, which is like that of Gwenddolau ap Ceidio which was the twelfth of the Thirteen Treasures of the Island of Britain.[28]

Equally Celtic, or at least very unlike the French, is the narrative style. It is in general much less discursive and descriptive than the French, although the style is not totally consistent throughout *Peredur*. The style of the Circular Valley episode is, for example, a little more expansive than that of the earlier episode of the Maiden of the Tent. Both, however, exhibit the concentration on event which is characteristic of, for example, the *Four Branches*. Sometimes there are echoes of the same phraseology: 'When they thought it more timely to sleep than to carouse they went to bed' (*Peredur*); 'That night they continued to talk and to sing and carouse as long as they liked, and when they saw that it was better to sleep than to continue to sit up they went to bed' (*Branwen verch Lŷr*).

This style may be indicative of the oral nature of *Peredur*, although one must be careful here: the description of Olwen in *Culhwch ac Olwen* is certainly not skimped, and *Breuddwyd Rhonabwy* seems to be mocking a more extensive style of description. There are more significant pointers to an oral tradition lying behind our versions of *Peredur*, such as the use of formulae. Major sections are introduced with a variant of 'Arthur was at Caer Llion ar Wysc', while twice Peredur's meeting with a knight is based on the pattern '"Are you Arthur's man?" "By my faith, I am." "This is a good place to declare that."' Equally indicative of such a tradition are the events which come (usually incrementally) in threes: three blows against the column, three fights in the Circular Valley, three summonses from the Empress, three challenges from three men with three cups, and a need to seek a man who will fight three times.

As well as differing in style and extent from the French, *Peredur* also differs in the order of some episodes. In Chrétien's poem the Blancheflor episode comes between Perceval's meetings with Gornement and the Fisher King; in *Peredur* the hero stays with his two uncles on successive nights, and only afterwards does he have the adventure with the Maiden of the Castle. It is arguable that Chrétien's order is, as D.D.R. Owen claims,[29] suited to his purpose of showing the development of his hero; in *Peredur* it is no more than another story.

The greater integration of the French version can be seen at the end of the Blancheflor episode. Perceval is most decidedly in love with Blancheflor; he leaves her only because he has decided to seek his mother, whom he had left in a faint.[30] This not only ties the story into the earlier part of the poem, and provides at least a plausible excuse for the hero's departure, but also illustrates a step in his moral progress in that he recognizes that his behaviour to his mother was wrong. In *Peredur*, however, the logic of the story again points to the hero falling in love with and marrying the lady — and he does indeed stay a while for love of her. His departure, however, is abrupt and without excuse; no mention is made of his mother. Despite having spent three weeks with the girl, it is only on his departure that he gives his name. This part strikes a false note, as if it has been changed because the rest of the tale cannot take place if the hero marries at this point. The ending:

> 'Friend, who are you?' 'Peredur son of Efrawg, from the north. If you are ever threatened with danger or distress, tell me, and I will rescue you if I can.'

is reminiscent of those television series where each episode is complete in itself, but has to leave the hero unchanged for the start of the next episode.

A quick glance at the number of ladies with whom Peredur is to become involved to some degree shows why he needs to start each episode without previous entanglements. Looking at the endings of such episodes shows in the main the same pattern of a break in the narrative logic which leads to marriage. Peredur says to Angharad Law Eurawg he could 'love you best of all women, if you liked'; he then makes a vow with the intention of persuading her to love him best of all men. Yet when this is achieved, the obvious consequence — marriage — is avoided; instead, 'he became the companion of Gwalchmai, and Owain son of Urien, and of all Arthur's retinue, and he stayed at court'. The Countess of the Feats, later, is conveniently married off to Etlym.

Even more interesting, because it shows very clearly the process of amalgamation of stories, is the tale of the Circular Valley. The story comes within the Angharad section, but could itself stand alone (hero tricked into danger, warned by a lady who has fallen in love with him, wins out against all the odds). Again the lack of the natural conclusion — marriage — is a pointer to modification to fit either within the Angharad story or within *Peredur* as a whole; even more telling, however, is the clumsy connection to the framework story through the baptism of the inhabitants of the valley. This is not demanded by the narrative, but is essential to the safeguarding of Peredur's vow to Angharad. The hero rams the point home rather obviously:

'Diolchaf inheu ydaw na thorreis vy llw wrth y wreic uwyhaf a garaf na dywedwn vn geir wrth gristyawn' (I am thankful that I have not broken my vow to the woman I love best, not to speak a word to a Christian). Had the Circular Valley episode been originally conceived of within the context of the Angharad story the hero would not have been so willing to talk with the inhabitants in the first place. If this section is an independent story modified to be brought within the Angharad tale, there must be a strong possibility that the other places where the ending has been modified indicate episodes brought into, but not fully integrated with, *Peredur*.

In the context of the changes made to potential marriages to prevent problems on the surface narrative level, the reign of Peredur with the Empress of Constantinople stands out even more strongly. If the redactor had wanted to lead into the final section of the story, he could surely have found a way to do so rather than the abrupt switch from Constantinople to Caerleon. Mary Williams thought that the MS Peniarth 7 version, which ends at this point, and which is of at least equal antiquity to that of MS Peniarth 4, was the 'original' form of the story. Jean Marx disagrees: 'Cet épisode n'a jamais pu être la fin d'un conte.'[31] His certainty seems based on the need for explanation of the strange procession, which is to be found only in the final section.

However, looking at the final section of *Peredur* (*WM* 165.26-178; *Mab*. 217-27) it is immediately apparent that it bears a much closer resemblance to the French poem, at least up to the meeting with the priest, than is evident elsewhere in the tale. The pattern is similar: the denunciation of the hero in Arthur's court, the introduction of the twin themes behind Gauvain/Gwalchmai's quest and the first episodes of it (considerably less elaborate in *Peredur*, omitting all the tournaments and the courtly love elements) and Perceval/Peredur's meeting with a hermit/priest. Interestingly, although the priest in *Peredur* lives in a castle there is no sign of any other human being. From this point the Welsh and French diverge, and any remaining comparisons are on the level of motifs rather than stories.

Nevertheless these parallels are striking and significant. It is true that Gwalchmai has appeared earlier as Peredur's sponsor at Arthur's court but it is hard to account for the insertion of the one brief adventure recounted here; in the French, however, this is part of a much longer theme, which also reflects back on the differences between Gauvain and Perceval. Even more striking is the correspondence between the French and the Welsh versions of the denunciation speech. In *Peredur* this does not at all match with the events which have been described earlier: the ugly maiden places the incident in the court of the wrong uncle (the lame one), halves the number of youths carrying the spear, and reduces by two the drops of blood on it. Each of these discrepancies tallies with the story as it appears in Chrétien's poem.

It is hard to avoid the impression that this last section of *Peredur* is very poorly written. Apart from the unexplained presence of the Gwalchmai story, with its less-than-satisfactory ending: 'but that is all the story has to say about Gwalchmai and this adventure', and the introduction of Good Friday without any specific purpose, how can any sense be made of the events following the hero's arrival at the Fortress of Marvels? He throws a *gwyddbwyll* board through a window, is set a task which he does not quite fulfil, goes back and completes it, is set another task the completion of which offends another(?) lady who sets a further task. In this last he is cheated, but walks to what is obviously his rightful place, receives an 'explanation' of the strange procession, and with Arthur's help avenges his first cousin by killing the Witches of Gloucester.

Yet this redactor is not incapable of writing well: between the meeting with the priest and the hero's arrival at the Fortress of Marvels comes a story, similar in many ways to that of the Maiden of the Court, which flows easily on a narrative level. In contrast with other originally independent stories, this even shows an attempt at integration into the quest for the Fortress of Marvels: this quest is acknowledged by the lady to be a higher one than that of marriage.

It is difficult to account for this muddle except as an attempt by a redactor to draw together confused or half-remembered stories about the hero. Jean Marx made comparisons with the *Continuations* of the *Conte du graal* and with the Didot *Perceval*,[32] although there is no indication that the redactor of *Peredur* knew those works. What is difficult to accept, however, is that this muddle was in any sense necessary to 'explain' or complete anything in the first part of *Peredur*.

It is normally said that this section resolves the vengeance theme, but this raises more questions than it answers. The first vengeance theme is that related to the dwarfs, and this is accomplished early in the tale. No other vengeance theme exists until it is raised by Peredur's cousin right at the end, and applied retrospectively to the procession. In any event, why should Peredur do the avenging? It is in Chrétien's version that Perceval's father was wrongfully dispossessed of his land; in *Peredur* his death seems to be accepted as natural, and his widow seeks to protect her son from his own natural instincts rather than from any treachery. Anyway, the head is that of Peredur's *cousin*, and it is carried by another cousin; who must also have been at least cousin, if not brother, to the dead man. Why should Peredur have to do the dirty work? 'It was prophesied that you would take revenge'; a lame excuse.

Nor does the cousin's explanation relate either to the denunciation (there is no suggestion now of the need to ask a question) or to the description of the events in the court of Peredur's second uncle. *Two* youths, not one, carried the spear, and *two* maidens carried the head. I am not convinced by the cousin's claimed ability to appear as a woman.

Indeed, that change of sex is just one of a number of unexplained strange events, threads left dangling. In the course of the narrative one or two loose ends may be tied up — the death of Peredur's mother, the avenging of Syberw's lady — but much passes without comment. Marvels abound in this environment: lions guarding castles, giants, serpents on gold rings, dead men who can be revived in tubs of warm water, magic stones. If one is looking for unexplained — and perhaps inexplicable — episodes, that of the black and white sheep and the half-burning tree ought to be sufficient: it plays no part in the narrative, and nowhere is there any attempt to ascribe significance to it. The strange procession is just another such occurrence; the oddity is not the event itself but the fact that an attempt is made to 'explain' what it was about. It may well be that the attempt to put an explanation into the mouth of Peredur's cousin is an afterthought itself influenced by the Grail legends.

In this context, to look for an underlying theme in *Peredur* is doomed to failure. The tale is made up from a number of stories connected by the identity of the hero and little else, with the addition of a part of a Gwalchmai story which is there because the redactor found it with other material. Some of the episodes may, I believe, actually be doublets of each other from varying traditions. The serpent on the ring and the *addanc* may be such a pair; the two fights with Cai are surely such a case. There is evidence, I think, that this collection of material originally existed without the final section, as in MS Peniarth 7, and that the addition of this material was the work of a redactor who, with a distinct lack of success, was trying to pull together various threads under the influence of what had been done on the Continent. In comparison with Chrétien's *Conte du graal*, *Peredur* is a failure; looked at on its own terms, as a series of exciting adventures, it is in the main as good as its modern television counterparts.

NOTES:

1. Unless otherwise stated, references are to MS Peniarth 4, *WM* col. 117-78. Also edited by Glenys Goetinck, *Historia Peredur vab Efrawc* (Cardiff, 1976). *Peredur* is translated in *Mab.* 183-227.

2. Glenys Goetinck, *Peredur: a Study of Welsh Tradition in the Grail Legends* (Cardiff, 1975), 304-17, and references therein.

3. Mary Williams, *Essai sur la composition du roman gallois de Peredur* (Paris, 1909).

4. Leo Weisgerber, 'Die Handschriften des Peredur ab Efrawc in ihrer Bedeutung für die kymrische Sprach- und Literaturgeschichte', *ZCP*, 15 (1925), 66-186; p.79.

5. Glenys Goetinck, op.cit., 313-16.

6. Sir Edward Anwyl, *RC*, 31 (1910), 382-3.

7. *TYP*, 303-6.

8. R. Thurneysen, *ZCP*, 8 (1912), 185-9.

9. Mary Williams, op.cit., 18.

10. L. Muhlhausen, 'Untersuchung über das gegenseitige Verhaltnis von Chrestiens Conte du Graal und dem kymrischen Prosaroman von Peredur', *Z.f. rom. Phil.*, 44 (1924), 465-543.

11. Jean Marx, 'Observations sur la structure du roman gallois de Peredur', *ÉC*, 10 (1962-3), 88-108.

12. I.C. Lovecy, 'The Celtic Sovereignty Theme and the Structure of *Peredur*', *SC*, 12-13 (1977-8), 133-46.

13. A.C.L. Brown, *The Origin of the Grail Legends* (New York, 1966); W.A. Nitze, *Perceval and the Holy Grail* (Berkeley, 1949); ATC.

14. Glenys Goetinck, op.cit.

15. E.g. *Echtra mac nEchach*, ed. W. Stokes, *RC*, 24 (1903), 190-207; trans. Cross and Slover, *Ancient Irish Tales* (rev. ed. Dublin, 1969), 508-13.

16. Rachel Bromwich, 'Celtic Dynastic Themes and the Breton Lays', *ÉC*, 9 (1960), 439-74.

17. Glenys Goetinck, op.cit, 20.

18. Ceridwen Lloyd-Morgan, 'Narrative Structure in *Peredur*', *ZCP*, 38 (1981), 187-231.

19. Chrétien de Troyes, *Le Roman de Perceval ou le Conte du Graal*, ed. William Roach (Paris, 1959); *Perceval: the Story of the Grail*, trans. Nigel Bryant (Cambridge, 1982).

20. *EWGT*, index *sub* 'Peredur'.

21. Ibid. 43. Cf. *TYP* no. 70 and n. p.188.

22. *EWGT*, 11.

23. *TYP* 489.

24. R. Fawtier, *La Vie de Saint Samson* (Paris, 1912); T. Taylor, *Life of St Samson* (London, 1925). Cf. above p. 45 and *CO*(1) lxxiv.

25. *Tochmarc Emire*, ed. A.G. van Hamel, *Compert Con Culainn and other stories* (Dublin, 1933), 16-68.

26. *LlDC* no. 31. Cf. *CO*(1) lxxiii-iv.

27. Rachel Bromwich, art. cit. and below p. 285.

28. *TYP* 241-2; cf. above p. 86.

29. D.D.R. Owen, *The Evolution of the Grail Legend* (Edinburgh, 1968), 140.

30. *Conte du graal* 11.2910-2932; Bryant, *Pereceval: the Story of the Grail*, 32.

31. Jean Marx, art. cit., 100.

32. Ibid., 104.

9

BREUDDWYD RHONABWY AND LATER ARTHURIAN LITERATURE

Ceridwen Lloyd-Morgan

A'r ystorya honn a elwir Breidwyt Ronabwy. (A llyma yr achaws na wyr
neb y breidwyt, na bard na chyfarwyd, heb lyuyr, o achaws y geniuer
lliw a oed ar y meirch, a hynny o amrauael liw odidawc ac ar yr aruev
ac eu kyweirdebeu, ac ar y llenneu gwerthuawr a'r mein rinwedawl).
                                                              (*BR* 21.9-14)

*And this story is called the Dream of Rhonabwy. And here is the
reason why no one, neither bard nor storyteller, knows the Dream
without a book — by reason of the number of colours that were on
the horses, and all that variety of rare colours both on the arms and
their trappings, and on the precious mantles, and the magic stones.*
                                                              (*Mab.* 152)

So ends *Breuddwyd Rhonabwy* (The Dream of Rhonabwy),[1] with a colophon as
ambiguous and tantalizing as Geoffrey of Monmouth's reference to the 'ancient British
book'. Whatever the ironic intent of this statement, the very emphasis on dependence
on a book, a written copy of the tale, provides an important indication that with this
text Middle Welsh Arthurian literature begins to move into a new phase.

Although modern scholars tend to group *Breuddwyd Rhonabwy* with the
Mabinogion group, it stands somewhat apart from the other tales, in terms of
manuscript tradition, mode of composition, structure, and its treatment of King
Arthur. Whereas all the other tales of the *Mabinogion* series are preserved both in
Llyfr Gwyn Rhydderch (the White Book of Rhydderch) and in *Llyfr Coch Hergest*
(the Red Book of Hergest), *Breuddwyd Rhonabwy* is exceptional in that it survives in
the Red Book only (*RM*, cols. 555.10-571). No fragments survive in any other
medieval manuscript. Although it has been assumed in the past that this tale was
once included in the White Book, in that portion of it which is now missing, there is
no evidence at all in the White Book itself to indicate such a possibility. Moreover,
in the unique Red Book copy, this text is grouped with *Chwedleu Seith Doethon
Rufein* (a version of the popular tale of the Seven Sages) and a vaticinatory text,
Proffwydoliaeth Sibli Doeth, some fifty-six columns separating it from the nearest
tale of the *Mabinogion, Owain*.[2] None the less, the kind of errors found in the Red
Book text of *Breuddwyd Rhonabwy* demonstrate that the scribe was working from a

written source,[3] and scholars have consistently maintained that this tale is essentially a written one, composed by a single author, even if he cannot be identified. As such, *Breuddwyd Rhonabwy* represents a new departure.

In their present state the earlier Middle Welsh prose tales are essentially written texts, in so far as they display certain narrative techniques and procedures that are more or less incompatible with oral composition, but the story material itself had evolved originally in an oral context, and that heritage can still be discerned in certain aspects of textual construction and the manner of story-telling. 'Revising' or 'editing' might take place when the tale was first written down, or during subsequent copyings, but the concept of the single author with absolute freedom to control his material had not yet developed. In *Breuddwyd Rhonabwy*, however, we appear to be faced with this new phenomenon, rather than with multiple or collective authorship over a period of time.

The outline of the story is simple enough. It opens with Rhonabwy, a purely fictional character not previously attested, setting out to seek the historical figure Iorwerth ap Maredudd, on behalf of Iorwerth's brother Madog, who ruled over Powys from 1130 to 1160. Rhonabwy and his followers seek lodgings for the night in the house of Heilyn Goch, and find themselves in such uncomfortable, cold and flea-ridden quarters that Rhonabwy, unable to sleep in the bedding provided, goes to lie down on a yellow heifer-skin on the dais at one end of the house. Here he sleeps and is granted a *drych* or vision, the dream of the title. He is transported from the twelfth century of Madog ap Maredudd into the Arthurian world, although this too is rooted with remarkable geographic precision in Powys. Here he meets Iddawg Cordd· Prydain (Iddawg Embroiler of Britain), who acts as his guide, explaining who other protagonists are and giving a limited commentary on events. Iddawg leads Rhonabwy to where Arthur is encamped, whilst troops arrive for battle. Arthur and Owain ab Urien become engrossed in the board-game *gwyddbwyll*, despite repeated reports from messengers that Arthur's men are attacking Owain's ravens, and then that Owain's ravens are slaying Arthur's men, with repeated requests that they be called off. Finally a truce is called, without any proper battle taking place, and Arthur's followers are told to assemble with him in Cornwall. With that Rhonabwy awakes, having slept for three days and nights, and the story ends with the colophon quoted above. Nothing further is said of Rhonabwy's search for Iorwerth ap Maredudd, nor is any commentary made upon the content or significance of the dream: that is left to the audience or reader.

Much of the subject matter of *Breuddwyd Rhonabwy* is both traditional and native; much of the interest of the text lies in the way in which that subject matter is given a new twist. In terms of content, the tale contributes comparatively little to the depth or breadth of our knowledge of the stock of medieval Welsh Arthurian tradition, in contrast with *Culhwch ac Olwen*, therefore, which is richly informative in that respect. Traditional material is still used in *Breuddwyd Rhonabwy* but not as an end in itself. Instead it is manipulated carefully to create something new, a completely original Arthurian tale, lacking any close parallels, and composed in a satiric rather than heroic vein, with a highly complex interplay of ambiguities and ironies.

King Arthur himself retains some of his trappings from earlier tradition, but the depiction is anything but heroic. When, through Rhonabwy's eyes, we first glimpse him seated on an island in the River Severn, no physical description is given of him, nor of his bishop, whereas a youth of lower status, standing nearby, is described in some detail, despite not even being named at this point (*BR* 6.10-20). Arthur's first words immediately suggest that the heroic Arthurian world is a thing of the past, for he contrasts present warriors with their predecessors:

> 'nyt chwerthin a wnaf, namyn truanet gennyf vot dynyon ky vawhet a hynny yn gwarchadw yr ynys honn gwedy gwyr kystal ac a'e gwarchetwis gynt'.
>
> (*BR* 6.27-7.3)
>
> *'I am not laughing; but rather how sad I feel that men as mean as these keep this Island, after men as fine as those that kept it of yore.'*   (*Mab.* 141)

Shortly afterwards, both he and the bishop, Bedwin, are drenched by Addaon fab Telessin, who spurs his horse over the ford to splash them. That the Arthurian world has truly turned upside down is confirmed by Iddawg describing Addaon in terms of praise, and Elphin, who rebuked the discourteous rider and struck his horse, in terms of abuse. These events set the tone for the rest of the tale. Arthur and Owain play *gwyddbwyll* rather than getting on with fighting the important Battle of Badon against Osla Gyllellfawr, as they are supposed to be doing. Instead, a battle of sorts is fought out between Arthur's men and Owain's ravens, who should presumably be on the same side. Both Arthur and Owain repeatedly refuse to end this conflict by calling off their respective supporters, and the result of both the *gwyddbwyll* game and the carnage offstage is nothing but a truce, and a postponement of the intended battle with Osla. All this is a far cry from the heroic Arthur leading his men into the fray, but in Rhonabwy's dream the Battle of Camlan is already past history, more than seven years old.[4] The fact that the Battle of Badon has not yet taken place whereas traditionally Camlan was the last Arthurian battle further demonstrates that here all the normal rules are broken.[5] Although the Arthur of *Culhwch ac Olwen* does not take an active role in every adventure and is sometimes overshadowed by his companions, he is still accorded proper status as a leader. The Arthur of Rhonabwy's dream, for all his being repeatedly addressed or referred to as Emperor, plays instead of fighting: crushing the *gwyddbwyll* pieces is his only physical action, and he shows little interest or involvement in what is going on around him. Rather than sources in Welsh this evokes the Welsh Saints' lives of the twelfth century, where Arthur as a temporal lord has to be presented in less favourable a light than the saint.

It is significant too that what fighting does take place is offstage, and only reported briefly, and, being a skirmish between men and ravens, is hardly an orthodox Arthurian battle. Nothing is achieved in the course of the dream-tale. At first sight it seems full of movement: the arrival of troops, the fighting between the men and the ravens, but the narrative is essentially static. Many of the actions are simply repeated with minor variation, as in the case of the three squires arriving to report on the fighting when Arthur's men are gaining the upper hand over Owain's ravens, and their three counterparts when the tide of battle has turned. Actions have little, if any, outcome. The Arthurian world does not change during the dream, nothing is won or lost. Some actions, such as splashing Arthur and the bishop, invite reaction, but this is discouraged. That the fighting which does occur is only reported indirectly, and that the battle with Osla is put off, immediately sets *Breuddwyd Rhonabwy* apart from the norm of Middle Welsh story-telling, where the lively description of such scenes formed an integral part of the story-teller's stock-in-trade.

None the less, many of the story elements are traditional, and familiar from other Middle Welsh tales. In *Breuddwyd Rhonabwy* as in *Culhwch ac Olwen*, Arthur is associated with Cornwall, thus reflecting the pre-Geoffrey localization of his court. Owain ab Urien, one of the oldest heroes to be linked with Arthur, is a prominent figure in the dream just as he is in the three romantic tales of *Geraint*, *Owain* and *Peredur*. The association of Owain with ravens seems likewise to have a long history in Welsh tradition,[6] as does the *topos* of the *gwyddbwyll* game,[7] and although the French *Didot Perceval* also includes the motifs of a fight at a ford involving ravens, and a chess-game[8] (the equivalent of *gwyddbwyll*), there seems no reason to doubt that in *Breuddwyd Rhonabwy* they are derived from Welsh indigenous sources. Yet here again, the redactor has made unusual use of these elements, for Owain plays *against* Arthur, just as the ravens fight the emperor's men: they are no longer on the same side. Although in *Owain* and *Peredur* we find similar passages where the hero of the title, one of Arthur's knights, fights Arthur's men one by one, this motif usually hinges on the hero's being incognito, his true identity only being revealed once he has been brought back into the Arthurian fold after a period of wandering.[9] In *Breuddwyd Rhonabwy* the circumstances are quite different, for there is no disguise and Owain has not left the court, yet Owain is overtly opposed to Arthur, rather than the two being united against a common enemy. Similarly, whereas in *Culhwch ac Olwen* Osla Gyllellfawr is one of the band of warriors who help Arthur in the hunt for the Twrch Trwyth, here he is to be Arthur's opponent at the Battle of Badon, whereas a Saxon enemy would have been more appropriate.[10]

Such violation of the normal rules of Arthurian narrative is ironically underlined by the introduction of the kind of local colour characteristic of earlier tales, such as the magic ring which will enable Rhonabwy to remember what he has seen in the dream (*BR* 7.3-8), and Arthur's magical mantle of invisibility (*BR* 11.13-23 and cf. above pp. 86-8). Although this suggests that the redactor was well steeped in Welsh story-telling tradition, whether Arthurian or otherwise, he was apparently particularly familiar with *Culhwch ac Olwen*, as witness the extensive borrowings from that text. The most notable example is the list of Arthur's counsellors (*BR* 19.10-20.5), which not only appears to be modelled in form on the list found in *Culhwch*, but includes a number of names lifted from there, such as Ffleudwr Fflam, Edern mab Nudd, Menw mab Teirgwaedd, Nerth mab Kadarn. Other personal names which appear elsewhere in *Culhwch*, such as Mabon mab Modron, and Gorau mab Custennin, are also mentioned, although some, such as *March uab Meirchiawn, Gilbert mab Katgyffro, Kadyrieith mab Seidi, Karadawc Vreichuras* and the latter's son *Kawrdaf*, appear to have been borrowed from the Triads. The one brief reference to Cai (*BR* 10.18-20), as the fairest man who rides in Arthur's court, recalls the favourable description of him given in *Culhwch*, rather than the surly character ascribed to him in tales such as *Peredur*. That the author also knew Geoffrey of Monmouth's *Historia Regum Britanniae* through one of the Welsh versions is indicated by his references to Cadwr, Earl of Cornwall and to Howel fab Emyr Llydaw.[11]

In style and narrative technique too, the redactor reveals a confident familiarity with the native tradition. The use of *rhethreg*, with its strings of compound adjectives recalls the style of other Arthurian tales such as *Geraint*, and the use of parallels and repetitions provides a further example. The repetition in threes of the squires' requests first to Arthur then to Owain to call off their supporters conforms to the incremental pattern so characteristic of Middle Welsh story-telling, where each repeat brings a greater intensity, with a climax or new step on the third occasion. Thus after the third vain request to Arthur, Owain gives orders for the standard to be raised, thus changing the course of the fighting, whilst the third request to Owain, in the second, parallel sequence, leads to the ravens being called off and peace being resumed. But whereas in normal practice the third repeat would significantly change the circumstances, and advance the narrative, in *Breuddwyd Rhonabwy* no progress is made thereby.

The descriptions of the squires and tents in this section are likewise carefully constructed, for although at first reading they may seem to be fairly arbitrary, and rather complex, on closer examination, as John Bollard has shown, they can be seen to follow a predetermined pattern.[12]   In turn the tent, the squire himself, and his dress are all described according to the selfsame formula, the same kind of detail being given in the same order each time (but for one single exception).   The descriptions of Arthur's knights, although more complex, still follow the same kind of pattern, starting with the horse, then the armour of horse and rider, and finally the sword, helmet and spear.   As Bollard stresses, the precise colour choice or detail might not be of vital importance, and although they could in theory be used to distinguish characters, this is not necessary.   Apart from Rhonabwy, Iddawg, Owain and Arthur, there is no attempt at characterization of even the crudest kind. Characters are given a formulaic physical description and perhaps a name, but play no significant part in the narrative, and once mentioned fade out of it.   The use of this regular pattern for descriptions would provide an important mnemonic aid in an oral telling of the story, as well as providing scope for variation by the story-teller. This strongly suggests several layers of irony in the colophon, where the redactor apparently boasts that no poet or *cyfarwydd* (story-teller) could tell the story without a book, because of the descriptions.   Bollard's analysis shows that this statement is simply untrue.   Moreover, although *Breuddwyd Rhonabwy* has all the marks of having been composed *ab initio* as a written text, we now find that it is still theoretically capable of being transmitted orally.   Not only is the redactor playing fast and loose with the components of the traditional Arthurian tale, he is also playing against each other the characteristics of the story for oral transmission and of the tale composed in a written context.   Once again expectations are built up only to be undercut, and we begin to realize that parody, rather than the usual straightforward type of narrative, is the pivot of *Breuddwyd Rhonabwy*.

The text begins with a classic opening formula, 'Madawc uab Maredud a oed idaw Powys yn y theruyneu' ('Madawg son of Maredudd held Powys from end to end'), following the model of the Four Branches of the *Mabinogi*, and other tales. But after this strong and positive note, our attention is drawn to the shortcomings of his brother Iorwerth, and from then on it is negative rather than positive characteristics that are stressed, both in the waking world of Rhonabwy in twelfth-century Powys, and in the Arthurian world of his dream, so that the expectations raised by the first line of *Breuddwyd Rhonabwy* are dashed by what follows, just as our assumption that Arthur will be presented in a heroic light is swiftly undercut.   Whilst Rhonabwy and his companions find their lodgings in the house of Heilyn Goch scarcely worthy of the name, so too is Arthur scarcely deserving of his title as Emperor.

Similarly, despite the opening formula, the tale is not about Madog.   Moreover, the quest for Iorwerth is not only unfulfilled, it is simply abandoned, and not even referred to when Rhonabwy wakes up after his dream. In retrospect it can be seen as a device for bringing Rhonabwy into the dream and for stressing the contrast between the two brothers, or between Madog's strong rule of Powys and the passivity of Arthur in the dream; in itself it is of little significance in the end, and as such can be laid aside.

The same elements of ambiguity, parody and irony can be seen in the use of the dream framework. Sleeping on an ox-hide occurs in Irish sources as a prelude to a dream, especially a prophetic vision,[13] but not normally in circumstances of such squalor as those in Heilyn's house. Moreover, Rhonabwy does not sleep on the hide in order to have such a dream, but because he is uncomfortable elsewhere. The dream is unwilled and unexpected. In the mainstream of Middle Welsh prose we have another important dream tale, *Breuddwyd Macsen Wledig* (The Dream of Maxen), which has close affinities with *Breuddwyd Rhonabwy* in one particular aspect. Macsen in his dream is transported to another world, which mimics the world of his waking, but where the rules are subtly changed. Macsen's dream journey from Rome to Caernarfon is depicted with exactly the same geographical precision as Rhonabwy's journey through Powys both waking and sleeping; in both tales the journey can be followed today on a map. But whereas Macsen's dream later becomes a part of his reality, it is the fictional aspect of Rhonabwy's dream that comes to the fore. The prosaic, historical world of Madog's Powys is contrasted with the topsy-turvy nature of the Arthurian world in Rhonabwy's dream, and it may be that parody of the usual tradition, where the dream is of serious intent, is involved.

Nevertheless there are clear Celtic parallels with Rhonabwy's type of dream. The Irish *Aislinge Meic Conglinne* (The Vision of Mac Conglinne),[14] the earliest manuscript of which is fourteenth century (though the longer redaction goes back to at least the twelfth century) not only contains a very similar description of poor lodgings and grudging hospitality in the introductory passage before the actual dream vision, but also has a satirical intent. But the Irish tale is full of overt burlesque elements, in contrast with *Breuddwyd Rhonabwy* which relies more on failing to fulfil the expectations it builds up. Two of the Welsh *Areithiau Pros*[15] also display similarities to our text. *Araith Wgon* provides an account of unpleasant lodgings of the type endured by Rhonabwy and his companions, whilst *Breuddwyd Gruffydd ap Adda ap Dafydd* describes another dream vision. But here again the parallels with *Breuddwyd Rhonabwy* are limited. In *Araith Wgon* the description of the lodgings is an end in itself and leads to no vision, whilst Gruffydd ap Adda in a richly decorated bed experiences a dream in which he sees, like Macsen, a beautiful lady in a castle. And although a battle takes place which includes *dvi branes* ('two flocks of ravens'), recalling the ravens of Rhonabwy's dream, this is actually witnessed by the dreamer, rather than being reported. These *Areithiau Pros* have been described as literary exercises composed by apprentices, and no manuscript copy predates 1560.[16] Although they have much in common with *Breuddwyd Rhonabwy*, it seems that they were inspired by that tale rather than vice versa.

It is particularly in the use of the dream framework that the unusually careful construction of *Breuddwyd Rhonabwy* emerges. Many Middle Welsh tales have a narrative structure which is comparatively loose and free, where excursions from the chief narrative thread are acceptable, a flexible form well suited to oral delivery. In *Breuddwyd Rhonabwy*, in contrast, we find a tale that comes closer to what we find in English or Continental literature in a purely written context, a text which can boast a beginning, middle and end, provided by the dream itself. The brief historical introduction provides the motivation for Rhonabwy's journey and his arrival at the house of Heilyn Goch, and the reason for his lying down to sleep on the heifer's skin is carefully given. In this way, the introductory passage provides the context for the dream itself, the dream providing the main narrative framework. The tale thus ends when Rhonabwy wakes. Since the search for Iorwerth ap Maredudd has served its structural function, it can be set aside, especially since its abandonment has its own role in the pattern of expectation and disappointment set up by the redactor, bringing into play tensions and similarities between the dream world and the 'historical' world.

Within the dream itself, too, the narrative has been carefully planned, with its sequence of non-events, parallels and repetitions discussed above. And although the actual circumstances which lead to Rhonabwy's dreaming have been taken from traditional stock, as suggested above, the structure of the dream may suggest reference to a wider body of literary tradition, since the dream sequence has structurally as much in common with the dream poems of French or English literature as with its Welsh or Celtic parallels. *Breuddwyd Rhonabwy* has the same specificity, the exactness in time and place in which the dream unfolds, as found in dream texts of other literatures — the opening of Guilaume de Lorris's *Roman de la Rose*, for example. As A.C. Spearing has stressed,[17] such specificity imparts a certain authority, spurious or otherwise, not only to the context of the dream but to the dream itself. And as the dream begins, the classic pattern, familiar from English and French, is employed: the dreamer finds himself once again in a precise geographical setting, where presently he meets the main interpreter or guide who conducts him on his way and provides a commentary on what he sees,[18] this role being played by Iddawg.

Not only was the redactor of *Breuddwyd Rhonabwy* well grounded in the traditions and techniques of native Welsh story-telling, therefore, but he was also aware of a wider body of literature, and written literature at that. Although the

Roman de la Rose was known in Wales by the early fourteenth century[19] and may have been known earlier, rather than suggesting direct influence from one specific text it may be more helpful to postulate an author with a general knowledge of literary trends outside Wales. Dafydd Glyn Jones, in the most detailed study to date of the satirical aspects of the tale, whilst attaching due importance to indigenous tradition, suggests that *Breuddwyd Rhonabwy* reveals familiarity with Continental satirical texts, and with specific *topoi*, such as that of the *monde bestorné*, commonly found in Old French.[20]   This indicates an author who has the detachment and sophistication to be able to pick elements of subject matter, exposition and technique from both the Welsh and the wider European traditions and put them together to create something new and original.

His precise purpose in so doing, and the meaning of the tale, are not immediately obvious. Scholars have agreed that *Breuddwyd Rhonabwy* is a written text, composed by a single author, in complete control of his material, who has built up an original Arthurian narrative from elements drawn partly from native tradition and partly from his own imagination. They have also agreed that his intention was to satirize and parody, but there has been less consensus with regard to the butt of such satire. The question is complicated by being closely related to considerations of dating. As with so many Middle Welsh tales, which survive only in comparatively late manuscripts, dating *Breuddwyd Rhonabwy* is fraught with difficulties, aggravated in this particular case by the lack of any copy predating the Red Book.

Dates between *c.* 1220 and 1309 have been suggested. Sir Thomas Parry and Melville Richards both based their cases on the opening section, set in twelfth-century Powys.[21]   Since a period of comparative stability during the reign of Madog ap Maredudd was followed after Madog's death in 1160 by a period of disunity and internal strife, as Powys was divided between Madog's sons, brother and nephew, they argued that *Breuddwyd Rhonabwy* reflected the nostalgia of a later period for what was perceived with hindsight as a golden age for Powys under Madog's rule. Richards suggested that since Powys entered a particularly unhappy period after the death of Gwenwynwyn in 1216, the tale might have been composed *c.* 1200-25, though Parry preferred a slightly later date. Both scholars concluded from the accuracy of the historical and geographical setting that the author came from Powys, and there is no reason to doubt this.[22]

Taking slightly different sets of perceived historical parallels, J. Angela Carson argued for a date in the late fourteenth century[23] and Mary Giffin, concentrating on the heraldic devices mentioned in the tale, for a date between 1293 and 1309.[24] The tale was certainly sufficiently well known by the second half of the fourteenth century for the poet Madog Dwygraig to compare himself to Rhonabwy the dreamer in an *awdl* to Morgan Dafydd ap Llywelyn.[25] No earlier reference in the poetry has come to light, and had *Breuddwyd Rhonabwy* been composed as early as the 1220s it might have been expected to be included in the White Book of Rhydderch or in one of the other medieval manuscripts which preserve fragments of Middle Welsh prose narrative.[26]

For Parry, Richards and others, considerations of dating have been based on the premise that the main theme of the tale is *laus temporis acti*, that the author intended a parallel between the inactivity in the Arthurian world and the lack of valour of his own time, in contrast with the golden age of Madog's rule. Dafydd Glyn Jones, however, has taken a broader view, seeing the tale first and foremost as a literary satire. The negative portrayal of Arthur here can be seen to follow in the tradition seen in the *Vitae* of the Welsh saints, such as the early twelfth-century *Vita Gildae*, but developed in the context of *Breuddwyd Rhonabwy* not only as a satire of Arthur himself, but of the Arthurian world. Since Dafydd Glyn Jones argues that the author was familiar with both native and Continental literary traditions, this raises the possibility that the intention was to satirize not simply the Arthurian legend in general but, rather more specifically, literary expressions of that legend.

Arthur's behaviour in the dream does seem to parody the accepted norm of Arthurian narrative: nothing in his behaviour suggests heroism or warrants the title Emperor. But literary parody implies familiarity with Arthurian tales on the part of the intended audience as well as of the author. The borrowings from *Culhwch ac Olwen* and from Geoffrey of Monmouth show that the author knew the earlier Arthurian texts well. But there is little to suggest parody of a specific text — the roll-call of names may be lifted partly from *Culhwch* but it does not contain burlesque elements as do the more obvious parodies of the later *Areithiau Pros*. The redactor seems to be satirizing the whole fabric of Arthurian literary conventions, which means he must have been working at a time when those conventions were already well developed. In that case, *Breuddwyd Rhonabwy* is likely to post-date the Welsh Arthurian tales of *Peredur*, *Owain* and *Geraint*,[27] which provide between them a reasonably consistent view of the Arthurian milieu and ethos. If *Breuddwyd Rhonabwy* was later than these texts and was composed partly to debunk the conventions which they accepted implicitly, this could explain why it does not appear in the earliest surviving manuscript compendia in Welsh. Assuming that the three romantic tales corresponding to three of Chrétien's romances achieved their present form in the first half of the thirteenth century, a date of composition in the late thirteenth or even early fourteenth century might be appropriate. Although satirical prose is attested at a later date, in the *Areithiau Pros*, and there is some Arthurian satire in the earlier Latin Lives of Welsh saints, *Breuddwyd Rhonabwy* appears to be the first example to survive in Welsh. This might be compared to analogous developments in Welsh poetry, where certain poets of the fourteenth and fifteenth centuries, such as Llywelyn ap y Moel and Llywelyn ap Gutun, parody the traditional style of heroic eulogy.

In all respects then, as a tale composed as a written text by a single author, in its selective use of traditional material within an original narrative, in its use of the dream framework and in its satirical intent, *Breuddwyd Rhonabwy* is essentially innovatory. In its move to the mode of written composition, and its awareness of non-Welsh literary traditions, the tale provides a foretaste of the way in which Arthurian narrative — and indeed prose narrative in general — was to develop. None of the later Welsh Arthurian texts display the inventiveness in terms of plot that we find in *Breuddwyd Rhonabwy*, but the influence of Continental literary traditions about Arthur and his court was to become increasingly important.

Later Arthurian Literature

Discussion of Welsh Arthurian literature has often focused mainly on the early poetry and prose narrative, with comparatively little attention being paid to material of the fourteenth, fifteenth and sixteenth centuries. Moreover, although many of these later texts are undoubtedly derived from French sources, the question of links between Welsh and Continental Arthurian literature has been approached most frequently in the context of the three romantic tales of *Geraint*, *Owain* and *Peredur*, and the problem of their respective relationships to the corresponding romances of *Erec*, *Yvain* and *Perceval* by Chrétien de Troyes. It is true that in recent years the view that those three Welsh texts have, at the very least, undergone French influence, may have become more widely accepted, but this remains a controversial issue. Yet it is in the later medieval period that we find concrete proof of the transmission of Arthurian material between the two cultures, albeit in the opposite direction, from France to Wales, with the production of texts closely and avowedly based on French sources or containing obvious borrowings.

Although during the fourteenth century earlier native tales continued to be copied, notably in the White Book of Rhydderch and Red Book of Hergest, and, presumably, to be transmitted orally,[28] no new native prose narrative from that period has survived and it is not now known whether any such texts ever existed. Instead, from the mid thirteenth century onwards, there appeared a whole body of translation into Welsh, based on original texts in French, English and Latin, and some of these were Arthurian. This was by no means an isolated phenomenon, for similar surges of translation into the vernacular took place in England and Ireland at the same period.[29] To take just one Arthurian example, the French *La Queste del Saint Graal* was translated into Welsh, English and Irish within the space of half a century. That Welsh patrons, redactors and scribes should have access to French Arthurian sources need not surprise us. Many French manuscripts may have come into Wales from England, for manuscripts of Continental French literature, including Arthurian texts such as the *Perlesvaus*, were circulating in England between the twelfth and the fourteenth century,[30] and the increasing political, economic and social integration between Wales and England from the early fourteenth century would have increased access. But Wales also had close direct ties with the Continent, throughout the medieval period, but especially following the Norman settlement of Wales in the late eleventh century, which led to even greater contact politically, and in economic and ecclesiastical affairs.[31] Furthermore, Anglo-Norman became, after Welsh and English, the third language spoken in certain regions, especially in the south-east, the area most rapidly and intensely settled, where noblemen found themselves having to employ professional interpreters fluent in all three languages in order to conduct their affairs.[32] French loan-words found their way into the Welsh language, as they did into English, and it is worth noting that the late fourteenth-century translator of *La Queste del Saint Graal* and the *Perlesvaus* possessed in his own current vocabulary a significant number of Romance loan-words quite apart from the ones that were suggested to him by the text before him.[33]

As in the case of earlier Welsh prose tales, few of these later texts can be dated with any certainty, for again the manuscript copies can only rarely be dated with precision, and normally we cannot tell how far the text predates the extant written copies. Setting aside the vexed question of the tales of *Geraint*, *Owain* and *Peredur* and their relationship to Chrétien's romances, however, the earliest examples of Welsh versions of French narratives are non-Arthurian; these include translations from the Charlemagne cycle of *chansons de geste*, probably from the period c. 1240-1340. It is in a fourteenth-century manuscript, NLW MS IA (formerly Llanstephan 201) in the National Library of Wales, that we find our earliest example of an Arthurian tale derived from a French romance.

This manuscript contains a fragment which was published by J.H. Davies in 1913 under the modern title 'The Birth of Arthur'.[34] The fragment opens with the arranging of a wedding between Uthyr and Eigyr, in order to bring peace between Uthyr and the followers of Gwrleis, Eigyr's first husband, and continues with Eigyr's confession that she is already pregnant. The birth of Arthur and his fostering are recounted, followed by the sword in the stone episode and the crowning of Arthur. The appearance of Blasius (Blaise), described as Myrddin's father confessor (his *dat eneit*) and secretary, immediately points to the French *Prose Merlin* as a source, and indeed for much of the narrative the redactor seems to have followed that text quite closely. Although he abridges or paraphrases from time to time, there are also passages of fairly close translation. This is not to suggest a slavish or unimaginative rendering, for the redactor has not only taken pains to supply personal names from native Welsh tradition but even to maintain a traditional style of narrative, faithful to the rhythms of Middle Welsh prose. Furthermore, he has effectively combined the narrative of these events in the *Prose Merlin* with the account of them given in versions of *Brut y Brenhinedd*, the Welsh versions of Geoffrey of Monmouth's *Historia Regum Britanniae*. Thus many of the proper names, and details of family relationships, given in the early part of the fragment, have been borrowed from the *Brutiau*, and Uthyr's death and the war which precedes it are referred to as being recounted in full in *Ystoria y Brytaniett*, a clear allusion to Geoffrey's account. The mention of an unnamed daughter of Uthyr being highly skilled in the seven arts and connected with *Ynys Avallach* may further indicate a knowledge of Geoffrey's *Vita Merlini* or perhaps native traditions. Although at this point in the narrative the *Prose Merlin* names the daughter as Morgue la fée, there is no mention there of Avalon.

In his careful dovetailing of French and Welsh accounts of the same basic narrative, and his substitution of familiar Welsh names for foreign ones, the redactor of 'The Birth of Arthur' shows his concern to adapt Continental material for a new audience. Apart from a lack of specialized training, and perhaps an imperfect knowledge of French at a period when Norman French had seriously declined as a living vernacular, the chief problem facing those adapting French Arthurian tales into Welsh was a cultural one. Although important characters such as Arthur, Owain, Peredur and Gwenhwyfar could easily be identified with their counterparts in Continental romances, the two literary traditions had developed in very different ways. Narrative structure and technique in Old French romances of, say, the early thirteenth century, were often incompatible with those characteristic of Middle Welsh story-telling, whilst the courtly life and ideals reflected in Continental Arthurian sources would sit uneasily in a Welsh context.

On a small scale, as in 'The Birth of Arthur', such difficulties can be overcome by concentrating on a single major episode and by judicious editing, but the task was more complex when the translation of complete French romances was attempted. Only one such example survives, now known for convenience as *Y Seint Greal*:[35] the earliest manuscripts bear no title as such, but in a colophon the redactor refers to his work as *ystoryaeu seint greal* (*SG* 433). *Y Seint Greal* is in fact two translations, for it includes Welsh versions of two French prose Grail romances of the early thirteenth century, *La Queste del Saint Graal* (one of the so-called Vulgate Cycle of French Arthurian romances) and the *Perlesvaus* or *Li Hauz Livre du Graal*. Despite their incompatibilities — Galaad is the Grail hero in the *Queste*, Perlesvaus in the second romance, and the concepts of Christian and knightly duty are strikingly different — these French romances are presented as two parts of a single whole.

The earliest surviving manuscript of *Y Seint Greal*, MS Peniarth 11 in the National Library of Wales, upon which all later copies are based, appears to be very close to the original translator's copy, judging by certain uncorrected mistakes. The scribe has been identified as the Hywel Fychan who was one of the three responsible for the Red Book of Hergest,[36] and both manuscripts are now believed to have been produced for Hopcyn ap Thomas, an important lay patron from Glamorgan, at the end of the fourteenth century.

As a rule, the translator of *Y Seint Greal* follows his French sources closely, to the extent that his work could never fail to be recognized as a translation, even had he not referred to himself as *trossyawdyr* (translator) at one point. None the less, additional detail given in the Welsh account of how Bohors lost his virginity demonstrates that he was adding to the version given in *La Queste del Saint Graal* information otherwise found only in the French *Prose Lancelot*, showing that another romance of the French Vulgate Cycle was also known in Wales.

The redactor of *Y Seint Greal*, furthermore, has made some attempt to adapt his foreign romances for a Welsh audience, albeit in a patchy and inconsistent manner. Despite the fact that, even taken separately, the two parts of *Y Seint Greal* are far longer than most Middle Welsh prose tales, some abridgement has taken place. This is particularly noticeable in the *Perlesvaus* section, where towards the end he paraphrases and condenses more and more, finally omitting entire episodes, even at the cost of leaving several ends untied. This inevitably results in a looser structure, which brings the narrative closer in form to earlier Welsh Arthurian tales such as *Culhwch ac Olwen* and *Peredur*, where the logical movement towards a carefully prepared conclusion is not regarded as necessary.

The abridgement also has its effect on the thematic development of the two narratives in *Y Seint Greal*, especially with reference to the elaboration of the ideologies of *courtoisie* and chivalry and their relation to the Christian faith. Since such discussions had less relevance in late fourteenth-century Wales, the translator has tended to omit or curtail those sections of his French texts which contain them. Greater emphasis is put on story-telling, particularly on battle scenes and action, with scant concern for the allegorical and mystical meanings which in the *Queste* provide the main motivation. But in so doing the redactor has gone some way to redefining the French knights as Welsh warrior heroes.

The French material is brought closer to the norms of native Welsh tradition in other ways too. Full use is made of the similarity between certain motifs and episodes in the French and those found in earlier Welsh tales, such as the magic chess-board and sword quest in the *Perlesvaus*, which evoke episodes in *Peredur* and *Culhwch* respectively. The choice of words in the translation often echoes earlier texts, especially *Peredur*. Wherever possible native proper names, which would be familiar to the Welsh audience, are substituted for the French ones. Thus Gwalchmai replaces Gauvain, and Cardueil gives way to Caerllion ar Wysg. Names that were less familiar could cause problems, however, and some were left as they stood. Occasionally the translator failed to find a Welsh equivalent the first time a name occurred, but made the connection later, so that Loholt, Arthur's son, retains his French name with Welsh spelling at first, but later receives his Welsh name, Llachau (*SG* 278.6, 304.29). Similarly Pennevoiseuse, where Arthur's court is sometimes held in the *Perlesvaus*, after much hesitation is rendered as Penwed (*SG* 380.37).

This kind of substitution also operates on other levels, as when the translator replaces a foreign element by something familiar from the Welsh way of life, for example in substituting *ae o vrethyn ae o hemp* ('either of woollen cloth or hemp') (*SG* 67.39) for 'de soie ou de lin' (*Queste* 105.2). Such local colour is also added to the Arthurian dimension of the tales: the identification of the French character with the Welsh Cai is strengthened by use of the traditional Welsh epithet, 'Cai hir' ('tall Cai', *SG* 340.8) which has no equivalent in the French, but recalls references in the tale of *Peredur* and *Ystorya Trystan*.[37]

Although an attempt was thus made to adapt the French romances for Welsh consumption, and although the prose style of *Y Seint Greal* follows as closely as possible standard Middle Welsh literary diction, with distinct echoes of the earlier prose tales, it could never be mistaken for anything other than a translation from the French. The world in which the action takes place remains closer to that of French romance than that of Welsh tradition, and King Arthur's portrayal has undergone little change in the translation. As in the French romances, the focus is more on the knights of Arthur's court rather than on the king himself: it is his duty to provide a context and motivation for the knights' deeds of prowess rather than to be constantly at their head in the field. Nevertheless, the *Perlesvaus* in particular explores how Arthur's inactivity and failure as a ruler affects adversely the whole of his kingdom, so that in the corresponding section of *Y Seint Greal* we find a thematic link back to the portrayal of Arthur in *Breuddwyd Rhonabwy*.

The evidence of other translations into Welsh suggests that French literature of all kinds was popular in Wales at this period, but in considering why *La Queste del Saint Graal* and *Perlesvaus* in particular were chosen, the discrepancies between the Graal narratives they relate make this decision at first sight a strange one. However, since Wales already had its own earlier Grail story (of sorts) in *Peredur*, it may have been felt that these texts would be more appropriate for their intended new audience than would a French romance which focused on a hero with no Welsh counterpart, such as one of the Lancelot romances. Even though in the *Queste* Perceval/Peredur is usurped as hero by Galaad, the older Grail-seeker still has an important role to play, even if in comparison with Galaad he becomes *y marchawc urdawl eil goreu or holl vyt* ('the next best knight in the whole world', *SG* 202.32-3).

In general, however, French material could be regarded as extending and enriching the native stock of stories about given Arthurian characters, rather than contradicting an accepted canon. Increased knowledge of Continental stories about characters also known in Welsh, and resultant borrowing, served to broaden considerably the scope of Welsh literary tradition, bringing new narrative material, new concepts, even new words. Although the decision to translate full-length romances more or less as they stood would obviously limit the potential input of the individual redactor, there was greater scope for the imagination when elements from a number of different texts were combined.

This was the procedure adopted by the anonymous redactor of a curious composite text of the early fifteenth century, *Darogan yr Olew Bendigaid*, where a Latin prophecy concerning Thomas Becket is skilfully combined with a veritable rag-bag of scraps of Arthurian tradition, to create a startling new tale.[38] In the introductory section, designed to provide a background for Becket's prophecy, the redactor returns to the Arthurian past, drawing on both native and French sources. Geoffrey of Monmouth and other sources available in Welsh such as *Y Seint Greal* were familiar to him, but he has lifted details from the French prose romances as well, notably the *Prose Merlin* and probably also the *Estoire del Saint Graal*, both belonging to the early twelfth century Vulgate Cycle of French Arthurian romances. Like the redactor of 'The Birth of Arthur', for example, he follows the *Prose Merlin* in presenting 'Blaes veudwy' (Blaise the hermit) as Myrddin's secretary, whilst some of the references to Nascien and the early history of the Grail seem to be derived from the *Estoire*.

Although the literary merits of *Darogan yr Olew Bendigaid* are, perhaps, limited, the text does provide further evidence of Welsh interest in Arthurian traditions which had developed on the Continent, and the ability to exploit this new material. Combining new narrative motifs and a fresh group of characters with familiar Welsh Arthurian tradition not only extended the repertoire of available stories, it also opened new possibilities in other ways. Whereas the traditional Welsh Arthurian stories would be passed on from one generation to the next, more or less intact, if subject to minor variation, combining native and foreign elements gave the redactor scope for providing something more than a story as an end in itself. The author of *Breuddwyd Rhonabwy* had recognized this potential when he put together materials drawn from various strands of native tradition to create an original satirical tale, whilst for the redactor of *Darogan yr Olew Bendigaid* it made a vehicle for political propaganda. In both cases enough use was made of native sources to create a familiar ambience within which the message could be conveyed.

The awareness of redactors of the differences between the native narrative tradition and the imported French romances, and of the need to adapt them for the new audience, is even more clearly demonstrated by a reworking of a single episode from *Y Seint Greal*, which is found only in the late fifteenth-century MS NLW Peniarth 15.[39] Here the redactor has taken as his starting point an incident in the second part of *Y Seint Greal*, based on the *Perlesvaus*, where Peredur comes to Arthur's court to collect his shield. The entire pasage, however, has been rewritten in such a way that all obviously non-native elements — including French loan-words and alien proper names — have been excluded, on the level of both subject matter and style, so that the result could be easily mistaken for a piece of purely indigenous prose.

During the fifteenth and sixteenth centuries no further literary Arthurian texts appeared and the antiquarianism already evident in *Darogan yr Olew Bendigaid* continued to assert itself, notably in such compilations as the Arthurian genealogies.[40] These are preserved only in manuscripts of the sixteenth and seventeenth centuries, and combine names familiar from Welsh tradition with others drawn from French written sources. Once again the Vulgate Cycle seems to be the main influence, with the *Estoire del Saint Graal*, *Prose Merlin* and *Prose Lancelot* providing practically all of the French borrowings, although some names also reveal familiarity with *Y Seint Greal*. Occasionally elements taken from both Welsh and French traditions are combined in a single individual, creating strange hybrid forms such as 'Predyr ap Efroc o verch Lambor ap Manael', where the Welsh hero has been made a direct descendant of the Fisher King.

Welsh interest in those French romances did not peter out amongst the antiquarians, however, for it came to the fore again in the early sixteenth century, in the work of Elis Gruffudd, the 'Soldier of Calais', who, despite his employment in the retinue of the English king, found time to compose a chronicle of the history of the world which is in many ways a work of medieval rather than Renaissance scholarship.[41] As well as drawing on Latin, Welsh and English sources, the section he devoted to the history of King Arthur is indebted to those same romances of the Vulgate Cycle used by his predecessors. Gruffudd's main interest here was to produce a comprehensive and coherent narrative of Arthur's career, using this variety of sources, but none the less this sometimes involved retelling substantial portions of those texts, especially the *Brut* and the *Prose Lancelot*. In order to impose unity on his material, however, and perhaps because he was not always working directly from the manuscripts, Elis Gruffudd retold it in his own style. His avowed role was that of a translator, interpreting for his fellow countrymen material in other languages to which they had no access, an aim shared, no doubt, by the translator of *Y Seint Greal*.

Although both narrative texts, from 'The Birth of Arthur' to Elis Gruffudd's chronicle, and compilations such as the Arthurian genealogies testify to the availability of French romances, especially those of the Vulgate Cycle, this does not necessarily mean that several manuscript copies of those French texts were circulating. Manuscripts of parts or the whole of the Vulgate Cycle are still numerous today, including some forty copies of *La Queste del Saint Graal*,[42] but far fewer manuscripts seem to have been produced of other texts. Only eight manuscripts of the *Perlesvaus* are attested, for example, and one early printed edition,[43] whilst of the Welsh translation of the *Perlesvaus* and *Queste*, *Y Seint Greal*, only two more or less complete manuscripts are known, the second being a fifteenth-century copy of the first.[44] Such evidence tells us little of the extent of the dissemination and popularity of such a work. The number of manuscript copies attested may not be a helpful index in the Welsh context, where many stories, including Arthurian ones, might well subsist in oral tradition for centuries, whilst at the same time compilers were copying from possibly a very small number of manuscripts, several redactors perhaps using the same volume at different times. Elis Gruffudd's practice of combining materials he had found in the manuscripts he had acquired or borrowed in England and France with oral traditions he had learned whilst growing up in Flintshire, perfectly illustrates the co-existence of these two strands of Arthurian tradition. Further evidence of the extent of the dissemination of such traditions is provided, however, by two important categories of written material, the Triads, and the references in the poetry of the *cywyddwyr*, the poets of the fourteenth, fifteenth and sixteenth centuries.

The Triads,[45] transmitted orally at first, formed the chief repository of literary tradition from the earliest times, with manuscript copies surviving from the thirteenth century onwards. One Triad manuscript in particular, Peniarth 50, which also contains *Darogan yr Olew Bendigaid*, includes a number of references to the Grail legend. In one example (*TYP* no. 81), an older triad has been reworked, so that Joseph of Arimathia has apparently been substituted for Caw o Brydyn, in a list of 'Three Saintly Lineages', most probably under the influence of *Y Seint Greal*.[46] Another triad in the same manuscript (*TYP* no. 86) even acknowledges its debt to *Y Seint Greal*:

Tri Marchawc o Lys Arthur a enillawd y Greal, ac eu duc y Nef:
>   Galaad vab Lawnslot y Lac,
>   a Pheredur vab Efrawc Iarll,
>   a Bort vab Brenhin Bort.

A'r ddeu gyntaf oeddynt wery o gyrff. A'r trydydd oedd ddiweir, am na wnaeth pechawt knawdawl ont unweith. A hynny drwy brovedigaeth yn yr amser y ennillawd ef . . . verch Brenyn Brangor, yr honn a vu Ymherodres yn Constinobyl, o'r honn y deuth y Genedlaeth vwyaf or byt; ag o'r genedlaeth Joseph o Arimathia y hanoedynt yll tri, ac o lin David brofwyt, mal y tystolaetha *Ystorya y Greal.*

(*Three Knights of Arthur's Court who won the Graal, and it brought them to Heaven:*
>   *Galaad son of Lawnslot of the Lake,*
>   *and Peredur son of Earl Efrawg,*
>   *and Bort son of King Bort.*

And the two first were virgin of body. And the third was chaste, for only once had he committed bodily sin; and that, through temptation, at the time he won . . . daughter of King Brangor, who was Empress in Constantinople and from whom was descended the greatest race in the world. All three were sprung of the race of Joseph of Arimathea, and of the lineage of the Prophet David, as the History of the Graal testifies.)   (*TYP* no. 86)

Here the names of the three knights are taken from the first part of *Y Seint Greal*, based on *La Queste del Saint Graal*, but the note which follows the triad contains information not included there, for the detail concerning King Brangoire's daughter is found only in the *Prose Lancelot*. Moreover, at that point in the *Prose Lancelot* the name of the king's daughter is not given, hence the Welsh scribe has left a gap in the manuscript.[47]

Y Seint Greal again seems to have been the source for a third triad:

>   Tri Diofnog Ynys Brydain:
>   Vn fv Walchmai ap Gwyar,
>   ar ail fv Llacheu ap Arthur,
>   ar trydydd fv Brydyr ap Efrog Iarll.

>   (*Three Fearless Men of the Island of Britain:*
>   *The first was Gwalchmai son of Gwyar,*
>   *the second was Llachau son of Arthur,*
>   *and the third was Peredur son of Earl Efrog.*)   (*TYP* no. 91)

Although these three names appear separately in earlier sources, it is only in the second part of *Y Seint Greal*, corresponding to the *Perlesvaus*, that they are combined, and again it appears that the scribe of the manuscript — in this case, Cardiff 6, *c.* 1550 — has invented a triad based on this particular Welsh text.[48]

A similar trend can be observed in the compilation of triads known as *Pedwar Marchog ar Hugain Llys Arthur* (the Twenty-four Knights of Arthur's Court), recalling the Arthurian genealogies, but where the names are grouped together in eight triads with a brief note accompanying each.[49] Rachel Bromwich has suggested that the text in its present form is unlikely to predate the mid fifteenth century, but that it remained popular until the seventeenth century, occurring frequently in the manuscripts used by the poets.   In the *XXIV Marchog*, as in the Arthurian genealogies, names from both native and Continental traditions have been combined, demonstrating the continuing interest in both strands. Thus the impeccably native list of Three Gold-Tongued Knights (Gwalchmai ap Llew ap Kenvarch, Drudwas ap Tryffin and Eliwlod ap Madog ap Uthur) is followed by a triad derived from either *Y Seint Greal* or *TYP* no. 86, which is itself based on the translation.

The references to Lanslod Lak and to Nasiens in the third and fifth groups respectively again suggest the influence of *Y Seint Greal* or the French Vulgate Cycle; it is worth noting that neither name appears in Welsh sources earlier than *Y Seint Greal*.   The sixth triad mentions Blaes, indicating further use of the *Prose Merlin*, and recalling examples in 'The Birth of Arthur' and *Darogan yr Olew Bendigaid*. Even if, as Rachel Bromwich has stressed, only one-third of the material in the *XXIV Marchog* is derived, directly or indirectly, from Geoffrey of Monmouth, *Y Seint Greal* and the French Vulgate Cycle,[50] traditions of non-native origin were evidently still being accepted into the native stock of tradition during the fifteenth and sixteenth centuries.

The Triads provided a useful quarry for the poets throughout the medieval period, providing as they did useful elements of story and tradition in a convenient and easily remembered form, but since some of the later ones were devised in much the same antiquarian spirit seen amongst later prose redactors, the mention of a character in a triad might not necessarily imply popularity with the poets of the fourteenth to sixteenth centuries.   On the other hand, a reference to an Arthurian name or incident in a poem might well be derived from a triad rather than directly from a written narrative or from an oral source. Certainly many of the poets could read and write: it was Gutun Owain, for example, who was the scribe of the oldest extant manuscript of the *XXIV Marchog*, Llanstephan 28, which bears the date 1455. Poets might gain access to manuscripts through their patrons, such as Hopcyn ap Thomas, who besides having various poems composed in his honour probably commissioned the translation of *Y Seint Greal* and the compiling and copying of the Red Book of Hergest.

The work of major poets from the fourteenth to the sixteenth century shows that they drew on a vast range of poetic and narrative tradition for epithets and comparisons to eulogize their patrons and adorn their work.[51]   Almost every type of material became grist to the poetic mill, from Old Welsh poetry and earlier prose tales to the newer, French borrowings.   The use of non-native traditions alongside Welsh ones shows that material like that of the French Graal romances had been assimilated to the extent that their basic subject matter and the names of their main characters had become familiar not only to the poets but to their patrons and public, for there would be little purpose in comparing one's patron to a hero if nobody could recognize the allusion. From the fourteenth century onwards Arthurian references become increasingly common in the poetry, reflecting a general trend of piling up names of characters from both romances and historiography. The practice appears to have tailed off in the sixteenth century, by which time it had, in any case, become conventional, with the same set phrases recurring constantly. Often whole lines from work of the first generations of *cywyddwyr* would be reproduced exactly, especially with names of non-native origin, such as Gala(a)th, which did not lend themselves so easily to the demands of metre and *cynghanedd*.

References to King Arthur are inevitably so general as to rule out any possibility of identifying a specific source. Gwalchmai and Cai are perhaps the commonest names amongst the knights, both being associated with native traditions as well as the newer, French-influenced or French-derived material, but whereas Cai is portrayed as a somewhat surly character in French romances — even as the murderer of Arthur's son in the *Perlesvaus* — during the later thirteenth century and into the fourteenth the Welsh poets present him in an extremely favourable light. Although later prose redactors, such as that of *Breuddwyd Rhonabwy*, made use of the names in *Culhwch ac Olwen*, curiously little reference is made to this tale in the poetry of the *cywyddwyr*, who seem to favour far more both the *Brutiau* and the later romantic tales of *Geraint*, *Owain* and *Peredur*. In many instances it can be impossible to establish whether the poet has a particular source in mind, although occasionally a hint may be given by the context or the use of an epithet, as in the reference by Tudur Aled (*c*. 1465-1525) to Owain as 'iarll y cawg' (the earl of the bowl), which must derive from *Iarlles y Ffynnawn*.[52] More minor characters are less problematic: Edlym, mentioned by Llywelyn ap y Moel (d. 1440),[53] must be borrowed from *Peredur*, Enid and Luned, named by Gruffudd ap Maredudd ap Dafydd (*fl*. 1352-82), from *Geraint* and *Owain* respectively.[54] Peredur himself appears frequently; in the case of the fourteenth-century poets we can usually assume that the prose tale of *Peredur* is the ultimate source, whether the poets had access to a written copy or had heard an oral version. In poetry from *c*. 1400 onwards, post-dating *Y Seint Greal*, it can be difficult to establish which of these texts lies behind the references, either because of the lack of narrative context or because of the overlap of subject matter between the texts themselves. References to the Grail itself, however, seem to be derived from *Y Seint Greal*, where the word *greal* appears in Welsh for the first time. Two poets even refer specifically to manuscripts of *Y Seint Greal*. Dafydd y Coed (*fl. c*. 1370) in a poem to Hopcyn ap Thomas lists 'Y Greal' among books in his patron's possession,[55] whilst Guto'r Glyn (*c*. 1412-93) mentions a manuscript of the

Grail twice, one *cywydd* being a request to Trahaearn ab Ieuan, on behalf of the Abbot of Valle Crucis, for the loan of the book, possibly MS Peniarth 11.[56] Other references are vaguer, for example that by Dafydd Llwyd o Fathafarn (*c.* 1420-90), revealing only familiarity with the general outline of the Grail story.[57]

Lancelot, Boort and Lionel, who play an important part in the French Grail traditions likewise appear only in poems post-dating the translation of *Y Seint Greal*. Lancelot even retains his epithet 'du Lac' in poems by Guto'r Glyn and Dafydd Nanmor, whilst Guto'r Glyn refers also to both 'Syr Liwnel' and 'Bwrd', the latter knight appearing again later in the work of Tudur Aled, in the late fifteenth or early sixteenth century.[58]

The unspecific nature of many of the references by the poets makes it difficult to pinpoint not only which tale they had in mind, but also how familiar they were with anything beyond the proper names and the broadest outline of the stories with which they were associated. In some cases the Triads may have been an important source, but the late date of most of the relevant triads, including the *XXIV Marchog*, suggests that this cannot be true for the fourteenth-century poets. None the less, even though the Arthurian names as such provide only a small proportion of the stock of proper names used by the *cywyddwyr*, their use, and their combination with native material, shows that throughout the later medieval period both native and Continental Arthurian traditions continued to be popular, with the tales of French origin — like the non-Arthurian ones such as *Guy of Warwick* or *Fouke le Fitz Waryn* — providing a useful new source. Even as late as the sixteenth century, Tudur Aled was evidently familiar with a number of Arthurian stories, whilst Dafydd Benwyn (1564-1634) not only refers to such characters as Galaeth, Bwrt and Lawncelot in his poetry, but also is the scribe of the Cardiff 10 manuscript of the Arthurian genealogies, indicating beyond doubt the overlapping interests of antiquarian, scribe and poet.[59] Nor did the interest in the Arthurian legend in general disappear from Welsh literature after the sixteenth century. Not only was Arthurian material still being copied in seventeenth-century manuscripts, albeit for purely antiquarian reasons; as late as 1716 Theophilus Evans, in his history *Drych y Prif Oesoedd*, retains his devotion to the 'British' history derived from Geoffrey of Monmouth.[60] Meanwhile, amongst the common people, *y werin*, Arthurian stories continued to circulate orally well into the nineteenth century, as witness the old woman who recited the story of *Owain* to Glasynys (Owen Wynne Jones, 1828-70).[61]

From the thirteenth century onwards, therefore, evidence appears of increasing interest in Continental versions of the Arthurian legend, an interest which persists well beyond the medieval period, whilst at the same time the earlier native traditions continued to circulate. Welsh story-telling remained vigorous, but adapted as necessary to changing circumstances, in particular to the growing importance of the written word and the influence of French Arthurian romances. It is significant that the redactors not only recognized that King Arthur and the knights in the imported romances could be identified with the characters with similar names in their own traditions, but were also able to relocate them in the Welsh story-telling context. This is all the more striking in view of the fact that, as Rachel Bromwich has stressed, in the majority of cases where elements of Celtic tradition had been drawn into Continental narrative by the twelfth century, the names did not pass hand in hand with the story themes with which those characters were originally associated.[62] In welcoming back familiar characters in foreign trappings, the Welsh redactors in the later Middle Ages realized — in both senses of the word — the potential for enriching and diversifying their work by combining Continental and native materials.

NOTES:

1. For general surveys see Idris Ll. Foster, *'Culhwch and Olwen* and *Rhonabwy's Dream'* in ALMA 31-43 (39-43); Dafydd Glyn Jones, 'A Literary Study of *Breuddwyd Rhonabwy'* (unpublished B.Phil. thesis, Oxford, 1966), and *'Breuddwyd Rhonabwy'* in TRh 176-95; Brynley F. Roberts, 'Tales and Romances' in Guide 203-43 (231-5).

2. For details of contents see RWM 1, 29, and Gifford Charles-Edwards, 'The Scribes of the Red Book of Hergest', *NLW Journal*, 21 (1980), 246-56 (254-6).

3. E.g. *BR* 8, n.1, 3; 12, n.1; cf. Thomas Jones, review of *BR*, *Y Llenor*, 27 (1948), 142-53 (146).

4. Iddawg's seven-year penance following Camlan is already over, *BR* 4.30-5.15.

5. Hence the suggestion by Edgar Slotkin that the narrative effectively runs backwards: 'The Fabula, Story and Text of *Breuddwyd Rhonabwy'*, *CMCS*, 18 (1989), 89-111 (97-8).

6. TYP 481, 520, 561; Melville Richards, 'Brain Owain ab Urien', *B*, 13 (1950), 136-7; N. Lukman, 'The Raven Banner and Changing Ravens, a Viking Miracle from Carolingian Court Poetry to Saga and Arthurian Romance', *Classica et Mediaevalia*, 19 (1958), 133-51.

7. *TYP* 240, 246-7; cf. A.G. van Hamel, 'The Game of the Gods', *Arkiv för Nordisk Filologi*, 50 (1934), 218-42.

8. *The Didot Perceval*, edited by William Roach (Philadelphia, 1941), ll.166-502, 966-1114. Here the knight associated with the ravens is called Urbain, recalling the Old Welsh form *Urbgen* (TYP 516-17), later Urien father of Owain, cf. Foster, ALMA 43.

9. *Owain* 18-19; Glenys Goetinck, *Historia Peredur fab Efrawg* (Cardiff, 1976).

10. But see also Foster, ALMA 42.

11. *BR* xv; Foster, ALMA 41-2. Cf. above p. 111.

12. 'Traddodiad a Dychan yn *Breuddwyd Rhonabwy*', *LlC*, 13 (1980-1), 155-63.

13. T.F. O'Rahilly, *Early Irish History and Mythology* (Dublin, 1971), 323-4.

14. Edited by Kuno Meyer (London, 1892, reprinted New York, 1974); see also *BR*, xv; Dafydd Glyn Jones, TRh 189-90.

15. *Yr Areithiau Pros*, edited by D. Gwenallt Jones (Cardiff, 1934).

16. *Yr Areithiau Pros*, xv, xix; Dafydd Glyn Jones, TRh 192.

17. *Medieval Dream-Poetry* (Cambridge, 1976), 5 and *passim*.

18. Ibid., 4.

19. A copy of it is mentioned in the inventory of the goods of Llywelyn Bren, executed in 1317. See J.H. Matthews, *Cardiff Records* (Cardiff, 1889-1911), 4, p.58.

20. D. Glyn Jones 'A Literary Study', *passim*.

21. Thomas Parry, *A History of Welsh Literature* (Oxford, 1955), 81-3; *BR* xxxvii-xxxix.

22. See also Enid Roberts, *Braslun o Hanes Llên Powys* (Denbigh, 1965), 42.

23. 'The Structure and Meaning of the Dream of Rhonabwy', *Philological Quarterly*, 53 (1974), 289-303.

24. 'The Date of the Dream of Rhonabwy', *THSC* (1958), 33-40.

25. *BR* xi.

26. E.g. the thirteenth century MS Peniarth 6; cf. *BR* xi.

27. Richards (*BR* xl-xli), admitted the possibility that *Breuddwyd Rhonabwy* post-dated these three texts.

28. This is indicated by the survival in very late manuscripts only of certain tales whose content was known to poets in the Middle Ages, such as the story of Tegau Eurfron, preserved in the late eighteenth-century NLW MS 2288B. See Graham Thomas, 'Chwedlau Tegau Eurfron a Thristfardd, bardd Urien Rheged', *B*, 24 (1970), 1-19; *TYP* 512-14, 564.

29. For general surveys see Stephen J. Williams, 'Rhai Cyfieithiadau', in TRh 303-11; Morfydd E. Owen, 'The Prose of the *Cywydd* Period' in Guide 338-75; Ceridwen Lloyd-Morgan, 'Rhai Agweddau ar Gyfieithu yng Nghymru yn yr Oesoedd Canol', *YB*, 13 (1985), 134-45, and 'Continuity and Change in the Transmission of Arthurian Material: Later Mediaeval Wales and the Continent', in *Actes du 14e Congrès International Arthurien* (Rennes 1985), ii, 397-405.

30. W.A. Nitze and T.A. Jenkins (eds.), *Le Haut Livre du Graal. Perlesvaus* (2 vols., Chicago, 1932-7, repr. New York, 1972), i, 3-4, ii, 3-11. A newly discovered fourteenth-century fragment of the text is also of English provenance: see James P. Carley, 'A Fragment of *Perlesvaus* at Wells Cathedral Library', *Zeitschrift für romanische Philologie* (forthcoming).

31. For a synopsis of the historical evidence, see Marie Surridge, 'Romance Linguistic Influence on Middle Welsh', *SC*, 1 (1966), 63-92.

32. Constance Bullock-Davies, *Professional Interpreters and the Matter of Britain* (Cardiff, 1966).

33. Ceridwen Lloyd-Morgan, 'A Study of *Y Seint Greal* in relation to *La Queste del Saint Graal* and *Perlesvaus*', unpublished D.Phil. thesis (Oxford, 1978), 64-70.

34. Ed. in *Cy.*, 24 (1913), 247-64.

35. *Y Seint Greal* edited by Robert Williams (London, 1876, reprinted Pwllheli, 1987) [*SG*]. See also Ceridwen Lloyd-Morgan, 'A Study of *Y Seint Greal*' and 'Perceval in Wales: Late Medieval Welsh Grail Traditions' in *The Changing Face of Arthurian Romance*, edited by Alison Adams, Armel H. Diverres, Karen Stern and Kenneth Varty (Cambridge, 1986), 78-91.

36. Gifford Charles-Edwards, 'The Scribes of the Red Book of Hergest', 250-1. See Introduction, p. 11.

37. *WM* col.122-3; Ifor Williams, 'Trystan ac Esyllt', *B*, 5 (1930), 115-29 (117, 122-3), and Jenny Rowland and Graham Thomas, 'Additional Versions of the Trystan *Englynion* and Prose', *NLW Journal*, 22 (1982), 241-53 (pp.244, 248). See ch.10, n.62 below.

38. R. Wallis Evans, 'Darogan yr Olew Bendigaid a Hystdori yr Olew Bendigaid', *LlC*, 14 (1981-2), 86-91; Ceridwen Lloyd-Morgan, 'Darogan yr Olew Bendigaid: Chwedl o'r Bymthegfed Ganrif', *ibid.*, 64-85, and 'Prophecy and Welsh Nationhood in the Fifteenth Century', *THSC* (1985), 9-26.

39. Ceridwen Lloyd-Morgan, 'The Peniarth 15 Fragment of *Y Seint Greal*: Arthurian Tradition in the Late Fifteenth Century', *B*, 28 (1978), 73-82.

40. P.C. Bartrum, 'Arthuriana from the Genealogical Manuscripts', *NLW Journal*, 14 (1965), 242-5; Ceridwen Lloyd-Morgan, 'Nodiadau Ychwanegol ar yr Achau Arthuraidd a'u Ffynonellau Ffrangeg', *ibid.*, 21 (1980), 329-39.

41. NLW MSS 5276D and 3054D; see Thomas Jones, 'A Welsh Chronicler in Tudor England', *Welsh History Review*, 1 (1960), 1-17; Prys Morgan, 'Elis Gruffudd of Gronant — Tudor Chronicler Extraordinary', *Proceedings of the Flintshire Historical Society*, 25 (1971-2), 9-20.

42. A. Pauphilet (ed.), *La Queste del Saint Graal* (repr. Paris, 1972), 111ff.

43. See above, n.3.

44. Ceridwen Lloyd-Morgan, 'A Study of *Y Seint Greal*', 7-11.

45. Rachel Bromwich (ed.), *TYP*.

46. *TYP* 201-3; Ceridwen Lloyd-Morgan, 'A Study of *Y Seint Greal*', 227.

47. *TYP* 213. For evidence of the Welsh connections of at least one manuscript of the *Prose Lancelot*, see John Scattergood, 'An Unrecorded Fragment of the *Prose Lancelot* in Trinity College Dublin MS 212', *Medium Aevum*, 53 (1984), 301-5.

48. *TYP* xxxviii, 219.

49. *TYP* cxxxv-cxxxix, 250-5; *THSC* (1946), 116-132.

50. *TYP* cxxxvii.

51. D. Myrddin Lloyd, *Rhai Agweddau ar Ddysg y Gogynfeirdd* (Cardiff, 1977); David Geraint Lewis, 'Mynegai i'r Enwau Priod Storiol yng Ngwaith Cyhoeddedig y Cywyddwyr', unpublished MA thesis (Aberystwyth, 1968); Ceridwen Lloyd-Morgan, 'A Study of *Y Seint Greal*', 234-40.

52. T. Gwynn Jones (ed), *Gwaith Tudur Aled* (2 vols, Cardiff, Wrexham and London, 1926), p. 40, line 49, p. 73, lines 2, 70, p. 246, line 63; see also R.M. Jones, 'Y Rhamantau Cymraeg', *LlC*, 4 (1956), 208-27 (pp.214-15). Two of these poems by Tudur Aled are dedicated to Syr Rhys ap Thomas (1449-1525), one of the most prominent Welshmen of the period, whose interest in Arthurian literature is demonstrated by his commissioning a copy to be made of *Y Seint Greal*: see Ceridwen Lloyd-Morgan, D.Phil. 'A Study of *Y Seint Greal*', 47-51. Tudur Aled also reveals knowledge of the tale of *Peredur* in his reference to Cai, *Gwaith Tudur Aled*, 41, line 83.

53. Henry Lewis, Thomas Roberts and Ifor Williams (eds.), *Cywyddau Iolo Goch ac Eraill* (2nd. ed., Cardiff, 1937), 166, line 2.

54. D. Myrddin Lloyd, *Rhai Agweddau ar Ddysg y Gogynfeirdd*, 10.

55. *RBP*, col.1376, lines 20-2.

56. John Llywelyn Williams and Ifor Williams (eds.), *Gwaith Guto'r Glyn* (Cardiff, repr. 1979), 303-4. It is probably to the same abbot of Valle Crucis that he refers in another *cywydd*, 'Marwnad Robert Trefor', *Gwaith Guto'r Glyn*, 50, lines 45-6; see also Ceridwen Lloyd-Morgan, 'A Study of *Y Seint Greal*', 237.

57. W. Leslie Richards (ed.), *Gwaith Dafydd Llwyd o Fathafarn* (Cardiff, 1964), p.120, lines 5-8; Ceridwen Lloyd-Morgan, 'A Study of *Y Seint Greal*', 236.

58. *Gwaith Guto'r Glyn*, 4, line 48, 122, line 37, 137, line 10; Thomas Roberts and Ifor Williams (eds.), *The Poetical Works of Dafydd Nanmor* (Cardiff, 1923), 59, line 58; *Gwaith Tudur Aled*, 246, line 70.

59. Ceridwen Lloyd-Morgan, 'Nodiadau Ychwanegol ar yr Achau Arthuraidd', 337-8 and note 19. Poets were also responsible for copying two other manuscripts of the Arthurian genealogies: Cardiff 4.265 is in the hand of Simwnt Fychan (1530-1606) and Peniarth 178 in that of Gruffydd Hiraethog (d. 1564).

60. *Drych y Prif Oesoedd*, ed. Garfield H. Hughes (Cardiff, 1961).

61. 'Yn yr encilion ym mysg pobl na fedrant air ar lyfr . . . clywais fy hun "Iarlles y Ffynnon" yn cael ei hadrodd gan hen wraig dros ei phedwar ugain oed. Dywedai mai ei thaid a glywsai yn ei hadrodd' (*Y Brython*, 1860, 231: 'In isolated places, amongst people who cannot read a single word, . . . I heard myself "The Lady of the Fountain" being recited by an old lady over eighty years of age. She said that she had heard her grandfather telling it.'

62. Rachel Bromwich, 'Celtic Elements in Arthurian Romance: a General Survey', *LAMA* 41-55.

10

THE *TRISTAN* OF THE WELSH

Rachel Bromwich

CLAIMS to have inspired the genesis of the Continental Tristan romances have been made on behalf of three Celtic lands — Cornwall, Wales, and Brittany: Irish parallels also need to be taken into account with respect to themes which appear in them. Yet apart from the Continental versions, it is in Welsh alone that stories and poems have come down from the Middle Ages which embody the names of the protagonists: *Drystan* or *Trystan, Es(s)yllt* and *March* are all clearly recognizable cognates of the French *Tristan, Iseut/Isolt* and *Mark.* The Welsh fragments offer a rare instance in which the names and story attached to the chief actors correspond in outline and situation to that portrayed in the Norman and Anglo-Norman poems of Béroul and Thomas, and the various foreign adaptations of Thomas's poem. Wherever correspondences of this kind are to be found — as is the case with the three Welsh Romances *Owain, Geraint fab Erbin* and *Peredur* and their French cognates — they have inevitably given rise to prolonged speculation as to the direction in which the borrowing has taken place between the Welsh and the Continental versions.[1] A similar problem exists in relation to the Welsh Tristan fragments. There can be no doubt as to the Brythonic forms in which the names of *Drystan, Esyllt* (Cornish *Eselt*) and *March* have come down: these names are all in origin either Welsh, Cornish, or Breton. But unfortunately the Welsh Tristan fragments cannot be given any precise date prior to the thirteenth-century manuscripts in which they first appear, and this is at least half a century later than the approximate dates which have been assigned to the poems of Béroul and Thomas.[2]

In contrast with the Continental poems, the Welsh fragments are all anonymous and the dates of the manuscripts which contain them offer no solution as to the date of the original composition of their contents, since it is characteristic of the medieval Welsh narrative tradition that a long antecedent oral and written transmission can usually be postulated before the earliest extant written texts. The Tristan fragments consist of i) an obscure and enigmatic poem (or parts of two poems) contained in the thirteenth-century Black Book of Carmarthen; ii) scattered allusions to Drystan, March, and Esyllt found in the Triads; iii) allusions made by the poets to the story of Drystan and Esyllt: these begin in the thirteenth century, but become very much more frequent from the fourteenth to sixteenth centuries; iv) the *Ystorya Trystan* ('Story of Tristan'), a medley of prose and verse which is extant in a number of manuscripts dating from the sixteenth to eighteenth centuries. I will consider these sources each in turn, but some preliminary discussion must be given in the first place to the names of the protagonists.

Drystan and *March* each bear a patronymic which is consistently attached to them in all Welsh sources: Drystan is always *ap Tallwch* and March is *ap Meirchiawn*. A single triad (*TYP* no.80) gives to Esyllt as father a certain *Culfanawyt Prydein*, but only in this one instance: otherwise she receives no parentage in Welsh. All of these patronymics are quite unknown in the Continental versions. In the Welsh sources Drystan and March already appear in association with Arthur, and this association may well go back to a much earlier period than that of the manuscripts concerned, since originally independent heroes appear to have been attracted into the orbit of Arthur from as early as the ninth or tenth century.[3]

Drystan or *Trystan*[4] derives from primitive Celtic *Drustagnos*.[5] The earliest recorded instance of this name is the famous inscription on the sixth-century memorial stone at Castle Dore in Cornwall: DRVSTA[N]VS HIC IACIT CVNOMORI FILIVS.[6] The cognate form in the Pictish language was *Drosten* (*Drostan* in manuscript sources): *Drosten* appears on an inscription at St Vigeans, Angus, dated to the middle or late ninth century.[7] This name and its shorter form *Drust* or *Drest* occur in seven instances in the Pictish regnal lists,[8] and since instances of them are rare elsewhere, they may be described as characteristically Pictish. These lists show a *Talorcan* (*Talargan*) *filius Drostan* in the eighth century, followed later by a *Drest* (*Drust*) *filius Talorgen* (*Thalargan*). The resemblance between this combination of names and *Drystan fab Tallwch* 'looks like more than a coincidence' as Oliver Padel has noted.[9] In Welsh a charter in the Book of Llandaf (*c.* 1135-50) records a certain *Avel mab Tristan* as the name of a witness.[10] Apart from *Carnedd Drystan*,[11] the name of a ridge on Carnedd Llywelyn in Gwynedd, there is no evidence that the name of *Drystan/Trystan* survived as a Welsh personal name, and all citations of the name (in either form) in poetry refer plainly to the hero of the romances. Nor has the name of *Tallwch* survived in the language.[12] In Brittany we find the place-name *insula Trestanni*[13] in the Bay of Douarnenez, and R.S. Loomis quoted Pierre le Baud (who had access to original documents now lost) for a 'Tristan' lord of Vitré in the early eleventh century.[14]

The name *Es(s)yllt* is no less rare.[15] It is attested from the tenth century both in the place-name *hryt eselt* ('E.'s Ford') in Cornwall (to be discussed later) and in the early form *Etthil*, *Ethellt*, and *Etil*,[16] preserved in several early versions of the genealogy of the ruling dynasty of Gwynedd, where it is bestowed on the heiress who was daughter to Cynan Tindaethwy.[17] Later versions of this genealogy give the name of this princess as *Es(s)yllt*, and her name was long commemorated by the bards in this form, as representing 'one of the three instances in which the descent of Gwynedd went by the distaff'.[18] The cryptic allusion to *Essyllt Vynwen ac Essyllt Vyngul* ('E. Fair Neck and E. Slender Neck'[19]) in the list of ladies at Arthur's Court in *Culhwch ac Olwen* must surely commemorate the romance heroine, not least because the Arthurian Court List also includes the name of *Drustwrn Hayarn* ('Drust Iron Fist'[20]) which looks like a remembrance or a misreading of *Drystan*. The duplication here of the name of *Essyllt* may appear somewhat suspicious in view of the existence of the two Isolts — Isolt of Cornwall and Isolt of Brittany — in the Continental poems. On the other hand, comparable doublets of alliterating names are to be found elsewhere in this list. The two Essyllts are the very last names among the ladies of Arthur's court, and it is not impossible that they are to be counted among the secondary additions to the list, made under the influence of the Continental romances. The names are exceptional also in that the two Essyllts receive no patronymic, as do all but one of the other ladies of Arthur's court in the list. Earlier in the list (l.253) *Culfanawyt mab Goryon* is included among Arthur's courtiers, and this name seems to be identifiable with *Culfanawyt Prydein*, who is named in the triad (*TYP* no.80) as Esyllt's father. Culfanawyt appears to have been a traditional character, since two poets of the twelfth and thirteenth centuries make allusion to *Cynon fab Kulvanawyt*.[21] In *Brut y Brenhinedd* the name *Esyllt* renders Geoffrey of Monmouth's *Estrildis*.[22] These are the only recorded instances of the name *Esyllt*, which was never adopted as a popular girl's name in Wales.

March (<*Marcus*) is attested as a personal name in early Welsh, Cornish and Breton,[23] and it occurs as an element in Welsh-Breton compound names.[24] There are a number of instances of *Meirchiawn* (<*Marciānus*) in the early genealogies and in the Book of Llandaf. The ninth-century *Vita* of the sixth-century St Paul Aurelian introduces a King Marcus who ruled either in the saint's home in Glamorgan or else in Cornwall as a contemporary of his, according to the saint's biographer Wrmonoc.[25] Other but less early sources name a tyrannical King Meirchiawn who ruled in Glamorgan at approximately the same period.[26] That March ap Meirchiawn held a recognized place in early Welsh heroic tradition is seen from the allusions to him in the Triads, in *Breuddwyd Rhonabwy*, and in the Stanzas of the Graves.[27] There is, further, a significant but enigmatic citation of his name in an ode to Owain Gwynedd (before 1170) by the poet Cynddelw Brydydd Mawr, who eulogizes his patron by describing him as one *a dyly Kymry ae kymer drwy barch / ual y kymerth march gwedy meirchyawn* 'who has a right to Wales and will possess her in honour, as

March possessed her after Meirchyawn'.[28]

Since *march* means 'horse' in Welsh, Cornish, and Breton, the name of *March /
Mark* attracted to itself in all these lands the familiar folk-tale of King Midas and his
horse's ears.[29] This association appears first in a garbled form in the twelfth century
in Béroul's *Tristan*.[30] But the story was already known in Irish in the tenth century,
attached to a king variously known as *Eochu Echcend* ('E. Horse Head') and *Labraid
Lorc* or *Loingsech* ('L. Seafarer').[31] Béroul's version must derive from a source in one
of the Brythonic languages, since in these alone the name *March* could account for it.
The only Welsh version which has come down attaches it to March ap Meirchiawn,
who is represented as the legendary ancestor of the family who in the seventeenth
century occupied the mansion of Castellmarch in Llŷn. The story is preserved in a
sixteenth-century genealogical tract,[32] and it may be translated as follows:

> Iarddur ap Egri ap Morien Mynac ap March ap Meirchion . . . He had horses'
> ears, and nobody knew that except the man who shaved him, and he did not
> dare to tell it for fear of his life. But the barber fell ill, and so had to seek a
> physician, who told him that a secret was killing him, and he told the barber to
> confess it to the ground. This he did, and became well. Fine reeds grew upon
> that spot. On a high feast-day the pipers of Maelgwn Gwynedd came to him
> and they saw the fine reeds and cut them and made them into their pipes.
> (When) they came to sing before the king, they could sing nothing but 'March
> ap Meirchiawn has horses' ears'.

This same story was recorded by or for Edward Lhuyd in 1693,[33] and it still
persisted in local tradition in the neighbourhood of Castellmarch in 1882, when a
blacksmith somewhat reluctantly told it to Sir John Rhŷs.[34] Variant forms of the
same story were known in western Brittany in the nineteenth century: in these the
king is known as *Marc'h* or alternatively *Guivarc'h*.[35] It has been suggested that
Béroul may have heard a Breton version current in the twelfth century, but this can
be no more than a conjecture. There is no evidence other than Béroul that the story
was known in Cornwall, attached to King Mark.

Castellmarch was a habitation site long before the present mansion was built in
the seventeenth century. This is proved by the poet Meilyr's reference to *cad rac
castell march*, 'a battle before Castell March', in his elegy for Gruffudd ap Cynan
(d.1137).[36] *March* in this place-name could of course have originally simply meant
'horse', and it may have been the later owners of Castellmarch who took it to be a
personal name which they identified with March ap Meirchiawn, known to them from
the Welsh versions of the popular Tristan romances. At almost any period from the
twelfth century the bizarre story of March's horses' ears may have been localized in
Gwynedd, just as it evidently was at some uncertain period in Brittany. But apart
from the few place-names already mentioned, there is no other evidence for the
localization of the Tristan story in Gwynedd.

II

In the early literature of Wales and Ireland, in which both prose and poetry have been preserved by oral means over long periods, metrical conventions have ensured that verse has been retained in a more stable form than prose, since it is better able to guard its original structure in spite of partial modernization and corruption through failure of memory or at the hands of successive copyists. Prose, on the other hand, being unfettered by metrical restraints, can transmit the substance of oral stories without recognizing any obligation to transmit them in the exact words in which they were received: prose is continually renewed and revitalized as the language itself develops. These considerations should be borne in mind in relation to the earliest Welsh references to the story of Tristan.

It is customary to look upon the fragmentary poem (or poems) in the thirteenth-century Black Book of Carmarthen[37] as containing the earliest of these references. This poem consists of two metrically distinct fragments: two and a half stanzas, each consisting of six nine-syllable lines, followed by two three-line *englynion milwr*. Stylistically both forms are fully integrated within the conventions of early *awdlau* and *englynion*, and they present archaic features in language and in rhyme.[38] These verses have been edited twice, first by J. Loth,[39] and more recently by myself.[40] Both editors have attempted to relate these highly-charged dramatic lines to episodes in the Tristan story as we know it from the Continental versions. The first stanzas appear to be a lament for a drowned warrior who bears the name of *Kyheic*. This is an extremely rare personal name,[41] and it is the only link which exists between the first stanzas and the two *englynion* which follow. I subjoin these with a tentative translation:[42]

Fechid diristan othiwod	*Drystan is enraged at your coming:*
mi nyth ervill im djod	*I will not accept my casting out (by you?),*
om parth guertheiss e	*For my part, I have sold (or 'betrayed')*
march irod.	*March for you.*
Dial kyheic am oet blis	*To avenge Kyheic would be my desire*
am y kywrev y melis	*because of his sweet words;*
och corr dy sorr de ymi bv ewnis.	*Alas, dwarf, your anger was hostile to me.*

This poem gives the earliest occurrence in a Welsh manuscript of the names of *D(i)ristan*[43] and *March* as characters belonging to a story — if indeed the latter is the personal name, and not the noun denoting a horse. The reference to a dwarf is also potentially a clue: here we have the earliest recorded instance of the word *corr* (dwarf) in Welsh. Both parts of the poem contain verbal echoes of an older tradition which link it in general, and closely in the case of the *englynion*, with a group of poems in the Black Book,[44] for the most part in this metre, and all implying a

narrative setting which has not come down.   They are all speech-poems, either
dialogues or monologues; their context being in each case incomprehensible in the
absence of supplementary information — whether or not this ever had a fixed form,
and whether or not it was ever written down.   Linguistic and metrical indications
point to a similar date for these poems to that which has been proposed for the
'Tristan' verses: that is, prior to c.1100.[45]

Yet for the reasons I have indicated above I would be uncertain about urging the
claim for an earlier date for this poem than for some of the Triads.   Drystan ap
Tallwch is named in three Triads which appear in both of the two main versions of
Trioedd Ynys Prydein, dating from the thirteenth and fourteenth centuries
respectively.[46]   Drystan is one of the *Tri Galofydd* (no.19, 'Enemy Subduers, lords of
hostility'), and he is one of the *Tri Thaleithiog Cad* (no.21), that is, warriors who
wore in battle a *talaith* (probably a coronet or chaplet) as a mark of distinction.   Both
of these epithets belong to the vocabulary of bardic praise-poetry, and in both Triads
Drystan is grouped with traditional figures whose names, like his own, appear in the
Arthurian Court List in *Culhwch ac Olwen* (*CO* ll.175-373).   Like the reference to
March as one of the *Tri Llynghesawg* or 'Seafarers' (*TYP* no.14), these references are
sufficient to indicate that Drystan held an accepted place in early heroic tradition.
And that he was remembered as a warrior, and not merely as a lover.

In contrast with these Triads, *Tri Gwrddfeichiad*[47] (*TYP* no.26, 'Mighty or
Powerful Swineherds') appears untraditional, and it is tempting to regard it as a
burlesque.   It is one of the few Triads which are extended to give brief synopses of
stories.   Two famous traditional figures, Pryderi and Drystan, are presented in the
incongruous and unbecoming role of pig-keepers:

> (The first Powerful Swineherd): Drystan ap Tallwch (who guarded) the swine of
> March ap Meirchiawn, while the swineherd went to ask Esyllt to come to a
> meeting with him.   Arthur, March, and Cei and Bedwyr were there all four, but
> they did not succeed in getting so much as one pigling, neither by force nor by
> deception, nor by stealth . . .   And Pryderi son of Pwyll, Lord of Annwfn, who
> guarded the swine of Pendaran Dyfed in Glyn Cuch in Emlyn.

The third entry in this Triad tells at some length how a certain enchanter, named Coll
fab Collfrewy, known only from the Triads, pursues a sow named Henwen ('Old
White') from Cornwall across the sea to Gwent and then to Pembroke.   At each
precisely named locality where she stops, she gives birth to a grain of wheat or
barley and to a bee (all items of economic value), but when afterwards she reaches
north Wales, she gives birth instead to a wolf, an eagle, and to the monstrous Cath
Palug, who in a brief appended Triad is described as 'one of the Three Scourges of
Anglesey'.[48]   In Triads, as in *englynion*, 'the sting comes in the tail', and the third
entry is apt to be the *raison d'être* of the whole.   It looks very much as though the

episode of Henwen not only satirizes north Wales and its produce in comparison with that of south Wales, but that it may also be a farcical response to the story of Arthur's hunt for the boar Twrch Trwyth, known in some form from at least the ninth century:[49] Henwen in fact reverses the elaborately detailed journey of the Twrch Trwyth as told in *Culhwch ac Olwen*, by travelling from Cornwall to Wales, instead of in the opposite direction.

For purposes of credibility this ironic fabrication has drawn to it the names of two prestigious figures, known to early story-telling — Pryderi and Drystan. My suggestion is that the episode attached to Drystan is as untraditional as that of Henwen, and that it may not recall any real story which was ever in existence. Its significance, however, lies in showing that episodes involving the triangular relationship between Drystan, Esyllt, and March were already familiar, and could be exploited as the setting for a comic and entirely fanciful incident which pointed up the ironic innuendo intended in the story of Henwen. The possibility of influence from the Norman romances of Tristan (n. 2 above) cannot be entirely excluded (cf. ch.13, p. 280).

A fifteenth-century manuscript[50] makes some additions to *Trioedd Ynys Prydein*, and shows a particular interest in the story of Trystan. It groups together the three Triads just discussed with three more which name him (*TYP* nos.71, 72, 73): he is one of the *Tri Serchawg* or 'Lovers', one of the *Tri Chyndynyawg* or 'Stubborn Men', and one of the *Tri Gogyfurdd Llys Arthur* or 'Peers of Arthur's Court'.[51] These additional Triads bear witness to the increasing interest in the figure of Trystan as the romances gained in popularity: he has become one of the three Lovers *par excellence*, but at the same time the earlier Welsh heroic concept is not lost sight of, and neither is his association with Arthur and his court. Later in the same manuscript (*TYP* no.80) the *Tair Aniwair Wraig* or 'Three Faithless Wives of the Island of Britain' name *Esyllt Fyngwen* ('E. Fair-hair'), Trystan's mistress, with two others of whom we know nothing. The three are all described as daughters of *Culfanawyt Prydein*, a character known to the early tradition, as was noted above. Esyllt's epithet 'Fair-hair' (*myngwen*) also has earlier authority, since it evidently derives from the epithet bestowed on one of the two Esyllts in *Culhwch ac Olwen* as noted above. Eight Triads grouped together under the title 'The Twenty-four Knights of Arthur's Court'[52] date also from the fifteenth century. Evidently this group enjoyed considerable popularity, judging from the number of manuscript copies. Two-thirds of the names belong to the native corpus of stories; the remaining third betray their origin as adaptations from *Brut y Brenhinedd* and the French prose Arthurian romances. Here *Trystan ap Tallwch* is grouped with *Menw ap Teirgwaedd* and *Eddilig Cor* ('the Dwarf') as one of the *Tri Lledrithiog Farchog* or 'Three

Enchanter Knights of Arthur's Court'.

The earliest references by medieval poets to *Drystan/Trystan* begin to be found from *c.* 1250-1350,[53] and these merely cite his name as a standard of excellence with which to compare the patron whom the poets are addressing — just as they might employ the names of Arthur, Rhydderch Hael, or any other well-known hero in the same way. March ap Meirchiawn, as we have seen, was known even earlier than this, and was mentioned by Cynddelw Brydydd Mawr in the twelfth century. Esyllt's name was also well known to the poets as that of the Gwynedd heiress, daughter of Cynan Tindaethwy, and it is not always clear whether it is she or the romance heroine whom the poets have in mind when they refer to *Esyllt*.[54] From the mid fourteenth century there begin to appear explicit references to the love-story of Trystan and Esyllt: Gruffudd ap Maredudd claims to have bestowed on a girl *trawstaer serchawl vryt trystan ar esyllt*,[55] 'the strong fervent love of Trystan for Esyllt'. Such allusions imply familiarity on the part of both the poet and of his listening audience with the famous love-story. Dafydd ap Gwilym is something of a pioneer in the frequency with which he speaks of a girl as *ail Esyllt*,[56] 'a second Esyllt' — an evocative comparison with an accepted paragon of beauty, to be used as were the names of the popular romance heroines *Luned*, *Enid* or *Eigr* (Arthur's mother). There is a suggestion that Dafydd ap Gwilym envisaged his own frustrations in the pursuit of love as comparable with those of Trystan, wandering the countryside in vain attempts to meet with the girl he is courting: *Unfryd wyf yn y fro deg / A Thrystan uthr ar osteg*[57] 'I am of one mind, in the fair land, with Trystan, famous in song'. In the fifteenth century Dafydd ab Edmwnd is the first Welsh poet to introduce the theme of the love-drink, which is otherwise unknown in Welsh sources: *Diod Trystan im anerch / a barafi lle bo'r ferch*[58] 'I shall make, wherever the girl may be, the drink of Trystan that she may greet me'. With the fifteenth- and sixteenth-century poets the term *cae Esyllt*, 'E.'s chaplet' or 'garland', came to be used for a treasure or any valuable object;[59] sometimes it is the equivalent of 'darling'. Dafydd ap Gwilym uses *llwyn Esyllt*,[60] 'E.'s thicket', for a girl's hair. But in the same period a more sombre note is sometimes struck by the poets in *marwnadau* (elegies) which compare a widow's grief for her husband (occasionally it is the poet's grief for the departed) with the grief of Esyllt for Trystan.[61]

The *Ystorya Trystan*,[62] 'Story of Trystan', is preserved in a number of manuscripts dating from the sixteenth to eighteenth centuries. A prose outline of the tale is the framework for speech-passages in *englynion*. The three principal actors are Trystan, Esyllt, and March: in addition Arthur, Cai, and Gwalchmai each play their part. As in the case of innumerable medieval *fabliaux*, the story demonstrates the trick by which the lovers win victory over the wronged husband. Trystan and Esyllt are presented as *ar herw*, 'in exile', in the famous legendary forest of Celyddon. Arthur goes with his *teulu* or warband to seek 'denial or compensation' on behalf of March ap Meirchiawn. Trystan is said to have a magical peculiarity which means that not only whoever he draws blood from will die, but whoever draws his own (Trystan's) blood will die also.[63] This effectively deters both March and Arthur's warband from confronting Trystan. But Arthur decides to placate him, first by sending to Trystan minstrels and poets to sing his praise, and then, when this proves insufficient, he sends Gwalchmai fab Gwyar 'of the golden tongue' as a further peacemaker. Gwalchmai enters upon a lengthy *ymddiddan* or dialogue with Trystan, each addressing the other in alternate *englynion*. His mission is successful, and Arthur then makes peace between the contestants. But since neither March nor Trystan is willing to live without Esyllt, Arthur pronounces judgement between them in a further *englyn*, which enjoins them that the one shall possess Esyllt while the leaves are on the trees and the other when they are leafless: the choice being given to the husband. In a final verse Esyllt joyfully pronounces the climax of the tale, which effectively turns the tables on her husband:

Tri ffren sy dda i rryw: *Three trees are of good kind*:
Kelyn ac eiddew ag yw,   *Holly and Ivy and Yew*
a ddeilian ddail yni byw —   *which keep their leaves while they live* —
Trystan pie fi yni fyw!   *Trystan will possess me while he lives!*

This verse is one of the two focal points of the *Ystorya*: it may have been already known to tradition two centuries earlier than the first manuscripts of the tale, if D.J. Bowen is right in his conjecture[64] that Dafydd ap Gwilym recalls Esyllt's words in a poem in which he describes the month of May as the time for lovers, while winter weather is appropriate only to the 'Jealous Husband'.[65] The other focal point of the *Ystorya* is the long exchange of verses between Gwalchmai and Trystan, which follows all the conventions of the *ymddiddan* or verse-dialogue as these are known from earlier examples[66] — it may indeed at one time have had a different context. At least one manuscript preserves the *ymddiddan* as a separate entity, without the accompanying prose.[67] Perhaps these two focal points in verse may have originated separately and have subsequently been brought together in a story invented for the purpose, since the differences are considerable between the various manuscripts as regards both the form and the length of the prose, and they seem to indicate differing attempts to explain the context of verses already in existence.

Apart from the general resemblance between the *mise en scène* of the lovers' retreat to the forest of Celyddon and their retreat to the forest of Morois in Béroul's poem, there is little indication of direct influence on the *Ystorya* from the French

Tristan romances.[68] But the *Ystorya* shows a clear affinity with the 'Twenty-four Knights of Arthur's Court' — the fifteenth-century group of Triads already mentioned. March ap Meirchiawn is introduced in some texts of the *Ystorya* as *un arall o'r marchogion*, 'another of the Knights', and Trystan's inclusion in the Triad of the *Tri Lledrithawc Varchog* or 'Enchanter Knights' may have influenced the magical *cynneddf* or 'peculiarity' assigned to him in the *Ystorya*. In both texts Gwalchmai receives the epithet *aurdafodiog* or *dafod aur*, 'golden-tongued', and his role as a peacemaker is familiar from other sources.[69] Dafydd ab Edmwnd compares himself to Trystan in terms which seem to refer to the Welsh *Ystorya* rather than to the Continental versions of the romance: *Trystan wyf yn wyllt / yn ymosod am Esyllt / March yw hwn a merch yw hi / am Meirchion y'w amherchi*, 'I am (like) Trystan, madly contending for Esyllt: he is (like) March ap Meirchiawn, dishonouring her.'[70]

The *Ystorya Trystan* has in common with the Triad of the 'Three Powerful Swineherds' the fact that both allude to stolen meetings between the lovers, and both recount an attempt by March, with the help of Arthur, to win back Esyllt. In my earlier discussion of the 'Tristan' poem in the Black Book of Carmarthen I advanced the view[71] that some such story of a stolen meeting between Trystan and Esyllt may have been the context for the fragment of dialogue which it contains. There is one episode which is common to all the Continental versions, and which is particularly suggestive.[72] Tristan throws chips of wood into the stream which passes through Isolt's room, as a sign that she should come to meet him in a nearby orchard: meanwhile a treacherous dwarf had caused Mark to hide in a tree in order to witness their assignation — but his design was frustrated because the moonlight disclosed Mark's shadow, and hence his presence, to the lovers. In the last line of the Black Book poem we meet with a hostile dwarf: earlier, there is an obscure and provocative allusion reminiscent of the 'chips in the stream': *kyweithit yd vam in dev / Menic it arwet duwir dalennev*,[73] 'we two were companions in the place where the water carries the leaves'. One may tentatively suggest that the Welsh poem is either a reflection or a precursor of this incident. Professor Newstead (loc. cit.) has pointed out that the immense popularity enjoyed by the 'Tryst beneath the Tree' is witnessed by the frequency with which it is represented in medieval art.

The 'Tryst beneath the Tree' is of course *fabliau* material, rather than high romance. But so, also, is the *Ystorya Trystan*: in both, the lovers outwit the husband by trickery. Of the nature of *fabliaux*, too, are the numerous incidents in the Continental romances in which Tristan adopts various subterfuges in order to visit Isolt, being disguised successively as a leper, a pilgrim, a minstrel, and a fool — or by making his presence known by imitating bird-song, or by leaving in Isolt's path a message on a hazel-twig. I have suggested that the Triad of the 'Three Powerful

Swineherds', far from evoking the memory of a known story about Drystan and Esyllt, is a burlesque upon all incidents of this kind, just as the other two episodes recalled in the Triad would have been recognized as burlesques upon familiar traditional stories. In contrast, the Black Book poem does not treat its subject in the *fabliau* vein: alone of the Welsh allusions to the 'Tristan' theme, its potential is tragic. Since the serious presentation of a story about known characters is likely to antedate its presentation as *fabliau*, it is more natural to regard the poem as a Welsh precursor of the 'Tryst beneath the Tree' episode, rather than as a derivative or a reflection of this incident as it appears in the Continental romances. In sum, the fragmentary Welsh evidence, while preserving partially submerged memories of Drystan/Trystan and March as heroic figures, implies an audience which was sufficiently informed as to the triangle situation between Trystan, March, and Esyllt to enable it to respond to the episodic treatment of this theme in any of the many variant ways in which it could be treated by individual poets and story-tellers — not least to its treatment as burlesque. The same might indeed be said of the background knowledge anticipated from the Anglo-Norman or French audience of Marie de France's *Chevrefoil* or of the two episodic *Folie Tristan* poems. This knowledge would have been equally within the range of a Welsh audience acquainted with either the Welsh or the Continental versions of the Tristan story. The patronymics borne by the main characters in the Welsh fragments are in themselves strong evidence for the indigenous growth and currency of the Tristan story in Wales.

As an essential accompaniment to my earlier study of the different versions of *Trioedd Ynys Prydein*, many years ago I undertook an investigation of the Celtic affinities of the Tristan story.[74] This investigation was of crucial relevance for the character of the 'Early Version' of *TYP*, since although the manuscripts of this version do not go back beyond the thirteenth century, there is evidence to show that some individual Triads are considerably older than this. It became clear that apart from the allusions to Drystan, Esyllt, and March in Triad 26, the 'Early Version' is wholly free from any suspicion of influence upon it either from the Welsh *Brut* or from French or Anglo-Norman romance. I therefore concluded that the three entries in Triad 26, like all the other Triads in the collection, must refer to native stories which were already in circulation in Welsh. I now feel much less certain about this, and I am inclined to regard the whole Triad as a farcical interpolation into the text of the 'Early Version' of the Triads, giving burlesque citations of the stories of Pryderi and Drystan, as a background to the elaborated story of the hunt for Henwen, which is the main point of the Triad, although its ironic overtones are by now perhaps barely comprehensible to us. As such the Triad would not be the only addition to *TYP* which appears in the 'Early Version'.[75] If a doubt on this matter remains, it rests wholly on the otherwise authentic and indigenous character of this version of *TYP*, as being free and independent of external influence. And the Black Book poem is equally devoid of the suspicion of any influence from outside. The contents of this manuscript — religious verse, prophecy, bardic praise-poetry and poems belonging to stories — are in the main several centuries older than the mid thirteenth-century date which has been assigned to the manuscript.[76] No trace of external literary influence has ever been discerned on the composition of the group of story-poems to which the 'Tristan' poem belongs. This poem therefore provides the only piece of corroborative evidence that Triad 26 refers to a love-story about Drystan, Esyllt, and March, which had developed in vernacular sources before it was further elaborated by Anglo-Norman narrators. The evidence for the existence of the native love-story is therefore at best circumstantial, depending as it does on one's estimation of the unadulterated character of the vernacular tradition as preserved both in the 'Early Version' of the Triads and in the Black Book of Carmarthen. When we come to the later period, the fifteenth-century Triads, the allusions by the poets and the *Ystorya Trystan* all testify to an imaginative elaboration of the 'Tristan' story in Wales which appears to owe quite as much to the indigenous resources of the literary tradition as it does to the external stimulus it received from the French Romances.

III

The years which have elapsed since the publication of my earlier essay 'Some Remarks on the Celtic Sources of "Tristan"' in *THSC* for 1953 have seen the appearance not only of ALMA but of other important landmarks in Tristan studies. One such landmark is Oliver Padel's article 'The Cornish Background of the Tristan Stories' which appeared in 1981 in the first volume of *CMCS*. Padel has shown very clearly that the Continental poets, and Béroul in particular, evidently derived their principal knowledge of the Tristan story from a Cornish source. In addition to the detailed and still identifiable Cornish localization of events which are found in Béroul's poem, it is significant that all the medieval poets — Thomas, Marie de France, Eilhart, Gottfried, and Béroul himself, place a court of King Mark (his principal court, in sources other than Béroul) at Tintagel. As ancillary evidence that the actual place of origin of the Tristan story was in Cornwall, Padel brings out the full significance of the place-name *hryt eselt* ('E.'s Ford') which is found in a tenth- or eleventh-century Anglo-Saxon charter[77] relating to a boundary near Porthallow in the parish of St Keverne on the Lizard Peninsula. Two prominent episodes in Béroul's poem associate Isolt with events which take place at a ford, and so the place-name may bear witness to an early localization of these events, since Béroul can hardly be supposed to have had any knowledge of the charter, or for it to have in any way influenced him. This suggests — though of course it cannot prove — that episodes belonging to the famous love-story were already known in Cornwall long before the late twelfth century when Béroul wrote. It should not be forgotten, however, that at very much the same period as Béroul wrote, his contemporary Marie de France claimed that Tristan's birthplace was in *Suhtwales*.[78]

There is, I think, no substantial disagreement between Oliver Padel and myself with regard to the place of the Castle Dore stone in the development of the Tristan story.[79] The stone commemorates a historical sixth-century *Drusta[n]us* (a form cognate with *Drystan*), and it is the earliest of all inscribed evidence for this name. Whether or not the man so named can really have been the prototype of the romance hero is an open question, and one which could be dismissed the more readily were it not that the stone stands within a few miles of Lantyan, near Fowey, the place where Béroul places the court of King Mark,[80] and near the adjacent church of St Samson, which he connects with the story. It is safer to conclude that Béroul was either himself responsible for associating the name on the stone with the hero of his poem, or that he found that this association had already been made in his hypothetical Cornish source. Padel makes an additional point, with which I would now agree: it is that *Cunomorus* (cognate with Welsh *Cynfawr*), the name given on the stone as that of the father of *Drusta[n]us*, is a Brittonic personal name which occurs too frequently in genealogies and elsewhere to be capable of bearing any particular significance in this instance.[81] I see no reason, however, why the names of the protagonists, and episodes illustrating their 'tug of love', could not have been current in both Wales and Cornwall in the tenth or eleventh centuries. The Cornish evidence reinforces that from Wales for the early evolution of the love-story of Trystan, Esyllt and March in both countries.

The ultimate origin of *Drystan ap Tallwch* as a heroic figure, long remembered from a remote past, is a far more obscure and intractable question. It is not easy to disregard the similarity between his name and patronymic and the Pictish names *Drust/Drest/Drosten* and *Talargan*. K.H. Jackson has shown that these are not unique instances of Pictish names which have their cognates in early Welsh sources.[82] German scholars were the first to recognize the parallel between an episode connected with Cú Chulainn in the Middle Irish tale *Tochmarc Emire*, 'The Wooing of Emer',[83] and the folk-tale of 'The Dragon Slayer'[84] which is duplicated in the Continental Tristan romances, first with the hero's contest with 'le Morholt' and again in Tristan's fight with the Irish dragon, by which he wins Isolt. The episode tells how Cú Chulainn freed a Hebridean princess from three *Fomóire* (mythical monsters emanating from the sea, who recur in Irish sources), but subsequently rejected the reward of this princess in marriage. It has been suggested[85] that this adventure was transferred from the greater hero to the less, from Cú Chulainn to an otherwise unknown *Drust mac Seirb*, who gets a single mention here as one of Cú Chulainn's followers on the expedition.   To conclude that the duplicated incident of Tristan's contest with a sea-borne monster could have been inherited from the heroic deeds of a remote Pictish prototype[86] requires a considerable leap of the imagination to account for it, since it implies a lost Brittonic intermediary between Pictland and Norman England to explain its reappearance in the Continental poems.   Yet this Irish version of 'The Dragon Slayer' (the earliest to be recorded) shows certain striking parallels in points of detail with the Tristan romances, which are not found in other versions of the tale.   Not least of these is the similarity, at least in their written forms, between the name of *le Morholt* and that of the *Fomóire*, together with the corresponding part played by these characters in the Irish tale and in *Tristan*.   There is no need to enlarge here on parallels to the transference to Wales at an early date of names and stories from the Brythonic kingdoms of the 'Old North'.

Another landmark for the study of the Celtic affinities of the Tristan romance was the publication in 1967 of Nessa Ní Shéaghdha's edition of the Early Modern Irish tale of 'The Pursuit of Diarmaid and Gráinne',[87] with a valuable introduction listing all the early fragments of the tale, which go back to the ninth or tenth century.   Since the time of Gertrude Schoepperle[88] this Irish tale has commonly been regarded as the source of much in the Continental Tristan romances, though Schoepperle herself only claimed that the source of these was 'a Celtic *aithed* (tale of elopement) *similar* to *Diarmaid and Gráinne*'.   The story tells how the young heroine Gráinne is destined to be the wife of the ageing warrior-leader Fionn mac Cumhaill, but elopes instead with his follower Diarmaid (in one version Diarmaid is his nephew), and they live in the wilderness, perpetually in fear of Fionn, who finally brings about the death of Diarmaid through treachery.   This new edition has given us a new perspective on the subject, and enables us to see that, apart from the relationship between the protagonists, the elopement to the wilderness, and Fionn's pursuit of the lovers, the outstanding points of detail between the two stories are found for the first time in the seventeenth-century 'Pursuit', which may not be much, if any, earlier than the text in which it appears.[89]   I would cite in particular the incidents in *Diarmaid and Gráinne* said to be parallel to the incidents of the 'Splashing Water' and of the 'Separating Sword' which as indications of a chaste relationship between the lovers are both clearly intrusive in a tale from a country where every second cromlech is popularly known as 'the bed of Diarmaid and Gráinne'.[90]   The 'Splashing Water' motif is found nowhere else but in this tale[91] and in *Tristan*.   Obviously *Diarmaid and Gráinne*, like the *Tristan* romances, collected to itself a number of repetitive incidents in the course of its development, and the folklore versions which have come down orally (particularly those from Scotland)[92] preserve several additional reverberations of the *Tristan* romances. As said in my study of the Black Book poem, but contrary to the view I expressed in 1953, I now believe that the *Tristan* romances have had a considerable influence in many points of detail on 'The Pursuit of Diarmaid and Gráinne' in the late form in which it has reached us.[93] Influence from the Continent on an Irish text of the seventeenth century is credible, in a way that it is not in the case of the twelfth-century 'Wooing of Emer'. The French and Anglo-Norman romances have, in a manner of speaking, given back to the Irish tale what they derived initially from a Celtic saga of which the original ingredients are found in early Brythonic sources.

In this brief survey there has been insufficient space to give due consideration to the important Breton dimension of the Tristan story, in which Tristan acquired new parents, Rivalen and Blanchefleur, and took the Breton princess Isolt to be his wife.[94] Nor has it been possible to examine other interesting Brythonic name-forms which appear in the French poems, as representing *disjecta membra* from the lost Celtic sources of the romance.[95]

NOTES:

1. For an outline see EAR ch.4 on 'The Mabinogion Controversy'; Jean Marx, 'Monde Brittonique et Matière de Bretagne', *ÉC*, 10 (1963), 478-88; chs.6, 7,8 above, ch.13, pp. 282-3 and n.52 below, and LAMA 170-82.

2. F. Whitehead, 'The Early Tristan Poems', ALMA 134-44. From a study of French personal names before 1220, Pierre Galais concludes that the Tristan story was known on the Continent by the early years of the twelfth century, *Actes du VIIᵉ Congrès nationale de Littérature comparée* (Poitiers, 1965), 79; see further ALMA 134-44, 393-9, and R. Lejeune in *Mélanges offerts à Jean Frappier* (Geneva, 1970), ii, 625-30.

3. Thomas Jones, 'The Early Evolution of the Legend of Arthur', *NMS*, 8 (1964), 19; = *B*, 17 (1958), 247-50; B.F. Roberts, Ast. H. 285-6. See ch.2 above.

4. T.J. Morgan, *Y Treigladau a'u Cystrawen* (Cardiff, 1952, repr. 1989), 460-1, gives instances of the variation in Welsh spelling between initial *Dr/Tr*. The spelling *Trystan* is more common than *Drystan* in the later texts.

5. K. Jackson, *WHR* (Special Number on Welsh Laws, 1963), 85.

6. R. Radford, 'Report on the Excavations at Castle Dore', *Journal of the Royal Institution of Cornwall*, New Series 1 (1951), Appendix, 117. According to Jackson, loc. cit., this reading 'is doubtful and begs the question'. The first name has been differently interpreted by others; see discussion by Oliver Padel, *CMCS*, 1 (1981), 55 n., and ch.11, p. 241 below.

7. K. Jackson in F.T. Wainright (ed.), *The Problem of the Picts* (Edinburgh, 1955), 140; E. Okasha, 'The Non-Ogam Inscriptions of Pictland', *CMCS*, 9 (1985), 60-1 and plate.

8. *Drest* is the form in Pictish corresponding to the Irish *Drust*: M.O. Anderson, *Kings and Kingship in Early Scotland* (Edinburgh, 1973), 90, 271-3, 299.

9. *CMCS*, 1, 55. The significance of the frequent occurrence of these names in the Pictish lists was first urged by Zimmer in 1891; see EAR i, 178; Vendryes, *ÉC*, 5 (1949), 36.

10. *LL* 279, 1.26.

11. *CF* 480; J. Lloyd-Jones, *Enwau Lleoedd Sir Gaernarfon* (Cardiff, 1928), 10.

12. Several sixteenth-century manuscripts name *Tallwch*, as follows, in a confused rendering of the female descent of Maelgwn Gwynedd: *Mam Meddyf merch Tallwch ap Kwch m. Kychwein chwaer y Drystann* (*EWGT* 91, 28(f); similarly *TYP* 329 and refs. cited; *LlC*, 4 (1957), 220; *B*, 18, 238).

13. Ch.Br. 235; J. Loth, *RC*, 32 (1911), 413; ibid., *Contributions à l'étude des romans de la Table Ronde* (Paris, 1912), 108.

14. *MLN*, 39 (1924), 326. Cf. J.C. Lozac'hmeur in HLCB 149.

15. K. Jackson explains *Esyllt* as derived from *Adsiltia*, 'she who is gazed upon', (Welsh *syllu*), LHEB 709.

16. According to Jackson (loc. cit.) these spellings 'seem to point to a Brittonic secondary by-form *Adthiltia* or *Atthiltia*, and to the rare survival of this dental affricate (in dialect?) in Wales, alongside *ss*, as late as the 9th or 10th century at least'. On the name *Esyllt* cf. also CF 480 n.

17. *EWGT* 9(i); 36(i); 47(22), etc. She was either the wife or the mother of Merfyn Frych, d. 844 (*EWGT* 151). The earliest version of the genealogy is in Harleian MS 3859, which was drawn up in the mid tenth century to illustrate the lines of descent of Owain son of Hywel Dda; see *EWGT* 9, and refs. there cited.

18. *EWGT* 90-1 (27c); *TYP* 257.

19. *CO* l.372 (=*WM* 470, 13-14). Cf. *TYP* 349.

20. *CO* l.191-2 (=*WM* 461, 8).

21. For refs. see *TYP* 311-12.

22. *HRB* II, 2-5. Cf. B.F. Roberts, *B*, 25 (1973), 279. Whatever may be the implication of the Welsh rendering of *Estrildis* by *Esyllt*, this name would have been known to the scribe of *BD*, since *Esyllt* occurs in Triad 26 in Peniarth MS 16, in the same hand and in the same manuscript as *BD*, see Introduction, p. 9 above and *TYP* xviii. Padel cites a (now lost) field-name *Dryll Esyllt* ('E's part' or 'fragment') in Denbighshire, attested in 1550 (*CMCS*, 1, 67 n).

23. *TYP* 444; Ch.Br. 150, 219. A Cornish *Marh*, *March*, is listed in the Bodmin Manumissions, *RC*, 1 (1870-2), 335, 338. For *March* in Breton see L. Fleuriot, *ÉC*, 18 (1981), 211.

24. See index to *LL*; *EWGT* 202; Ch.Br. 150.

25. *Vita S. Pauli Aureliani*, ed. Cuissard, *RC*, 5 (1883), 445. Summary in G.H. Doble, *The Saints of Cornwall: Part I* (Truro, 1960), 16. Cf. H. Newstead, 'King Mark of Cornwall', *Romance Philology*, 11 (1958), 240-1; *THSC* 1953, 46-7.

26. G.H. Doble, *Saint Illtud* (Cardiff, 1944), 23-4 (reprinted in D.S. Evans, *Lives of the Welsh Saints*, ed. G.H. Doble, Cardiff, 1971); index to *LL*.

27. *TYP* 444-8. In *TYP* no. 14 March is one of the *Tri Llynghesawg*, 'Fleet owners' or 'Sea-farers', hence this name was borrowed into the 'Dream of Rhonabwy' where March is described as leader of the *gwŷr Llychlyn* or Scandinavians (*BR* 9, 22).

28. *Hend*. 87, 13-14.

29. Stith-Thompson, *Motif-Index of Folk Literature* (Copenhagen, 1950-7), F.511.2.2.

30. Ed. A. Ewert (Oxford, 1939), ll.1306-47. Newstead, loc. cit., 253; ALMA 128 suggests a Breton source for Béroul's version, on the sole evidence of several much later Breton versions recorded in the late eighteenth and nineteenth centuries. See n.35 below. On the variants of the tale see J. Jones, 'March ap Meirchiawn', *Aberystwyth Studies*, 12 (1932).

31. For the story of *Eochu Echcend* see Newstead, *Romance Philology*, 11, 247, and refs. there cited. For the *Labraid Lorc/Loingsech* version see M. Dillon, *The Cycles of the Kings* (Oxford, 1946), 9-10; *TYP* 447.

32. RWM i, 887. Ed. P.C. Bartrum, *National Library of Wales Journal*, 20 (1978), 373 (from Peniarth MS 134, 131-3).

33. J. Rhŷs, *Cy*. 6 (1883), 181-3; CF 232-3. The text is printed in *Y Brython* for 1860, 431.

34. CF 572-3; Newstead, *Romance Philology*, 11, 250.

35. The earliest recorded version is by F. Cambry, *Voyage dans le Finistère en 1794* (ed. E. Souvestre, 1836); see also J. Loth, *Contributions* 108. The passage by Cambry is quoted by Loomis, *Comparative Literature*, 11 (1950), 290-1.

36. *Hend*. 5, 11.

37. BBC 100-1 (=*LIDC* no. 35). On the date of the Black Book see Introduction p. 7 above, and *LIDC* xxiii-iv.

38. See *LIDC* lxiv-lxv.

39. *RC*, 33 (1912), 403-13; Loth, *Contributions* 112-23.

40. 'The Tristan Poem in the Black Book of Carmarthen', *SC*, 14/15 (1979-80), 54-65.

41. A name unrecorded elsewhere except in two instances in *LL* 207, 5; 212, 5. See *SC*, 14/15; 56 n.

42. The interpretation of each of the three lines of the first *englyn* can only be conjectural.

43. As was first noted by J.G. Evans in an additional note to his edition, *BBC* 138, 160. Later confirmed by Lloyd-Jones, in G, 394 and by others; *SC*, 14/15, 55 n.

44. Most of these are edited by B.F. Roberts, 'Rhai o Gerddi Ymddiddan yn Llyfr Du Caerfyrddin', Ast. H. 281-325.

45. *SC*, 14/15, 55; *LIDC* lix, lxii; cf. T. Jones, *PBA*, 53 (1967), 100; cf. O. Padel, *CMCS*, 1, 58 n.

46. *TYP* nos. 19, 21, 26. The prototype of the 'Early Version' of *TYP*, like *BD*, can be taken back

on linguistic grounds to the early thirteenth century; see n.22 above; *TYP* xviii. The text of the later *'WR'* version dates from the middle and late fourteenth century. See Introduction pp. 7-12 above.

47. This is the only instance recorded in GPC of *meichiad*, 'swineherd', with the intensive *gwr(dd)*; unlike the epithets which introduce the two other triads naming Drystan, *gwrddfeichiad* has no place in the bardic vocabulary.

48. The reference to the Cath Palug or *'Palug's Cat'*, like the other two 'scourges of Anglesey' named in the triad, was evocative of an ancient and well-known tradition; *TYP* 484-7. See ch.2, p. 45 above.

49. In the Nennian *Mirabilia*, quoted by Thomas Jones, 'The Early Evolution of the Legend of Arthur', *NMS*, 8 (1964), 11; *B*, 17 (1958), 243. See *CO*(1) lxiii-lxvii.

50. Peniarth MS 47 (*TYP* xxviii-xxxi). This version of *TYP* preserves a number of triads (nos. 70-80) not found in either of the two main versions, together with interesting archaic features pointing to an earlier exemplar.

51. In this last triad Drystan is no longer *ap Tallwch*, but is described as *eil March*, 'heir' or 'successor' of March (unless *eil* is here a mistake for *nei*, 'nephew of March').

52. *Pedwar Marchog ar Hugain Llys Arthur; TYP* cxxxv-cxxxix, 250-5; *THSC* 1956, 116ff. See ch.9, pp. 201-2 above.

53. See *TYP* 333; G 394.

54. For refs. see G 491; *TYP* 349-50. But we are left in no doubt when the poets refer to Gwynedd as *tir Esyllt*, *brodir Esyllt*, or *gwlad Esyllt*, 'the land of E.'.

55. *RBP* 1327, 7-8.

56. Thomas Parry, *Gwaith Dafydd ap Gwilym* (Cardiff, 1963), 580, lists six instances.

57. T. Parry, op. cit. no. 33, 7-8. Cf. *YB*, 12 (1982), 62-3.

58. T. Roberts (ed.), *Gwaith Dafydd ab Edmwnd* (Bangor, 1914), no. 2, ll.25-6.

59. Cf. GPC 382; E. Bachellery, *L'Oeuvre Poétique de Gutun Owain* (Paris, 1951), LXIII, 36 and n.; T. Gwynn Jones, *Gwaith Tudur Aled* (Cardiff, 1926), cxxxviii, l.48; E.D. Jones, *Lewys Glyn Cothi (Detholiad)* (Cardiff, 1984), 28, l.38; etc.

60. T. Parry, op. cit. no. 45, l.41.

61. Ifor Williams, *Gwaith Guto'r Glyn* (Cardiff, 1961), XI, ll. 61-2; LII, ll. 31-2; T. Gwynn Jones, op. cit. X, l.26; LXXIV, ll. 27-8; E. Rowlands, *Gwaith Lewys Môn* (Cardiff, 1975), XXI, ll. 24-8; XXXV, ll. 33-4. Cf. Bachellery, op. cit. I, p.64 n.

62. Ed. Ifor Williams, *B*, 5 (1930), 115-29, and (from different MSS) by J. Rowland and G. Thomas, *National Library of Wales Journal*, 22 (1982), 241-53; J. Loth, *RC*, 34 (1913), 377-96 (text from Cardiff MS 6, printed RWM ii, 105-6). Trans. T.P. Cross, *Studies in Philology*, 17 (1920), 98-110, and by R.L. Thomson in *The Tristan Legend*, ed. J. Hill (Leeds, 1977), 1-5. Cf. *TYP* 332, and J. Rowland, *Ériu*, 36 (1985), 33. See now the latter's discussion in her *Early Welsh Saga Poetry* (Cambridge, 1990), 252-4.

63. J. Loth pointed out (loc. cit. 388-9) that this characteristic could have arisen from a

misunderstanding of the line spoken by Trystan in the verse-dialogue *Om lleddir mi ai llada*, 'if I am slain, I will slay'. Cf. *THSC*, 1953, 55 n.

64. *B*, 25 (1972), 21-2, citing T. Parry, *Gwaith Dafydd ap Gwilym*, no. 24. Cf. *YB*, 12 (1982), 62-3.

65. In one version alone, attributed to the seventeenth-century Edward Lhuyd, March is given a final obscure verse in which he states that he never thought Esyllt would be so cruel. Text printed in *Y Brython* (1860), 430-1. Cf. Rowland and Thomas, op. cit., 252 (text from Cwrtmawr MS 376 D).

66. Cf. *TYP* 383-4.

67. *B*, 13 (1950), 25-7.

68. Trystan's sword *Arkwlff* (named in two MSS) has been compared with the name of his bow *arc qui ne faut* in Béroul's poem, ed. A. Ewert, ll.1752, 1763.

69. This is Gwalchmai's role in the three romances *Owain*, *Geraint* and *Peredur*; *Mab.* 172, 202, 265. Cf. *TYP* 374, and cf. n.52 above.

70. T. Roberts, *Gwaith Dafydd ab Edmwnd* (Bangor, 1914), 56, ll. 27-30.

71. *SC*, 14/15 (1979-80), 61-5.

72. H. Newstead, 'The Tryst beneath the Tree: An Episode in the Tristan Legend', *Romance Philology*, 9 (1956), 269. For the many pictorial representations of this scene in medieval art see A. Ewert, *Romance of Tristan by Béroul*, ii (Commentary) (Oxford, 1970), 70.

73. *LlDC* 35, 15-16. Cf. *SC*, 14/15 (1979-80), 57.

74. 'Some Remarks on the Celtic Sources of "Tristan"', *THSC* (1953), 32-60.

75. Cf. *TYP* triad I and n. The farcical triad of the three fugitives from the Battle of Camlan may also be compared, *CO* ll.225-32; *TYP* xcii.

76. See *LlDC* xxviii.

77. *CMCS*, 1, 66-7 and n.

78. *Chrevrefoil* line 16 (*Poems of Marie de France*, ed. A. Ewert (Oxford, 1947), 123).

79. *THSC* 1953, 47-8; *CMCS*, 1, 77-8. See now pp. 240-3 below.

80. *CMCS*, 1, 60. See ch.11, p. 240 below.

81. The ninth-century *Vita* of St Paul Aurelian (ed. Cuissard, *RC*, 5 (1883)), 431 equates a King Marcus with *Quonomorius* (=*Conomorus*), but this may have been because the author had seen the stone, or — as Padel suggests — it could be a later gloss on his text. Cf. *THSC* (1953), 47-8.

82. K.H. Jackson, *YB*, 12, 21, instances Welsh *Taran* and *Gwrgwst* (Pictish *Uurguist*); cf. also F.T. Wainright (ed.), *The Problem of the Picts* (London, 1955), 145, 165. More striking, however, is the character of Caw of Prydyn (Pictland) and his son Hueil, who figure in *CO*, in *TYP* and in the Lives of the Saints.

83. O. Bergin and R.I. Best, *Lebor na Huidre: The Book of the Dun Cow* (Dublin, 1929), 315-16.

Ed. A.G. van Hamel, *Compert Con Culainn and Other Stories* (Dublin, 1933), 60-2; trans. Cross and Slover, *Ancient Irish Tales* (London, 1936, rev. ed. Dublin, 1969), 168-9. For a Breton version of 'The Dragon Slayer' see *RC*, 41 (1924), 331-49, and H. Newstead in ALMA 128-9.

84. Aarne Thompson, *The Types of the Folktale* (Helsinki, 1928, 1961), no. 300. Cf. IPT 13-14.

85. R. Thurneysen, *Die irische Helden- und Königsage* (Halle, 1921), 392 n.; Deutschbein, *Beiblatt zur Anglia* xv, 16ff.; Newstead, ALMA 126; *THSC* 1953, 38-40.

86. A twelfth-century date is usually accepted for *Tochmarc Emire*, but whether early or late in the century can only be adjudged in relation to other texts; on the question of date see D.N. Dumville, *Éigse*, 16 (1975), 22; idem, *CMCS*, 9 (1985), 91-8 and refs. there cited.

87. Nessa Ní Shéaghdha, *Tóruigheacht Dhiarmada agus Ghráinne: The Pursuit of Diarmaid and Gráinne* (Irish Texts Society, vol. xlviii: Dublin, 1967).

88. Gertrude Schoepperle, *Tristan and Isolt* (London, 1913), 391-446; H. Newstead, ALMA 127. First pointed out, independently, by J.F. Campbell, *Popular Tales of the West Highlands*, iv (1893), 240; cf. EAR i, 171 n.

89. As shown by Gerard Murphy, *The Ossianic Lore and Romantic Tales of Medieval Ireland* (Dublin, 1955, revised 1971), 14. Idem, *Duanaire Finn*, iii (Irish Texts Society, vol. xliii: Dublin, 1953), xxxvi.

90. Cf. A. Bruford, *Gaelic Folktales and Medieval Romances* (*Béaloideas*, 34: Dublin, 1966), 106; Murphy, *Duanaire Finn*, iii, xxxv.

91. N. Ní Shéaghdha, op. cit., ll. 785-93. Cf. Stith-Thompson, *Motif-Index of Folk Literature* (Copenhagen, 1952-7), V, 376, under T.315.2.1; Stith-Thompson and T.P. Cross, *Motif-Index of Early Irish Literature* (Bloomington, 1952); H. Newstead, 'Isolt of the White Hands', *Romance Philology*, 19 (1965), 156-8; Schoepperle, op. cit., ii, 415. See also *SC*, 14/15 (1979-80), 63-4.

92. N. Ní Shéaghdha, op. cit., xxvi-ix (from which instances I would draw the opposite conclusion from hers); Bruford, op. cit., 106-9.

93. A similar view is expressed by Padel, *CMCS*, 1, 57. Cf. also R.J. Cormier, 'Open Contrast: Tristan and Diarmaid', *Speculum*, 51 (1976), 589-601; idem, *ÉC*, 15 (1976-7), 303-15.

94. Cf. *THSC* (1953), 56-7; H. Newstead, 'Isolt of the White Hands' and ALMA 128-9; R.S. Loomis, *Comparative Literature* No. 4 (1950), 293-4. See J.R.F. Piette, 'Yr Agwedd Lydewig ar y Chwedlau Arthuraidd', *LlC*, 8 (1965), 183-90 (p. 188).

95. For *Brangien* and *Urgan* see *TYP* 287, 391; *THSC* (1953), 49-50, 55. For *Hu(s)dent* see J. Loth, *Contributions à l'étude des Romans de la Table Ronde* (Paris, 1912), 106, and for this group of names see ch.13 below, p. 280 and n.38. On *Urgan* < *Gwrgi* see p. 65 n.50 above.

I am grateful to Dr P. Sims-Williams for some useful comments on this chapter.

SOME SOUTH-WESTERN SITES WITH ARTHURIAN ASSOCIATIONS

O. J. Padel

THE aim of the present chapter is to summarize recent work on certain sites in the south-west, three in Cornwall and one in Somerset, which have achieved fame in connection with the Arthurian legend, and which have recently been reassessed. Unfortunately, for reasons of space, it is not possible to include various south-western sites, less well-known, which are more truly Arthurian, in the sense that they exemplify folklore of the kind found in the *Historia Brittonum*, but at much later dates. Similarly the site at Glastonbury, where it was claimed in 1191 that Arthur's grave had been found, has not undergone drastic revision recently, and so is not considered here.[1] The sites will be examined in chronological order — that is, in order of their datable Arthurian associations.

Tintagel (*c.* 1139)

The earliest record of the name of Tintagel, and also its earliest association with the Arthurian legend, are in Geoffrey of Monmouth's *History of the Kings of Britain*, completed before 1139. In that work its single appearance, as a site, is in the episode of the conception of Arthur, where it receives a vivid description giving the impression that Geoffrey had seen the place.[2] After Geoffrey's *History*, Tintagel does not play a very prominent part in later Arthurian romances, though it is mentioned occasionally; instead, its main fame in medieval literature was as the castle of King Mark in the legend of Tristan and Isolt.[3] Knowledge of the literary story about Arthur's conception continued meanwhile, and it was mentioned by antiquaries in connection with Tintagel; but the earliest evidence at present known to me of the name 'King Arthur's Castle' being locally current is in 1650, *King Arthur Castle alias Tintagell Castle*.[4]

Modern interpretation of Tintagel began with the interest which led to excavations there, starting in 1933.[5] There have been further minor excavations since the war, which have amplified but not drastically altered the information gained from the pre-war excavations.[6] It should be noted that some of the description which follows is provisional, for fresh excavations are due to take place there during 1990. These may well qualify, or render obsolete, some of the remarks which follow. Some of the questions which arise in connection with the site may be enlightened by careful investigation, using modern techniques.[6a]

The most important fact to emerge from the earlier excavations is that the area of Tintagel headland teems with fragments of pottery of a type manufactured in the Mediterranean area (mainly in North Africa and Asia Minor); these fragments are dated between the mid fifth century and the late sixth (c. 450–c. 600). Until found at Tintagel, this pottery had not previously been recognized in Britain, and it is to the pre-war excavator that the credit is due for identifying it.[7] The importance of Tintagel as a find-site for this pottery cannot be overemphasized. Since being identified there, it has been found to occur at other sites within Dark-Age western Britain and Ireland, including other sites in Cornwall and Devon, Cadbury–Congresbury and South Cadbury in Somerset (see below), places in Wales and south-west Ireland, and as far north as the Scottish Highlands.[8] But at many of those sites, the amounts found are trivial compared with those at Tintagel, and none of them comes near it in quantity. It occurs there in such density that even minor investigations in the area of the headland can be virtually assured of finding more pieces. Being imported from so far away, this pottery represents expensive, luxury, goods. Some of it may have been imported for the sake of its contents (probably either wine or oil), while other pieces can only have been brought for their own sake as items of high-class tableware.

What this shows, for certain (and this is the only certainty to be had), is that the headland at Tintagel was occupied for some or all of the period between c. 450 and c. 600; and that, at the time of its occupation, it was highly important, in some manner which can only be guessed at. For forty years the widespread theory was that the Dark-Age occupation represented a Celtic monastic community. This hypothesis is no longer accepted by most archaeologists.[9] The site has none of the attributes recognized as characteristic of Dark-Age monastic settlements in Wales and Cornwall, such as an enclosed curvilinear cemetery, a place-name suggesting ecclesiastical associations, perhaps a contemporary inscription, or indications in the historical record.[10]

With the collapse of the theory that Tintagel was a Dark-Age Celtic monastery, several questions arise. In addition, it has lately become apparent that the site of Tintagel church, one-third of a mile from the headland, is of considerable interest, and that the sites need to be considered as a group, and not individually. It could be said that the more information becomes available about Tintagel, the more complex and incomprehensible the place becomes.

The questions arise mainly in relation to the Mediterranean pottery. First, what is the pottery doing in Britain, at this and other sites? It must have been brought in the way of trade, and if an object for the trading connection is to be sought, then an obvious one would be Cornish tin, since it is in Cornwall that the greatest amount of the pottery is found. It is unknown whether the lesser amounts found elsewhere in western Britain were the result of similar trading-contacts all around the Irish Sea, or whether the trade was primarily with Cornwall, with a secondary distribution from there to other parts of the Celtic world.[11]

The next question is why the pottery is found in greatest quantity at Tintagel, and not at some other site in Cornwall. The answer to this is dependent upon another question, what kind of site Tintagel was in the Dark Age. The legends which first appear in the twelfth century portray Tintagel as a royal residence (King Mark's in the Tristan legend), or as a royal defensive site (that of Gorlois, Duke of Cornwall, in Geoffrey of Monmouth's *HRB*). One might surmise that the legends had preserved a folk-memory of a historical fact, and that the site was indeed a defensive royal residence in the fifth and sixth centuries. If so, it is most unlikely to have been the sole such site, partly because it is not pleasantly habitable in winter, and partly because such little as is known about Dark-Age Celtic kingship suggests that a king of Cornwall, or of the whole south-western peninsula, would have had more than one residence. One should perhaps think more in terms of seasonal or occasional occupation.

The idea of Tintagel as a defensive site is interesting, because at precisely the period of the imported pottery Cornwall, like western Wales and western Scotland, was subject to pressure from Irish raiders or settlers. In Cornwall there is no historical documentation for this, but it is demonstrated by ten Dark-Age inscriptions in Irish ogham script or bearing Irish names. Moreover, it is precisely the area near Tintagel which was particularly subject to this pressure, for the inscriptions, with one exception, all occur in an arc around Tintagel.[12] The occupation at Tintagel could have been intended to maintain a strong Cornish presence in precisely that area where Irish settlement was having its greatest impact at the same period. Tintagel headland is a splendidly defensive site, as noted by Geoffrey of Monmouth in *c.* 1139 and by Leland in *c.* 1540 ('almost *situ loci* inexpugnable'), and it might be surprising if the Dark-Age occupation were not sited there in order to take advantage of that fact. The name itself also seems to enshrine the defensive aim, since it is likely to be composed of Cornish **din*, 'fort' (variant **tin*), plus **tagell*, 'constriction': 'the fort of the narrow neck'.[13]

If Tintagel was a protective response to the Irish settlements in the area, there is an echo of that function in the Tristan romances, where the notion of Irish raids upon

Cornwall appears side by side with that of Tintagel as King Mark's residence; and that record of Irish attacks is all the more remarkable in view of the lack of historical documentation for them — their mention in the twelfth century can hardly be other than a folk-memory of the actual events. This makes it slightly more reasonable to suggest that the legendary nature of Tintagel as a royal site might be a similar survival, through folklore, of a historical fact.

Another question which needs to be answered is the nature of any structural remains which might be expected to have been associated with the Mediterranean pottery. The headland has been found to be covered with the remains of small rectangular huts, arranged in chains with shared walls. Some have been restored and are visible to the visitor; but careful survey in recent years, particularly after an area of the turf on the headland was destroyed by a fire in 1983, has shown that the number of these huts is far greater than that presently seen, and that they cover much of the available level ground and terraces on the headland.[14] Very few parallels for these structures have been found, and their date is uncertain. They were formerly considered to belong with the Dark-Age pottery, but in the absence of a full report of the excavations, some authorities now doubt that dating.[15] Further excavation may provide a definite answer to this question: it may be that the huts are not all of the same period.

The other area of archaeological significance for the present purpose is that around the parish church of Tintagel, one-third of a mile from the headland.[16] There are various earthworks outside the churchyard itself, suggesting that it overlies some earlier structure; and within it there are certain mounds, one of which has been found to contain a slab-sided grave. These are unlikely to be as late as the Norman period, and they would be most at home in the Dark Age, when parallels for them could be found in both Wales and Brittany, as noted by Dark.[17] The possibility therefore arises that, if Tintagel was indeed a royal residence or defensive site in the fifth to seventh centuries, these might be royal burial-mounds of the rulers of Cornwall at that period.

Tintagel seems largely to have gone out of use in the seventh century, and evidence for occupation during the succeeding five centuries is scanty: if it was occupied at all, it was not a site of significance, on present evidence. Any theory explaining the nature of the site at its peak ought also to be able to account for its disuse after that period. This abandonment comes too early to be explained by reference to English pressure upon east Cornwall, since that hardly began before the eighth century. If Tintagel is seen as a response to the Irish settlements in the area, then its abandonment might have been due to the assimilation of the settled Irish population (or to its no longer being felt to be a threat), or to the cessation of the attacks. Whatever the reason for the abandonment, it is interesting that five miles east of Tintagel is the Domesday manor of Lesnewth, 'new court' (Cornish *lys + noweth). This manor gave its name to a parish, and also to the medieval administrative hundred within which it and Tintagel both lie. It is tempting to understand the place-name as indicating the place which superseded Tintagel in the political geography of Dark-Age Cornwall.

Mention should also be made of the medieval castle at Tintagel, since theories about it, too, have recently been revised.[18] Formerly the accepted theory was that it was built before Geoffrey of Monmouth's History was written, and provided the inspiration for his literary use of the site; but there is no evidence, either historical or archaeological, to justify so early a date for the castle, and the presence of a Norman ring-work elsewhere within the same manor makes such a date very unlikely. The earliest historical hint that the local lord of the manor might have made Tintagel his residence appears in 1207, and the earliest mention of the castle in 1233. By that period the international fame of Tintagel was well established, and the best explanation for the creation of the castle is that it was done in response to the literary renown. The person responsible may well have been Richard, the brother of King Henry III. He was created Earl of Cornwall in 1227, and shortly afterwards, in 1233–6, he went to some lengths to acquire both the site of the castle and then the whole manor in whose lands the castle lay. Thus the historical evidence at present suggests that the castle was built in about 1230 or slightly later, and owed its existence from the start to the occurrence of the place in international romances.

It is also worth asking what visible remains the story-tellers might have had in mind in the twelfth century. What would a visitor have seen there at that date, before the castle was built? If it is right to guess that Cornish folklore lay behind the literary use of Tintagel, one would like to know around what remains the folklore had accumulated. The large ditch which protects the landward side of the castle is said to be contemporary with the Mediterranean pottery; such a ditch would have defended the narrow neck, and thus the whole of the headland, from landward attack. It is this feature which would probably have formed the chief visible structure in the twelfth century. If any of the huts belong with the imported pottery, then there is also the possibility that the foundations of these were also visible.

Finally, there is another slightly curious feature about Tintagel. If the Dark-Age occupation represents a royal promontory-fort, then it would fit into a type of monument which is well attested in Cornwall and elsewhere; but such promontory-forts are mainly Iron-Age (pre-Roman) in date. At Tintagel it is surprising that there is no evidence, from the pottery-finds, of any occupation at that earlier period. However, there is some evidence that the headland was so used in the late Roman period, since there have been finds there dating from the third or fourth centuries. It seems that the occupation represented by the Dark-Age pottery may have been simply the continuation of a slightly earlier occupation in the late Roman period.

In brief, from a literary point of view the use of Tintagel can be divided into three main phases: first, its occupation, as a site of considerable importance, between *c.* 450 and *c.* 600, followed by a period of apparent unimportance lasting for several centuries. Second, its appearance in international legend in the twelfth century, as a residence or defensive site of the supposed Dark-Age rulers of Cornwall; and third, a century *after* the first appearance of those legends in written texts, the building of a castle there, which does not seem to have served any function other than exemplifying the legends themselves.

It seems very likely, then, that when Geoffrey of Monmouth related that the Duke of Cornwall placed Igerna at Tintagel for protection against Uther Pendragon, he was following pre-existing legends which claimed that the place was a stronghold of the Cornish rulers. What is unknown is whether there was already a link between Arthur and Tintagel, or whether Geoffrey thereby created it. If Arthur was locally regarded as a Dark-Age ruler of Cornwall, then in that role he ought already to have been associated with the place. On the other hand, if one regards it as unlikely that Arthur was traditionally seen as a ruler of Cornwall (and there is certainly no evidence that he was ever so envisaged), then his association with Tintagel may have been incidental. It could be due merely to the fact that, in the story of Arthur's conception, Geoffrey was following a (hypothetical) Cornish tradition in making the fort a stronghold of Gorlois.

'Kelli wic in Cornwall' (twelfth century)

This is the name given in two early Welsh texts, *Culhwch ac Olwen* and the Welsh Triads, to Arthur's residence.[19] It demands identification, and there have been numerous attempts to do so.[20] Cornish antiquaries in the eighteenth and nineteenth centuries identified it with Callington — it is not clear why, but presumably because of the slight similarity of the names.[21]

There have been other, more recent, attempts to identify *Kelli wic*, again on the basis of the name; only one of these has received much currency, and it is examined below. Ferdinand Lot suggested that it meant Bodmin, because of a nearby place-name Calliwith;[22] and Joseph Loth suggested and then retracted Gweek Wood, near Helston, again because of the partial correspondence of the place-name to *Kelli wic*, and also because of a nearby earthwork in the wood.[23] Neither of these has received much attention, presumably because of a realization that the similarity of names was not sufficiently close, and that other names of a comparable degree of similarity might also be found; perhaps also because of a realization that the quest, as it stands, is too vague. It is unclear what one should actually be looking for, in trying to identify *Kelli wic*. In order to answer that, one would need to know how the early Welsh story-tellers came by the name, and what sort of place they might have had in mind as a suitable place for Arthur to have resided. It is not at all certain that they would have had a real site in mind, though, as will be seen below, there is some reason to think that *Kelli wic* was indeed a real place in Cornwall. There is an unexplained archaeological site, on Bodmin Moor, which has been known as King Arthur's Hall since *c.* 1600. It consists of a rectangular bank, enclosing marshy ground, and with a rectangle of upright stones within it.[24] This shows the kind of site which later folklore, at any rate, could envisage as a suitable residence for Arthur. However, it has generally been assumed that a conventional fort would be the most appropriate identification.

In 1900 it was suggested that the name might refer to a hill-fort called Castle Killibury.[25] There is actually no reason why this suggestion is any more likely than the others; but it has received greater currency, so the reasoning behind it must be explained. The process started with a different investigation, the attempt to identify a site mentioned by Geoffrey of Monmouth in connection with Tintagel and his episode of Arthur's conception. This is the site named *Dimilioc* in Geoffrey's text, and it is where Gorlois, Duke of Cornwall, was besieged and killed while Uther Pendragon was begetting Arthur at Tintagel. The place referred to by Geoffrey is that now called Domellick, where there is a suitable hill-fort close by, at St Dennis. It is about twenty miles from Tintagel.[26] Geoffrey's text is vague about the distance, but he seems to imply that it was within reach of Tintagel during the course of a single night. That is not actually stated, but the episode can be read so as to suggest it. In the eighteenth century, therefore, a suitable hill-fort was sought, near Tintagel, to be identified with Geoffrey's *Dimilioc*, and one such was found at the fort called Tregeare Rounds.[27] This suggestion is now seen to be misguided, in the light of place-name evidence which identifies *Dimilioc* securely with Domellick further away; but as a result, the spurious name 'Dameliock Castle' appeared upon Ordnance Survey maps as the name of Tregeare Rounds for a brief period.[28]

Even though the mistake was short-lived, it had a further consequence, in giving rise to the identification of *Kelli wic* with Castle Killibury, nearby. The suggestion was made on the basis of the similarity of the names, and for the invalid reason, which seemed cogent at the time, that Killibury is near to Tregeare Rounds.[29] The suggestion was taken up by Charles Henderson in 1925, and thereby gained currency in academic circles.[30] However, in the light of the re-identification of *Dimilioc*, there is now no reason for maintaining the suggestion, other than the vague similarity of the names.

Recent excavations have shown that Castle Killibury was an Iron-Age hill-fort, constructed probably in the third century BC. Two sherds of Mediterranean amphorae indicate that the fort was reoccupied in the Dark Age, but this reuse was probably on a very small scale, and the limited extent of the excavations did not show any sign that the site was refortified, as at South Cadbury and other forts at this period.[31] It should be noted that both the interior and the rampart of the fort had been heavily damaged by ploughing; the only section of the rampart to be examined had been virtually flattened, though other parts remain upstanding.

The identification of *Kelli wic* with Castle Killibury was slightly confused by a separate question, the identification of a manor mentioned in two tenth-century Anglo-Saxon sources under the name *Cællincg* or *Cællwic*.[32] This manor is unidentified. It ought to be found among the lands later belonging to the bishops of Exeter, but the problem is not helped by the discrepancy between the two forms of the name, *Cællincg* and *Cællwic*. Going by name alone, Callington might be a suitable candidate, but that was not episcopal property at a later date. Another possible place is the episcopal manor of Burneire, a mile north of Wadebridge; the difference of name can be resolved by pointing out that within the territory of that manor is a tenement called Kelly, which might be a descendant of the name *Cællincg* or *Cællwic*, and from which Killibury is in turn named.[33] At the moment, then, Burneire is the most likely identification of this mysterious estate, but the matter remains uncertain.

There is no need for the episcopal manor of *Cællincg* to be the same place as the legendary *Kelli wic*, but until lately there was a general assumption that they were to be equated, and that the identification of one would thus be affected by that of the other. On that assumption, it was felt that the two identifications, of *Cællincg* with Burneire, and of *Kelli wic* with Killibury (lying within the territory of Burneire), were mutually supportive of one another. That is not so, once the two problems are separated. Killibury remains a candidate for *Kelli wic*, but only by virtue of the association of a suggestive place-name and a hill-fort (assuming that a fort is the appropriate kind of site); and, as already seen, there are other sites in Cornwall which would qualify equally well on that basis. So the suggestion should be treated as very tentative, and as no more likely than other suggestions previously made.

The legendary *Kelli wic* is likely to remain unidentified, but there is a single reference to a real place in Cornwall with a name which seems to be identical: a man called Thomas de *Kellewik* was murdered at Lanestly (at Gulval, a mile north-east of Penzance), and two men were accused of his murder in 1302.[34]   For lack of other references to the place-name, the only inference that can be made about the residence of this Thomas is that it might have been near Gulval; but at the moment no later name is known to which the form could refer.   It would be rash to build any theories on the basis of a single form in a source which was not written locally, and which was therefore liable to corruptions in its spelling.   However, if the Welsh story-tellers had a genuine place and name in mind when they used the phrase *Kelli wic*, and if *Kellewik* was the correct name of a place in Cornwall in 1302, then it might well represent the one intended by the story-tellers.   If so, then surmise can go a little further.   The sole hint as to the whereabouts of *Kellewik* is that it may have been in the Gulval area, in the far west of the county.   If a significant archaeological site were to be suggested with which *Kelli wic* could be identified, then the prominent nearby hill-fort called Castle-an-Dinas would be an obvious choice.[35]   However, the unlucky Thomas might have come from further afield, so that there is not enough evidence at present to say more than that.   What is needed is further references to this tantalizing Cornish place-name.   At the moment all that can be said is that there is this one indication that *Kelli wic* may indeed have referred to a genuine place in Cornwall; and, if so, that it was probably in the hundred of Penwith, the westernmost district of Cornwall.   This would be in keeping with the suggestion of Rachel Bromwich that *Kelli wic* could perhaps be equated with another place mentioned in the same story of *Culhwch ac Olwen*, called *Penn Pengwaed yg Kernyw*, 'the end (or top) of Penwith in Cornwall'.[36]

The meaning of the place-name causes some difficulty.   Since it occurs in a Welsh text, it has usually been interpreted as if it were a name in Welsh, rather than Cornish.   Indeed, part of the problem in trying to identify it as a Cornish place has been whether the name, occurring exclusively in Welsh legend, should be regarded as an actual Cornish place-name at all, though the form *Kellewik* in 1302 shows that it could be so.   Its form in the Welsh texts, usually as two words rather than one, indicates that it should be treated as a name-phrase (with the second, stressed, word qualifying the first), not as a compound.   As a Welsh place-name, it can then be translated as 'grove of a forest, forest grove', though it is unclear exactly what that would mean: a *celli* or grove is a small wood, and a 'small wood in a forest' is a rather unclear concept. There are two places in Wales with the same name, one in the north-west and one in the south-east.[37]   There are also two places in Brittany called Quillivic, both with documentation going back several centuries.[38]   The meaning of the Breton names is not clear.   On the one hand, they would seem likely to be the same as the Welsh examples, but *gwik* in Breton means 'village', not 'forest'. (The meaning 'forest' of *gwig* in Welsh is unexplained, for the word comes from Latin *vicus*, 'community, habitation'.)[39]   Similarly, the meaning of *Kelli wic* as a Cornish name would be uncertain, for the meaning of Cornish **gwik* is not known.   It might have meant 'forest', as in Welsh, or 'village', as in Breton.[40]   The temptation to give it its Welsh meaning is strong (and that is no doubt how the author and audience of *Culhwch* understood it), but it should perhaps be resisted, if only because the sense in Welsh is not wholly clear.   It might be added that both of the possible locations preferred here for *Kelli wic*, King Arthur's Hall on Bodmin Moor, or somewhere in the West Penwith district of Cornwall, are unlikely districts for a place-name containing the meaning 'forest', because they are not heavily wooded parts of the county; however, small areas of woodland ('groves') are possible in both areas.

Finally, one must ask how the Welsh story-tellers would have obtained the name, if it was a real Cornish place-name that they were using.   The only likely explanation seems to be that the name had first become current in Arthurian stories or folklore within Cornwall, and that these, or part of them, were borrowed into Welsh story-telling.   The alternative would be that the name was a purely Welsh invention, that they never had any actual Cornish place in mind, and that the real Cornish *Kellewik* is a mere coincidence.

South Cadbury, Somerset (sixteenth century)

This is an important Iron-Age hill-fort, which continued to be used in the Roman period, and which was reoccupied, with major refortification, in the late fifth or sixth century.   Its Arthurian association is first found in the sixteenth century, when Leland, a noted apologist for a historical Arthur, referred to it as Arthur's residence. There is another possible legendary association with Arthur in the same century; this will be given below.   Leland's description, in *c.* 1540, is as follows:

> At the very south ende of the chirch of South-Cadbyri standith Camallate, sumtyme a famose toun or castelle, apon a very torre or hille, wunderfully enstrengtheid of nature . . .   The people can telle nothing ther but that they have hard say that Arture much resortid to Camalat.[41]

Elsewhere, Leland says:

> Popular legend of the *Murotriges*, who inhabit the foot of the hill of Camalet, proclaims, exalts, and keeps reciting the name of Arthur, the one-time inhabitant of a fort, which same was formerly situated, most magnificent, most strongly-fortified, and on a most lofty eminence, where the hill rises up.[42]

The excavations of this spectacular site in 1966–70 were very fruitful in information.[43]   They showed that South Cadbury had been a strongly-defended site in the late Iron Age, and that activity there continued through much of the Roman period, though the defences were not maintained.   After a hiatus, the fort was reoccupied in the late fifth century, and this reoccupation continued through the sixth century, but seemingly ceased in the seventh century and later; after that date, there was again reuse in the late Saxon period (eleventh century).

The investigations produced information about the Dark-Age use of both the defences and the interior of the fort. The innermost of the four ramparts was extensively rebuilt, over its length of three-quarters of a mile. It was lavishly strengthened with timbers, and in places Roman stone was reused; there may have been more than one Dark-Age phase of repairs. The whole operation represents a formidable undertaking, such as could only have been carried out by people who commanded extensive resources. Owing to the difference between a hill-fort and a promontory-fort, the work involved was far greater than that required to fortify an equivalent area of land at Tintagel.

In the interior, a large number of post-holes were found; some of these were interpreted as representing a Dark-Age timber hall of considerable size (over sixty feet long). The dating of both the defences and the hall was provided by imported Mediterranean pottery, which was found in fair quantities on the site, though rarely in a context which would have enabled it to provide a date for particular structures. Curiously, on a site of such importance, no Celtic metal-work was found, nor any evidence for metal-working activities, unlike comparable sites elsewhere in Somerset (Cadbury–Congresbury, below) and in Wales and Scotland. It may be that such activities occurred, but in a part of the site which was not excavated.

The excavator has emphasized that the uniqueness of South Cadbury, within its period, makes it hard to know at present how to interpret these results. However, there is a site which forms a useful parallel in the county some thirty miles away, at another hill-fort known as Cadbury–Congresbury. Here, too, there had been activity during the Roman period, but the substantial hill-fort was a Dark-Age creation. Again, considerable quantities of imported Mediterranean pottery were found, and several Celtic brooches. This is instructive, in showing that there were other important sites which experienced the same kind of activity, and at the same period, as South Cadbury, but where there is no hint of an Arthurian connection.[44]

When South Cadbury was excavated twenty years ago, the interpretation of the site played a part in a theory involving a historical Arthur who was a battle-leader against the English invaders, along the lines of the *Historia Brittonum*, chapter 56.[45] More recently, the excavator has laid less emphasis on the Arthurian connection, and pointed out that the reoccupation probably lasted for more than a century. Without excluding the possibility of a military role, he would now see South Cadbury in the later fifth and the sixth centuries more as an administrative centre of a large British estate.[46]

The other sixteenth-century Arthurian legend which may refer to South Cadbury appears in the writings of the Welsh antiquary Elis Gruffudd, who died in 1552. He related, in Welsh, two English versions of the legend that Arthur lies sleeping in a cave, and will rise up again to save the island of Britain.[47] One of his versions, the more detailed, is located 'in the region of Gloucester'; the other, mentioned only in passing, says that '[the English] say and firmly believe that he [*sc.* Arthur] will rise again to be king. They in their opinion say that he is asleep in a cave under a hill near Glastonbury.' The most natural interpretation of the last phrase would be that it refers to Glastonbury Tor; but Thomas Jones has suggested instead that it could mean South Cadbury, eleven miles away.[48] If so, it would confirm the strength of the Arthurian folklore at South Cadbury in the sixteenth century. However, there are many other sites, in England as well as Wales, claiming a link with Arthur by that date. In view of the lateness of the connection, the importance of South Cadbury as an Arthurian site depends upon one's view of the historicity of Arthur. That does not, of course, lessen the value of the excavations at South Cadbury, which remains one of the most important sites of the period to have been investigated.

Castle Dore (*c.* 1930)

The supposed connections of this site are, strictly speaking, not with the Arthurian legend, but with that of Tristan. However, the two legends have themselves been associated since the twelfth century. The literary association here arose from a place-name found in one version of the Tristan legend, that of the Anglo-Norman poet Béroul, whose poem probably dates from the late twelfth century. Most texts of the Tristan legend at that period place King Mark's palace at Tintagel, but Béroul's poem places it both there and also at a place called *Lancien*, the modern farm of Lantyan in south Cornwall.[49] That is not the only feature which distinguishes Béroul's poem from other early versions: in other respects, too, the text is surprisingly well informed concerning twelfth-century Cornish geography and, apparently, folklore.[50] However, the poet also took liberties, one of which consisted in describing *Lancien* as a 'city', with some two thousand inhabitants, something which the real Lantyan cannot have been.

Castle Dore is the only obvious fortified site near to Lantyan; it is situated a mile and a half to the south of the farm.[51] Lantyan was a manor, first recorded in Domesday Book (1086); the fort is within the territory of that manor, and within thesame parish of St Sampson, Golant.[52] In ground-plan Castle Dore is a small double-ramparted hill-fort. An excavation was carried out there in 1936–7, with the specific aim of finding 'the palace known to have existed in this part of Cornwall and connected with the name of King Mark'.[53]   This aim was based on two unstated assumptions: first, that Béroul's poem was closer to sixth-century history than the other twelfth-century texts; and second, that a fortified site is the kind of place which should be envisaged, either as what Béroul had in mind, or as the sixth-century reality lying behind his reference.   As has been seen, a similar assumption has been made in trying to identify *Kelli wic*.

The name of Castle Dore is first recorded in 1478, in the form *C(astellum) Dirford*; other early spellings include *Castelldurward* (1525), *Casteldour* (c. 1540), *Castell Dorwarde* (1573), and *Castell Dore* (1612).[54]   It is unclear what this represents.   Evidently the first element is Cornish *castell*, 'fort'.   The final syllable, which appears in some early spellings but is now absent, looks as if it were an English word, added to a pre-existing Cornish name.   If so, then the second element might be Cornish *dour*, 'water', but no obvious reason for such a name is apparent.   A small stream rises near the fort, but that hardly seems a distinguishing feature. (Compare, however, the Breton place-name Castel Dour, four miles north-north-west of Loudéac.)   None of the early references contains any hint of legends connected with the site, nor are there any recorded until the twentieth century.   Indeed, the legendary status which Castle Dore now has appears to be entirely the result of the excavations.

However, the problem over the legendary status of Lantyan, and the possible relevance of Castle Dore, is further complicated by the fact that a Dark-Age inscribed stone from a site a mile and a half to the south of Castle Dore (and thus three miles from Lantyan) bears a name which is probably an early form of *Tristan*.[55]   The reading of the crucial first name on the stone is uncertain, but the inscription may read DRVSTAVS HIC IACIT CVNOMORI FILIVS, thus commemorating a man called *Drustanus* (assuming that the ligatured AV in the first name could be expanded as ANV), son of a man called *Cunomorus*.   The relevance of this is apparent when it is recalled that the ninth-century Breton *Life* of St Paul Aurelian mentions a King *Marcus*, ruling somewhere in Britain, *quem alio nomine Quonomorium vocant*, 'whom by another name they call Quonomorius'.[56]   If this information is accurate, and taking it in conjunction with the legend and the inscription, it could show that the man commemorated on the stone was effectively the son of a man called Mark.   He could be equated with the legendary Tristan, nephew and heir of King Mark, on the assumption that the original relationship between the two men, father and son, had been altered to uncle and nephew in order to make the story more acceptable to European ears.   However, it might instead be the case that this remark, in the ninth-century *Life*, was somehow due to knowledge of the inscription; and it may also be that the inscription is partly responsible for Béroul's localization of the legend nearby at Lantyan, and not at Tintagel as with other authors.[57] If that were so, then the stone would still be of significance for providing the earliest evidence of the name of Tristan, but it would not provide independent evidence for the historicity of the main characters, nor for the localization at Lantyan.   Alternatively, it could reasonably be claimed that the inscription constitutes evidence that the legend of Tristan, as localized in Cornwall, was attached to a historical figure of the sixth century, who had survived in traditional memory, and whose gravestone we still have.

The excavations carried out in 1936–7 were fully reported in 1951.[58]   The main discovery was of Iron-Age pottery, and of a considerable number of post-holes in the interior of the fort.   Although most of the pottery dated from the Iron Age, one fragment and two more possible ones were considered to be of Dark-Age date, as was one of several glass beads found there.   It was therefore considered that the site represented an Iron-Age fort, with reoccupation in the Dark Age, as has since been found elsewhere (for example, at Castle Killibury and South Cadbury, above).   The reuse of the site was demonstrated by the rebuilding of certain features (but not extensive refortification, as at South Cadbury); and the date of that reuse was provided by the evidence of the two or three fragments of pottery.   The post-holes were interpreted as showing a timber-framed hall, which has been widely cited as 'King Mark's palace'.

These interpretations are no longer tenable.   In the forty years since the report was produced, much more has become known about Iron-Age and Dark-Age sites in the south-west.[59]   Precise dating of the various structural phases at Castle Dore is not possible, because extensive ploughing in the interior of the fort has destroyed the stratigraphy, so that the datable finds cannot be associated with the evidence for particular structures.   All that can be given is an overall range of dates for the occupation, from the evidence provided by those finds.   As a result of recent work, the Iron-Age chronology has been extended backwards, and the earlier pottery-finds are now dated to the third or fourth centuries BC, and not to the second century as previously.   This, in turn, provides more time in the pre-Roman period for the later rebuilding of certain features at the site.   This rebuilding could thus be a part of the Iron-Age occupation, and not Dark-Age as was formerly suggested.

Such a scheme would accord much better with the pottery found at the site, for that has proved to be exclusively Iron-Age in date, as far as a re-examination can tell. For present purposes, the most significant fact to emerge from a reconsideration of the excavations is that there are no finds from Castle Dore which indicate a Dark-Age occupation there.   The two or three fragments claimed to be post-Roman in date cannot now be distinguished among the pieces of Iron-Age pottery; but, in any case, their dating was extremely tentative, and they were never claimed actually to be of the imported Mediterranean type.[60]   The glass bead, too, has proved to be of Iron-Age date.[61] This reassessment can go a stage further, for more is now known than in 1951 about the finds to be expected on a Cornish site which was occupied in the fifth or sixth century; the progress is partly due to the valuable contributions of Radford himself, who excavated Castle Dore.   In particular, the imported Mediterranean pottery had not been clearly identified, even at Tintagel, at the time when the report on Castle Dore was published.   It is now clear that even quite insignificant Dark-Age sites in Cornwall are liable to produce sherds of these wares;[62] a site of the importance claimed for Castle Dore would be expected to have produced considerable quantities, as at Tintagel and South Cadbury.   The complete absence of this pottery is a powerful argument against any significant occupation in the fifth to seventh centuries.   It had been suggested that the ploughing of the interior might have destroyed such remains; however, that did not happen elsewhere (at Killibury and South Cadbury, for instance), and similarly the Iron-Age pottery itself had survived at Castle Dore.   Insofar as such a negative point can be proved, it may be stated that, on present evidence, Castle Dore was not occupied in the fifth to seventh centuries.

It is also open to question whether the post-holes found in excavation actually represent a timber-framed hall, as originally interpreted, or a group of smaller structures.   Again, the lack of stratified finds makes it difficult to know which particular post-holes are to be associated with one another.   Since any structures would now be considered Iron-Age rather than Dark-Age in date, the point may seem to have little relevance in the present context; but it does have some significance, since Castle Dore was the site which, as it were, set the fashion for finding timber-framed halls on supposed Dark-Age royal sites, and the excavations here have been widely quoted as providing virtually the type-site for such structures.[63] The loss of this type-site should therefore be borne in mind when other, similar, examples are cited.

To sum up the evidence from Castle Dore: there is no indication of any Dark-Age occupation there, and its role as King Mark's palace must be abandoned. The proximity of Lantyan to the inscribed stone which probably bears a form of the name of Tristan is highly suggestive, but it is much harder to know what it actually suggests. In considering Lantyan, the important question is why Béroul mentions the place-name, and what sort of place he envisaged as King Mark's residence, rather than any implications for archaeological investigations at present.

NOTES:

1. For a recent account of the Arthurian connection at Glastonbury, see A. Gransden, 'The Growth of the Glastonbury Traditions and Legends in the Twelfth Century', *Journal of Ecclesiastical History*, 27 (1976), 337-58 (at pp. 349-57).

2. O.J. Padel, 'Geoffrey of Monmouth and Cornwall', *CMCS*, 8 (1984), 1-28 (at p. 11).

3. O.J. Padel, 'The Cornish Background of the Tristan Stories', *CMCS*, 1 (1981), 53-81 (at pp. 71-2).

4. *The Parliamentary Survey of the Duchy of Cornwall*, edited by Norman J.G. Pounds, Devon and Cornwall Record Society, vols. 25 and 27, 1982-4 (at II, 180).

5. C.A.R. Radford, 'Tintagel: the Castle and Celtic Monastery: Interim Report', *The Antiquaries Journal*, 15 (1935), 401-19, and 'Tintagel in History and Legend', *Journal of the Royal Institution of Cornwall*, 26 (1937-42), Appendix, 25-41; for summaries and further references see K.R. Dark, 'The Plan and Interpretation of Tintagel', *CMCS*, 9 (1985), 1-17, and Charles Thomas, 'Tintagel Castle', *Antiquity*, 62 (1988), 421-34; also now *Cornish Studies*, 16 (1988), Special Issue: Tintagel Papers. There is a useful summary of informed opinion at the time just before the excavations took place: Henry Jenner, 'Tintagel Castle in History and Romance', *Journal of the Royal Institution of Cornwall*, 22 (1926-8), 190-200.

6. See notably S. Hartgroves and R. Walker, 'Excavations in the Lower Ward, Tintagel Castle, 1986', *Cornish Studies*, 16 (1988), 9-30; and Charles Thomas, 'The 1988 C.A.U. Excavations at Tintagel Island: Discoveries and their Implications', ibid. 49-57.

6a. See now Jacqueline A. Nowakowski and Charles Thomas, *Excavations at Tintagel Parish Churchyard, Cornwall, Spring 1990. Interim Report* (Truro, 1990). Further excavations are due to take place in 1991.

7. C.A.R. Radford, 'Imported Pottery found at Tintagel, Cornwall', in *Dark-Age Britain: Studies Presented to E.T. Leeds*, edited by D.B. Harden (London, 1956), 59-70; Charles Thomas, *A Provisional List of Imported Pottery in Post-Roman Western Britain and Ireland* (Redruth, 1981); and Lynette Olson, *Early Monasteries in Cornwall* (Woodbridge, 1989), 41-8.

8. At Iona and Dumbarton: Thomas, *Provisional List*, 9, 11 and 13.

9. Ian Burrow, 'Tintagel — Some Problems', *Scottish Archaeological Forum*, 5 (Edinburgh, 1974), 99-103; Charles Thomas, 'East and West: Tintagel, Mediterranean Imports and the early Insular Church', in *The Early Church in Western Britain and Ireland*, edited by S.M. Pearce (Oxford, 1982), 17-34.

10. For an excellent recent discussion of the attributes of Dark-Age Cornish monastic sites, see Olson, *Early Monasteries in Cornwall* (pp. 34-5 for discussion of Tintagel).

11. A 'deliberately minimalist' view, speculating on the possible course of a single trading-voyage, is hypothesized by Charles Thomas, 'The Context of Tintagel: a New Model for the Diffusion of Post-Roman Mediterranean Imports', *Cornish Archaeology*, 27 (1988), 7-25; but he allows the possibility of regular trade.

12. R.A.S. Macalister, *Corpus Inscriptionum Insularum Celticarum*, 2 vols. (Dublin, 1945-9), I, nos. 457, 466-7, 470, 472, 484, 488-9 and 492, all in north or east Cornwall or west Devon; the outlier is no. 463, bearing an Irish name (not oghams) but being in west Cornwall. Nos. 473 and 478, on which Macalister claimed to have seen traces of ogham inscriptions, do not bear such traces now, if

they ever did. Compare Charles Thomas, 'The Irish Settlements in Post-Roman Western Britain: a Survey of the Evidence', *Journal of the Royal Institution of Cornwall*, n.s. 6 (1969-72), 251-74 (map, p. 264).

13. O.J. Padel, 'Tintagel: an Alternative View', Appendix 2 (pp. 28-9) of Thomas, *Provisional List of Imported Pottery*, at p. 29.

14. A.C. Thomas and P.J. Fowler, 'Tintagel: a New Survey of the "Island"', *Annual Report of the Royal Commission on Historical Monuments (England)*, 1984-5, 16-22.

15. Thomas, 'Tintagel Castle', 425a; Thomas and Fowler, 'New Survey', 21.

16. Dark, 'Plan and Interpretation of Tintagel', 13-14; Charles Thomas, 'The Archaeology of Tintagel Parish Churchyard', *Cornish Studies*, 16 (1988), 79-91.

17. 'Plan and Interpretation of Tintagel', 14.

18. O.J. Padel, 'Tintagel in the Twelfth and Thirteenth Centuries', *Cornish Studies*, 16 (1988), 61-6.

19. *CO*(1) lxxix-lxxx and n.218, and index, p. 77; *TYP* nos. 1, 54 and 85, and pp. 3-4. There may be a further reference in the phrase *pan colled Kelli*, 'when *Kelli* was lost', in the Arthurian poem 'Pa gur': *LIDC* 61, line 33.

20. Summarized by Peter Moreton, 'Killibury Hillfort and Kelli Wic in Antiquarian Studies', *Cornish Archaeology*, 16 (1977), 118-19. What follows is based upon Moreton's summary, and is also an expansion of my note, 'Kelli Wic in Cornwall', ibid., 115-18 and 119.

21. The earliest known instance of this identification is that of W. Hals, c. 1735, printed in [Joseph Polsue], *A Complete Parochial History of the County of Cornwall*, 4 vols. (Truro, 1867-73), I, 168.

22. F. Lot, 'Kelliwic, résidence d'Arthur', *Romania*, 30 (1901), 13-14.

23. Joseph Loth, 'Le Cornwall et le Roman de Tristan', *RC*, 33 (1912), 258-310 (at p. 262); = J. Loth, *Contributions à l'étude des romans de la Table Ronde* (Paris, 1912), 64. In 1924 he withdrew his suggestion of Gweek Wood and preferred Killibury, on the unpublished advice of Charles Henderson: 'Un parallèle au Roman de Tristan, en irlandais, au dixième siècle', *Comptes rendus de l'Académie des Inscriptions et Belles-lettres*, 1924, 122-33 (at p. 132n.).

24. John Norden, *Speculi Brittaniae Pars: A Topographic and Historical Description of Cornwall* (London, 1728), 71 (with illustration). Norden surveyed in Cornwall in about 1584, and wrote his description in about 1605. See also John Barnatt, *Prehistoric Cornwall: The Ceremonial Monuments* (Wellingborough, 1982), 196-7 (with illustration). Is it possible that this could itself be the site meant by *Kelli wic*? If so, the loss of the Cornish name, and its replacement with an English one, would be readily explained in this moorland area of east Cornwall. But, as shown below, there are other possibilities.

25. Grid reference SX 0073; the fort is also called Kelly Rounds. The suggestion appears first in W. Howship Dickinson, *King Arthur in Cornwall* (London, 1900), 4, 40, 70-4 and 80-1.

26. Domellick is at grid reference SW 943585; for discussion and references, see Padel, 'Geoffrey of Monmouth and Cornwall', 12.

27. Grid reference SX 0380, five and a half miles from Tintagel.

28. On the Ordnance Survey Six-Inch map of Cornwall, sheet no. XIX North-East, 1st Edition (1888); replaced by 'Tregeare Rounds' on the 2nd Edition, 1907, and subsequently. For the removal

of the spurious name, see S. Baring-Gould and others, 'An Exploration of Tregaer Rounds', *Journal of the Royal Institution of Cornwall*, 16 (1904-6), 73-83.

29. Dickinson, *King Arthur in Cornwall*, 70-4.

30. Charles Henderson, in *The Cornish Church Guide* (Truro, 1925), 24 and 87; and Charles Henderson, *Essays in Cornish History* (Oxford, 1935), 121 and 146. He was followed, for instance, by H. O'Neill Hencken, *The Archaeology of Cornwall and Scilly* (London, 1932), 249, and Bromwich, *TYP* 3-4.

31. Henrietta Miles and others, 'Excavations at Killibury Hillfort, Egloshayle 1975-6', *Cornish Archaeology*, 16 (1977), 89-121. The Dark-Age reoccupation is discussed on p. 115.

32. J. Armitage Robinson, *The Saxon Bishops of Wells* (London, British Academy, n.d.), 22-3; and A.S. Napier and W.H. Stevenson, *The Crawford Collection of Early Charters and Documents* (Oxford, 1895), no. 7, 18-19. For discussion, see also W.M.M. Picken, 'Callington and Kelliwic', *Devon and Cornwall Notes and Queries*, 27 (1956-8), 225-7.

33. Henderson, *Cornish Church Guide*, 87, and *Essays*, 146.

34. Public Record Office, Eyre roll, JUST 1/117, m. 68. I owe this reference, and the name itself, to the kindness of W.M.M. Picken. Lanestly or Gulval is at grid reference SW 484317.

35. Grid reference SW 484350; not the same as the better-known Castle-an-Dinas on Goss Moor, grid ref. SW 9462, which had Arthurian associations at a later date.

36. *CO*(1), line 106 (p. 4), and Introduction, p. lxxix, n.218.

37. Gelliwig (Caernarfonshire) is at grid reference SH 257302; the manor of Gelli-wig (Monmouthshire) is listed by Melville Richards, *Welsh Administrative and Territorial Units* (Cardiff, 1969), 74. Note that GPC, s.v. *celliwig*, says that the first of these names is stressed on the second syllable, presumably making it a close-compound (compare *coedwig*); but that will not do for the Arthurian place-name, and, judging by his hyphen, Richards evidently interpreted the Monmouthshire name like the medieval *Kelli wic*.

38. Joseph Loth, 'Gallois *Celliwig*; breton moyen *Quilliuuic*, [etc.]', *RC*, 41 (1924), 390-3.

39. There may be other possibilities for the second part of the name. Loth, ibid., pointed out a possible instance of *gwig* meaning 'battle', and he suggested comparing Irish *fich*, 'enmity, anger'; see also K. Jackson, *Early Welsh Gnomic Poems*, 2nd impression (Cardiff, 1961), 51-2. Compare Middle Welsh *gwydwic*, perhaps meaning 'heap of slaughter' (?), *PKM* 210-11; also Welsh *cleddiwig*, 'quarry', and maybe *coedwig*, 'wood'.

40. O.J. Padel, *Cornish Place-name Elements* (Nottingham, 1985), 119.

41. *The Itinerary of John Leland in or about the Years 1534-43*, edited by Lucy Toulmin Smith, 5 vols. (London, 1906-10), I, 151.

42. John Leland, *De Rebus Britannicis Collectanea*, edited by T. Hearne, 2nd edition, 6 vols. (London, 1770), V, 28-9 (my translation).

43. Leslie Alcock '*By South Cadbury is that Camelot . . .*', *The Excavation of Cadbury Castle 1966-70* (London, 1972); Leslie Alcock, 'Cadbury-Camelot: a Fifteen-year Perspective', *PBA*, 68 (1982), 355-88.

44. P. Rahtz and P. Fowler, 'Somerset AD 400-700', in *Archaeology and the Landscape. Essays for*

L.V. Grinsell, ed. P.J. Fowler (London, 1972), 187-221 (at pp. 194-7); P. Rahtz, 'Celtic Society in Somerset AD 400-700', *B*, 30 (1982-3), 176-200 (at pp. 191-5).

45. Alcock, *Excavation of Cadbury*, 193-4.

46. Alcock, 'Perspective', 384-5.

47. Thomas Jones, 'A Sixteenth Century Version of the Arthurian Cave Legend', in *Studies in Language and Literature in Honour of Margaret Schlauch*, edited by Miecyslaw Brahmer and others (Warsaw, 1966), 175-85.

48. Jones, 'Arthurian Cave Legend', 179-81.

49. Grid reference SX 105572. The identification was first made by Loth, 'Le Cornwall et le Roman de Tristan', 270-1 (= Loth, *Contributions*, 72-3); see also O.J. Padel, 'Cornish Background of the Tristan Stories', 60, for detailed references to the text.

50. Padel, 'Cornish Background', 59-68; O.J. Padel, 'Béroul's Geography and Patronage', *Reading Medieval Studies*, 9 (1983), 84-94.

51. Grid reference SX 1054.

52. The church dedicated to St Sampson is mentioned by Béroul: for references, see Padel, 'Cornish Background', 60.

53. C.A.R. Radford, 'Report on the Excavations at Castle Dore', *Journal of the Royal Institution of Cornwall*, n.s., 1 (1946-52), Appendix (1951), 6.

54. These forms come from my survey of Cornish place-names deposited at the Institute of Cornish Studies, University of Exeter.

55. Macalister, *Corpus Inscriptionum*, I, no. 487; for the reading, see Radford, 'Castle Dore', 117-19, and plate II (p. 6); Padel, 'Cornish Background', 55 n.8 and 77 n.59. For a good account of the history of the stone, and an attempt to draw far-reaching conclusions from the inscription, see A. de Mandach, 'Aux portes de Lantien en Cornouailles: une tombe du VIe siècle portant le nom de Tristan', *Le Moyen Age*, 4th series, 27 (1972), 389-425; also his 'The Shrinking Tombstone of Tristan and Isolt', *Journal of Medieval History*, 4 (1978), 227-42, and his 'Legend and Reality', *Tristania*, 4, no. 2 (1979), 3-24. But the inscription never had three lines, as against the present-day two: Leland simply misread one line.

56. Ch. Cuissard, 'Vie de Saint Paul de Léon en Bretagne', *RC*, 5 (1881-3), 413-59 (at p. 431).

57. But see . Padel, 'Béroul's geography and patronage', 91-2, for another possible reason for the localization at Lantyan, connected with the twelfth-century ownership of the manor.

58. Radford, 'Castle Dore'.

59. Henrietta Quinnell and Daphne Harris, 'Castle Dore: the Chronology Reconsidered', *Cornish Archaeology*, 24 (1985), 123-32. For an earlier reassessment, see P. Rahtz, 'Castle Dore — a Reappraisal of the Post-Roman Structures', ibid., 10 (1971), 49-54.

60. Radford, 'Castle Dore', 93-4.

61. Quinnell and Harris, 'Castle Dore', 130.

62. H. and T. Miles, 'Excavations at Trethurgy, St Austell: Interim Report', *Cornish Archaeology*, 12

(1973), 25-9 (at p. 28).

63. For instance, as recently as Alcock, 'Perspective', 377; cf. 370-1 for a frank and useful discussion of the way in which such factors might unconsciously have affected the interpretation of the post-holes at South Cadbury.   Compare Nicholas Reynolds, 'Dark Age Timber Halls and the Background to Excavation at Balbridie', *Scottish Archaeological Forum*, 10 (1980), 44-5.

Note. The author is most grateful to Henrietta Quinnell and Charles Thomas for reading parts of this article and making helpful comments; but they are not responsible for any remaining errors, or for the opinions expressed.   He is also grateful to Rachel Bromwich for making several useful suggestions.

12

BRITTANY AND THE ARTHURIAN LEGEND

J. E. Caerwyn Williams

As its name implies, Brittany had at one time a very close connection with Britain. Even its earlier name Armorica implied a connection, for the adjective *Armoricae* was applied at one time to all the *civitates* of the north-west coast of Europe.[1] One reason for this connection was the physical proximity of the two countries. Another was their remoteness from the rest of Europe. True, they shared the advantages of being accessible by the western sea-routes. We are told that in Caesar's time, the most important tribe of Armorica, the Veneti, enjoyed their exalted position by virtue of their navigational skills and their numerous ships on which, we are told, *in Britanniam navigare consuerunt*.[2] The English Channel was one of the main routes of the western seas and was used not only by the Celts of Brittany but also by their kindred to the east.[3] Even in pre-Roman times there was a Belgic presence on both sides of the Channel. Caesar informs us that the maritime part of mainland Britain was inhabited by people who had crossed from Belgic Gaul for war and plunder, and had remained to settle there and to till the land.[4] Elsewhere he says that within living memory Diviciacus, King of the Suessiones (around Soissons), had held sway in Britain also.[5] It is not surprising then that Tacitus tells us that the Brittani *proximi Gallis et similes sunt, . . . sermo haud multum diversus*.[6] We should not, however, assume that the tribes of Armorica were culturally indistinct from the Belgic tribes: there were differences, and it may not be foolhardy to suggest that the Armoricans had more affinities with Highland than with Lowland Zone Britain. This would be in keeping with the suggestion that the south-western parts of Cornwall had been colonized by the Veneti rather than come under the influence of their culture, which had features in common with a south-western Iron Age B culture to be found in Devon, Somerset and Dorset as well as in much of the south-eastern borderland of Wales.[7] It would also explain to some extent the fact that, although the Britons who emigrated from Britain some time after the Romans had left went to other parts of the Continent, their migration to Brittany was apparently the one that involved the largest number and that resulted in the most permanent settlement.[8] Their migration is usually related to the Anglo-Saxon onslaughts on Britain.[9]

Scholars have failed to agree on the dating of the Brittonic emigration to Brittany, possibly because they have failed to agree on its causes and its points of departure. It seems that it was at its height in the first half of the sixth century, and that it continued throughout the seventh into the eighth century.[10] It must have started in the fifth century, if not earlier. During the sixth century *Britannia* and *Britannia Minor* as names for the country became general,[11] and as the country emerges into the light of history, we find two provinces called *Domnonia* and *Cornobia*, tribal names which had been in use in the mother country before the emigration.[12]

If the emigration was at its height in the sixth century, it was at its height when the British Church embraced monasticism with a fervour reminiscent of the early Desert Fathers, and when the foundations of the Celtic Church, which included the churches of Brittany, Cornwall, Ireland and Britain, were being laid. One peculiarity of the Celtic Church was the emergence of great monastic churches and of great abbots who overshadowed the bishops when they did not combine the office of bishop with their own.[13] Another peculiarity was the irresistible urge which many of the monks had to leave not only their monastery but also their country *pro Christo peregrinari volentes*.[14] It is not surprising, then, to find among these monks or, as they were often called, 'saints',[15] a considerable number of pan-Celtic 'saints' who are said to have travelled between the Celtic countries, and not a few pan-Brittonic ones.[16]

That 'saints' travelled along the same ways as, if not with, the Britons who emigrated to Brittany, is not to be denied. One important piece of evidence is the toponomy of the Brittonic settlements which are, as Nora Chadwick remarked, ecclesiastical 'to a degree which is perhaps unique in any country. A very large proportion (of place names) consists of two elements, [one] denoting a place or settlement such as *plou-*, *trev*, *lann-*, *loc-*, to which are added the names of various early Celtic saints.'[17]

The frequency of such place-names and the prominence of ecclesiastical traditions coupled with the comparative absence of any record of military clashes between the immigrants and the natives leave us with the impression that the 'saints' played a prominent part in the emigrations from Britain to Brittany. One must remember that we are dealing with an age in which the monk or hermit was the 'saint' *par excellence*, that 'saintship itself was, to the popular mind, a concept of the magical order. Its essential characteristic was not moral goodness but the possession of that mysterious power which works miracles'.[18] The 'saints' for the most part belonged to the nobility, that is to the class which provided the leaders of the community, and by and large they were better educated than any other class.[19] St

Germanus of Auxerre (c. 380-c. 448) had been one of the imperial administrators of Gaul before he became a bishop, and his subsequent career shows how easy and imperative it was to assume secular as well as ecclesiastical leadership when need arose. St Patrick, a Briton, was commonly represented as a disciple of St Germanus, and although this can hardly be true, his leadership, like that of St Germanus, was a combination of the secular and the spiritual. We should not, therefore, be surprised that the 'saints' played a prominent part in establishing the British settlements in Brittany and that the ecclesiastics who succeeded to their power continued to play an important role in the affairs of their country.

One of the peculiarities of the Celtic Church was the emphasis laid by its leaders on learning and the tolerant attitude they took towards native lore.[20] This is better attested in the history of the Irish Church than in the history of any other Celtic church, but it is attested in the Welsh Church: the story of Asser (died 909) and, years later, the story of Sulien (1011-91) and his sons illustrate the importance attached to learning.

It is usual to regard the fact that Landévennec by the middle of the ninth century had become the most intellectual centre in Brittany as the result of the influence of the Carolingian Renaissance, but is it not possible that scholarship was already cultivated there as at other centres of the Celtic Church in Ireland and Wales?[21] It is well known that the Carolingian Renaissance owed a great deal directly to the Irish Church and indirectly to it through the Anglo-Saxon Church which had come under Irish influence,[22] and it is surely possible that Landévennec's eminence in scholarship owed as much to native tradition as to foreign influence.[23] That Landévennec was firmly part of the Celtic Church until 818, we have proof in the report that when its Abbot Matmonoc was questioned that year by Louis the Pious on the discipline and the tonsure observed in the Breton monasteries, he replied that they were conforming to Irish usage.[24] If this was the case, it is not likely that Landévennec and other Breton monasteries forgot their connection with the Irish Church as soon as the Carolingian Renaissance had begun to exercise its influence on the Continent. If, as we may assume, some of the Irish monks who travelled abroad entered the Continent through Brittany, and if they returned to their homeland the same way, they must have been carrying with them some of their characteristic books, such as the Irish penitentials and the *Collectio Canonum Hibernensis*.[25] We know that the latter was well received and frequently copied in Brittany, for an important group of the extant copies are of Breton origin. Henry Bradshaw argued that Brittany was the chief, if not the sole, route by which the work entered the Continent, and even if, as Kenney thought, he was overstating his case, his argument is none the less significant for us. Of greater significance, however, is the fact that his researches in French and Breton libraries enabled him to say:

> All these results seem to me to point to a time when there were schools of learning in Brittany such as we read of in the lives of the Breton saints, and that after the decay and extinction of these, many of their books passed into the hands of others who knew how to treat them with the reverence they deserved.[26]

Whichever way we explain the phenomenon, and the influence of the Carolingian Renaissance cannot be discounted after the middle of the ninth century, there can be no doubt that scholarship flourished in Brittany, and there can be no better proof than the number of *magistri* and *grammatici* whose names have been preserved. One of their precursors in the tenth century was Israel (fl. 947-60),[27] monk, bishop and grammarian. Kerlouégan[28] mentions some of the *magistri*: Cariou 'magister Conani comitis' (1005); Guilhelmus, *magister* of Alan Fergant; Andronic, *magister* of Geoffrey de Penthièvre (c. 1084); Aymo, *magister* of Alan III, and Eudon (c. 1100). His list of *grammatici* is longer: Arembert (1032), Ascelin, beginning of the eleventh century, Ingomar, grammarian and historian (c. 1000), Gurgoret and Adgan (1029), Gradlon (1030), Aldroen (1084), Iudical (1066), Herbert (c. 1100), Berhald (1037), Berthuald (1021), Kerou (1082).

These scholars and the schools in which some of them were successively pupils and masters were primarily concerned with ecclesiastical studies, but it would be a mistake not to recognize that their interests extended to the secular, and that the secular must have exercised the minds of the less spiritual, not to mention the less able, to a large extent. Caesarius of Heisterbach (c. 1180–1240) tells us that when Abbot Gevard was once preaching and found his audience of monks sleeping and even snoring, he interrupted his sermon with the remark, 'There was once a king called Arthur . . .', whereupon they all awoke and were all ears.[29] But the inveterate lovers of stories among the monks could find satisfaction, without recourse to stories about secular heroes, in the lives of the saints and there were other kinds of literature which were an odd mixture of the spiritual and the secular.[30]

In early Irish literature there was a literary genre of pagan origin called *immrama*, accounts of voyages, but, presumably under ecclesiastical influence, there arose a Christian voyage literature including the 'Voyage of Mael-dúin', the 'Voyage of Snedgus and Mac Riagla', the 'Voyage of the Uí Corra', and above all, the 'Voyage of St Brendan'.[31]

The 'Voyage of St Brendan' is of particular interest not only because of its hybrid nature but also because in its appeal to the peoples of the Continent it seems to have paved the way for the popularity of the *matière de Bretagne*. It appears to have passed to the Continent from Ireland by way of Britain (that is Wales and

Cornwall) and Brittany. By the early tenth century at the latest it had contributed in both of its chief forms to the *Acta* of St Malo. It was translated into Norman French, Old French, Middle English, Flemish, Dutch, German, Provençal, Italian and Norse. An often quoted passage in the Old French *Roman de Renard* suggests either that there was also a Breton tale of Brendan or simply that the verse translation of the 'Voyage' was regarded as forming part of the Arthurian cycle of Romances.[32] Even if we reject the 'Voyage' as part of the Arthurian legend, it seems reasonable to regard it as part of the *matière de Bretagne* and to look on its popularity on the Continent as indicating the way in which the *matière* was to be welcomed there.

The language of ecclesiastical scholarship, needless to say, was Latin, but Brittany was connected with early Britain by the language which the British immigrants brought with them. We have mentioned the place-name elements *plou-*, *trev-*, *lann-*, *loc-*, which recall the Cornish *plu-*, *tre*, *lann*, **log* and the Welsh *plwy(f)*, *tref*, *llan*, and *llog* (*mynachlog*, etc.). Brittany, or rather Armorica, had its own dialect of Celtic or Gaulish before the first Britons set foot on its soil, and some have argued that Modern Breton is descended from that dialect,[33] but the orthodox view is that Breton was taken over to Brittany by the British immigrants.[34] It has been suggested that Roman records distinguish between the Britons of the 'Lowland Zone' and those of the 'Highland Zone' (that is north and west Britain)[35] by calling the former *Britanni*, the latter *Brit(t)ones*. Perhaps a reflection of this distinction is preserved in the practice of some writers of much later date in calling the Britons of Brittany 'Britones' and those of Britain 'Britanni'.

The Britons of the Highland Zone must have called themselves *Brittones* for this is the form which gave Welsh *Brython*, a name applied to all the western Britons from southern Scotland to Brittany, and they must have called their language *Brittonikā* which gave W. *Brythoneg*.[36] The Bretons still call their language *Brezhoneg*, and although the Cornish people have adopted a new name for their language, *Kernewek*, it seems that they called it *Brethonec* until it died. Nowadays Welsh people use the term *Brythoneg* to denote the language from which their language is descended. This development was to be expected, once the Welsh and their northern neighbours had begun to call themselves **Kombrogī* (sg. **Kombrogos*) whence the Welsh *Cymry* (sg. *Cymro*).[37] The Bretons did not need to change the name of their language for they call their land *Breizh* which comes from *Brittia*, a diminutive of *Britannia*, and a form attested by Procopius.[38]

The Welsh and the Bretons have never forgotten completely that they speak languages which are related, and indications that they could understand each other's languages down to the Middle Ages are not lacking. The oldest life of St Magloire of Dol tells us that he crossed the sea from Britain and made haste to the borders of the territory of Dol to preach to the people settled in the West who had the same language as himself.[39]   At a date probably in the second half of the ninth century a Welsh prince Guidnerth went to Dol to do the public penance that had been imposed upon him, 'for Guidnerth himself and the Bretons and the archbishop of this country were of the same language, although separated by distance . . .'[40]   Giraldus Cambrensis, who instances Bretons among the Normans, states that in his day Cornishmen and Bretons spoke languages very similar to each other — *Cornubia uero, et Armorica Britannia, lingua utuntur fere persimili,* 'In both Cornwall and Armorican Brittany they speak almost the same language as in Wales' — and he adds that Cornish and Breton were both fairly easily intelligible to Welshmen: *Kambris . . . in multis adhuc et fere cunctis intelligibil(es),* 'to the Welsh it is intelligible in many instances, and almost in all'.[41]

There is ample evidence, then, that Breton was similar enough to Cornish and Welsh for the three to be considered fundamentally one and the same language, and for their speakers to feel themselves to be related for a long time after the British settlement of Brittany.   One of the most striking expressions of this relationship is provided by the Welsh prophecy *Armes Prydein.*[42]   Written apparently by a monk in a south Wales monastery sometime before the Battle of Brunanburh (937), after which united opposition to Athelstan would have appeared futile even to the most optimistic, the poem sees the Britons in Brittany, Cornwall, Wales and the Old North, as joined by the Norsemen of Dublin and the Irish to drive back the English across the sea.   If one of the two princes whose prophesied return would deliver the Welsh from the English invaders was Cynan Meiriadog, the legendary founder of the Breton colony, as Dr Rachel Bromwich suggests, this feeling of relationship must have been deep not only for the author of the prophecy but also for his audience.

Although the author was in all probability a monk he must have learnt the rules of Welsh poetic composition and to do that he must have associated with the Welsh bards.   These like the *filid* in Ireland, and like the earlier druids and their bards from whom they were both derived, formed a secular learned order whose existence side by side with the Church in the Celtic countries seems to have distinguished those countries from others in Europe.   There is every reason to believe that the Celts of Armorica, like the other Gauls, had a learned order comprising *druids, bards* and *vates,* which is referred to by classical authors,[43] but even if they did not, it is virtually certain that the Britons who emigrated from Britain took over with them its representatives, and that with those representatives they took over a great deal of their traditional culture.   In other words, they must have been accompanied by bards who had learnt their poetic craft as well as a great deal of traditional lore in Britain and who were equipped not only to sing the praise of their chieftains but also to recite the praise sung to their ancestors in the mother country. We assume that they would have performed the same function as the bards who, we may presume, came with Cunedda from Manaw Gododdin, and the later bards who brought or borrowed the *Gododdin* poem to form a corner-stone of the poetic heritage of Wales.[44]

One should, however, remember that in early times there was some rivalry between the bardic order and the ecclesiastical intelligentsia, and take cognizance of the possibility that the Britons who emigrated to Brittany were so dominated by the 'saints' that neither the bards nor their patrons, the kings or princes, were allowed to play their traditional roles in their new homeland. Evidence for the existence of the bardic order in Brittany, to say the least, is not ample, and compared with the evidence of its existence in Wales it is meagre. The reason for this, we would like to suggest, lies in the difference in the history of the two countries in the eleventh and twelfth centuries.

Very little is known of the Welsh bards in the centuries preceding the Norman invasion of Wales. Less is known of the Breton bards preceding the Norman incursions into their lands. At the beginning of the twelfth century there was in Wales, under pressure from the Normans, a resurgence of national feeling: the princes of the country resisted Norman aggression and their bards sang the praises of those princes, breaking what appears to have been the bardic silence which had lasted almost without interruption through the preceding three or four centuries, and thus bringing to an end the *bwlch* or hiatus in the Welsh poetic tradition which seems to have occurred during this period. That so-called hiatus was probably not real: it appears real to us because of the loss of so much of its poetic output. But the loss would have been even greater had we not the work of the twelfth- and thirteenth-century Poets of the Princes, which gives essential assistance to us in our understanding of that of the earliest Welsh poets.

If we turn to Brittany we find that the native princes there went on the offensive and not only fought off the Normans but also extended their territory at Norman expense with the result that they became lords of a French-speaking as well as a Breton-speaking population, and eventually became more like their French counterparts than their own predecessors; this resulted in an end to whatever patronage they had once given to the Breton language and to the bards who sang in it.[45] It is possible, too, that as Brittany had to abandon its 'heroic age' view of life and became progressively, especially in its higher echelons, more assimilated to French civilization, the bardic order found that it had to undergo the same change as that which its counterpart in Wales underwent, when the Poets of the Princes gave way to the Poets of the Nobility, and the poets abandoned their semi-sacral role to assume that of entertainers, when the *awdl* yielded its primacy to the *cywydd*. This is probably one reason why Brittany seems to lack a precise nomenclature for its poets, and does not seem to draw a distinction between them and more popular entertainers. Although there is a reference to *bard* — Riuallonus is described as *filius an Bard* about 1131-9 — and a reference to *cerddoran* which seems to be a diminutive of *cerddor* and could mean 'a little singer' or 'a little poet',[46] there was apparently a tendency to identify the bards with the entertainers known elsewhere in other parts of France, with the *jongleurs* (*ioculatores*), and to distinguish between those whose appeal lay mainly in their words and those whose appeal lay mainly in their music, whether produced vocally (*cantores*) or instrumentally (*citharistae*).[47] Both categories could also be poets or bards in our sense of the word. Fleuriot, who did not distinguish between the *jongleurs* and poets proper, presented us with a not unimpressive list, such as Hoarvan 'the father of St Hervé', 'le premier des "jongleurs" bretons connus', ?Radulphus 'poeta' (*c.* 1110), Cadiou 'citharista' (1069), Dunguallon 'cantor' (1074-6), Petrus 'cantor', Sciou 'cantor' (*c.* 1160), Norman 'citharedus' (*c.* 1065), Pontellus, 'ioculator comitis', Riuallonus filius an Bard (*c.* 1131-9), Fru Roudu, a famous Breton poetess *c.* 1070.[48] There is a strong presumption that some, at least, of these used the Breton language.

There is a Latin Life of King Iudicael composed at the beginning of the eleventh century by Ingomar, a monk of Saint Méen, and in it we find a Latin poem which must have existed before the Life as it refers to Iudicael's military exploits as a youth.[49] Although it is in Latin, it is the sort of poem that we would have expected to find in Breton, for its motifs, as Fleuriot has shown, can be paralleled in the *gorchanau* affixed to the *Gododdin* poem, and in *Moliant Cadwallon* sung by a poet of a later age than Aneirin.[50] The composer of the Latin poem was obviously following a native Breton tradition, and it is interesting to note that Ingomar tells us that the poet Taliesin sojourned for a while in Brittany. We are reminded that Iudhael, son of Aidan, who appears in the *Cartulaire de Quimperlé*, recites the genealogy of Gurthiern, not for an earthly but for a heavenly reward.[51]

Although no Breton poetry of an earlier date than the fourteenth century has survived, the earliest poetry in the language that has come down is composed in metres so intricate and complex that they must be the result of cultivation and development over a long period, most probably by bards trained in the same kind of schools as their counterparts in Ireland and Wales.[52] Here is a typical example of the rhyming complexity of the system:

> Quenomp *cuff* hac *uvhel* Nou*el* da Roe'n *vell-y*,
> Ha din*am* de m*am* chu*ec* choant*ec* hep di*eguy*
> He dev*eus* n'en d*eus* sy.[53]

But the Celtic bards were not simply poets. They had charge of the traditional lore of their people, a lore which included genealogy and history, although neither poets nor people conceived of history as we do. Still, it would be a matter of pride for them not to forget the rock from which they had been hewn, and as we could have expected, 'origin' stories were an important part of the traditional lore of most peoples in early times.

It is strange to find that although the Bretons traced their origins back to Britain, they have little to say of the series of British migrations which must have occurred. They and their bards probably subscribed to the foundation story which connected their origin with Magnus Maximus, the Spaniard whom the Roman army in Britain proclaimed Emperor in 383.[54] Under the name of Macsen, Maximus played an important part, according to tradition, in the history of Britain and of Brittany. The ninth-century *Historia Brittonum* tells us that Brittany was settled by the British troops whom Macsen had taken with him to Gaul and to Rome. From Geoffrey of Monmouth's *Historia Regum Britanniae* we learn that *Conanus Meriadocus* (later known in Welsh as *Cynan fab Eudaf*) remained with his troops on the Continent as founder of the Breton settlement.[55]

As we shall see, Léon Fleuriot cogently argued the case for presuming the existence at one time of a *Historia Britannica* which showed that the Bretons and the Britons shared a common view of their early history, and this is not unlikely seeing that the Bretons were an offshoot, as it were, of the Britons.[56] It should not occasion any surprise that other elements not directly concerned with their history should be found in the traditions of both peoples. There are Breton versions of a story of the Welsh 'Ysgolan' who figures in a poem in the Black Book of Carmarthen. The two scholars who have discussed these stories, A.O.H. Jarman and Donatien Laurent,[57] are agreed that their original must have been in circulation first among the insular Britons. Even if it was taken over to Brittany at a later date than that of the Breton migrations, as Professor Jarman believes, it constitutes significant evidence that cultural contact was maintained between the two countries. In one way it is easier to assume that the traditions shared by Bretons and Britons are all derived from the time when they were one people or had just separated from each other. But the possibility that they took over from each other traditional elements at later periods seems to be indicated by the following facts: (i) that Alan IV or Alannus Fergannus, Duke of Brittany 1084-1112, who died in 1119, and who was first an opponent and then an ally of William the Conqueror, is referred to in *Trioedd Ynys Prydein*,[58] and (ii) that 'Sberin mab Flergant brenhin Llydaw' is mentioned in *Culhwch ac Olwen*,[59] and (iii) that *Llonyaw Llawhir* son of *Alan Fyrgan m. Emyr Llydaw* is mentioned in *Bonedd y Saint*.[60]

Here two questions present themselves. Assuming, as we must, that Arthur was originally a Brythonic hero, when did the Bretons begin to take an interest in the deeds he was said to have done? It is hardly credible that the earliest Britons who emigrated to Brittany carried with them stories of his exploits. On the other hand, it is not inconceivable that the latest did so. Is it possible that by the time the *Historia Brittonum* was compiled the Bretons knew of him and loved to tell tales of him?

The second question is indirectly related to the first. Can we postulate, as Jean Marx does, *un monde brittonique*?

> C'est-à-dire en Grande Bretagne, le pays de Galles, le Domnonée (Cornwall et partie de Devonshire) . . . Strathclyde . . . l'Armorique constitue en fait une culture, une civilisation, une ensemble de tradition, une langue.[61]

One can understand why Jean Marx postulated *un monde brittonique*. Various scholars have isolated successive stages in the development of the *Tristan* story, each stage involving contributions from various parts of this *monde brittonique*, that is a Pictish or Scottish stage, a Welsh stage, a Cornish stage, a Breton stage, and finally a French stage.[62] The Breton stage is characterized by the introduction of the second Isolt (the Breton princess), by a version of the hero's dragon fight, perhaps by the story of King Mark's horse's ears,[63] and by the episode of the black and white sails, which is found in a Breton folk-tale. The latter motif occurs in the ancient classical tale of Perseus and Andromeda, and Sidney Hartland showed that it is found in many European and several Breton folk-tales.[64] Van Hamel studied a representative of the latter, and concluded that the Breton versions were not an offshoot of the Tristan and Isolt romance, although their ancestors in a much earlier period must have contributed to the formation of the romance.

It is well known that Breton Brittany, like Gaelic Scotland, and other countries where literacy in the native language was not achieved until comparatively recent times, had until the beginning of the twentieth century a very lively folk-tale tradition. Unfortunately Breton folk-tales have not yet been systematically collected, nor fully studied.[65] Occasionally scholars have examined some of the published tales in search of motifs which could be regarded as the originals of those included in the medieval Arthurian romances, but the results have been indecisive.[66] One would like to know how peculiar to Breton folk-tales are many of the motifs they contain, and how peculiar to their ancestors were the motifs they had in common with the romances. It is reasonable to believe that the Celts of Gaul had their fund of folk-tales and that they transmitted some of them to the invaders who supplanted them. Another important consideration is that there is a two-way traffic between the oral folk-tale and the literary tradition. If the literary story-teller is prepared to borrow from the oral story-teller, the oral story-teller is prepared to borrow from the literary story-teller, given the opportunity.[67]

Of all the Celtic peoples in the eleventh century the Bretons were probably the most advanced economically and the most flourishing politically. By the middle of the century their possessions south of the Loire had reached La Roche-sur-Yon and Les Sables-d'Olonne.[68] Moreover, they were used as auxiliaries by the Normans not only in their conquests of Italy in the south but also of England in the north; indeed, they are said to have had more land in England after the Conquest than the native English.[69] This is not surprising, if, as it has been said, they were William the Conqueror's chief auxiliaries.

The prominence of the Bretons among the Celts must be viewed against the background of the Norman world, a world which at the end of the eleventh century stretched from Abernethy to Syracuse, and from Brittany to Antioch, as well as against the background of a certain community of sentiment based partly on self-interest, but partly also on genuine political and religious emotions.[70] But it should be pointed out that this prominence of the Bretons among the Celts had not been of very long duration and that it did not mean that the Breton language and its culture enjoyed the same eminent position. The Breton dukes may have patronized the Breton language in the previous centuries but by the eleventh century they had been long accustomed to the French language and its culture. This, however, should not be taken to mean that many of the Breton leading families, those who remained in Brittany as well as those who settled in Britain, were not bilingual in Breton and French. Indeed, it may well be that the fact that they spoke Breton as well as French was what distinguished them in the eyes of contemporary observers from the Normans and the French. Unfortunately the languages used by these observers — Latin and French — tend to blur the distinction they drew between the Bretons and the Britons, that is between them and the Cornish and the Welsh of Britain, with the result that scholars have been engaged in a long debate over the question whether the *Bretagne* of the *matière de Bretagne*, in so far as it is used to indicate provenance, refers to Brittany or to Britain.[71] According to some scholars, it was from the Bretons that the Normans and the French learnt of the *matière de Bretagne*; according to others,[72] it was from the Welsh and to a lesser degree from the Cornish. Perhaps the best-known advocate of the view that it was the Bretons, and in particular Breton entertainers, who made the French aware of the *matière de Bretagne* was the late R.S. Loomis in his numerous writings; while the late Jean Marx and others have advocated the equal, if not greater, importance of direct transmission from the Welsh to the Anglo-Normans.

The debate revolves around such questions as the precise meanings of *Britones* and *li Bretun* in the twelfth century, and what meaning we should attach, for instance, to Marie de France's use of the latter. Marie de France wrote in the third quarter of the twelfth century, and composed her *lais* some time before 1189. She was writing after the appearance of Geoffrey of Monmouth's *Historia Regum Britanniae*, and some of her references to *li Bretun* may have been made under the influence of the conventions of her day, but these references cannot be ignored in any attempt to assess the Breton contribution to the *matìere de Bretagne*.[73] We may allow Alfred Ewert to summarize their significance for us:

> From all these statements taken together it appears that there existed in Marie's time Breton *lais*, some reputed to be of great antiquity, which could be heard or read, and which comprised a melody and a narrative of some kind, the melody being carried by the Breton *rote* (a sort of harp). Marie's object is to retell the story, to reproduce the narrative content (or accompaniment) of this musical composition. The propagators of the Breton *lais* . . . were clearly the Breton jongleurs of whose activity there is ample evidence in the twelfth century and even much earlier.[74]

The fact that two of the titles Marie de France gives are Breton[75] and that the alternative title given to *Eliduc* is 'Guildeluec ha Gualadun', which contains the Breton conjunction *ha*, 'and', suggests very strongly that she had heard *jongleurs* announce their songs in this way, and that they may have sung them in Breton, giving a resumé in French.[76] Indeed, the late Dr Constance Bullock-Davies argued that about half of Marie de France's *lais* and a majority of the anonymous *lais* are of Breton provenance.[77]

It should be noted that Robert Biket's *Lai du Cor* (c. 1175) has a hero named *Garadue*, known to Chrétien de Troyes as *Karadues Briebras*. He would have been known to the Bretons as *Caradoc Brechbras* and to the Welsh as *Caradawc Freichfras*.[78] Perhaps it is more likely that Biket got the name from Breton than from Welsh. In any case, it has assumed in French as remote a form as other Welsh or Breton names tend to do in the romances.[79]

One of Marie de France's *lais*, *Chevrefoil*, is a form of the story of Tristan and Iseult, a story which apparently started its existence quite unrelated to the Arthurian Cycle, and which she situated in Cornwall (though she mentions that 'Suhtwales' was Tristan's birthplace). Oliver Padel has recently made a most convincing case for locating in Cornwall the genesis of the Tristan story in the form given to it by the poet Béroul.[80] Of even greater interest is the fact that Marie asserts that she had seen stories of Tristan in written form, and that she implies a written form for the *lai* of *Guigemar*.

Chrétien de Troyes tells us a little more about the sources of his Arthurian romances.[81] Of *Erec* he asserts that it is 'a story which those who desire to earn their living by telling tales are wont to dismember and spoil in the presence of kings and counts'. The suggestion that Chrétien, in referring to the source of his tales as a *conte* or a book (*livre*), is merely using a conventional formula to add authority to his work may have some validity, and it is true that he had nothing but contempt for the ordinary run of story-tellers (*fableors, conteurs*). However, he does not suggest anywhere that these story-tellers were Bretons, although, as we have seen, there is reason to believe that Breton story-tellers enjoyed a reputation second to none, and there are several considerations which suggest that the French heard the tales of Arthur and his knights from them rather than from the story-tellers of the other Celtic nations. It was these and similar considerations that persuaded Loomis and others that it was from Brittany that the *matière de Bretagne* was disseminated throughout Europe.[82]

We have referred to some of the evidence for believing that Breton *jongleurs* were famous for their songs. Fleuriot has used Gottfried von Strassburg's *Tristan und Isolde* to show that the Breton language was held in high esteem as were the Breton *jongleurs*.[83] According to this version of the romance, the words of the *lai* of Guirun and his paramour were composed by Bretons and its music was played by Welsh harpists. Elsewhere in the poem, Tristan played the *lai* of Grallon on the harp in the Breton manner, so wonderfully that many who heard it forgot their own names. Then he sang the *lai* of Thisbe in Breton, Welsh, Latin and French. When asked whether he knew the four languages, Tristan answered, 'Yes, tolerably well'. Later in the tale, Tristan's friend speaks to him in French, and is answered in Breton. Tristan is not only a reciter of *lais*: he is also a composer of love-songs. In Thomas's version of *Tristan* (*Tristran*), *Iseut* (*Ysold*) is said to compose 'un lai piteus d'amour'.[84] Wace in his *Brut* refers to an instrumentalist called *Blegabred*, a Breton name, and to a warrior called *Balduf* who was disguised as a Breton *jongleur*.[85] It may be, however, that in emphasizing the role played by Breton *jongleurs* in spreading Arthurian traditions, we are doing less than justice to two other classes in the Breton population, the soldiers and the clerics. That Breton soldiers fought side by side with the Normans we have already seen, and if the Church recruited from among the Bretons as many clerics at this time as it did later, the number of Breton clerics serving outside Brittany must have been considerable.

Geoffrey of Monmouth leaves us largely in the dark as to the stories of Arthur and others which were in circulation among the Welsh, Cornish, and Bretons before he wrote his *Historia Regum Britanniae*. He tells us that he was surprised to find no records beyond the references in Gildas and Bede, either to the pre-Christian kings of Britain, or to Arthur, although their deeds were 'told abroad as if inscribed in the jocund memories of many peoples'. He refers, of course, to the *liber vetustissimus*, the very ancient book in the British tongue (*Britannici sermonis*) which proved to contain a continuous and elegant narrative of all those kings down to Cadwallader.[86] He does not claim that the 'ancient book' was his sole authority, but it supplemented for him what he had learnt from Gildas and Bede, from the 'jocund tales' and from oral information supplied by Archdeacon Walter.

It is not impossible that the *Britannicus sermo* was Breton rather than the Welsh it is generally assumed to be, and that the tales told abroad about Arthur were tales which Geoffrey had heard among the Bretons who had crossed to Britain with the Normans and had settled there in several places including Cornwall and the vicinity of Monmouth, where, born apparently of Breton parents, he had been reared.[87]

It has been argued that interest in Arthur at the beginning of the twelfth century was greater in Cornwall and Brittany than in Wales. The evidence for this revolves around the belief that Arthur is not dead but biding his time in hiding to appear when his people need him. This belief, it appears, was alive in Cornwall in 1113. There a man with a withered arm maintained that Arthur was still living. Herman of Laon who records this, probably soon after 1145, introduced his narrative with the words *sicut Britones solent jurgari cum Francis pro rege Arturo.*[88] Here we presume that by Britons he meant Bretons. Giraldus Cambrensis testifies that it was the *fabulosi Britones*, not the Welsh, who told that Arthur had been borne away by the *dea phantastica* called Morganis to the isle of Avalon.[89] However, a commentary on the *Prophetiae Merlini* which can be dated to the second half of the twelfth century informs us that the belief in Arthur's departure was common to the Bretons, the Welsh and the Cornish (*Omnium scilicet haec est superstitio, Britonum, Guallorum et Cornubiencium*).[90] Perhaps the most interesting feature of this *superstitio* is that it was shared by the three Brittonic peoples, for the motif of the hidden saviour is found attached to the names of several heroes,[91] and it is obviously an accretion to the tales of Arthur. On the other hand, the Breton belief was so vivid that it assumed a political aspect. Étienne de Rouen in his *Draco Normannicus* gives an account of Henry II Plantagenet in Brittany in 1167, and relates that when he was preparing to attack Brittany he received a letter from Arthur announcing his return![92]

It is surely natural to conclude that Geoffrey of Monmouth obtained some of his material from Breton sources, and some from Cornish and Welsh sources. That Geoffrey accumulated some of his knowledge piecemeal is shown by the fact that he is said to have interrupted his writing of the *Historia* to write the *Prophetiae Merlini*,[93] which was then incorporated in the *Historia*, and again later in the *Vita Merlini*. It would be very satisfactory if we could conclude that Geoffrey had derived some information regarding Merlin from his compatriot Bretons, and that he had then acquired additional information from someone well versed in the Welsh sources, but here we would be begging the question as to whether the seer was known as Merlin. It is certainly of some significance that the oldest complete composition in Breton literature that has come down to us involved Arthur and a character resembling Merlin, namely the *Dialog etre Arzur roe dan Bretounet ha Guinglaff*,[94] written c. 1450. Guinglaff is a wise 'wild man' who lives in a forest. He is also a prophet and is prepared to prophesy about anything which Arthur names 'except thy death and mine'. In other words, although he is not known by that name, he has several of the features associated with Merlin/Myrddin.

That Geoffrey did not use all the information which was available concerning Arthur and his 'knights' is shown by Wace in his *Roman de Brut*,[95] and in particular by his mention of the 'Round Table', and of the tales told by *li Bretun* about Arthur. There can be no question about Wace's sources: he tells us that *li Bretun* told tales — *mainte fable* — of the Round Table, and that so much had been related of the 'mervelles provées' and the 'aventures trovées' of Arthur that they had turned all 'à fable': 'Ne tot mençonge ne tot voir / Tot folie, ne tot savoir' (vv.10,038-9). His knowledge of Arthur's Round Table, which Geoffrey does not mention, was derived, then, from oral tradition, from legends told by *li Bretun*.[96] Notwithstanding the ambiguity in Wace's use of the word 'Bretun', and the possibility that the reference to *li Bretun* and the Round Table may be an allusion to insular rather than to Continental Britons, the reference to *li Bretun* in connection with the return of Arthur seems to be the latter. We know that Wace was a native of Jersey — as such he has been claimed by Fleuriot as a 'demi-breton'[97] — and that he was familiar with Brittany and especially with the forest of Brocéliande, and with its famous fountain of Barenton, which he mentions in the *Roman de Rou*, so that, all in all, he, like Marie de France, may be taken as another witness to the popularity of tales emanating from Brittany.[98]

However this may be, the evidence that Wales knew a good deal about Arthur independently of Geoffrey is considerable, and outweighs the evidence for any comparable knowledge among the Bretons.[99] It is well known that Geoffrey had no high regard for the Welsh people of his day and presumably he would not have been anxious to use whatever material they could have given him.[100] There is, on the other hand, ample evidence that he esteemed highly his compatriots the Bretons, that he was prepared to promote their fame, and that he would have used any material concerning Arthur that they could provide. It is, therefore, rather surprising that until recently few have been concerned to show how much Breton material could have been absorbed in Geoffrey's *Historia* and in the Arthurian Legend, especially as there is reason to believe that he knew Brittany personally.[101]

J.R.F. Piette led the way with 'Yr Agwedd Lydewig ar y Chwedlau Arthuraidd' in *LlC*, 8 (1965). Since the appearance of his article there has been a great deal of activity among Breton scholars and Léon Fleuriot, in particular, has addressed the problem of Geoffrey's indebtedness to Breton sources.[102]   According to the latter, Geoffrey's use of proper names shows the influence of Breton, for, whereas in Welsh after the tenth century a prosthetic y- appeared before words beginning with st, sp, sq, it did not appear in Breton, so that when Geoffrey uses such forms as *Spaden*, *Stadhiald*, he uses the Breton forms, not the corresponding Welsh ones. By that time the termination -*auc* remained in Welsh, whereas in Brittany it had become -*oc*, and Geoffrey uses -*oc* more frequently than -*auc*, e.g. *Budoc*, *Chinmarocus*, *Caradocus*.[103] Assuming, however, that Geoffrey knew more Breton than Welsh, we can imagine that he would be tempted to adapt the Welsh forms to their Breton equivalents.

As J.E. Lloyd pointed out, the name 'Arthur', probably a patronymic of Geoffrey himself, as a personal name was of rare occurrence in Wales, but it seems to have had a vogue in Brittany.[104] And it is interesting to note that in Geoffrey's *Historia* Arthur's grandfather Constantinus is a Breton. His mother, the world's greatest beauty, is Duchess of Cornwall. His wife, his heir and successor also come from Cornwall. His most distinguished vassal is his nephew, King Hoelus of Brittany, who is appealed to by common consent when young Arthur is hard pressed by the Saxons. Another of Arthur's most distinguished vassals is Cador, Duke of Cornwall. Other features in the *Historia* could be mentioned to show how Geoffrey highlights Arthur's connections with Brittany and Cornwall, and to understand his coupling of Cornwall with Brittany one needs to remember not only the close connection which existed between the two countries from the earliest times, but also the considerable number of Bretons who had been granted lands in Cornwall after the Norman Conquest.[105]

The name Arthur itself is interesting. Since the name is derived from *Artorius*, it is strange that no Latin sources refer to him as such: only to a Latinized Welsh or Breton name *Arthurus*.[106] In French the form *Arzur* apparently occurs only once — in Biket's *Lai du Cor*. (c. 1175). In Modern Breton *Arzur* is pronounced (*arzur*), but in the twelfth century the Breton pronunciation of the written form *Arzur* would have been almost the same as the Welsh, that is [Arθur] or [Arður]. If Biket's *Arzur* was from a written source, it was Breton: if it was from an oral source, it could be Breton or Welsh. Almost without exception, Arthur's name in French is *Artu*[s], a form which cannot be derived from Breton. J.R.F. Piette,[107] whom I am following here, thought that French *Artus* had come from a written source with the *th* or even *t* (*Arthur*, *Artur*) taken to have the same phonetic value as French *t*. If this was so, Piette thought that a Welsh source would be more probable than a Breton one, although the latter would not be impossible.

Piette called attention to the frequency of names ending in *-us, -ie* and *-uc,* corresponding to Welsh names in *-og,* Ml. W. *-awc,* for example *Caradues, Garadues: Caradawc; Meriadus, Meriaduc: Meiriadawc.* In Old Breton the termination was *-oc* which became [oek] at the beginning of the medieval period, a sound represented by *-uc* in the eleventh- and twelfth-century Breton charters, and he adds 'it is quite likely that those names were borrowed from Breton'.

Piette thought that some names were borrowed into French from written sources. He himself did not think it possible that the forms in *u(e)s* noted above represented a Breton pronunciation as heard by Frenchmen; they were rather taken from written sources. This is true also, according to him, of forms in which mutations are not shown. He derives *Garadues Briebras* to a written early Middle Breton form *Caraduc Brechbras,* corresponding to the Middle Welsh *Caradawc Vreichvras.* He refers also to the form *Meriadus* which occurs in Marie de France's *Guigemar,* a *lai* of which the authoress says 'Sulunc la lettre e l'escriture, / Vos mosterai un' aventure . . .', with the clear suggestion that she was drawing on a written source.

Loth derived the name *Erec* from *Bro-(w)erec*[108] and Rachel Bromwich has since derived *Enide* from *Bro-(w)ened.*[109] These derivations suggest oral rather than literary transmission, and they argue a strong case for assuming Breton intermediaries. But if the Arthurian tales were spread solely or even mainly by Breton intermediaries, one would expect a more regular pattern of Breton linguistic influence on the nomenclature of the Arthurian tales, and so far, as Piette has shown (art. cit.), the existence of such a pattern has not been proved.

Léon Fleuriot has argued the case for assuming the existence of a *Historia Britannica* which showed that the Bretons like the Britons had 'une vision d'ensemble de leur histoire'.[110] His case rests mainly on the material found in a passage in the Cartulary of Quimperlé which uses sources from the beginning of the ninth century although it is itself to be dated to the twelfth,[111] and in the prologue to the Life of St Goueznou,[112] a composition dating from 1019, the second year of the episcopacy of Eudon, which contains material additional to and in some respects different from that of the British source, the *Historia Brittonum,* and the use made of that source by Geoffrey in the *Historia Regum Britanniae.*

Fleuriot also refers to *Le Livre des faits d'Arthur,* so named by Le Baud, who knew a fuller version than the one known to us in the miserable fragments that have survived. It has been studied in an important article by Gw. Le Duc, 'L'*Historia Britannica* avant Geoffrey de Monmouth'.[113] The book was apparently dedicated to Arthur II of Brittany (1305-12). Fleuriot thinks there are reasons for regarding it as a 'mise en vers d'un texte plus ancien'. It is, as we have said, in a fragmentary condition, but the fragments show that the history they relate differs from Geoffrey's in some places and supplements it in others. In Fleuriot's words, 'Geoffrey donne en général un texte bien plus court que le livre, dont la perte est très regrettable. Tout indique que la préface et l'arrangement en vers sont postérieurs à la rédaction du texte primitif.'[114] The fragments should, as Fleuriot suggests, be compared with the *Historia Britannorum Versificata* composed probably by a certain Guillaume de Rennes between 1234 and 1237[115] and dedicated to Bishop Cadioc of Vannes, and both works should be compared for similarities and differences with Geoffrey's *Historia*, since the Breton tradition may give us better clues to Geoffrey's sources.

However, the evidence that we have discussed is sufficient to demonstrate that Brittany and the Bretons did play a significant part in the transmission of the *matière de Bretagne*, and to provide grounds for hoping, if not for expecting, that further research will disclose still more evidence.[116]

NOTES:

1. Caesar, *De Bello Gallico*, vii, 57; cf. Bede, *Historia Ecclesiastica*, i.1.

2. Caesar, op. cit., iii, 8.

3. C. Fox, *The Personality of Britain* (Cardiff, 1932), 13, 15. Cf. E.G. Bowen, *Saints, Seaways, and Settlements* (Cardiff, 1969), 6.

4. Caesar, op.cit., v, 12. There were tribes bearing the same names on both sides of the Channel, e.g. the Parisii, Brigantes, etc.

5. Ibid., ii, 4. For suggestions that at a much later date rulers in Brittany held sway at the same time over parts of south-west England, see N.K. Chadwick, *Early Brittany* (Cardiff, 1969), 212, 220.

6. Tacitus, *Agricola*, 11.

7. E.G. Bowen, op. cit., 165.

8. André Chédeville and Hubert Guillotel, *La Bretagne des saints et des rois, V–X siècles* (Ouest-France, 1984), 33.

9. For another view, relating the migration to the Irish settlements in Wales and the south-west, see Chadwick, op.cit., 172-92.

10. LHEB 15; Chadwick, op.cit., 193-237. We find the inhabitants of Brittany called by the name of *Britanni*, apparently for the first time, in a letter written by Sidonius Apollinaris, referring to a trial for treason which occurred in 468, ibid., 195.

11. Ibid., 197.

12. Ibid., 217-18.

13. J.F. Kenney, *The Sources for the Early History of Ireland*, I, Ecclesiastical (New York, 1929; Dublin, 1979), 291 ff.

14. Ibid., 487-9.

15. Kenney, loc. cit.

16. F. Kerlouégan, 'Les Vies des saints bretons les plus anciennes dans leurs rapports avec les Îles britanniques', in Michael Herren (ed.), *Insular Latin Studies* (Toronto, 1981), 195-213.

17. N.K. Chadwick, op. cit., 208. She is here citing the testimony of R. Largiilière, *Les Saints et l'organisation primitive dans l'Armorique bretonne* (Rennes, 1925).

18. Kenney, *The Sources*, 303.

19. Chadwick, op. cit., 209.

20. J. MacNeill, 'The Pioneer of Nations', *Studies*, 11 (1922), 13-28, 435-46.

21. Kenney, *The Sources*, 530ff.

22. S.J. Crawford, *Anglo-Saxon Influence on Western Christendom 600-800* (Cambridge and New York, 1933).

23. *Landévennec et le monachisme breton dans le haut moyen âge. Actes du colloque du 15ème centenaire de l'abbaye de Landévennec, 25-26-27 avril 1985* (Association Finistère, 1985).

24. Kenney, *The Sources*, 175. The Abbey of Redon during Nominoë's reign (d.851) adopted the Rule of St Benedict and became a powerful influence in favour of submission to Roman practice.

25. Kenney, *The Sources*, 248. After saying that the remoter history of many of the Irish MSS in foreign libraries is difficult to determine, Kenney, op.cit.,10, expressly states the possibility that Brittany and Tours served as entrepôts for Irish MSS.

26. *Collected Papers of Henry Bradshaw* (Cambridge, 1889), 474.

27. Colette Jeudy, 'Israel le Grammairien et la tradition manuscrite du Commentaire de Réme d'Auxerre à l'Ars Minor de Donat', *Studi Medievali*, 3e Série, 18 (1977), 195-248.

28. HLCB 61.

29. J. Stange, (ed.), *Dialogus Miraculorum* IV, 36 (Köln, 1850), 205. The *Dialogus* is dated c. 1223. It is suggested that the Cistercians were very fond of romances; see F.M. Powicke, *Ailred of Rievaulx and his Biographer Walter Daniel* (Manchester, 1922), 65-6.

30. See H. Sparnaay, *Verschmelzung legendärischer und weltlicher Motive in der Poesie des Mittelalters* (Gröningen, 1922); J.E.C. Williams, 'Bucheddau'r Saint', B, 11 (1944), 149-57, especially p.153.

31. Kenney, op.cit., 409-12.

32. Kenney, op.cit., 412, and n.147. See Martin (ed.), *Roman de Renart* (Strasbourg, 1882), especially vol. i, 66-7, and Fleuriot in HLCB 23.

33. See F. Falc'hun 'Le Breton, forme moderne du Gaulois', *AB*, 69 (1962), 413 ff.; idem, *Histoire de langue bretonne d'après la géographie linguistique* (Rennes, 1951, Paris, 1963). Falc'hun

followed the views of La Villemarqué and the earlier view of La Borderie.

34. K.H. Jackson, *A Historical Phonology of Breton* (Dublin, 1967), 32. Jackson enlarged on the views of Aurelien de Courson and J. Loth. See also André Chédeville and Hubert Guillotel, *La Bretagne des saints*, 43-5, Léon Fleuriot and Charles Evans, *A Dictionary of Old Breton*, ii (Toronto, 1985), introduction.

35. For these terms see Cyril Fox, op.cit., note 3 above.

36. Herman of Laon seems to differentiate between the Britons of Britanny and those of Britain by calling the former *Britones* and the latter *Britanni*. See E.K. Chambers, *Arthur of Britain* (Cambridge, New York, 1927, 1964), 249.

37. For the terms *Brython* and *Cymry* see J. Morris Jones, *A Welsh Grammar* (Oxford, 1913), 5. On the name *Cymry* see *AP* 20.

38. See W. Edwards, 'The Settlement of Brittany', *Cy.*, 11 (1892), 78 and n.4 by E. Phillimore.

39. Cited by L. Fleuriot in HLCB 12 (from B.N. MS Lat. 15436, fol.52^V, col.2).

40. *LL* 181.

41. *Giraldi Cambrensis Opera*, vol.VI, *Descriptio Kambriae*, ed. J.F. Dimock (R.S. 1868), I, vi. Trans. L. Thorpe, *Gerald of Wales* (Harmondsworth, 1978), 231.

42. See notes on Kynan and Kadwaladyr, *AP* 44, 46.

43. See J.J. Tierney, 'The Celtic Ethnography of Posidonius', *Proc. Royal Irish Academy*, 60 C5 (1960). On the old priest Phoebicius, of Armorican druidical stock, see N.K. Chadwick, op.cit., 85-7.

44. On the Gododdin poem see Ifor Williams, BWP 50-69; K.H. Jackson, *The Gododdin* (Edinburgh, 1969, 1978); A.O.H. Jarman, *Aneirin: Y Gododdin* (Llandysul, Dyfed, 1988).

45. It has been said that the Breton language lost ground to French. The case seems to have been that the territory of Brittany was extended eastwards in the ninth century by the conquests of Nominoë to include parts of France and a French-speaking population and that the leaders of the Breton community were thereby brought into close contact with the French aristocracy, and were thus the more readily induced to adopt the language and customs of France. See A. Rebillon, *Histoire de Bretagne* (Paris, 1957), 37-8. Cf. Caroline Brett 'Breton Latin Literature as Evidence for Literature in the Vernacular', *CMCS*, 18 (1989), 1-25.

46. HLCB 15-16, 23; Fleuriot and Evans, *Dictionary of Old Breton*, i, s.v. *Cerddoran*.

47. H. Waquet, *Histoire de la Bretagne* (Paris, 1948), 46, discovered the name *Cadiou citharista* in a list of Duke Hoel's protégés in the tenth century.

48. HLCB 12, 15-16.

49. Ibid., 104. Cf. L. Fleuriot 'Sur quatre textes bretons en latin', *ÉC*, 18 (1981), 179-213, esp. 207-13.

50. L. Fleuriot, *Documents de l'histoire de la Bretagne sous la direction de Delumeau* (Toulouse, 1971), 156-9.

51. L. Fleuriot, 'Old Breton Genealogies and Early British Traditions', *B*, 26 (1974-5), 1-6.

52. F. Gourvil, *Langue et littérature bretonnes* (Paris, 1952), 115-16, points out that early Breton poetry, composed in a variety of metres which utilize both internal and final rhyme, implies a written tradition which must go back to an early date. See L. Fleuriot, 'L'Ancienne métrique', in HLCB 19-21, and J. Loth, *La Métrique Galloise depuis les plus anciens textes jusqu'à nos jours* (Paris, 1900-2).

53. Gourvil, op.cit., 116.

54. See C.E. Stevens, 'Magnus Maximus in British History', *ÉC*, 3 (1938), 86-94; *TYP* 451-4. On the importance of 'Origin' stories see P.P. Sims-Williams, 'Some Functions of Origin Stories in Early Medieval Wales', in *History and Heroic Tales*, ed. by Tore Nyberg *et al.* (Odense, 1985), 97-131; esp. 102-111.

55. *HRB*, vi, 4-5. After its original settlement by Conanus Meriadocus, Armorica provides a founder for the Arthurian dynasty in Constantine, a brother of Conanus's descendant Aldroenus (hence Arthur's grandfather), and Budecius of Armorica protects Aurelius and Uther in the time of Vortigern. Duke Hoelus of Armorica is Arthur's faithful ally.

56. A similar view was expressed earlier by A. de la Borderie; see E.K. Chambers, *Arthur of Britain* (London, 1927, 1965), 92-3. Cf. notes 110 and 111 below.

57. See A.O.H. Jarman, 'Cerdd Ysgolan', *YB*, 10 (1977), 51-78, D. Laurent, 'La Guerz de Skolan et la légende de Merlin', *Ethnologie française*, 1, 19-54, and ch.5, n.25 above.

58. *TYP*, 270-1.

59. *CO*(1) lxxxiii, and line 216.

60. *EWGT* 64, no. 58.

61. Jean Marx, *ÉC*, 10 (1963), 479; repr. in his *Nouvelles recherches sur la littérature arthurienne* (Paris, 1965), 78.

62. The whole subject is surveyed in R. Bromwich, 'Some Remarks on the Celtic Sources of "Tristan"', *THSC* (1955), 32-60. See further ch.10 above, and general bibliographies of Tristan scholarship, such as that of R. Picozzi, *A History of Tristan Scholarship* (Berne and Frankfurt, 1971).

63. In the French versions Tristan's father has a Breton name, Rivalen — in place of the Welsh Tallwch (see p. 210). For a Breton version of the hero's dragon fight see A.G. van Hamel, *RC*, 41 (1924), 331-49, and on Breton versions of King Mark's horse's ears see p. 212 above and n.35.

64. S. Hartland, *Legend of Perseus* (London, 1894-6), 111. See also R.S. Loomis, *Comparative Literature*, 2 (1950), 293 and refs. cited.

65. Hersart de la Villemarqué in his *Contes populaires des ancien bretons* tried to collect folk-tale items which could be considered to be the originals of the *romans chevaleresques*. On his work see now Donatien Laurent, *Aux sources du Barzaz Breiz* (Paris, 1989). P. Sebillot, *Le Folklore de France*, 4 vols. (Paris, 1904-7), etc. and F.M. Luzel, *Contes populaires de la Basse Bretagne* (Paris, 1887), etc. were the greatest collectors of Breton folklore in the last century whose work has become widely known, and the latter was highly critical of the work of La Villemarqué; see his book *De l'authenticité des chants de Barzaz-Breiz* (Paris, 1872), and P. Batany, *Luzel, poète et folkloriste breton 1821-1895* (Rennes, 1941).

66. R.S. Loomis 'Breton Folklore and Arthurian Romance', *Comparative Literature*, 2 (1950), 289-306. The indexes of Anti Aarne and Stith Thompson to the Types and Motifs of Folk-tales are,

of course, of fundamental importance for this study.

67. Cf. J.E. Caerwyn Williams, *Y Storïwr Gwyddeleg a'i Chwedlau* (Caerdydd, 1972), 112-16.

68. A. de la Borderie, *Histoire de Bretagne* (1898-1906), 407-8.

69. See HLCB 8, and M. Jones, 'Notes sur quelques familles en Angleterre après la conquête normande', *Mémoires de la Société Historique et Archéologique de Bretagne*, 58 (1981), 75-97. Cf. ch.13 below.

70. R. Allen Brown, *The Normans* (London, 1984), 154, and J. Le Patourel, *The Norman Empire* (Oxford, 1976). On the sentiment of community see Gaston Paris, *La Littérature normande* (Paris, 1899).

71. For useful summaries of this controversy see J.R.F. Piette, 'Yr Agwedd Lydewig ar y Chwedlau Arthuraidd', *LlC*, 8 (1965), 183; ALMA ch.6; Karl Voretzsch, *Introduction to the Study of Old French Literature*, trans. F.M. du Mont (New York, 1931); K.O. Brogsitter, *Artusepik* (Stuttgart, 1965).

72. Prominent among these were Jean Marx, 'Monde brittonique et matière de Bretagne' (see n.61 above), and J. Loth, *Contributions à l'étude des romans de la Table Ronde* (Paris, 1912); idem, introduction to *Les Mabinogion* (Paris, 1913). See ch.13 below.

73. C. Foulon, 'Marie de France et la Bretagne', *AB*, 60 (1953), 243-58; F. Lot, 'La Patrie des lais bretons', *Romania*, 28 (1899), 1-48. See ch.13, n.81 below.

74. A. Ewert (ed.), *Lays of Marie de France* (Oxford, 1944), xi.

75. *Laüstic* (<Breton *eostic* = 'nightingale') and *Bisclavret* (?= *bleid lavaret* 'talking wolf'). See Th.M. Chotzen, *ÉC*, 2 (1937), 33-44; H.W. Bailey, *CMCS*, 1 (1981), 95-7.

76. On the meaning of 'Breton' and 'Bretagne' in the twelfth century see H. Zimmer, 'Beiträge zur Namenforschung in den altfranzösischen Arthurepen', *Zeitschrift für französischen Sprache und Literatur*, 13 (1891), 1-117; F. Lot, 'Études sur la provenance du cycle arthurien: (i) Le sens du mot breton au XIIe siècle; (ii) de la provenance des lais dits bretons', *Romania*, 24 (1895), 497-528, esp. 524-8.

77. C. Bullock-Davies, 'Marie de France and South Wales', Ph.D. Diss. (Univ. of Wales, Bangor, 1963), Pt.iia, 226-326. See also idem, 'The Form of the Breton Lay', *Medium Aevum*, 42 (1973), 18-31; idem, 'Marie de France: A Reassessment of her Narrative Technique in the Lais', in *Court and Poet*, ed. Glyn Burgess (Liverpool, 1981), 93-9.

78. J.R.F. Piette, 'Yr Agwedd Lydewig ar y Chwedlau Arthuraidd', *LlC*, 8 (1965), 187, derives *Garadues Briebras* from an early Middle Breton form *Caraduc Brechbras*, corresponding to Middle Welsh *Caradawc Freichfras*; see also *TYP* 98, 299-300. On the *Lai du Cor* see ALMA 113-16.

79. See G.D. West, *An Index of Proper Names in French Arthurian Verse Romances* (Toronto, 1969); idem, *An Index of Proper Names in French Arthurian Prose Romances* (Toronto, 1978).

80. Oliver Padel, 'The Cornish Background of the Tristan Stories', *CMCS*, 1 (1981), 53-80. See ch.10 above.

81. Of crucial importance for this question are the three Welsh romances *Peredur*, *Owain*, and *Geraint ab Erbin* and their relation to Chrétien's poems *Perceval*, *Yvain*, and *Erec et Enide*. See chs.6, 7, 8 above, and pp. 282-3 below.

82. R.S. Loomis, *Celtic Myth and Arthurian Romance* (New York, 1927), 27; idem, *The Grail: From Celtic Myth to Christian Symbol* (Cardiff, 1963), 13, and elsewhere throughout his writings. The evidence concerning the Welshman *Breri* or *Bleddri* goes far towards modifying this view; on him see ALMA 57; *TYP* cxv and refs. cited, and ch.13, notes 74, 75, 76 below.

83. L. Fleuriot in HLCB 149. See A.T. Hatto (trans.), *Gottfried von Strassburg: Tristan* (Harmondsworth, 1960).

84. A.T. Hatto, op. cit., 313.

85. Ivor Arnold (ed.), *Le Roman de Brut* (Paris, 1938), i, 3693ff.; ii (Paris, 1940), 9101ff.

86. Geoffrey's *liber vetustissimus* had been brought *ex Britannia* and *Britannia* could refer to Brittany, as Geoffrey himself tells us *'Armoricum regnum quod nunc Britannia dicitur'*, or to the island of Britain, or to the British part of the island. Cf. C. Brett, 'Breton Latin Literature', *CMCS*, 18 (1989), 12.

87. J.E. Lloyd, 'Geoffrey of Monmouth', *EHR*, 57 (1942), 460-8. See further O.J. Padel, 'Geoffrey of Monmouth and Cornwall', *CMCS*, 8 (1984), 1-28.

88. See E.K. Chambers, *Arthur of Britain* (London, 1927, 1964), 18, 249; R.S. Loomis, 'The Legend of Arthur's Survival', ALMA 64-73; J.S.P. Tatlock, 'The English Journey of the Laon Canons', *Speculum*, 8 (1933), 454-65.

89. Giraldus Cambrensis, *Speculum Ecclesiae*, ch.ix (*Opera*, IV, 47); repr. Chambers, op.cit., 272.

90. J. Hammer, 'A Commentary on the *Prophetiae Merlini*', *Speculum*, 10 (1935), 3-30; *Speculum*, 15 (1940), 409-31, esp. 414-15.

91. See Gunter Lanczkowski, *Verborgene Heilbringer* (Darmstadt, 1977).

92. E.K. Chambers, op.cit., 110-12, 264-5, quoting from *Draco Normannicus*, ed. R. Howlett in *Chronicles of the Reigns of Stephen, Henry II and Richard I*, (R.S., vol.ii, 695).

93. On the *Prophetiae Merlini* see ch.5 above, and ALMA 75-80.

94. Ed. in *AB*, 38 (1928-9), 627-8. J.R.F. Piette points out (*LIC*, 8, 190) that in the orthography of the time when the manuscript was written a final *-ff* marked the nasal quality of the preceding vowel, and so *Guinglaff* may be the original of the name *Guinglain* of *Le Bel Inconnu* and other romances.

95. See Jean Marx, 'Wace et la Matière de Bretagne', *Mélanges Jean Frappier* (Genève, 1970), ii, 771-4; M. Houck, *The Sources of the Roman de Brut of Wace* (Berkeley, California; Cambridge, England, 1941).

96. On the ambiguity of 'Breton' in Wace see M. Houck, op. cit.

97. HLCB 118.

98. On the fountain of Barenton see Chantal Cornoche-Bourgne, 'La Fontaine de Barenton dans 'L'image du Monde" de Goppin de Metz', *Mélanges Charles Foulon* (1980), 37-48; Chadwick, *Early Brittany*, 299 and refs.; Tatlock, Leg. Hist., 468, is sceptical with regard to Wace's Celtic sources.

99. The evidence is considerable: see K. Jackson, ALMA, chs.1 and 2; Thomas Jones, 'The Early Evolution of the Legend of Arthur', *NMS*, 8 (1964), 8-21; A.O.H. Jarman, 'The Delineation of

Arthur in Early Welsh Verse' in K. Varty (ed.), *An Arthurian Tapestry* (Glasgow, 1981), 1-21; R. Bromwich, 'Concepts of Arthur', *SC*, 10/11 (1975-6), 163-81; ch.13 below and elsewhere in this book.

100. See refs. in n.87 above. Cf. Tatlock, Leg. Hist., 396-400.

101. On the reasons for believing that Geoffrey had it in mind after finishing the *HRB* to write some kind of history of Brittany — to translate (as he says) *librum de exulatione eorum* (XI, 10) — see Leg. Hist. 443.

102. L. Fleuriot, *Les Origines de la Bretagne* (Paris, 1980), 269-86; idem, 'Sur quatre textes bretons en latin, le *Liber vetustissimus* de Geoffrey de Monmouth et le séjour de Taliesin en Bretagne', *EC*, 18 (1981), 197-213; idem, 'Sur trois textes bretons en latin du Xe et du début du XIe siècle. Leur date, leur contenue et les sources de Geoffrey de Monmouth', *Archéologie en Bretagne*, 27 (1980), 16-27.

103. HLCB 117.

104. J.E. Lloyd, 'Geoffrey of Monmouth', *EHR*, 57 (1942), 460-8. As a witness to documents Geoffrey signed himself *Galfridus Arturus* which undoubtedly meant 'Geoffrey son of Arthur'.

105. E.M.R. Ditmas, 'A Reappraisal of Geoffrey of Monmouth's Allusions to Cornwall', *Speculum*, 48 (1973), 510-24; idem, 'Geoffrey of Monmouth and the Breton Families in Cornwall after the Norman Conquest', *THSC* (1977), 11-39; O.J. Padel, 'Geoffrey of Monmouth and Cornwall', *CMCS*, 8 (1984), 1-28. See ch.13 below.

106. *LIC*, 8 (1964-5), 186.

107. Ibid., 187; A.O.H. Jarman, 'Y Darlun o Arthur', *LIC*, 15 (1984-6), 3-17.

108. *RC*, 13 (1892), 483-4.

109. *B*, 17 (1956-8), 181-2; idem, 'Celtic Dynastic Themes and the Breton Lays', *ÉC*, 11 (1961), 464-6; *TYP*, 347-8. See ch.6, p. 148 above, and ch.13, p. 279 below.

110. Fleuriot in HLCB 98 refers to P.C. Bartrum's article 'Was there a British Book of Conquests?', *B*, 23 (1968), 1-6. Cf. B.F. Roberts, 'Geoffrey of Monmouth and Welsh Historical Tradition', *NMS*, 20 (1976), 29-40.

111. See L. Fleuriot, 'Old Breton Genealogies and Early British Traditions', *B*, 26 (1974-5), 1-6.

112. Claude Sterckx and Gwenael Le Duc, 'Les Fragments inédits de la Vie de Saint Goeznou', *AB*, 88 (1971), 227-85.

113. See Gw. Le Duc, 'L'Historia Britannica avant Geoffrey de Monmouth', *AB*, 79 (1972), 819-35.

114. HLCB 99. See also Fleuriot, 'Brittonica . . . 6. L'Historia Brittonum versificata . . .', *ÉC*, 19 (1982), 259-74.

115. On the Latin poem of Guillaume de Rennes see now R. Morris, 'The *Gesta Regum Britannie* of William of Rennes: An Arthurian Epic?', in R. Barber (ed.) *Arthurian Literature*, 6 (1986), 60-123.

116. I should like to thank the editors, in particular Professor A.O.H. Jarman for some additional references and Dr R. Bromwich for condensing parts of an otherwise too lengthy chapter.

13

FIRST TRANSMISSION TO ENGLAND AND FRANCE

Rachel Bromwich

IN the eleventh century the Normans extended their rule over Britain by means of dynastic marriages no less than by conquest. From as early as 1002 when King Ethelred (the 'Unready') married Emma,[1] daughter of Duke Richard I of Normandy, Norman influences had pervaded England through all kinds of commercial and familial channels. In due course Emma became the great-aunt of William the Conqueror, and Emma's half-Norman son Edward (the 'Confessor') spent years of exile in Normandy at the court of his uncle Duke Richard II. When later he became King of England he maintained his close contact with the duchy by encouraging Norman settlements in Britain, and by instigating trade relations with the duchy. (The Third Branch of the *Mabinogi*, the tale of Manawydan, gives us a glimpse of one such pre-Conquest Norman settlement at Hereford.)[2] In 1066, when William the Conqueror won the Battle of Hastings, his victory was achieved with the substantial aid of a mixed army of recruits drawn from Normandy, Brittany, Boulonnais, Flanders, Picardy and even further afield. It has been said that 'all Normans were French, but all Frenchmen in England were not Normans'.[3] Even though the Norman strain was undoubtedly the dominant one among the Conqueror's aristocratic companions and their followers, it is important to remember the mixed composition of the invading army as well as of the subsequent settlers who arrived in its wake. In Latin and in Anglo-Norman the terms *Franci, Franceis* served as a comprehensive description of the nationality of all these new arrivals in Britain, so that the generic term 'French' tended from the outset to obscure the separate ethnic and racial origins of the newcomers.[4]

It appears that the largest group of auxiliaries in the Conqueror's army was the one which came from Brittany, and that this had long-lasting consequences both in England and in Wales. According to F.M. Stenton: 'There is, in fact, hardly a county (in England) in which the Breton element is not found, and in some counties its influence was deep and permanent.'[5] William's followers were handsomely rewarded with gifts of land for the help they had given him at Hastings. Their assimilation into British life and culture was assisted by the fact that men from the same parts of

France were not grouped together in isolated settlements, but the lands given to them were often placed in separate holdings dispersed widely over the country. Often the Conqueror's most faithful followers were given property in places of strategic importance. One of these was the lordship of Richmond in Yorkshire, which William bestowed on Alan Rufus,[6] a cadet of the Breton ducal house, who may have been the leader of the Breton contingent which formed a third division of his army at Hastings.[7] The castle at Richmond was built by Alan Rufus and his brothers, and at that date its strategic importance as a stronghold against the Scots was no less than its importance had been four and a half centuries earlier, when Britons and English had fought so savagely for the possession of 'Catraeth'.[8] With the addition of separate territorial holdings in Lincolnshire and East Anglia, Alan Rufus became one of the most wealthy and powerful of landowners in the whole of England. Throughout the twelfth century Norman lords were frequently the possessors of land on both sides of the Channel.

From the late eleventh century Scotland also became progressively Normanized by a series of intermarriages between members of its ruling family and that of the Norman kings of England.[9] Before his death in 1087 William I had made forays into Scotland as far north as the Firth of Tay,[10] and into Wales as far west as St David's,[11] and he had established powerful Norman barons as custodians of the Marches of Wales, just as he had in the north of England for defence against the Scots. Both the Scottish King Malcolm Canmore and Rhys ap Tewdwr of Deheubarth had accepted William's overlordship (Gwynedd was the only Welsh kingdom which resisted subservience to the Normans for a further two centuries). By 1120 three of the four Welsh bishoprics were in Norman hands.[12] In the middle of the century the marriage of William's great-grandson Henry II to Eleanor of Aquitaine led to Henry's overlordship of an empire which encompassed not only England, Normandy, and Brittany,[13] but nearly the whole of France south of the Loire. The consequences which followed from this were of the greatest importance for the subject which is to be discussed in this chapter. Ireland, too, was brought within the bounds of Henry's Angevin empire (at least nominally) when Pope Adrian IV gave Henry his express permission for its conquest, and in due course Henry landed with his army at Waterford in 1171.[14]

On the Continent, as in Britain and Ireland, Normans and Britons lived in close proximity and were continually involved in each other's affairs. Ever since the original settlement of Normandy, which had taken place more than a century before the conquest of England, the Norman and Breton duchies had been closely interlocked both on hostile and on friendly terms. At the time when the Conqueror's army brought young Breton aristocrats and junior members of the ducal house to settle here with their followers, the Continental Britons still remembered their ancestral origins in Wales and Cornwall. Evidently a strong urge was felt by Normans and Bretons alike to nurture a sense of 'belonging' to their new country, by investigating its traditions, imaginatively re-creating its legendary history, and collecting its ancient stories and the Lives of its early church-founders, or 'saints'.[15]

The close connection between Normans and Bretons continued throughout the turbulent years of the twelfth century. In 1166 Henry II acquired direct rule over Brittany through the betrothal of his young son Geoffrey to the infant Duchess Constance of Brittany, daughter of Duke Conan IV. Their ill-fated offspring was a posthumous son named Arthur (1187-1203), whom the Bretons welcomed as their promised deliverer from foreign rule, the embodiment of the 'Breton hope' that Arthur, the long-awaited leader would return again to succour his people.[16]

This twelfth-century Norman world was the world in which the Arthurian Legend crystallized in the work of a series of Norman and Anglo-Norman chroniclers and poets — Geoffrey of Monmouth (whose Breton sympathies suggest that he may himself have been a Breton),[17] Wace — the Channel Islander who rendered Geoffrey's story into his own Norman dialect, the two 'Tristan' poets Béroul and Thomas, Marie de France (who lived and wrote partly in England — a fact which by itself may account for her self-styled epithet 'of France')[18] and the French poet from Champagne, Chrétien de Troyes. In addition to these the several French continuators of Chrétien's unfinished *Conte du graal* deserve important mention, particularly the anonymous author of the 'First Continuation', which contains the *Livre de Carados*.[19] At the hands of these poets, together with many tellers of tales by word of mouth, whose ephemeral work can only be deduced from scattered allusions, the Arthurian story evolved permanent and irreversible features: Arthur's birth, his far-flung conquests in foreign lands, his band of heroic companions (of whom a number were the subject of separate stories in their own right), his betrayal through domestic infidelity, and the disastrous battle which brought about his downfall, and with it the downfall of the Arthurian kingdom.

Geoffrey of Monmouth was the first to systematize this story, but it is evident that he derived many of its constituent features from pre-existing documents (such as genealogies) and oral traditions, whether these came from Wales, Cornwall, or Brittany.[20] Together with the poets just named, Geoffrey is our primary source for the transmission of Celtic tradition to the outside world. These authors are also, with rare exceptions, our only source of evidence for the wide diffusion among the different branches of the Celtic peoples themselves of the traditions relating to their ancestors. The subject-matter of their poems derived from Britain and from Brittany, but as the Arthurian legend developed it progressively incorporated new themes from every kind of additional source, whether from classical literature, international popular tales, or from the epic *chansons de geste* of France. The diffusion of the Arthurian stories was not coterminous with the limits of the Angevin Empire, for there is evidence that during this century, and occasionally even before 1100, the stories of Arthur had become known in Italy and Sicily, and before the twelfth century ended the Crusades had carried Arthur's fame to the other side of the Mediterranean.[21]

Earlier chapters in this book have shown that the portrayal of Arthur as the centre of a cycle of tales and the leader of a band of famous heroes had been in the process of gradual development in Welsh and in Welsh-Latin sources since even before the Norman Conquest. The relatively late date of the Welsh manuscripts means that there is at all stages an area of doubt as to the extent to which Welsh literature may really be described as indigenous, in the sense of being unaffected by cosmopolitan Latin learning or by the literature of neighbouring countries. The close connections between Britain and Normandy go back to a date which is quite as early as that for any evidence for the literary recording of the Welsh tales: prior to *c.* 1100 the antiquity of antecedent British oral tradition and written literature can at best be only a nebulous and uncharted area. Yet it is precisely this uncharted area of submerged and unrecorded tradition, whether before or after the Conquest, that must have provided the matrix for such fragments of Celtic narrative as were collected by the Normans, and were subsequently channeled by them into the poetry of the Angevin Empire and of France (to be found before 1170 as far south as in the poetry of the Troubadours),[22] and then into the literature of most other European countries.

Irrefutable evidence for the transmission of Celtic stories to the Normans at an early date is to be found in the large number of personal names of Brythonic derivation which have come down in the work of French and Latin writers. A number of these are clearly recognizable as belonging to Welsh traditional characters, whether or not these were independent heroes or heroes who had been previously associated with Arthur. Yet such easily identifiable names as *Yvain, Gauvain, Carados* are only a tantalizing, small minority in the midst of the great number of obscure personal names in the French Arthurian poems which may conceal the name of a traditional Brythonic hero who is no longer known to us, or one whose name is unrecognizable because of the degree of corruption it has suffered in the course of long transmission through many hands, and originally, perhaps, through oral channels alone. With place-names we are generally on less insecure ground, since these normally corroborate the Welsh-Cornish-Breton background of the tales, and present fewer difficulties. They are nearly all recognizable as the Anglo-Norman forms of place-names in Britain or in Brittany: *Caradigan, Caruent, Carlion, Tintagel, Breceliande, Carahès* (Carhaix), Nantes. A few, such as *Excestre* (Exeter), *Cestre*

(Chester), *Carduel* (Carlisle) and *Gleucester* (Gloucester) are in England, but are on the 'Celtic fringe'. Chrétien de Troyes has also an interesting group of Scottish names: *Danebroc/Tenebroc* (Edinburgh), *Galvoie* (Galloway), *Cotoatre* ('Scots' water, that is the Firth of Forth), *Orcanie* (Orkney), *Estregales* (Strathclyde).[23] Only a few of the above names originated with Geoffrey of Monmouth, however, and these were derived by the French poets from Wace, or another of the French renderings of *Historia Regum Britanniae* which has since been lost. But there is little reason to believe that the authors of these poems had any specific knowledge of the places in 'Arthurian' Britain to which they allude.[24]

We can say, however, that of the poets whose work has survived, Chrétien de Troyes has preserved many more than any other of the personal names of Brythonic legendary and mythical figures, all of whom have in his poems been absorbed into Arthur's entourage.[25] The process which had already begun in vernacular Welsh sources, of drawing the names of independent legendary figures into Arthur's orbit, is greatly extended in his work. Jean Frappier designated Chrétien 'the Ovid of a disintegrating Celtic mythology' (ALMA 164) and the implied allusion to the *Metamorphoses* is apt, even though it is impossible to be certain how far Chrétien himself was directly responsible for this great influx into his poems of Brythonic names. Chrétien's Arthurian ambience and Arthurian nomenclature may have derived its initial inspiration from just such intermediaries as those to whom he alludes disparagingly in a famous passage in *Erec et Enide*, when he describes his story as one *Que devant rois et devant contes/ Depecier et corronpre suelent/ Cil qui de conter vivre vuelent*,[26] 'a tale which those who wish to make their living by story-telling habitually fragment and corrupt in the presence of kings and counts'. However this may be, Chrétien drew upon Wace, or a parallel Anglo-Norman version of *HRB* (such as the lost *Brut* of Gaimar) for the framework of his Arthurian court, and for its more prominent figures. Names which appear in earlier forms in *HRB* are Keu, Kai, Kei (in *HRB* Caius), Bedoier (*Beduerus*), Gauvain (*Gualguanus*), Guenièvre (*Guenhuuara, Guenhumara*), Yvain fiz Uriens (*Hiwenus filius Uriani*),[27]Pandragon (*Utherpendragon*). With these names Geoffrey of Monmouth had established for all time the nuclear Arthurian court, as it continued to be delineated by every author who followed him — a permanent group which could be progressively expanded as each new story demanded a new hero, even if such a hero existed for the purposes of that one story alone.

Yet this nuclear group of names, initially derived from *HRB*, represents only a small proportion of the number of recognizable names from antecedent Brythonic heroic and mythical sources which Chrétien, his contemporaries and successors drew into their poetry. By far the greatest number of these names are found in Chrétien's earliest poem, *Erec et Enide* (c. 1170). Examples of names in this poem which have identifiable antecedents in Welsh sources are *Yder fiz Nut* (Edern fab Nud in *Culhwch*, CO 1.182, *Hiderus filius Nucii* in *HRB*), *Gi(r)flet fiz Do* (Gilfaethwy fab Don in the *Mabinogi*, PKM 67); *Karadues/Carados Briebras* (Caradawc Freichfras in the Triads and elsewhere). The first two of these — in addition to *Yvain fiz Uriens* (<*Hiwenus filius Uriani* in *HRB*) — are especially interesting, as being the only instances in which the names of father and son combined together have survived the transition from a Welsh into a French context. As has often been pointed out, *Karadues Briebras* has an interest of a different kind, in that his epithet preserves a corrupt form of Caradawc's original Welsh epithet *Brecbras* (*Breichfras*), 'Strong Arm'.[28] Similarly Geoffrey of Monmouth's *Uther Pendragon* retains the epithet 'Chief of Warriors' which had previously been bestowed on him in the poem 'Pa gur' (ch.2, pp. 40-6 above; cf. *TYP* 520).

These names have come down in one or other of the two Arthurian court-lists which Chrétien introduces in *Erec et Enide* (lines 1691-750; 1934-2008), or they are found elsewhere in the same poem. Certain names recur individually in Chrétien's later poems, but nowhere else are they found in so great a profusion as in *Erec et Enide*. The first of these lists is given on the occasion of Enide's initial reception at Arthur's court, the second on the occasion of her wedding, held at Arthur's court at the following Pentecost. Both lists are reminiscent of the extended Arthurian Court-list in *Culhwch ac Olwen* (*CO* ll.175-372), and though there is virtually no overlap between the names in Chrétien's lists and those in *Culhwch*, certain structural similarities can be observed between them: numerical exaggeration (four men named *Yvain*, ll.1706-9), with elements of farce, and echoes of mythology — a good example is Chrétien's citation of one of the least-known of mythical Welsh figures, *Maheloas . . . Li sire de l'Isle de Voirre* (*Erec et Enide*, ll.1946-7), that is *Melwas*,[29] who is known in Welsh sources as a legendary ruler at Glastonbury: Chrétien attributes to *l'Isle de Voirre*, 'the Island of Glass', features which elsewhere characterize the Celtic Otherworld scene, 'an island where thunder is not heard, no lightning strikes or tempest blows, no toads or snakes stay, and it is never too hot or too cold' (*Erec et Enide*, ll.1946-51). Elsewhere in this poem a character named *Mabonagrain* plays a significant part as both prisoner and guardian of an enchanted garden-prison: this name must conceal in corrupt form the identity of *Mabon fab Modron*, the Romano-British deity and the mythical prisoner of *Culhwch ac Olwen*.[30]

In his review of ALMA (*ÉC*, 9 (1960), 257) and again more forcefully in his 'Monde Brittonique et Matière de Bretagne' (*ÉC*, 10 (1963), 483-4) the late Jean Marx denied that there was any appreciable amount of two-way traffic between Brittany and Wales in the field of narrative ('Rien ne permet de penser qu'un rôle de création ait appartenu a la Petite-Bretagne') and he points out that Arthur, the royal British hero and supposed descendant of the Breton founder Conan Meriadoc,[31] received far more lasting fame in Brittany than did either Conan or any other of the early legendary Breton rulers such as Gradlon Mor, Guiomar, Cunomorus, who figure in the *lais bretun* or in the Lives of the Breton saints. The substitution of the traditional Welsh or Cornish hero Geraint ab Erbin for Erec (*Gueroc*) in the Welsh tale cognate with Chrétien's poem is significant in this respect, and it has been discussed above (ch.6, p. 148). Some years ago I conjectured that the name of the heroine *Enide* derived from *Bro (W)ened*, 'the land of **Ened*',[32] attested as an old name for the district of Vannes (the old tribal territory of the *Veneti*), which is also regularly named (after Erec) *Broerec*. The name of Erec's wife was thus transferred, from an original in Breton or in French, by the composer of the Welsh version of the tale, to become that of the wife of Geraint. If this is the true explanation of the name of *Enid(e)*, such a return to Wales of the name of a legendary or mythical figure would constitute a wholly exceptional occurrence, as Jean Marx himself recognized it to be, while giving it his support (*ÉC*, 10 (1963), 482). Some further support for this suggestion is however to be derived from the fact that memories of other legendary founders of the Breton kingdoms — Cornouailles (*Grallon Mor*) and Léon (*Guiamar, Guigemar*)[33] — have come down in the anonymous Breton lays (and one in Marie de France's lay of *Guigemar*). By alluding to *Graislemiers de Fine Posterne. . . Et Guigomars, ses frère (Erec et Enide*, 1952-5), Chrétien shows that he too knew of these lays or of their sources. But there is no known instance other than *Enid(e)* in which a distinctively Breton mythical figure has been adopted into Welsh tradition at the same time that the name of her 'husband' Erec/Gueroc, the ruler of Broerec and conqueror of Nantes, was decisively rejected in favour of the insular hero Geraint fab Erbin. Apart from the historical Breton duke Alan Fergant,[34] who has become a legendary figure in a single Welsh triad (which portrays him *en route* for the Battle of Camlan), early Welsh sources seem to have been satisfied with employing the indeterminate generic name 'Emyr Llydaw'[35] which means 'a ruler (ie. 'some ruler or other') of Brittany' to denote an unspecified compatriot from across the sea. The surviving genealogies of the Breton 'saints' or founders of the Church in Brittany, tend to concentrate on their traditional links with progenitors of royal birth in Wales, Cornwall, or the 'Old North' rather than with ancestors in Brittany.[36]

Some names were cited above from Chrétien's *Erec et Enide* as belonging to recognizable figures of earlier Welsh tradition. Though *Yder fils Nut/Hiderus filius Nucii/Edern fab Nudd* was known to Geoffrey of Monmouth, the following Arthurian figures were known neither to him nor to his adapters: *Maheloas/Melwas*,

Mabonagrain/Mabon, Gi(r)flet fis Do/Gilfaethwy fab Don, Caradues (Carados)
Briebras/Caradawc Freichfras. Each of these characters plays only a very minor
part in extant Welsh sources, yet *Yder* and *Carados* are both the subject of complete
poems by Chrétien's successors, in the romances of *Yder*[37] and the *Livre de Carados*.
The French poems suggest that very much more may once have been known and told
about these heroes in Wales, and that both are figures who have declined in status in
the existing Welsh records. This points to a very early date (before 1100?) for the
transmission of their names, and the vestiges of narratives concerning them to
Brittany. Evidence of a similar kind is to be deduced from the Brythonic names
preserved by Chrétien's near contemporaries, the 'Tristan' poets Béroul and Thomas.
Both preserve the interesting forms *Brengain (Brengven, Brengian, Brigvain)* as the
name of Isolt's maid-servant.   This is the Welsh *Branwen*, familiar from the
Mabinogi, but completely unknown in Brittany, and unknown also in any other Welsh
source.   Like the name of *Tristan* itself, it must have been derived from an Old
Welsh written intermediary *Branguen*. Béroul also offers us the names of Tristan's
hunting hound *Hu(s)dent*, 'of the good teeth', and of Tristan's seneschal *Dinas de*
Lidan — evidently a misunderstanding of the compound noun and adjective *dinas*
lydan, 'broad fortress'.[38]

.The appearance in French sources of several other rare and enigmatic names
from Welsh tradition seems also to point to their early transmission into French.   In
Erec et Enide three references are made to Gauvain's horse *le Guingalet/Gringalet*
— a name which (allowing for the variation between *guin/kein*) undoubtedly
corresponds to the name of Gwalchmai's horse *Kein Calet*, the 'Hard-Backed',[39] in the
Triads of Horses.   It is remarkable that this name for Gwalchmai's horse does not
appear in *Geraint fab Erbin*, nor anywhere else in the Welsh tales.   Another name
from the Triads of Horses is that of *Lluagor*,[40] horse of Caradawc Freichfras, which
reappears in the *Livre de Carados* as *Lorzagor*, the foal born at one birth with his
master *Caradues Briebras*, together with a boar named *Tortain*.[41]   In the earlier of
Chrétien's two court-lists we find the name *Torz, le fiz le roi Arés* (*Erec* 1.1728):
both *Torz* and *Tortain* have been recognized as corruptions of the name of the
monster boar *Twrch Trwyth* in *Culhwch ac Olwen*.   Several French sources make
allusion to the savage *Cath Paluc*,[42] a monster cat known from a Welsh poem and
from a triad (ch.2, pp. 45-6) and who reappears in a Norman poem of the late twelfth
century as *Le Capalu*.   In the poem this monster cat is said to have killed Arthur in a
bog (French *palu*): evidently this is a variant (and possibly an early variant) of the
more familiar account given of Arthur's end in *HRB*, which is reproduced with
romantic accretions in the later prose romances.

The early transmission of these names into Anglo-Norman and later into French sources appears thus to have been through both written and oral channels. A few names beside those already mentioned show orthographical evidence of having been early written borrowings: *Caradauc Brecbras* (*TYP* 299-300), *Yvain* (*TYP* 480), *Guenhuiuar* (*TYP* 381), but oral transmission, at least in the first instance, is likely to have been mainly responsible for the large number of enigmatic and unrecognizable name-forms which proliferate in the poems of Chrétien and, to a lesser degree, in those of his successors. A number of these may belong to Welsh heroic and mythical figures of whom all other trace has been lost. We would not be able to recognize the names of the animals given above in their French forms, were it not for the unique survivals of their Welsh prototypes in the very few instances which have been quoted.

All this serves to indicate how great must have been the quantity of names and stories which were passed into Normandy and thence into France during the eleventh or twelfth century, perhaps in some instances even earlier. The names of certain originally independent, traditional (and some, at least, historical) figures who later became leading Arthurian heroes, such as Owain/*Yvain*, Gwalchmai/*Gauvain*, Peredur/*Perceval*, Drystan/*Tristan* and (I venture to suggest) Caradawc Freichfras/*Carados Briebras*,[43] and perhaps the mythical Edern fab Nudd/*Yder filius Nut*, may even have been carried overseas at as early a date as was Arthur's own fame (see ch.12, p. 261), though the French romances rarely seem to preserve any possible traces of original insular traditions concerning them. This is hardly surprising, since it is exceptional for names and stories to pass in combination from one culture into another: in the field of Arthurian romance, as in that of folklore, it is far more usual for story-themes to move about freely, and to become freshly associated with a succession of characters.[44] The Brythonic names themselves are the survival of an oral literature which was presumably still very much alive in Britain in the eleventh and early twelfth centuries, when parts of it were carried overseas to Brittany. This mainly oral literature, only rarely and partially committed to writing, must once have been fully comparable in richness and variety with that which has come down from early Ireland.[45] Its sparse traces are preserved only in the most provocative of allusions: in the Welsh Triads, in the Stanzas of the Graves, in the Arthurian Court-list in *Culhwch ac Olwen*, and — not to be forgotten or neglected — in the wealth of personal names which Chrétien de Troyes, his contemporaries and successors, have handed down to us in French and Latin.[46] This body of names constitutes the most important and incontrovertible evidence for the Celtic contribution to Arthurian romance. As Léon Fleuriot phrased it, 'Ce n'est que par des fragments en Latin ou des noms propres que la Bretagne (i.e. Brittany) connaissait des variantes des traditions connues outre Manche. La littérature de la Matière de Bretagne le montre surabondamment.'[47]

II

In chapters 6, 7 and 8 of this book the three tales of *Geraint*, *Owain*, and *Peredur* have been considered in relation to the continuous Welsh literary tradition, and as primarily expressive of the style and idiom of the works which had preceded them, in particular the *Four Branches of the Mabinogi*. Here it will be necessary to discuss these same tales, however briefly, in relation to their French cognates, the three poems of Chrétien de Troyes, *Erec et Enide*, *Yvain*, and *Perceval: Le Conte du graal*. Each of the three pairs of stories relates the career of a traditional Brythonic hero: *Yvain* (Owain) and *Perceval* (Peredur) both emanate from the 'Old North', while *Erec* is a Breton hero, supplanted in the Welsh tale by the Dumnonian Geraint fab Erbin, and given a new orientation in the south-western peninsula of Britain. The audience of the Welsh tales might be expected to have had sufficient previous knowledge to enable them to recognize the identity of these heroes, perhaps regarding them as in some sense ancestral figures. Though differences in style and structure preclude any likelihood that the Welsh versions, like the French poems, were composed by a single author,[48] they nevertheless betray an awareness of external literary models[49] and, to varying degrees (greatest perhaps in *Geraint*) of an underlying source in the French language.[50] But this source need not necessarily have been the corresponding poem by Chrétien de Troyes.

We have Chrétien's own testimony that he knew of anterior oral versions of *Erec*, and that he obtained the story of *Perceval* from a book given to him by the Count of Flanders: in each of his poems Chrétien claims to be retelling a tale which is already in existence. Either oral traditions or literary redactions of the tales in Anglo-Norman could as well have been at the disposal of the Welsh narrators of the tales as they were of Chrétien himself. While the Welsh versions generally follow the same sequence of incidents as the French, it was pointed out above (pp. 166, 176) that there are instances in both *Owain* and *Peredur* of deviation from the French versions in the order in which certain incidents are presented: such deviations could easily be explained if the Welsh author were summarizing from memory a story which he had heard narrated or read aloud.[51] Opinions may always diverge as to whether the Welsh tales are the more likely to be directly indebted to Chrétien's poems, or whether both Welsh and French versions have derived their common features from earlier redactions of the tales which have since been lost. B.F. Roberts[52] envisages Chrétien's poems as having been the actual source of *Owain*, *Geraint*, and *Peredur*, their selection by the Welsh redactors being dictated by the 'receivability' of these tales for a Welsh audience, since they related to recognizable traditional figures. In contrast, Chrétien's *Lancelot: Le Chevalier de la Charette* would have been utterly alien to such an audience: Lancelot was untraditional, and probably an invented character (*TYP* 415). Another suggestion, put forward some years ago by R.M. Jones,[53] is that the three stories were evolved in a bilingual milieu near the south Wales border (Glamorgan, Monmouth or Archenfield) in the early post-Conquest period, a milieu in which they could have been narrated either in Welsh or in French as the occasion demanded. Such a situation would suit well with the activities of the *latimarii* or highly-placed professional interpreters, to whose activities on the Welsh border the late Dr Bullock-Davies directed attention.[54] But with respect to the three tales as they have come down, it is a theory better suited to the diffuse construction of *Peredur* than to the more closely-knit sequel of events in *Owain* and *Geraint*. The 'common source' theory has received a good deal of support in recent years, but it has usually been taken to imply a common written source, rather than impromptu narration of the stories. The closeness in the order of incidents with which each one of the three stories complements its pair in the other language would be difficult to explain except on the assumption that both versions are retellings of a written original. Such an original must surely have been in Norman or Anglo-Norman, although Chrétien's poems appear to derive ultimately from Breton sources, in which insular traditions had previously been acclimatized — in addition, of course, to the 'Arthur's court' framework inherited from *HRB via* Wace. But the question of indebtedness to earlier recensions could well have been different in the case of each of the three tales: *Peredur* is perhaps the most likely to have included Chrétien's poem as one among its several sources.[55]

Certain resemblances in design between the three tales are nevertheless unquestionable, as has frequently been pointed out.[56] Each of the three treats of the growth and development of an individual hero, and conducts him to maturity through a series of trials or tests. *Erec/Geraint* and *Yvain/Owain* treat of the conflict between the hero's love for his wife and his loyalty to Arthur and to the fellowship of the court. *Peredur/Perceval* illustrates the theme (subsequently to be repeated more than once in Arthurian romance)[57] of the awkward initiate's first arrival at the court; on the other hand it is implied that Erec/Geraint and Yvain/Owain are heroes who are already established there. The careers of the two latter pairs follow along similar lines, in that both experience marriage, estrangement from their wives, and eventual reconciliation.

At a deeper lever there has been some measure of agreement in distinguishing the pan-Celtic myth of the 'Sovereignty'[58] as the ultimate but submerged theme underlying all three stories. Irish sources[59] which date from very early times embody the belief that a ruler was conceived to be mated to the tutelary goddess of his kingdom, whether this kingdom was Ireland herself, one of her *tuatha* or sub-kingdoms, or a lesser lordship. As Proinsias Mac Cana has shown,[60] this myth has pervaded Irish literature through all periods of Irish history, virtually down to the present day. It may take one or other of two customary forms (though in the earliest Irish versions the two are combined): one is the 'Transformed Hag' who bestows sovereignty on a destined ruler after having been restored to beauty by sexual intercourse or by a kiss, and the other is the hunt for a white animal (usually a stag) who may itself be a manifestation of the transformed 'Sovereignty'.[61]

If it were not for the very striking prototypes for this theme which are found in early Irish sources, it seems unlikely that the Welsh tales or their French cognates would ever have been interpreted as incorporating the myth of the 'Sovereignty'. The significance of the Irish prototypes comes out most clearly in relation to the figure of *Enid(e)* in the two cognate versions of her story. As indicated above (p. 279) they invite the conclusion that *Enid/Enide* was once conceived to be the tutelary goddess of the eastern Breton kingdom of Bro Weroc (Bro Wened), over which her spouse, the kingdom's historical/legendary founder Erec (*Gueroc*) is crowned king at Nantes, his capital city, at the end of Chrétien's poem. Significantly, Enid(e)'s name remains undivulged in both versions right up until the occasion of her wedding to Erec/Geraint.

The parallel survival of the theme of the 'Sovereignty' in the Welsh tales *Peredur* (*Perceval*) and (more doubtfully) in *Owain (Yvain)* has been advocated by several writers, most notably by Glenys Goetinck.[62] But this is not to suggest that the significance of the ancient myth was in any way recognizable to the redactors of these tales, either in their Welsh or their French form, nor is it even likely that it was comprehended by the authors of any of their hypothetical sources. Mac Cana has suggested that the implications of the Sovereignty theme were still in some sense intelligible to early Irish story-tellers.[63] But however this may be, it is inconceivable that Chrétien or the authors of the Welsh tales had any comprehension of the significance of this theme. The myth was so old and so deeply submerged that its meaning had been lost and forgotten long before the composition of the extant tales and poems, though Mac Cana observes in relation to them that 'certain basic concepts seem to have survived the social system which had generated them'. One is led to conclude that these stories have come down through such an infinite number of retellings as to recall the famous words of the poet Wace: *Tant ont li conteor conte/ Et li fableor tant fable/ Pour lor contes ambeleter/ que tout ont feit fables sanbler*. But if the myth of the 'Sovereignty' has left its traces on the three tales as they have been transmitted in both languages it must have been present in their ultimate Brythonic sources, whatever these may have been. Sometimes the underlying mythical features are more clearly recognizable in Chrétien's poems, and sometimes in the cognate Welsh tales. And we saw above (p. 279 and n.33) that significant corroborative evidence for the existence of this theme in a Brythonic milieu is to be found in the Breton lays which relate to the foundation of the early Breton kingdoms.

The surviving traces of the 'Sovereignty' in these stories have led some investigators to detect their traces elsewhere in early Welsh literature.[64] Whether or not these further instances are felt to be convincing, the twin themes of the Transformed Hag and, more frequently, the Chase of the White Stag, recur throughout Arthurian romance as prologues to magical adventures. Indeed I would class them as the most significant of the Celtic motifs which were destined to develop into 'Arthurian commonplaces.' Such themes were originally highly meaningful in terms of pagan Celtic religious belief, but they possessed a momentum of their own, and this has brought about their continued reappearance in Arthurian literature, in however garbled and sometimes even distorted a form. It is not too much to say that the persistence of such obliterated themes of Celtic mythology has contributed largely to defining the special character of Arthurian romance. The evocation of ancient concepts which were no longer fully comprehended has constituted its most powerful attraction.

Other such 'Arthurian commonplaces' are not far to seek. These are of necessity more abundantly illustrated by reference to early Irish literature than to that of Wales, and for reasons of the earlier and more abundant preservation of Irish tales which are by now well recognized.[65] A common fund of narrative circulated among the Celtic nations, and this included international tale-types and story-motifs, while the mutual inheritance of Celtic pre-Christian sacred beliefs is sufficient explanation for the similarity of mythical concepts which have come down in early sources from both Ireland and Wales. The fact that the theme of the Sovereignty is more fully and clearly exemplified in Ireland than in Wales is not an adequate reason to conclude that there has been direct borrowing from Irish into Welsh sources: such borrowing can never be proven, nor can it rightly be assumed.

Even though so much of lost Welsh tradition can only be inferred from the recording of names and allusions in lists and catalogues such as those which have been alluded to above (p. 281), yet the *Four Branches of the Mabinogi* preserve a selection of motifs which may be regarded as emblematic of the richness of myth and story from which these tales originally sprang. At the outset of the First Branch the chase for a white stag preludes a magical adventure; later we encounter the theme of love for a person who has not been seen (the supernatural Rhiannon for the 'mortal' Pwyll), the 'unspecified boon', the supernatural time-lapse, a magic mist and a magic fountain, a magic cauldron of rebirth, the Waste Land, transformations of men and women into animals and a bird. And there is the ever-present Otherworld, which may materialize in unexpected places, and which men may visit, and encounter delights which are familiar from Celtic accounts given elsewhere of *Annwfn, insula Avallonis, Ynys Afallach*,[66] or *Magh Mell* — sometimes returning with Otherworld treasures (see ch.3, p. 87 above). Some of these motifs contain in them the germ of later 'Arthurian commonplaces'.[67] On the other hand the personal names of the *Mabinogi* have left little trace on Arthurian romance in any contexts which are recognizable (I have referred above to Chrétien's perpetuation of the name of *Branwen* and *Gi(r)flet fils Do* = Gilfaethwy fab Don). But one possible instance of the retention of a name in combination with a story-element from the *Mabinogi* is that of *Bendigeidfran*, who in the *Mabinogi Branwen* was wounded in the foot with a poisoned spear. Some have seen in Bendigeidfran the prototype of Chrétien's 'Fisher King' who in the poem of *Perceval: Le Conte du graal* (1.3509-13) was incapacitated by a disabling wound through the thighs: later versions of the *Graal* story (such as the *Didot Perceval*) actually give the name of *Brons* (with variants) to the 'Fisher King'. In Cai's churlish behaviour to Peredur/Perceval and subsequently to other new arrivals at Arthur's court, it is difficult not to see an ironic echo of Cai's ungracious reception of the young Culhwch on his arrival there (*CO* ll.134-5), and Chrétien's presentation of *Mabonagrain* (unnamed in *Geraint*) as a self-imposed prisoner in an enchanted garden must ultimately recall the mythical Welsh prisoner Mabon fab Modron of *Culhwch* and a triad (see n.30 above). But these are exceptions: on the whole, specific attributes which in later romances become attached consistently to Arthurian characters are hard to trace back to Welsh sources. The predominantly Brythonic character of the Celtic names in Arthurian romance offers far more cogent evidence for the Brythonic source of Arthurian narrative than do such migratory story-patterns in themselves.

Some further corroboration for the insular genesis of Arthurian romance is to be derived from a fact whose significance it is hard to assess — it may, after all, be no more than a mere coincidence, or an expression of the medieval fondness for asserting prior authority. The only man whose name has come down as having told Arthurian stories on the Continent in the twelfth century was a Welshman, named in the Second Continuation of Chrétien's *Conte du graal* (c. 1200)[68] as *Bleheris. . . qui fu nés et angenuis en Galles* 'who was born and nurtured in Wales', and who is said to have related to a Count of Poitiers[69] stories about the Arthurian quest for the *Graal*, on which he was regarded as a supreme authority. Further testimony to his wide knowledge on such matters (if, as is generally belived, the allusion is to the same man) has been adduced from the words of the Anglo-Norman poet Thomas. About the mid-twelfth century, Thomas cited a certain *Breri* as his authority (not necessarily received at first hand) for the best version of the *Tristan* story. He further praises Breri with the tribute *ky solt les gestes e les cuntes/ de tuz les reis, de tuz les cuntes/ ki orent esté en Bretaingne,* 'who knew the deeds and the stories of all the kings and all the counts who were formerly in Britain'.[70]

As long as a century ago both Gaston Paris[71] and John Rhŷs[72] proposed the identification of *Bleheris/Breri* with the *famosus ille Bledhericus fabulator qui tempora nostra paulo praevenit,* to whom Giraldus Cambrensis attributes a joke about the Carmarthen coracle-fishermen.[73] This is an attractive speculation, but unfortunately it can be no more than a speculation, for although the Welsh name *Bleddri* ('king of wolves', 'wolf-like king') is easily discernible as underlying all three of these name-forms (*Bleddri* being easily corrupted to *Bleri* and then by assimilation to *Breri*), the name is not by itself sufficiently distinctive to be understood as denoting any specific individual of the early twelfth century, the period which is indicated by these references.[74] Yet it is possible to take the suggested identification a step further. In 1912 W.J. Gruffydd proposed to identify Breri/Bledericus with a certain *Bleddri ap Kadifor ap Gollwyn,* whose name is preserved in a genealogy.[75] A certain *bledri latimer* ('interpreter') *ap Kadifor*[76] is listed in a Carmarthen cartulary as having made a gift of land to the Priory of St John at Carmarthen about the year 1130, and he is said to have been the guardian of a nearby castle for King Henry I). Evidently Bleddri was a supporter of Norman interests in the neighbourhood of Carmarthen in the early years of the century, and the date would certainly agree with his conjectural identification with the *Bledhericus* of Giraldus — whether or not he could also be the *Breri/Bleheris* of the poets. In her essay referred to above (n.54) Dr Bullock-Davies has amply demonstrated the high status held by the *latimarii* or professional interpreters on the Welsh Marches in the century following the Conquest. And she emphasizes:

> It is necessary to try to distinguish between first transmission and subsequent repetition. The latter can be regarded as primarily the work of minstrels, but it is to be questioned whether they were generally responsible for transmitting the tales in the first place, because original transmission of Celtic story presupposes translation; and if minstrels were the only people responsible for transmission, then it has to be assumed that they were very capable linguists.
>
> (*Professional Interpreters*, p.5)

What we know of Bleddri *lladmerydd* or *latimarius* suggests that he and men like him could have been key figures in the transmission of Arthurian stories, as representatives of a class of highly trained and cultured professionals, capable of translating both into and out of their own first language, and therefore in the best possible position to act as liaison officers on every kind of level between the Normans and their neighbours, whether in England, Wales, Scotland, or Brittany.

Others have cited the evidence for the bilingualism of the Continental Bretons, which resulted from their long and intimate contact with Normandy on both hostile and friendly terms, and they have referred to the enhancement this received in the ninth century when the kingdom of Bro Weroc extended Breton rule eastwards to encompass a large tract of French-speaking territory, so that besides Vannes it included the towns of Rennes and Nantes.[77] Much bilingualism must have still existed among the post-Conquest Breton settlers who came to Britain in the wake of the Conqueror's ally Alan Rufus and his like. These Bretons settled in England, in Cornwall, on the Welsh Marches and in south-east Wales (for instance at Monmouth), and, as Giraldus assures us, they could have communicated easily enough with the indigenous inhabitants in their own language. The episode of the monks of Laon (pp. 49, 262 above) is one of several reminders that Brittany retained a vivid interest in the subject of Arthur in the early twelfth century, and, if we are to believe the evidence of Chrétien and his contemporaries, this interest brought with it a wide knowledge of Welsh legend concerning other heroes besides Arthur — Owain, Peredur, Drystan (Tristan), Gwalchmai, Caradawc — whose fame had in the course of the previous century become established in Brittany, and had developed there, frequently to become the genesis of new stories which in their turn were carried back to Wales and to Cornwall.

But there is not any direct evidence that the Bretons made use of their bilingualism for the purpose of story-telling in French. Chrétien alludes from time to time to the *conteurs* who retailed his stories, but he does not anywhere describe these as Bretons.[78] The great emphasis which has been placed on Breton *conteurs* is due to a misunderstanding which is increased by the complete ambiguity as to the meaning of the words *Bretaigne* and *Bretun* in twelfth-century usage: they may equally well relate either to Britain or to Brittany. *Conteur* and *jongleur* are presumably in this context the French equivalents of the Welsh term *cyfarwydd* in its extended meaning of 'story-teller'[79] (originally 'guide, expert', etc.) — a word which has none of the slightly disparaging connotations with which Chrétien and Wace sometimes endow the corresponding French words. That there must have been Breton equivalents to the Welsh *cyfarwyddiaid* goes without saying: we have the whole corpus of Chrétien's Arthurian names and stories as evidence for this. In further support for it we have the evidence brought forward by Fleuriot and quoted in ch.12 (p.256) for the existence of poets and minstrels of different grades in eleventh- and twelfth-century Brittany; men whose names have actually come down and are now accessible to us.[80] The Bretons were particularly famous for their 'lays', to which Chrétien alludes (*Erec et Enide*, 1.6187-8) among his sources, and as to the nature of which there has been much discussion. Fleuriot points out that in certain respects the lays are nearer to their Celtic origins than are the romances, and we have seen that this is true with respect to their preservation of dynastic myths concerning the foundation of the Breton kingdoms. And, quite apart from mythology, certain of the lays (*Bisclavret* and *Le Fresne*) exhibit narrative devices which are akin to those employed for similar effect in the *Mabinogi*: the importunate wife's questioning of her husband, which leads to his destruction (cf. Blodeuwedd in *Math*), the vassals' pressure on their lord to take a wife from whom to obtain an heir, and the foundling's rich clothing as indicative of noble origin (in *Le Fresne*, as in *Pwyll*). But in spite of their thematic importance with respect to lost Breton literature, the lays are only marginally 'Arthurian', and they played no part in disseminating Arthurian nomenclature. Various scholars have urged, no doubt rightly, that the *lais bretun* were chiefly famous as musical compositions, and that their narrative content was merely auxiliary.[81]

Who, then, were the primary transmitters of Brythonic stories to the outside world? Evidently this transmission took place in considerable profusion on both popular and learned levels. For the popular, oral dissemination of the stories we may conclude that informal social contacts were in large measure responsible: in addition to the cultural results of intermarriages, stories would have been carried abroad by merchants, soldiers, Crusaders, and, no doubt (remembering Chaucer), by pilgrims on their extended travels. On the slightly more formal, but no less important level, of literate transmission, we have the potential importance of interpreters such as Bleddri. Not all of the *latimarii* were ecclesiastics, though no doubt some of them were, and ecclesiastics must have played a very important part, if not the crucial part, in the dissemination of Arthurian stories. The Lives of the Welsh saints offer vital testimony to the bringing together of secular and ecclesiastical traditions under religious auspices. Although their portrayal of Arthur tends to be ironic (see ch.3, pp. 82-3) the Arthur they depict is at times highly reminiscent of the Arthur of *Culhwch ac Olwen*. (The Life of St Illtud[82] portrays its hero as Arthur's first cousin, drawing on a genealogical fiction which we find also in *Culhwch*.) Geoffrey of Monmouth was the first of a line of Norman clerics who occupied themselves in the task of collecting and transmitting both secular and ecclesiastical Brythonic tradition in a literate and learned milieu. Others, such as Geoffrey's contemporary Caradoc of Llancarfan, were primarily concerned with the traditions of the Welsh saints, but in recording them they drew to a considerable extent on secular traditions.[83] These ecclesiastical collectors and writers were a very important medium — perhaps, in the last resort, the most important of all — for the collection and transmission of early secular Arthurian material to England and to the European Continent.

Inevitably we are drawn back to the contemplation of the widely extended

Norman and Angevin Empire of the twelfth century, whose cultural centre was to be found in the courts of Henry II and of Eleanor of Aquitaine, whether in England or at Poitiers.[84] Political alliances, intermarriage, Norman conquests and the Crusades, all enhanced the need and the desire for movement, from Britain to Europe, and from north to south of the Continent. Extended travel carried in its wake the Arthurian stories and the men of every kind who propagated them; from Wales to Flanders and to Poitiers, from Scotland to Brittany, from Britain to the Alps and to Italy and Sicily. Norman-French was the *lingua franca* of this whole world; and in the twelfth century it was a French dialect of considerable cultural prestige.[85] Before the century began Brythonic traditions from both Devon-Cornwall and the 'Old North' were in process of being drawn together in Wales, particularly in the south, the area of Wales first to be Normanized. Though it is right to regard insular Britain as the birthplace of the Arthurian Legend,[86] the colony settled by the Britons in Armorica was at least as much responsible as Norman and Angevin Britain for its development. As the saga developed, the much-travelled Bretons were in a particularly favourable position to blend new themes and new stories with the names of Arthur and others of the old traditional insular heroes which the emigrants had at various periods carried with them overseas. Both in Brittany itself, and after the Norman Conquest in Britain as well, the Bretons enjoyed an especial advantage in the field of transmission by reason of their consequent ease of communication, not only with their Norman neighbours, but also with their Welsh and Cornish-speaking compatriots in this Island.

NOTES:

1. F.M. Stenton, *Anglo-Saxon England* (Oxford, 1943, repr. 1971), 379; H.R. Loyn, *The Norman Conquest* (London, 1967), 50-1. It was on the basis of his collateral descent from Emma that William I placed his rather tenuous claim to the English throne; see M. Chibnall, *Anglo-Norman England* (Oxford, 1986), 55, and cf. J. Le Patourel, *Feudal Empires: Norman and Plantagenet* (London, 1984), VI, 4.

2. *PKM* xxxiv, 52; HW 363.

3. R.L. Graeme Ritchie, *The Normans in Scotland* (Edinburgh 1954), xviii-xix; Cf. Stenton, *Anglo-Saxon England*, 629-30.

4. F.M. Stenton, *The First Century of English Feudalism* (Oxford, 1932), 29; Ritchie, *The Normans*, xx.

5. Stenton, *First Century*, 25. He draws attention to the long survival of some Breton personal names in one such settlement in Lincolnshire. On William's land-gifts to Normans and Bretons who had helped him at Hastings see also Stenton, *Anglo-Saxon England*, 628-9, and cf. ch.12, p. 259 above. For Breton settlers in Cornwall see E.M.R. Ditmas, *WHR*, 6 (1973), 451-61; ibid., 'Breton Settlers in Cornwall after the Norman Conquest', *THSC* (1977), 11-39 (citing some Cornish/Breton personal names).

6. On Alan Rufus see Stenton, *First Century*, 24-5; and a note by J.F.A. Mason, *EHR*, 78 (1963), 703-4. He belonged to a junior branch of the Breton ducal dynasty, though he has sometimes been wrongly identified (as shown by Loth, *RC*, 13 (1892), 491) with his cousin Duke Alan IV (Alan Fergant), who entered into Welsh Arthurian tradition (see n.34 below, and cf. ch.12, p. 257 above). For a genealogy of the Counts of Richmond which clarifies the relationship between them see C.T. Clay, *Early Yorkshire Charters IV: The Honour of Richmond* (Yorks. Arch. Soc. Record Series 1935), IV, 84.

7. Either Alan Rufus or his brother Brian may have led the Breton forces at Hastings; Ritchie, *The Normans*, 69-70 and nn.; F. Barlow, *The Feudal Kingdom of England* 1042-1216 (London, 1988), 83. H.R. Loyn, *The Normans*, 121 notes the importance of the brothers in the settlement, whether or not they were present at Hastings.

8. BWP chs.4 and 5; A.O.H. Jarman, *Aneirin: Y Gododdin* (Llandysul, 1988); K. Jackson, *The Gododdin: The Oldest Scottish Poem* (Edinburgh, 1969). Cf. Ritchie, *The Normans*, 69-70.

9. Ritchie, *The Normans*, xi-xiv; *passim*. Edith Maud, d. of Malcolm Canmore, who married King Henry I of England, made one of the five Norman dynastic marriages with Scottish rulers which are here listed.

10. Ritchie, *The Normans*, 30.

11. HW 393-4.

12. HW 455.

13. By the Treaty of Gisors in 1113, Louis VI of France relinquished the overlordship of Brittany to Henry I of England, who was concurrently Duke of Normandy. E. Durtelle de Saint Sauveur, *Histoire de Bretagne* (Paris, 1946), 118-21; A.L. Poole, *From Domesday Book to Magna Carta* (Oxford, 1951), 124. Under King John the lordship of Brittany was again lost to England in 1204.

14. The primary sources for Henry's conquest, apart from the Irish Annals, are Giraldus Cambrensis, *Expugnatio Hibernii* (*The Conquest of Ireland*), ed. and trans. by A.B. Scott and F.X. Martin (Dublin, Royal Irish Academy, 1978), and the Anglo–Norman poem *The Song of Dermot the Earl*, ed. G.H. Orpen (Oxford, 1892).

15. M.D. Legge, *Anglo-Norman Literature and its Background* (Oxford, 1963), 4. Cf. Chibnall, *Anglo-Norman England*, 5, and ch.3, pp. 82-4, ch.4, p. 100 above.

16. J. Le Patourel, 'Henri II Plantagenet et la Bretagne', *Feudal Empires*, X, 101-4; E. Durtelle de Saint Sauveur, *Histoire*, 124-5; A.L. Poole, *From Domesday Book to Magna Carta*, 381-2. On the 'Breton hope' of Arthur's return see ch.12, p. 262 above; Leg. Hist. 471, ALMA ch.7; C. Bullock-Davies, 'Arthur and the Messianic Hope', *B*, 29 (1981), 432-40. L. Fleuriot in HLCB 112-14 argues that for the Bretons Arthur was a symbol of Brythonic unity and of hope for the future, a memorial of their ancient power and strength during and after their original migrations. Arthur's name remained for them a powerful symbol until at least the fourteenth century. The widespread motif of the 'Hero's Expected Return' is listed by Stith Thompson, *Motif Index of Folk Literature* (Copenhagen, 1955-8), as A. 580.

17. As proposed by J.E. Lloyd, *EHR*, 57 (1942), 466-8; HW 523-4. On Geoffrey's national affiliations see above, ch.4, p. 98 and n.9.

18. A. Ewert, ed., *Marie de France: Lais* (Oxford, 1947), vi, ix-x; Legge, *Anglo-Norman Literature*, 72-3, EAR i, 56. See ch.12, p. 260 above. Marie has been conjecturally identified with Marie, Abbess of Shaftesbury, who was a half-sister to Henry II; *EHR*, 25 (1910) 303-6; A.L. Poole, *From Domesday Book to Magna Carta*, 243. The oldest manuscript (13th cent. Harley 978) is in Anglo-Norman orthography. On the 'Breton Lays' see now especially L. Fleuriot in HLCB ch.5., 131-8, and n.81 below.

19. For the *Livre de Carados* see W.J. Roach, *The Continuations of Perceval* (Philadelphia, 1949); A.W. Thompson, 'Additions to Chrétien's Perceval', ALMA ch.17, 212. See n.43 below.

20. See above ch.4, pp. 108-9 and refs. cited in ch.4, n.31.

21. ALMA ch.6 'The Oral Diffusion'; R.S. Loomis, *The Grail* (Cardiff, 1963), 8. If the passage quoted (ALMA 62) from the pseudo-Alanus de Insulis is to be believed, it indicates that by the latter half of the twelfth century Arthur's fame had been carried as far as the Crusader states of Carthage and Antioch, and even to Palestine. For the early diffusion of some Arthurian names on the Continent see in particular Pierre Gallais, 'Bleheri, la cour de Poitiers et la diffusion des récits arthuriens sur le continent', *Extraits des actes du VIIe. Congrès national de Littérature Comparée* (Poitiers, 1965), 61-79.

22. On Arthurian references by the Troubadours see R. Lejeune, ALMA ch.29; ibid. in *Mélanges Offerts à Jean Frappier* (Geneva, 1970), ii, 625-30.

23. On these and other names in Scotland employed by Chrétien see R.L. Graeme Ritchie, 'Chrétien de Troyes and Scotland', The *Zaharoff* Lecture (Oxford, 1952). Chrétien shows considerable knowledge of Scotland, though it is not clear how this was gained. With *Estregales* (Strathclyde) cf. *Straecled Wealas*, 'the Strathclyde Welsh', *Anglo-Saxon Chronicle* (*C text*) ann. 875.

24. In 'Chrétien de Troyes and England' in R. Barber (ed.), *Arthurian Literature* 1, (1981) the late C. Bullock-Davies makes a valid distinction between such names as those listed above, and Chrétien's English place-names in *Cligés*, which show a detailed and apparently familiar knowledge of places in the south of England.

25. Both personal and place-names in the poems of Chrétien de Troyes are conveniently listed in R.S. Loomis, ATC, Appendix 477-92. The forms of the names vary considerably between the

numerous MSS (none of which is earlier than thirty years after Chrétien's life-time, Legge, *Anglo-Norman Literature*, 31). Many of the derivations proposed by Loomis are unacceptable to modern scholarship, and any approach to their satisfactory elucidation must depend on a full collation of the MSS. See n.46 below.

26. Wendelin Foerster (ed.), *Kristian von Troyes: Erec und Enide* (Halle, 1934), lines 20-2. Cf. Frappier, ALMA 162-3.

27. Geoffrey makes clear in *HRB* XI, 1 that he knew *Hiwenus filius Uriani* (ie. Owain fab Urien, *TYP* 479-83) belonged to a later generation than that of Arthur, but for subsequent writers, including Chrétien, *Yvain* became a customary member of Arthur's court. See ch.4, p. 109 above.

28. *Karadues Briebras* gives the Breton spelling of the name *Caradawc Freichfras* (earlier *Brecbras*), who figures in the Triads and Genealogies and in the Life of St Padarn (*TYP* 299-300). This is a well-known instance of misinterpretation, in which the Old Welsh epithet *brecbras* (*breichfras*), 'Strong Arm', was misread and misunderstood as containing the French *bras*, 'arm', and *brie(f)*, giving the meaning 'Short Arm'. *Karadues Briebras* (*sic*) is the hero of the twelfth-century Anglo-Norman *Lai du Cor* by Biket (ALMA 114). See above ch.12 p. 260 and n.78. On Caradawc in Breton tradition see n.43, and cf. n.39 for Caradawc's horse in a triad.

29. See above, ch.2, 58-90 and ch.3, p. 83, *TYP* 381-2 and ALMA 178 for the story of the abduction of Gwenhwyfar by Melwas to Glastonbury (*Ynys Wydrin* or the *Isle de Voirre*), according to Caradoc of Llancarfan's *Vita Gildae*: evidently Chrétien had somehow heard of this story, which was unknown to Geoffrey of Monmouth. In his *Conte de la Charette* Chrétien denotes *Melwas* by the name *Meleagant*, but the two allusions both clearly refer to the same character: the difference in the two forms of the name merely points up the confusion to which Welsh names were subjected in the course of their adoption and transmission in French.

30. On Mabon fab Modron see *TYP* 433-6, *CO*(1), xlvi. On the name *Mabonagrain* see J. Lozac'hmeur, 'A propos de l'origine du nom de Mabonagrain', *ÉC*, 17 (1980), 257-62 (deriving it from *Mabon a(c) Owein*), and superseding the earlier discussion by W.J. Gruffydd, *Rhiannon* (Cardiff, 1953), 92-5. See Fleuriot (HCLB 133) for a suggestion as to another corrupt form of the name Mabon in the Prose *Tristan*.

31. On Conan Meriadoc (the Welsh *Cynan*) see above chs.4, p. 103; 12, p. 257 and n.55; *AP* 46n., *TYP* 316-18. In *B*, 26 (1974), 2, L. Fleuriot quotes a passage from the Cart. de Quimperlé (*c.* 1120) concerning the story of *Kenan filius Outam Senis* (Cynan son of Euddaf the Old), and points out in *ÉC*, 19, (1982), 271-2 that this allusion confirms that the tradition of *Kenan/Cynan (Meriadoc)* was known in Brittany before *HRB*, and before *Breuddwyd Maxen*. See further C. Brett 'Breton Latin Literature as Evidence for Literature in the Vernacular, AD 800-1300', *CMCS*, 18 (1989), 16, (indicating that the tradition was known both orally and in writing). In 'Brittany and *Armes Prydein Vawr* (*ÉC*, 20 (1983), 156) D.N. Dumville points out that the linking of Cynan and Cadwaladr in *Armes Prydein* as messianic deliverers appears to be 'so automatic' as to suggest that it had an earlier precedent in Welsh poetic tradition.

32. *B*, 17 (1958), 181-2; *TYP* 347-8; R. Bromwich 'Celtic Dynastic Themes and the Breton Lays', *ÉC*, 9 (1961), 464-5. For agreement on this point and on the significance of the name *Enide* see J.C. Lozac'hmeur, 'Les romans bretons', HLCB ch.5, 151. Chrétien claims a *lai breton* as his source for this part of the romance (*Erec et Enide* ll.6187-8). On *Gweroc/Erec*, the sixth-century prince, conqueror and eponym of *Bro Weroc*, or Vannes, see Chedeville and Guillotel, *La Bretagne des saints et des rois* (Ouest-France, 1984) 72, 78. Cf. above ch.6, n.5. On the name *Bro Uuerec/Guerec* see K. Jackson, *Historical Phonology of Breton* (DIAS, 1967), 139.33; R.Bromwich, 'Celtic Elements in Arthurian Romance; A General Survey', LAMA 41-55.

33. On *Guiamar*, *Guigemar* < *Guihomarc'h* (O.B. Uuiuhomarch), 'horse worthy', see L. Fleuriot 'Les lais bretons', HCLB 132, 134, and J.Loth, *Chrestomathie Bretonne* (Paris, 1890), 176. This name

appears to have belonged to several of the Counts of Léon in the eleventh and twelfth centuries (H. Zimmer, *Z. für Fr. Sprache und Litteratur*, 13, 80, HCLB loc.cit). *Gradlon Mor (Grallon, Graelent*, Chrétien's *Graislemier*) was a legendary ruler of Cornouailles, whose name was borne subsequently by more than one of its rulers (Fleuriot, HLCB 115, 134).

34. *TYP* no.30 and 270-1. Cf. n.6 above.

35. See above ch.4, p. 111; *TYP* 346-7.

36. Cf. L. Fleuriot, 'Old Breton Genealogies and Early British Traditions', *B*, 26 (1974), 1-6; P.C. Bartrum, *EWGT*.

37. A. Adams (ed. and trans.), *The Romance of Yder* (Woodbridge, 1983), (early thirteenth century).

38. For *Brengain < Branguen (Branwen)* see J. Loth, *RC*, 32 (1912) 301-2, reproduced in his *Contributions à l'étude des Romans de la Table Ronde* (Paris, 1912), 103-4; *Dinas de Lidan*, ibid.,90-2; *Husdent*, ibid.,106. Chrétien lists *Brangien* in *Erec et Enide*, l.2077.

39. *TYP* civ and n., p.106; *LIDC* no.6, 1.12. 'Hard-Back(ed)' is the meaning proposed by Ifor Williams, *CLIH* 100, cf. also A.O.H. Jarman, LAMA 105, *Guingalet* 'Fair and Hard'. Variants such as that between *guin/kein* can be paralleled elsewhere among the names and epithets in the Triads of Horses, *TYP* nos.38-44.

40. On *Lluagor > Lorzagor* (var. *Loriagor*) see *TYP* no 38, ibid., p.98 and refs. cited. The 'Congenital Helpful Animal' is listed as motif B.311 in Stith Thomson, *Motif Index*.

41. This recalls the name of the monster-boar *Twrch Trwyth* in *Culhwch ac Olwen*; see Ruth Roberts, 'Tors fils Ares, Tortain', *BBIAS*, 14 (1962), 91-8, and ALMA 39, *CO*(1) lxxii, n.

42. For *Cath Paluc* see above, ch.2, p. 45 and n.; *TYP* no.26 and pp. 484-7; ALMA 15, n.4; 323.

43. For Caradawc Freichfras see n.28 above, and Fleuriot, *Les Lais bretons*, HLCB ch.5, 134. The matter relating to him in the *Livre de Carados* and elsewhere is summarized by R.S. Loomis, 'The Strange History of Caradoc of Vannes', *Medieval Studies in Honour of F.P. Magoun*, ed. Bessinger and Creed (New York, 1965), 232-9. For *Yder* see n.37 above. *Yder fils Nut = Edern mab Nud CO*(1) l.182 (?brother of *Gwyn mab Nud*), *Hidernus filius Nucii* in HRB, *Ider filius Nuth* in Wm. of Malmesbury's *De Antiquitate*, and possibly the *Isdernus* of the Modena archivolt (ALMA 61). Lozac'hmeur ('Les romans bretons', HLCB 149-50) notes a *Hedern filius Nut* in a charter in the *Cart. de Quimperlé* of the year 1128. Evidently this was a namesake of the legendary hero, who clearly developed as a more prominent figure in Breton than in insular tradition.

44. R. Bromwich, 'The Celtic Inheritance of Medieval Literature', *Modern Language Quarterly*, 26 (1965), 203-27.

45. Cf. Proinsias Mac Cana, *The Mabinogi* (Cardiff, 1977), 19-20.

46. In spite of the lists of names compiled by Flutré (*Tables des noms propres dans les romans de la Moyen Age*, Poitiers, 1962) and G.D. West, *Index of Proper Names in French Arthurian Verse Romances* (Toronto, 1969*)*, idem., *Index. . . Arthurian Prose Romances* (Toronto, 1978), no full etymological study exists as yet of the Celtic proper names in the French romances. Both Fleuriot and Lozac'hmeur note ('Lais et romans bretons', HLCB ch.5, 132, 139) that many of the MSS preserve better variant forms of the names than those which have been printed. Lozac'hmeur has made a useful start to this much-needed study in his analysis and discussion of the names *Mabon/Mabuz/Mabonagrain* (see n.30 above). Additional evidence for the knowledge of early Welsh traditions in Brittany was noted above in ch.5 p. 127 and n.25. L. Fleuriot showed in *ÉC*, 18 (1981), 207-13 that Taliesin was known by reputation as an early prophetic poet at the

monastery of Rhuys in the Vannes district in the eleventh century. See above ch.12, p. 256, and n.49.

47. *ÉC*, 18 (1981), 210.

48. P. Mac Cana, *The Mabinogi* (Cardiff, 1977), 101. Cf. I.Ll. Foster, ALMA ch.16.

49. Cf. B.F. Roberts, 'The Welsh Romance of *Owain*', LAMA 182; ibid., 'Dosbarthu'r Chwedlau Cymraeg Canol', *YB*, 15 (1980), 19-46.

50. See ch.6 above, and cf. M. Surridge, 'Romance Linguistic Influence on Middle Welsh', *SC*, 1 (1966), 63-92; especially 88; idem, *ÉC*, 21 (1984), 249.

51. On 'aural copying' see B.F. Roberts, LAMA 171 and cf. I.Ll. Foster, ALMA 204. This possibility would perhaps be consistent with M.D. Legge's assertion (*Anglo-Norman Literature* 366) that the works of Chrétien de Troyes were 'unknown in England for some time after they were written'. Her deduction is based on the lack of reference to, or influence from, Chrétien's works in the work of Anglo-Norman writers during this period.

52. LAMA 181-2.

53. R.M. Jones, 'Y Rhamantau Cymraeg a'u Cysylltiad â'r Rhamantau Ffrangeg', *LlC*, 4 (1957), 208-27. Cf. P. Mac Cana, *The Mabinogi*, 100, and R. Bromwich 'Dwy Chwedl a Thair Rhamant', TRh 160.

54. C. Bullock-Davies, *Professional Interpreters and the Matter of Britain* (Cardiff 1966). A story capable of being adequately narrated in more than one language must have possessed some degree of fluidity as to its form and content. The bilingual titles which Marie de France cites as equivalent for two of her *lais Bretun (Gotelef/Chevrefoil; Laustic/Russignol/ Nihtegale)* offer a suggestive parallel (see below p. 289), as does the fact that Gottfried von Strassbourg attributes to his hero the ability to sing his lays in four languages — Breton, Welsh, Latin, and French (*Tristan*, 11.3625-6).

55. Cf. ch.8, pp. 171-82 above. In *Owein* xxvi R.L. Thomson emphasizes the difference between the texts of the three tales as they appear in the White Book, and points out that *Geraint* preserves a greater number of archaic spellings than do either of the others. This suggests that there was a distinct and separate prototype for each of the three.

56. ATC *passim*. Cf. Mac Cana, *The Mabinogi*, 114-15 on 'the tension between love and loyalty which underlies much of Arthurian romance and which is central to our three Welsh tales'.

57. Notably in Malory's *Tale of Sir Gareth* (E. Vinaver, *The Works of Sir Thomas Malory* (Oxford, 1967) I, 293-363) which is derived from lost French sources (see F. Lyons, 'The Changing Face of Arthurian Romance' = *Arthurian Studies* xvi, ed. Diverres *et al.* (Woodbridge, 1986), 137-47), and Vinaver, *Commentary*, ibid. III, 1427-42.

58. P. Mac Cana, *Celtic Mythology* (London 1970), 94. Cf. T.F. O'Rahilly, *Ériu*, 4 (1946), 14; R. Bromwich, 'Celtic Elements in Arthurian Romance', LAMA 51, TRh 167-9. See above ch.6, p. 148 and ch.8, p. 173.

59. *Echtra mac n-Echach*, 'The Adventure of the Sons of Eochaid Mugmedon', *RC*, 24 (1903), 190-207, trans. Cross and Slover, *Ancient Irish Tales* (London, 1936), 508-13, and the tale of Lugaid Laigde in *Cóir Anmann* (ed. E. Windisch, *Irische Texte* iii, 317 ff.). Discussion: R. Bromwich, 'Celtic Dynastic Themes and the Breton Lays', *ÉC*, 9 (1961), 439-74, especially 449-51; I.C. Lovecy, 'The Celtic Sovereignty Theme and the Structure of *Peredur*', *SC*, 12/13 (1977-8), 133-5.

60. *The Mabinogi*, 115-16. Mac Cana defines the theme as 'the land personified as a woman, a goddess, whose willing union with its ruler confers legitimacy on his rule and peace and fruitfulness on his kingdom'.

61. Cf. n.32 above, and ch.6, p. 148 and n.5; ch.8, p. 173 and n.16.

62. Glenys Goetinck, 'Historia Peredur', *LlC*, 6 (1961), 138-53; ibid., *Peredur: A Study of Welsh Tradition in the Grail Legends* (Cardiff, 1975). See also Gerald Morgan, *Y Tair Rhamant* (Llandybïe, 1965), 10. For modified views see I.C. Lovecy, loc.cit (n.59), and C. Lloyd-Morgan, 'Narrative Structure in *Peredur*', *ZCP*, 38 (1981), 188.

63. According to Mac Cana, 'Aspects of the Theme of King and Goddess in Irish Literature', *ÉC*, 7 (1956), 357, it was a theme 'of which the early Irish story-teller understood the implications, and (it) was one which he would not hesitate to attach to characters, be they historical or unhistorical, which literature and tradition set in the seventh century'. Cf. ibid. *ÉC*, 8 (1958), 59.

64. G. Goetinck, 'Gwenhwyfar, Guinevere, and Guenièvre', *ÉC*, 11 (1966-7), 351-60; Rhian Andrews, 'Rhai Agweddau ar Sofraniaeth yng Ngherddi'r Gogynfeirdd', *B*, 27 (1976), 23-30; C.A. McKenna, 'The Theme of Sovereignty in *Pwyll*', *B*, 29 (1980), 35-52. As the latter points out (p. 46, n.) the recurrent collocation *Prydein priawt* in the poetry of the Gogynfeirdd need not mean 'Britain's spouse' rather than simply 'Britain's (lawful) owner'. The force of the phrase lay in its ambiguity.

65. P. Mac Cana, *The Mabinogi*, 19-20.

66. See *TYP* 267-8 and refs. cited.

67. Cf. J. Frappier, *Chrétien de Troyes: L'Homme et L'Oeuvre* (Paris, 1957), 59-60. Most of the 'thèmes fondamentaux demeurent reconnaissables' which he cites are found in the above list from the *Mabinogi*, the others are found elsewhere in Welsh or Irish sources, and all reappear in Arthurian romance. Cf. also Jean Marx, *ÉC*, 10 (1963), 483, and *ÉC*, 11 (1967), 511 (review of Jean Marx, *Nouvelles recherches sur la littérature arthurienne*, Paris, 1965); R. Bromwich, 'The Celtic Inheritance of Medieval Literature', *Modern Language Quarterly*, 26 (1965), 216, TRh 169. The *tynged* or taboo imposed by one person on another (=Ir. *geis*) is exemplified in *Culhwch ac Olwen CO*, 1.50-1.

68. Ed. Potvin 1.31674 (quoted P. Gallais, ref. in n.75 below).

69. Presumed to be William VII (1071-1127), the Troubadour poet, grandfather of Eleanor of Aquitaine, who became William IX of Aquitaine in 1086.

70. B.H. Wind, *Les Fragments du Tristan de Thomas* (Leiden, 1950), 1.848-51. *Bretaigne, Britannia* etc. were applied indifferently in the twelfth century to Britain or to Brittany (cf. Leg.Hist. 85; Ewert, *Lays of Marie de France*, xv).

71. *Romania*, 8 (1879), 425-8.

72. *The Arthurian Legend* (1891), 370-3. The views of Paris are there summarized and endorsed by J. Rhŷs.

73. *Descr. Kam.* i, 17. D. Legge, *Anglo-Norman Literature*, 52 is sceptical as to the identification of *Breri* with the *Bledericus* of Giraldus Cambrensis.

74. On the name *Bledericus* see K. Jackson in the compendium *Les Romans du Graal dans la littérature des XII à XIII siècles* (*Colloques Internationaux du Centre national de la Recherche Scientifique*, Paris, 1956), 148 (as quoted in n. to *TYP*(2) 528).

75. *RC*, 33 (1912), 180-3, see *EWGT* 106(18(b)). According to HW 398 Cadifor ap Collwyn died in 1091. For discussion of *Breri/Bledericus* see P. Gallais, *Breri, la cour de Poitiers et la diffusion des récits arthuriens sur le continent* (Poitiers, 1965 = Paris, 1967), and C. Bullock-Davies, *Professional Interpreters*, 12-14, *passim*. See also *TYP* cxv and refs. cited, TRh 160-1, and cf. ch.12, n.82 above.

76. For *Bledri latimer* (=*latinier*) *ap Kadifor* see HW 428 and n.; P.C. Bartrum, *Welsh Genealogies AD300-1400* (Cardiff, 1974), I, 187; RWM i, 826, no.173. (On grounds of date Lloyd rejects identification of the latter with Bleddri ap Cadifor, d.1091. See preceding note.).

77. Cf. Jean Marx, 'Monde Brittonique et Matière de Bretagne', *ÉC*, 10 (1963), 481, and L.Fleuriot in HLCB 23-5. The latter emphasizes the twofold linguistic facility of the Bretons resulting from the closeness of their speech to that of Cornwall and Wales, together with their close proximity to the Normans throughout their history, and the innate propensity of the Bretons to travel, which caused them to follow the Normans on their furthest conquests, for instance to southern Italy.

78. This point is made very strongly by C. Bullock-Davies, *Professional Interpreters*, 5. Writing before the publication of Fleuriot's work (see HLCB 15-16, and ch.12, p. 252 above) she points out that 'it seems odd that when French and English harpers . . . are mentioned in our records, the name of no Breton poet or minstrel of any kind has survived'. See also R.L. Graeme Ritchie, *Chrétien de Troyes and Scotland*, 15-16, who emphasizes the absence of any reference to *conteurs bretons* in any account relating to Scotland, such as that of the wedding of Malcolm Canmore's sister Margaret to Duke Conan IV of Brittany, which took place in 1160.

79. On the functions of the *cyfarwyddiaid* or oral story-tellers and the relation of their art to the literary redactions of the Welsh tales see B.F. Roberts, 'Tales and Romances', *Guide* ch.9, 203-6. On the ambiguity of the terms *Bretaigne, Bretun* see n.70 above. Cf. ch.12, p. 253.

80. See ch.12 above, p. 256. Fleuriot renders *jongleurs* by 'bardes vagabonds', HLCB 23-6, and gives for *cantores historici* (such as Iudhael) the O.B. equivalent *anhuariatan*. He regards Breri as one of these.

81. As was urged by Brugger, *Z.f.Fr. Sprache*, 49 (1927), 126 ff. For fresh light on this subject see C. Bullock-Davies, 'The Form of the Breton Lay', *Medium Aevum*, 42 (1973), 18-31, and cf. n.54 above. For the extensive literature on the Breton lays see Pickford and Last, *The Arthurian Bibliography i and ii* (Woodbridge, 1981, 1983), and more recently the bibliography to Glyn S. Burgess, *The Lais of Marie de France* (Manchester 1987), 221 ff. Fleuriot's important article 'Les Lais bretons' (HLCB ch.5, 131-8) regards the *lais féeriques* (such as *Lanval, Yonec, Guigemar*) as the most ancient in their content and adds that while these derive ultimately from Celtic mythology 'il est frappant que les poètes ont attribué ces aventures à des personnages des dynasties de Cornouailles, Léon, Nantes ou Vannes' (p.134). Cf. p. 279 above and refs. cited in n.32.

82. See above ch.3, p. 82 and n.31. In 'More about Bleddri', *ÉC*, 2 (1937), 221, M. Williams stressed the potential importance of the Welsh 'saints' in carrying stories between S. Wales, Devon-Cornwall, and Brittany.

83. See Elissa R. Henken, *Traditions of the Welsh Saints* (Cambridge, 1987). See above ch.3, pp. 82-3; and ch.12, p. 251 on the general tolerance of the Celtic Church towards native lore.

84. J. Frappier, *Chrétien de Troyes*, 56, and Fleuriot, HLCB 118-19, show that the court of Eleanor, patroness of Troubadours and (in all probability) of Wace, was a cultural centre of supreme importance where the dialects of north and south France were brought together with Breton and (if we are to believe Bleheris) with Welsh. Her daughter, Marie de Champagne, was the patroness of Chrétien de Troyes, and Marie's court succeeded that of her mother as a cultural centre. See further Legge, *Anglo-Norman Literature*, ch.4 'The Court of Henry II', and ibid., p.366.

85. On the cultural prestige of the Normans and Anglo-Normans see Legge, *Anglo-Norman Literature*, 3-4: 'Anglo-Norman taste was not lagging behind continental, it was in the van'; ibid. 366 makes plain that it is not easy to distinguish between works produced in England and Normandy. Their common dialect united the Normans on both sides of the Channel, and distinguished both from speakers who came from central France (Leg.Hist. 467).

86. Cf. ch.12, p. 256 above.

INDEX

Hopcyn ap Thomas 11, 12, 14 n.25, 196, 202-3
hryt eselt 210, 220, *see* E(s)syllt
Huail (fab Caw) 83, 84, 95
Hu(s)dent (Tristan's hound) 280
Hywel ap Goronwy 35
Hywel fab Emyr Llydaw 149, 187
Hywel Fychan (scribe) 11, 14 n.27, 196

Iarll y Kawg, y Cawg ('Earl of the Bowl') 160, 203, *see Owain*, story of
Iarlles y Ffynnawn, *see Owain: Chwedl Iarlles y Ffynnon*
Ida of Bernicia (king) 22
Iddawg Cordd Prydain 184-5, 188, 190
Igerna 104, 111, 234; *see also* Eig(y)r (Arthur's queen)
Illtud, St, Life of 82, 83, 94 n.31, 225 n.26, 289
immrama 252
'incremental repetition' 46
Ingomar 256
insula Avallonis 110, *see also* Isle of Avalon, *Ynys Afallach*
insula Trestanni 210
insular script 35
international popular tales 276
Iorwerth ap Maredudd 184, 188, 190; *see also Breuddwyd Rhonabwy*
Ireland 17, 20, 35, 55, 56, 76, 78, 107, 117, 126, 128, 129, 132, 230, 250, 252, 254, 274, 281, 284, 285; Chronicle of Ireland 26, 27; Marvels of 89-90; Irish Ogham script 231; Irish raids and settlements 231-2; Irish literature and tradition 130, 212, 252, 285; literary analogues 2, 87, 194, 209, 222, 283-4; traditional history 17; Irish scholars 18; story-tellers 284, *see also filid*; 'Irish rhyme' 36
Iron-Age hill-forts 236, 238; pottery 243
Isidore (of Seville) 54
'Island of Britain' / *Ynys Prydain* 6, 80-1, 89, 100-4, 151, 240; *see also* 'Names of the Island of Britain'/ *Enwau Ynys Prydain*
Isle of Avalon 108; *see also insula Avallonis*, *Ynys Afallach*
Isle of Man 57
Isolt / Iseut of Brittany 258, 261; 'Isolt of the White Hands' 228 n.91, n.94; *see* Es(s)yllt
Italy 276
Itinerarium Kambriae 136; *see also* Giraldus Cambrensis
Iudeu (fortress) 24
Iudicael (king) 256

Joceline of Furness 121-2, 137, 139; *see also* Kentigern, St, Life of
jongleurs (Breton) 261, 288, 297 n.80; *see also cyfarwyddiaid*
Joseph of Arimathia 200, 201
Julius Caesar 100, 105
Juvencus *englynion* 35, 36

Kadeir Teyrnon (poem) 52
Kaer Sidi 57; *see also* Annw(f)n
Kai 277, Kaius 108, 109, 112, Keu 59; *see also* Cai (Cei fab Cynyr)
Kamber (alleged eponym of *Cymru*) 102
Kanu y Meirch (poem) 53
Karadawc Vreichfras 187; *see also* Caradauc Brecbras, Caradawc Freichfras, *Carados Briebras*
Kat Godeu (poem) 51-2
Kein Calet (Gwalchmai's horse) (*le Guingalet*) 280
Kelli 40, 64; *see* Celli Wig
Kelli wic 234-8; *see* Celli Wig
Kent 23-4
Kentigern, St, Life of 122-4, 126, 137, 139, 141 n.8, n. 9, 161; *Lailoken and Kentigern* 123
Kernyw, *see* Cornwall
Killibury, *see* Castle Killibury; *see also* Celli Wig
'King Arthur's Castle' 229; King Arthur's Hall 235, 238
king-lists 101
Kyheic 231

Labraid Lorc / Loingsech 212
Lady of the Fountain, The 154; *see also Owain*, story of
lai, lais Bretun 274, 289; *see also* Marie de France
Lai du Cor (Biket) 206, 264
Laigin 17
Laloecen, Lailoken 121-6, 128-30, 134-5, 138, 142 n.32; *Lailoken and Kentigern* 122-3; *Lailoken and Meldred* 122; *see also* Kentigern, St, Myrddin
Lancelot (du Lac) 60, 69, 198, 204, Lawnslot y lac 201, 283; *Lancelot: Le Chevalier de la Charette* 283; *see also* Chrétien de Troyes
Landevennec 251, 267
Land's End 76
Lantyan *(Lancien)* 221, 240-3
Laon, monks of 262, 271 n.88, 288
Later Arthurian literature 193-205
latimarii 283, 287, 289; *see also* Professional Interpreters
Laudine 166
Laustic (Breton *lai*) 270 n.75; *see also* Marie de France, *lais Bretun*
Layamon 111
Lebor Gabála Érenn ('Book of Invasions of Ireland') 19, 55, 69
Le Fresne 289; *see also lais Bretun*
Leland 231, 238, 246
Léon (Brittany) 279, 297
Lesnewth 233
liber vetustissimus 100-1, 261, 271 n.86, 272 n.102
Liber Historiae Francorum 20, 21
Licat Amr (Llygad Amr) 91
Lifris of Llancarfan 39, 83
Limwris, Earl 149, 152, 153
Li Hauz livre du Graal 195
Livre de Carados 275, 280, 292 n.19
Livre des faits d'Arthur 265